Aikido Exercises

for Teaching and Training

by C. M. Shifflett

Round Earth Publishing
P. O. Box 3855
Merrifield, Virginia 22116-3855
http://round-earth.com

Aikido Exercises
for Teaching and Training

By C. M. Shifflett

Copyright © 1999, 2004 by C. M. Shifflett
Printed in the United States of America
First Edition, Fourth Printing (revised)
Cover design and full-color scan by The Bluemont Company
Illustrated by the author.

Publisher's Cataloging in Publication
Shifflett, C. M.
Aikido exercises for teaching and training / by C. M. Shifflett.
p. cm.
Includes bibliographic references and index.
ISBN 1-55643-314-x
LOC 99-70555
796.8'154
1. Aikido. 2. Aikido--training. 3. Ch'i (chinese philosophy)
I. Title.

Published by:
Round Earth Publishing, P. O. Box 10728, Pittsburgh, PA 15203
(412) 381-4148 / FAX (412) 381-4060 / http://round-earth.com

Distributed by:
North Atlantic Books
P. O. Box 12327
Berkeley, California 94712
http://www.northatlanticbooks.com

Distributed to the book trade by Publishers Group West

Aikido-L quotes are reproduced with the permission of the Aikido FAQ and Aikido List maintainers, Kjarten Clausen and Jun Akiyama.

Although the basic exercises contained herein are not dangerous, improper rolling and throws can be dangerous and damaging. Undertake these exercises only under the guidance of a qualified instructor, using good sense, good judgement, and personal responsibility.

Contents

Foreword

I wish I'd had a book like this one available to me when I started teaching 25 years ago! While most books on Aikido are focused on a particular point of view and fairly narrow in scope, this book is quite open in its approach to the teaching of Aikido exercises, the operation of a school and myriad details that many forget. Drawing on experience in the Virginia Ki Society and past martial art studies as well as international associations created through the Internet and the Aikido-L ListServ, the author has woven a rich tapestry of Aikido and related topics which is easy to read and surprisingly easy to comprehend.

Sources for observations, suggested approaches, and additional resources are liberally quoted and referenced. While this work clearly reflects the impact of Master Koichi Tohei and Ki Society teachings it also includes information from physics and anatomy and practices from judo and other Aikido systems (such as Aikikai and Yoshinkan) to help the reader to better understand the material.

The author has an easy writing style with a flair for detail which should satisfy even the most discriminating of readers. While the book was written primarily to help people who are new to Aikido, it will be a valuable resource for more senior students and teachers of the art. A fitting adjunct to the author's first volume, *Ki in Aikido*.

George Simcox, November 1999
Virginia Ki Society
Merrifield, Virginia

Preface

Practice is like honing a knife. You start with a ragged piece of steel. You put it on the grinder, but two or three passes won't do the job. It has to be honed and honed and honed. Even then you aren't done, because with use, you still have to hone and sharpen. It is a never-ending process.

— *William Thorndike, Jr.*

The more I train, the more I realize that there are no "advanced techniques," just basics applied well.

—*Peter W. Boylan*

The first rule of writing is to "Know Your Audience" yet you will notice that this book switches relentlessly between "you the student" and "you the instructor." This seems to me to be a fairly accurate analogy of any Aikido class.

Student is teacher.

Teacher is student.

What we know we can teach to another.

And we never stop learning.

This book is not intended to teach Aikido. It is certainly not intended to teach the One True Right Way (of many right ways) of doing exercises or techniques. It is intended only to provide exercises and insights into the processes and tools of training and learning, regardless of style. A ball is useful for demonstrating spherical movement whether you are coming from karate, judo, Aikikai, Ki Society or Yoshinkan. As Sensei Casey Stengal pointed out: "You don't have to belong to a ballteam to steal their signals."

Aikido is a complex discipline. It is never so uncomplicated as simply punching an opponent. In any given Aikido technique, there are at least three different things going on. And that's just at the beginning levels. Yet many new students assume that they should be able to stroll onto the mat and perform a throw perfectly the first or second time they try it. If unable to do so, the problem is that Aikido is "too difficult." Actually, the problem is the underlying assumption. The beginning math student does not begin with calculus. The beginning skier does not start on the black slopes.

The beginning music student quickly learns that the best way to learn music is not to struggle and crash through the entire piece.

Although any student will want to see and hear the entire form to understand just where it is going and how it should be approached, not even the most superlative musician will tackle a complex work in its entirety.

Instead it is broken down into workable segments. A few notes, a single phrase, then a single measure. Then a new phrase and when this is correct, adding it onto the first and continuing only when these — and all their parts — are correct. When the parts are mastered they are combined and practiced. Then another measure is added, then another and another . . . .

When I began piano lessons at the age of seven, standard equipment on the piano was the music, the metronome, me — and five pennies. Each practice segment had to be done correctly five times. On playing a measure correctly, one penny was moved to the other side of the piano. On playing it correctly a second time, the second penny moved to the left and so on through five correct renditions. If I stumbled or made an error, all the pennies went back to the right and the process began all over again.

In Aikido, it is tempting to practice by zooming through an entire technique before the individual components are mastered or even understood. Continuing through to the throw is as satisfying as whipping through the written music to a crash-bang finale but the end result is years of poor technique, bad habits, and poor performance. On a very practical note, this approach decreases your practice time by unnecessarily tiring even the most helpful of partners. Lisa Tomoleoni of Tokyo's Shindo Dojo advises:

Quality of training is important, not just quantity. I'm not speaking of quality of instruction. I'm speaking of quality of one's own training. Yes, there is value to pushing through the exhaustion, the pain. But also important is truly focused intense training. And this type of training comes in many flavors — "hard fast through the mat" flavor, "slow and conscious" flavor, "smooth and connected" flavor, "big movement flavor," "small movement" flavor, and many many more. I can train for an hour very slowly and focus on one or two points only, and be just as tired, if not more so, than going at it throwing each other through the mat for an hour. Think quality, not quantity!

While learning new skills, better to break down a technique into the component parts. This approach has the added benefit of allowing work with injured partners who cannot take falls but can "dance" the individual sections. But practice! Not, "Oh, I'll have to work on that [later]," not three or four attempts followed by chit-chat, but real practice. Having trouble with the "Standard Response"? *Tenkan*? Rolls? Don't just practice it 4 or 5 times, practice it 40 or 50, or 400 or 500 times. Was it perfect? If not, do it again.

Guitarist Frederick M. Noad tells of "a very famous concert guitarist, whose name is today a household word," who was conscripted into the army.

Afraid of losing his technique, he evolved an exercise routine covering the main aspects of playing, which could be completed in forty minutes — the maximum time he felt sure of being able to secure daily without fail. After two years of military service he found that he had not only maintained his ability to play, but actually improved it. As he said afterwards, technique seldom stands still — it either advances or retreats.

This book offers a collection of exercises, games, tools, and equipment that can be used to develop and practice basic Aikido skills. It does not represent official policy or procedure for Ki Society or any other style. It is not intended to teach actual throwing techniques beyond what is necessary to illustrate the why, what, and how of the exercises. On the other hand, the exercises and demonstrations can be adapted, in one way or another, to all styles. And, while nothing replaces practice, understanding can greatly speed the process and eliminate errors, misunderstandings, and other pointless blocks to progress.

Oddly enough, many students and instructors approach the study of Aikido in a way which largely ignores written reference materials. Few of us would consider studying computer programming, auto mechanics, music or mathematics in this manner. Nor is there the slightest need to do so as excellent texts are available.

With no intent to slight other styles, keys in the following material refer to the Aikikai, Ki Society, and Yoshinkan reference materials below. *Aikido and the Dynamic Sphere* is the long-time standard Aikido textbook. Shioda's Yoshinkan text, *Total Aikido*, is radically different in approach, but extremely valuable for technical information which applies to the body mechanics of any style.

- **ADS — *Aikido and the Dynamic Sphere*** (Westbrook & Ratti, 1970): This is the classic Aikido text, written when Koichi Tohei (founder of the Ki Society) was Chief Instructor at Aikikai *Honbu Dojo*. In Ki Society and other styles which have spun off since the 1970's, techniques have changed somewhat, but essentials remain. It is 30 years old, a standard, and so widely used that if you are discussing a technique with someone in a different style with different terms and perhaps over the Internet, you may want to reference this book. Meanwhile, see key on pages 152-153.

- **KIA — *Ki in Aikido*** (Shifflett, 1997): *Ki* exercises for balance, coordination, and focus in step-by-step format designed for actual practice.

- **KDL — *Ki in Daily Life*** (Tohei, 1978): Basic exercises applied to Ki-Aikido and to daily living.

- **TOT — *Total Aikido*** (Shioda, 1996): Yoshinkan-style Aikido with beautiful illustrations and clear instructions. Excellent commentaries on "common mistakes" which regardless of style, will always be the same as the physics, physiology and body mechanics will always be the same.

- **ZC— *Zen Combat*** (Gluck, 1997): Jay Gluck was the first American exchange student to post-WWII Japan.He set off on a tour of Japan's ancient martial arts. Here you will find many familiar stories of the formative years of Aikido, from Ueshiba to Tohei to Rube Goldberg. Wonderful eye-witness history.

There are other excellent references, but if you are trying to discuss a technique in words (with names that vary between styles) over the Internet, it can be enormously useful to have these books on hand. Also note the following abbreviations, used because they are faster to read when attempting to follow directions.

LH = Left Hand, **RH** = Right Hand, **LF** = Left Foot, **RF** = Right Foot

Acknowledgements

Many thanks to George Simcox, Chief Instructor of the Virginia Ki Society, Merrifield, Virginia, and Father of Books. Thanks also to Kjartan Clausen of Norway and Jun Akiyama of Colorado, U. S. A., maintainers and keepers of the Aikido List (begun by Gary Santaro) on the Internet. They are responsible for a world-wide web of Aikido friends and contributors who occasionally grumble about "trivia and lack of useful material on The List," while helping me to write this book a line and a thought and a nugget of information at a time.

Thanks again to fellow travelers, helpers, and contributors including: Philip Akin, Jim Baker, Margo Ballou, Mike ["Insert Quote Here"] Bartman, Kevin Beck, David Berger, Jan Beyen, Leonard Bohanan, Bruce Bookman, Peter Boylan the Budo Bum, Chris Brogden, David C. Buchanan, Ben Calvert, Gloria Campbell, Vicky Chiang, Mark and Margie Dean, Kirk Demaree, Katherine Derbyshire, Serban Derlogea, Guy de Wolf, Emily Dolan, Suzette Hayden Elgin, Jay Dunn, Matt Firor for editing, Tony Fitts, Robert E. Gardner, John Garner, Tarik J. Ghbeish, Stephen Gilligan, Tim Gion, Jay Gluck, Cady Goldfield, Chuck Gordon, Paul Gowder, Tim Griffiths, Wendy Gunther, Judy Halloran, Daniel M. Henry, Julie Herbert, Dennis Hooker, Patrick L. Jones, Beate Kawelke, Ed Keith, Steve Kendall, Neil McKellar, Wiley Nelson, Monica Norman, John Oldenburg, Greg Olson, Robert Pavese, the late Hilda Perkins, Minh Pham, Chris Pierce, John Pinkman, Will Reed, Janet Rosen, Karl Schmidt, Yael Shahar, Dex Sinister, Michael Speece, Hal Singer, Stefan Stenudd, Chizuko Suzuki, Ben Swett, Jim Templeman, William Thorndike, Jr., Joseph Toman, Lisa Tomoleoni, Laura Walton, David Wang, John Wiley, Steve Wolf, Maxine Wright, and Joel and Janice Zimba.

Aikido is a relatively new martial art dating from the 1920's when its founder, Morihei Ueshiba (*O-Sensei*[1]), began to develop what he eventually came to call *Aikido*.[2] Aikido can mean "the way (*do*) to harmony (*ai*) with *ki*."

Aikido is rooted in the Japanese *samurai* warrior tradition and incorporates concepts from the Yagyu school of swordsmanship. It is also based on Ueshiba's nearly 20-year study of *Daito-Ryu jujutsu* which was gentled and transformed by his attachment to the Omoto religion and its celebration of life, creation, and loving protection of others. Aikido replaced the maiming and destruction of classic *jujutsu* with control and compassion. It is, for example, the only martial art recommended to parents of abusive children.

Internal principles aim to subdue and control rather than damage or destroy the opponent while protecting the attacker and the attacked. The Aikidoist does not punch or kick to injure or harm unnecessarily, does not block or resist attacks but blends with, redirects and transforms the attacker's energy, maintaining the flow. The result is devastating softness, invisible technique and an art that makes no sense to most observers accustomed to force against force. There are surely more questions about the hows and whys of Aikido than for any other martial art. Some thoughts on these follow.

---

1. "Honored Teacher."
2. Like Judo, Kendo, *Daito-ryu,* and Karate (actually Okinawan rather than Japanese), all are *gendai* ("modern") styles with roots in *koryu*, the traditional ("old flow") schools of classical *budo*. The division between the traditional and the modern is the end of the Shogunate and the Meiji restoration of 1868.

Some Common Questions and Observations

"Oh, He's Just Falling Down for Her."

To start the lesson, your instructor will . . . ski a short distance down the mountain, just to the point where it gets very steep, and swoosh to a graceful stop, making it look absurdly easy. It IS absurdly easy for [him], because underneath his outfit he's wearing an antigravity device. All the expert skiers wear them. You don't actually believe that "ski jumpers" can leap off those ridiculously high ramps and just float to the ground unassisted without breaking into walnut-sized pieces, do you?

— Dave Barry

An Aikido throw can look so improbably and impossibly smooth and effortless that it is easy to believe that it is faked. It isn't. It's physics.

The laws of physics are just as strictly enforced at Aikido schools as they are on motorcycles or on ski slopes. If you have ever been a beginning skier, you know from painful experience just how devastating the forces of physics can be. Saying that the attacker fell down "for" the Aikidoist is like saying that the beginning skier fell down "for" the mountain.

The advanced cyclist or skier has learned to use these forces; a small shift in weight or position is the difference between crashing into a tree or swooshing effortlessly through a turn and down the slope.

An accomplished skier flying across the snow is as wildly improbable to the frustrated beginner as an accomplished Aikidoist flying across the mat — but neither one is faking.

Skiing is real and motorcycles are real. As long as ski slopes are littered with the bodies of fallen and frustrated beginners, as long as motorcyclists drop their bikes[3] and as long as Aikidoists align with the law of physics and the universe, Aikido will be real.

---

3. It is said that there are three groups of bikers: those who have dropped their bikes, those who haven't yet, and those who lie about it. Bikes fall on the street for exactly the same reasons that *ukes* fall on the mat and motorcycle classes are eerily similar to Aikido classes. See "On Zen and The Art of Motorcycles" on page 82.

Q. What is Aikido?

A. It is . . . .

Walking 10 steps down a flight of stairs when there are only 9.
Pushing a door just as someone opens it from the other side.
Reaching out to shake someone's hand just as they step back.

— *David Buchanan, Ki Society*

Did you ever . . .
Pull a chair out from under someone just as they were sitting down?
Try to kiss a girl on the lips just to have her turn her head at the last moment so the kiss landed on her cheek?
Hold something out to someone and snatch it away at the last moment?
Lead an animal around using bait?
Hold a child's hand to keep them from straying off?
It's not a touch you develop, it's a feeling you hone.

— *Dennis Hooker, Aikido Schools of Ueshiba*

Aikido is origami with people, instead of paper.

— *Kjartan Clausen, Aikikai*

The art of hitting people with planets.

— *Anon.*

Actually, I have had people look at me oddly when I say I study Aikido and ask "Isn't that one of those Japanese dogs?"
I have learned to reply with a straight face: "Yes. This is an art in which, when someone attacks, you pick up a dog and hurl it at them. Very effective."

— *Janet Rosen, Aikikai*

Aikido is a way of unifying the world.

— *O-Sensei (Morihei Ueshiba)*

Q. How is Aikido different from karate?

A. In the variety of responses and in the end goal.

...In many martial arts there is really very little choice, since the techniques themselves and the methods by which they are employed all work toward and are intended to injure if not actually destroy an attacker...in Aikido the student is given the freedom and responsibility of choice.

— A. Westbrook and O.Ratti, Aikido and the Dynamic Sphere

Because Aikido uses the energy and motion of the attacker, there must be a wide variety of possible responses to the wide variety of possible attacking energies and motions. Hal Singer gives this demonstration based on a single wrist grab.

Attack	Karate	Aikido
Pull wrist in, response is:	Punch/Kick	*enter (irimi).*
Push wrist in, response is:	Punch/Kick	*turn around (tenkan)*
Turn wrist in, response is:	Punch/Kick	*shiho-nage*
Turn wrist out, response is:	Punch/Kick	*sankyo*

And so on . . . with a different response to every different attack.And in the end, because the Aikidoist is blending with the motions, they are easier to deflect, to redirect, to neutralize and control the attacker without causing actual harm.

It's Too Much Like Dancing — It'll Never Work

The genius of Aikido is to transform the most violent attack, by embracing it, into a dance.

— *George Leonard*

I think [Aikido] is the most difficult of all the martial arts to learn. Its demands for skill, grace and timing rival those of classical ballet.

— *Jearle Walker, Physicist*

What is dancing?

It is controlled motion.

Consider Fred Astaire and Ginger Rogers, the two moving in harmony, whirling around the floor in perfect control.

What would have happened if Fred had let go at a critical moment?

She would have gone flying across the room and fallen.

What happens when the Aikidoist lets go of an attacker at a critical moment?

The attacker goes flying across the room and falls.

Yes, it is like dancing, but so is everything else.

Conversation is like dancing. Teamwork is like dancing.

Any form of cooperation is like dancing.

You can do it well or you can do it badly.

Yes, Aikido it like dancing.

Yes, it works.

Q. Why protect an attacker?
A. For his sake — *and* for yours.

Whoever fights monsters must beware that in the process he does not become a monster. For when you look long into the abyss, the abyss also looks into you.

— *Nietzsche*

The doors of heaven and hell are adjacent and identical.

— *Nikos Kazantzakis*

It is often gratifying to think that an attacker deserves anything you can dish out. From both legal and practical standpoints this is untrue[4].

Legally you are limited to a type and degree of defense appropriate to the incoming attack, to do what is necessary to control the situation and keep yourself safe.

Practically, you are more likely to face assault from someone you care for, such as a drunken friend, than from a malevolent stranger.

Aikido *skills* allow you to deal with either one but you must practice for that contingency. Aikido *attitudes* are practical self-defense against ending up in jail yourself for assault or murder. Regardless of the attacker's identity, do what is necessary to control the situation and protect those concerned. No less, no more.

As Hollywood knows so very well, hatred, fear, vengeance and anger are exciting, exhilarating and energizing. Because they invoke mankind's favorite mind-altering drug of choice — adrenaline — these emotions are extremely seductive and they are the fast track to the Dark Side. The one who feeds on the thrill of violence and assault is little different from the one who relishes and feeds on the thrill of vengeance and hatred.

Destroying an attacker because "he attacked and therefore deserves whatever he gets" *is not* "self defense." What, then, *is* self defense? The late Bruce Tegner wrote an essay on this topic that is remarkable for its grace and good sense.[5]

One way of defining self-defense is to explain what it is not. Personal self-defense is not warfare; it is not vengeance; it is not an art; it is not a sporting event; it is not a movie or television fight scene.

[It] is training to learn and use appropriate and effective physical actions if there is no practical available alternative.

Many victims of assault are victims not because they lack the capacity to win fights but because they have been given absolutely no preparation to cope with this special kind of emergency.

The old-fashioned view that self-defense instruction is training to reach a high level of fighting skill has the effect of eliminating those individuals who have the greatest need. It is precisely those people who are unable or unwilling to become fierce

---

4. See Sullivan, Edward F. (1993).
5. The introduction to *Self-Defense Nerve Centers and Pressure Points for Karate, Jujitsu and Atemi-waza.* Reproduced by kind permission of Thor Publishing Company, Ventura, California.

fighting machines who benefit from practical self-defense instruction to the greatest degree.

Our capabilities ought to bear some relationship to real-life objectives. People learning to defend themselves against assault ought not to be trained as though they were preparing for warfare.

The legal and moral definition of self-defense expressly limits the degree of force to the least which can be used to avert, stop, or escape from an intended assault.

In old-style self-defense, every assault is viewed as a very vicious assault. Real life is different. There are degrees of danger. Assault intentions range from mildly threatening to the intent to do great bodily harm. More important, there are mildly threatening situations which, if handled properly with assertive self-control, can be prevented from escalating into physical violence.

There must be a full range of responses to correspond to the range of possible situations. Otherwise there is only the all-or-nothing response, which is not a choice — it is a dilemma. The person who cannot cope with a mildly threatening hostile act does nothing, or responds to the mild threat as if it were a vicious assault. If the intended victim is passive it encourages the assailant and assaultive action is more likely to occur. Reacting to a mild threat as though it were a vicious assault is inappropriate.

The objective of ethical self-defense instruction is to teach appropriate and effective responses.

Q. Is Aikido the Ultimate Martial Art?
A. No.

Thermonuclear warfare is the Ultimate Martial Art, followed by long range artillery, armor, guns, knives, and large guys named Bubba. If you want to defend yourself in the street, buy a tank. Aikido isn't about that, neither is real Budo.

— Jim Baker, Aikikai

Q. Does Aikido work "on the street"?
A. Why do you ask?

If you have a fantasy of becoming the invincible ultimate fighting warrior, learning a martial art won't help you achieve it. That's a fantasy, remember? To become "effective" first you have to drop the nonsense and meet Mr. Reality. He's the only one you have to defeat. Unfortunately, he always wins. Aikido isn't a quick course in self defense. It takes a while before you could use the techniques.

In Brooklyn, we'd answer this question with, "Look, you live in New York City. Sometime in the next five years you'll probably be mugged. They'll take your money, and maybe they'll hurt you.

Or you can study Aikido. Here we will take your money every month, and guarantee to hurt you every time you come!"

— Jim Baker, Aikikai

Q. How come it didn't work? (1)
A. Did it not? Define "It Worked."

Aikido works. Your aikido doesn't. Don't confuse the two.

— Hiroshi Ikeda, Aikikai

It is useful to define what you mean by "it worked" or "it didn't work." If someone grabs you and you prefer that he not do that, you have many options. Some techniques (especially those known as *kokyu-nage*) depend on the attacker holding on to the defender; the attacker is in danger of being thrown only so long as he holds on. If he lets go, you have no throw. But, if your purpose was to persuade the attacker to let go and he did, then the technique "worked." You do not have to put him on the ground to achieve that purpose.

In class, when the purpose is to learn a technique, there are other considerations. The technique may proceed too slowly to "work" as a *throw*; it "works" as patterning and as part of the learning process, just as you would learn a new dance step.

New students often see throwing as "winning" and falling as "losing." The attacker (*uke*) may counter every move that the thrower (*nage*) makes, or let go as soon as they feel themselves in danger of falling, then confuse the cessation or change of their own attack with failure of the technique — and of Aikido.[6]

In Aikido, falling is not "losing." It is *uke*'s time for *ukemi* (rolling and falling) practice. *Uke* is not loser but teacher. The ability to fall safely is a valuable self-defense technique and a valuable tool for helping your partner to learn. We learn to give the appropriate attack and we learn to fall so that we can help others to learn. You "win" by being a good teacher.

Winning means winning over the discord in yourself. Those who have a warped mind, a mind of discord, have been defeated from the beginning

— Morihei Ueshiba

Q. How come it didn't work? (2)
A. Aikido is defensive. Were you defending or attacking?

Aikido is primarily a defensive technique. It counters, neutralizes, and redirects attacks; it rarely offers them. Because the defender is using the attacker's weight and power and inertia, rather than his own strength, a smaller defender has a tremendous advantage — so long as he avoids a weight and strength contest.

When someone at home or office asks you to show them what Aikido is about, new students will usually ask the questioner to "grab my wrist." They "do" something, the "attacker" counters, and it often ends up as wrestling match, not Aikido. Why?

---

6. See "Nage and Uke — Partners in the Dance" on page 159.

- The attacker isn't really attacking (this is the office after all, he doesn't know what's going to happen to him, and is feeling apprehensive) so there is limited energy to work with.

- Meanwhile, the student is trying to "do" a technique from a limited repertoire, rather than what might be most appropriate for the energy given.

- When the attacker counters, the student tries to force the technique, the attacker forces back — to the weight and strength contest.

"Real Aikido techniques" require "real attacks." But on the street or on the mat, there should only be one attacker.

Q. Is Aikido really practical for self-defense?
A. Yes.

What we are all striving for is complete control over an attacker, a perfect combination of timing and sensitivity and power that allows us to go untouched as we "move" our attacker wherever we want. This may be onto his head or this may be simply to the other side of the room where he is, temporarily, no longer a threat — your choice. But at that level of control, you have that choice. I think that Aikido suggests what you do with that control.

— David Berger, Aikikai

Practical is exactly the right word.

We go to see fantasy adventure slice&dice movies with Bad Guys and crazed psychotics lurking behind every bush, where the only hope of survival is superior firepower and muzzle velocity and where the monster never dies.

Besides legal considerations, in Real Life an attacker is much more likely to be someone you know and care about, where firepower, muzzle velocity, death-dealing blows are simply not desirable or sensible options. While many martial arts are designed to kill or maim, Aikido gives you the choice of control and a range of options regardless of the attacker.

The word "attacker" usually conjures up the movie version. Consider at least two categories of attacker that are far more likely to appear in the course of life.

Drunken Buddies. A *Tae Kwon Do* blackbelt came to us because of drunken fraternity brothers who came home throwing punches and kicks so he would "show them his moves." Because "his moves" were designed to smash and kill, they were not an option. Meanwhile, his unwillingness to harm was getting him beaten up.

Abusive Children. When my husband's 12-year old son came to live with us, he hit, slapped, or kicked me at every opportunity. When I spoke to him, he "wasn't doing anything" or he was "just playing." Not surprising. He loves his Mom and loves his Dad and although they had already been divorced for over seven years when I first met his father, it is obvious to a child that if only this strange other person would *just go away*, then Mom and Dad could get back together again.

Very wrong — but very understandable. Problem was, the "kid" was as big as I was, weighed more, and was being abusive. What was I to do?

Yell "Just wait 'til your father gets home!" at every incident? — an abdication of authority and responsibility.

Pull out my handy sidearm — carefully selected for firepower and muzzle velocity— and blow him away?

Neither of these were options. Aikido was.

The next punch got him flipped onto the couch. The next grab got him rolled across the rug and the next slap got him a firm *ikkyo* plant with pin. Any combination of these got him out of breath (as he was also fighting gravity) but he was allowed to live and I did not get arrested for child abuse or murder. When he started purposely doing these things for the *fun* of getting rolled across the rug or flipped onto the sofa, we enrolled him in Aikido class.

Think of a favorite uncle who's had a bit too much to drink after the party, the wedding, the divorce, the layoff. This is your child, your brother, your friend. This is also your attacker. Are you going to:

- Smash and destroy a person you care for?
- Be rendered completely helpless by unwillingness to harm? (While your attacker takes full advantage of your kindness . . .)
- Be effective and very glad that effectiveness and control come with the option *not* to smash and destroy?

How you *train* is how you will *do* Aikido. Choose a *range* of appropriate tools. And train for that.

. . . Thus the attacked is saved from harm, and the attacker is saved from sin.

— *Morihei Ueshiba*

Q. Can a woman ever beat a man?

A. Yes.

Most of my Aikido heroes were under 5'4"; tall, under 130 pounds, and over 65 years old. Our friend Vicky is about 4'9" and threw a beefy prison guard so far that he asked if it qualified him for frequent flyer mileage.

— *Jim Baker, Aikikai*

I've often heard men gravely discussing some encounter with a hostile fellow "who must have been heavier by 20 pounds and at least 2 inches taller" while his listener nods seriously in sympathy and understanding. It's strange to hear big strong fellows worry about a few inches and a few pounds when women who have been assaulted by men a couple inches to a couple feet taller and heavier by several pounds to several hundred pounds, are often dismissed with the suspicion that they didn't "Just Say No" firmly enough.

In Aikido the tables are turned. Aikido uses the attacker's own weight, inertia, strength, and energy in such a way that smaller persons actually have an advantage. It may seem impossible but it is very real. [7]

My favorite martial artist within the narrow limits of Aikido is Vicky Chiang. She's Chinese Cuban, has a sandan, rows like O-Sensei, does bookkeeping, teaches reiki, weighs 80 lbs, measures 4' 9", and in my presence beat up a Rikers Island prison cop who benches 300+ who had decided to learn Aikido. And there was nothing he could do about it, either. And she giggled off and on as she did it. He came over to me after about the fifth fall:

"Did you see that?"

"Yes, Mike, I saw it."

"I was flyin'!"

"Yes, Mike, you were."

He went back, and she beat him up again.

Sometimes the terrifying downswing on her muscleless irimi-nage reminds me of a story Hal once told me about falling so far, for so long, from one of Sugano Sensei's throws that he had time to actually begin to worry that there was no ground, that he was on the descent into hell and was going to go on downward forever; and when he did hit the mat, he almost kissed it, he was so grateful it was there.

— *Wendy Gunther, Aikikai*

---

7. See Chapter 3 for the physics of Aikido and the power of small or large bodies.

Q. But doesn't size matter?

A. No.

You humans! When you gonna learn that size doesn't matter?

— Frank "The Dog" in Men in Black

I spent ten years getting my ass kicked by Japanese people who weighed one-third of what I did. There's not one person I fear more than anybody else. Size or sex have nothing to do with it.

— Terry Dobson, It's a Lot Like Dancing

One day I received a shipment of fan-foot geckos, small lizards about six inches long. Suddenly, while I was digging around in the box, one of the lizards ran up my arm and clamped itself onto the skin right over my carotid artery. Startled, I clamped my hand over the lizard, and sat up suddenly. But the back of the chair that I was sitting in was broken.

I fell backwards out of the chair, in the process, kicking the box, sending a couple dozen lizards airborne in a diffuse pattern that covered most of the room. I ended up on the floor, clutching my throat, in a futile attempt to defend myself from this one-ounce lizard who had quite cleanly thrown and pinned me and who even liberated his comrades in the process.

— Wiley Nelson

Aikido is remarkable in that size does *not* matter except for the times when the smaller you are, the more of an advantage you have. On the other hand, some techniques are awkward for partners of radically different sizes. For example, *shiho-nage* which involves ducking under your partner's arm, is difficult for a tall person to perform on a shortie. For the shortie, it's a cinch[8].

Differences in height often cause problems due to different perceptions of "up" and "down." For example, a very tall person may think he is dropping *waaay* down to a point that is still "up" to a shorter person. Sometimes the technique must be subtly altered. For *ikkyo irimi*, a shorter person must concentrate on control of the wrist and fingers that control the arm rather than trying to control the arm directly. Taller partners can do the technique kneeling. Working with these differences is one of the advantages of practice partners of various shapes and sizes.

---

8. Michael Bartman is approximately my height when he kneels. I have a tremendous advantage over poor Mike in *shiho-nage* (which allows me to be relatively sloppy). But if Mike drops to his knees, the whole equation changes.

Q. What about physical disabilities?

A. They can be adapted.

Almost everyone has some sort of disability, from bad knees, to vision, to other conditions. In the end it isn't the condition that matters as much as determination and persistence.

A young woman apparently doomed to life in a wheelchair was somehow dragged into Aikido. She went on to become a *nidan* with her own *dojo*.

One of our students, Jim Templeman, has no arms and he has taught us so much. No one has a more compelling *tenkan* than Jim! — he isn't distracted by trying to muscle *uke* to the mat with his arms like the rest of us.

Jim started out taking classes in Ki Development and Mind and Body Coordination. One evening at the beginning of the second hour I started to teach ryokata-tori techniques — both of uke's hands holding onto nage's gi. I got a gi top from our closet and invited Jim to participate in the first three techniques since they didn't use arms. The rest is history.

We don't change the class much to accommodate Jim but I usually work with him and his partner after the general instruction and figure out how to use the principles being taught with the "technique of the hour" into something Jim can do. He now has his 5th Kyu and is working toward 4th Kyu. Last month he was a member of a demonstration group for a local middle school and wowed the kids with his skill. Jim has taught us much about our art and ourselves. Blessings come in many shapes and guises. Jim is one of ours.

— George Simcox, Ki Society

My mother-in-law, over 50, portly, with persistent myalgia, has asked me to teach her Aikido. She is a Great Lady and the mother of my favorite person, so this is quite an honor. We went to the pool, and worked on tenkan from same side grab, spinning each other about in the warm water. She cannot sit seiza on land, her knees aren't strong enough. But she can do it on the steps in the pool, and I have taught her how to rise properly so she can practice it with the water's support.

I don't know how long we will persist, but I am learning a lot, and I think "pool-kido" for those with physical obstacles has potential. At least as a start!

— Emily Dolan, Seidokan

Q. How long will it take me to get a black belt?
A. About 10 minutes.

There's a martial arts store nearby and you can pick one up for about $6.00. On the other hand, if you want to learn Aikido . . . .

— *George Simcox, Ki Society*

How long is a piece of string?

— *Emily Dolan, Seidokan*

How long does it take to catch a fish?

— *Michael Bartman, Ki Society*

Q. I've heard it's six months to a year before Aikido is practical as a self defense and up to 3 or 4 years until one is proficient . . . .
A. . . . Which is typical of real stuff that real humans do.

Think about it. Does a person with a two-year junior college degree know as much as one with a four-year degree? What does the job market say to that?

If you want to learn cooking, how good are you in six months? Decent, but nobody's going to hire you into the kitchen of a four-star restaurant, are they? With just six months of experience, nobody's going to hire you to run the microwave at the local diner because in just six months you are not yet good enough to go pro.

Whether you want to learn how to restore old cars, shoot skeet, or run a business, just how good are you in just six months?

Most real things take people about four years to get moderately competent at, and several years later they get some degree of mastery. (Aikido, being more complex, kind of up there with ballet or pro basketball, takes a few years longer.) But we all have this fantasy that somehow self defense is going to come faster than other human endeavors. Why? Because we might need it sooner? Hey, I can hear Mr. Reality laughing at us!

What would you think if you heard I was going around to medical schools, saying, "You tell me I can get an MD in four years, but MediQuick U. has offered me one in three. Can you promise to give me one in two and a half?" Then when your HMO assigns me to you against your will as your personal doctor how happy are you going to be if you find out I did just two and a half years of MD training, and went straight from that into practice?

Why should a black belt be any different from that? In any art?

It takes several years to get good at Aikido, just as it takes several years to get good at basketball, skiing, piloting a plane, or learning a language.

That's because Aikido is real.

— *Dr. Wendy Gunther, Aikikai*

Q. What if I need a self-defense class now?
A. Take a self-defense class now.

Martial arts are a long-term investment in time, money, effort, and passion. Aikido does not provide instant self-defense. Neither does any other martial art. Neither does signing up for Drawing 101 make you an artist.

An excellent short-term self-defense series is the renowned Model Mugging (now called Impact Self Defense) which features full-impact training and skills in attitude, response, and technique. Most martial arts, developed by and for men, rely on arms and upper body strength. This system and classes available from the American Women's Self-Defense Association emphasize women's stronger hips and legs while emphasizing the types of attacks which women are most likely to face.[9] Classes are also available tailored to children and to men. All emphasize full-contact practice with a fully padded attacker.

Meanwhile, be aware of your own strengths and weaknesses. As an exercise, consider: if you were a mugger, who would you pick and why? Professional muggers have repeatedly stated that their choice of target is heavily dependent on walk and carriage.

Women wobbling along in tight skirts and high heels (the Western version of Chinese bound feet) are a natural, as are men who walk in a vague, foot-flopping sort of way, as are persons who are inattentive to surroundings and those with a poor sense of personal space. If in doubt, attackers will actually "interview" potential targets to confirm their potential as low-risk victims[10] but the initial selection takes about seven seconds and is heavily based on walk and carriage.

In a classic study[11] prisoners convicted of street assault were shown videos of people walking down the street and asked to rate their vulnerability. Those rated as highly vulnerable shared the following basic characteristics.

1. Abnormally long or short strides.
2. Lifting and placing the whole foot rather than normal heel-to-toe motion.
3. Moving same-side leg and arm at same time, rather than opposite arm and leg[12].
4. Moving upper body independent of lower body with random arm and leg movements; not moving from center.

Your best short and long-term self-defense?

Awareness, mind-body coordination, and confidence.

What we learn in Aikido.

---

9. See Chapter 6 on attacks.
10. See "Life Etiquette" on page 245.
11. Grayson and Morris (1981).
12. This appears to describe the "*samurai* walk" (page 43) but also describes the walk of severely overweight persons whose legs must roll around one another rather than moving directly past.

Q. If you aren't in Aikido for self-defense, why are you here?
A. Because there's more.

When I was in my third year of theatre school we got a new voice teacher. He had individual sessions with each student to evaluate their voice work. I went in and did my best big, deep, full theatre-resonant type voice. Beautifully supported and all. He looked at me and said "Well that's very nice Philip. What else can you do?" I have kind of adopted that as one of my mottoes.

— Philip Akin, Aikido Yoshinkai Canada

People who have been in aikido for more than a year or so seem rarely to be still in it only for application "on the street." That was on the list initially, but not at the top. It is now pretty much at the bottom, and under consideration for being dropped entirely. So why study? A lot of reasons.

It's different from everything else I do, and I often need to be boosted out of my rut. There are aspects of it that I can't explain, and I love puzzles.

I find the basic principles satisfying. They fit well with my outlook on things, and I love the way they are simple yet subtly complex.

I can use any exercise, but I hate gerbil-like activities like stationary bikes and treadmills.

I've found the things I learn at the dojo useful in all areas of life, including working with my boss, undergoing surgery, opening heavy doors, not falling down on ice, and falling down a short flight of stairs without getting hurt in the least (not even a bruise!)[13]

Being around the sort of folks who show up at the dojo is pleasant and relaxing. They are friendly, cheerful, helpful, kind, and interested in at least one of the things I'm interested in: Aikido!

— Michael Bartman, Ki Society

---

13. Mike was thrown by his Sunday newspaper. See page 120.

Q. But what if he . . .

Q. But in the Real World wouldn't you . . . ?

A. It depends.

Dennis: OK, but what if the other guy has a tank, and you're on foot and unarmed?

Wendy: Yeah, well what if my guy has a flame thrower, is mounted on the back of a horse, and you are on the space station Mir?

Janet: It depends. What day of the week is it?

— Aikido-L

The possibilities of attack and defense are unlimited. Beginning Aikido is like beginning arithmetic: we stage a particular attack with particular energy in order to practice a particular response or its variations. Calculus, with its multiple variables, comes later. For now, give the appropriate energy, respond with the appropriate response. This is how we learn. It is never wrong to ask questions or experiment, but meanwhile, practice, test and learn what is presented. (See "Nage and Uke — Partners in the Dance" on page 159.)

Q. But what if this were a *real* attack?

A. Make it real *now*.

Although what happens on the mat is staged practice, the attacks should be quite real in terms of an attack having a particular direction, force, or momentum. Hence "real" is probably best interpreted as "what happens in an attack or counter with a different direction, or force."

Good question. Try it and see. Practicing different possibilities and options will raise your techniques from the level of staged Aikido to real Aikido.

Not all attacks to the hand are the same and the different techniques are designed for different types of energy. You can practice all the *katate-tori* techniques to develop a repertoire of techniques for apparently similar attacks. One technique designed for a wrist grab may deal with pulling forward, another with pulling back. Practice the alternatives because every Aikido technique can be countered.[14] In fact, the advanced Aikidoist will often set up a situation that invites a counter. These are known as "conversions" and are part of the fun of advanced Aikido.

---

14. See "The Cycle of Katame-Waza (Wrist Locks)" on page 184.

Q. But instead I could . . .
A. Yes, but please don't.

We start by practicing basic attacks, basic skills and basic solutions to basic problems. Practice what you are practicing.

New students sometimes want to spend time debating intricate nuances of this or that, theoretical or theatrical comparisons with other styles, or pronouncements on why the basic technique they've been assigned to practice couldn't possibly work in the Real World™.

Better to get up and practice. There are things about driving a car with a manual transmission which simply cannot be explained in words to someone who has never driven anything but an automatic — or who has never driven at all. Please practice what your teacher is teaching you. Mat time is precious and short.

I think training hard, often and diligently is the only philosophy. After 23 some-odd years (yeah, some of 'em very odd), I find that the more I talk about philosophy, the more it eludes me. As long as I train, all that takes care of itself. Ki, harmony, love, whatever. All the same. All useless without good training to take you there. Without a solid foundation in the basics, nothing else is really pertinent anyway.

Talk about it and it slips away.

Ignore it and it comes to you. Kind of like a cat.

— Chuck Gordon, Kokoro Ryu Aiki Budo

Q. But it's all staged. It isn't Real!
A. Neither is Terminator, Freddy, Rambo, or Dirty Harry.

The trick, Fletcher, is that we are trying to overcome our limitations in order, patiently. We don't tackle flying through rock until a little later in the program.

— Richard Bach, Jonathan Livingston Seagull

New students can't help but compare their first beginning steps with what they have seen in carefully choreographed movies. They just aren't the same. Movies have the advantage of extensive rehearsals, a set script, multiple shots, camera angles, stuntmen, safety equipment, skillful editing, and few surprises. Learning Aikido is no different from learning other skills, from piano to basketball. Here's how it works in Real Life.

Level 1: Beginning Practice.

In school, it's learning to print big block letters and do basic arithmetic. In motorcycle class, it's the "duck walk," learning balance and how to shift gears. In skiing it's the bunny slope and "snowplow," proper foot position, weighting and posture.

In beginning Aikido, attacks are staged and static; techniques are done slowly and haltingly with emphasis on following the lines of force and leading energy. The purpose is not to smash *uke* to the ground, but to progress through the technique to its conclusion at which point *uke* is given the opportunity to practice *ukemi*.

It is not the time to carp about how the situation would be handled in other martial arts or to list the reasons why this or that would or would not work "On the Street." In truth the technique may not yet "work" as a technique, because there is little movement, little compelling reason for *uke* to be off-balance[15]. The compelling task at hand is not so much to Make Uke Fall Down as it is to learn the letters and the alphabet of Aikido that will later be formed into words, and still later into entire sentences and books of knowledge.

The alphabet of fencing, if you will allow the expression, is as fixed and immutable as any other alphabet. Is characters are ascertained and definite motions, which are combined in accordance with the structure and balance of our organism, the natural action of the muscles and the flexibility possible to the limbs and body.

— Baron César de Bazancourt, Secrets of the Sword

Level 2: Intermediate Practice

Printing is more fluid as the student is thinking and writing in words rather than individual letters. This child can also walk and run, but is amazed by older children on bicycles and skates. In motorcycling it is developing balance and the ability to lean into a curve and apply brakes without falling over on a highway surface. In skiing it is carved turns and controlled movement in a controlled environment, but no idea how to handle moguls.

In the intermediate levels of Aikido, the student begins to grasp processes rather than one-step operations. This level emphasizes moving and leading *uke's* center and balance. The "real" effects of flow and centrifugal forces begin to appear. Many throws still do not work. Many throws do.

Level 3: Advanced Practice

Calligraphy and calculus. Knowing the forms and building blocks, challenging them, enjoying them, playing among them. In motorcycling it's motocross. In skiing it's hitting the mogul fields — and loving it.

Advanced Aikido combines leading and moving in response to dynamic, forceful attacks. Minute adjustments in position and direction lead and move *uke* into positions that are subject to powerful but invisible forces of the Universe, of gravity, centripetal force, inertia, and balance.

---

15. See the discussion on the physics of traffic on page 75 and suppose that the tight circular curve presented there is on a race-course and you are allowed to view the course to familiarize yourself with the layout before the race. *Walking* through that curve and the forces that act upon you as you do this will be very different compared to *running* through the curve at full speed — in a fully loaded dump truck.

Q. But "On The Street . . ."
A. . . . Is mostly Hollywood and is mostly bunk.

Bad things happen and yes, some of them happen On The Street, but most of them happen in Hollywood.

Do not base training on a theatrical scenario designed to sell adrenaline and tickets.

Do not use it to excuse or cultivate a mindset of justified vengeance and murder or to shortcut or alter techniques on the mat.

Do consider a little statistical reality. Contrary to the popular media, most deadly injuries are not due to muggers with handguns, they are due to motor vehicle accidents and they are due to falls, usually at home or close to it.

What's really on the street is cars. You may be in a hurry, lost, angry or frightened — and so may the other person. Therefore practice *ma-ai,* patience, awareness, flowing and blending. Practice etiquette, good manners, good sense, kindness and consideration. Observe the laws of physics to keep yourself and others safe.

What's really on the street is concrete. You may trip on the curb, slip on the ice, miss a step, break a wrist, an arm, a leg, a head. Therefore practice your rolls and *ukemi*; it can save your life as it once saved mine.

The leading cause of death in America? Not psychopathic killers, gangs, or drugs, although you'd never know it from the headlines.

It is automobile accidents[16], barbecue and "biscuit poisoning," that is, too much speed, too little awareness, too much fat, too much sugar, too little exercise, too much alcohol[17] and too little good sense. It is sticking your head in an alligator's mouth and yelling: "Bite me and you've had it!"

Effective self-defense is surviving daily life using all your tools. It is careful driving, eating right, using your body as it was designed to be used. It's soap and water and flu shots. It's doing your homework, paying bills on time, dealing honorably with others. It's batteries in the fire alarm, knowing how to swim, all the bits and pieces that make up daily life. Real life.

Practice Aikido on the mat, on the street, and at home.

Practice good sense and sensible living.

---

16. True even for policemen.

17. Almost one-third of all accidental deaths including homicides, suicides, fire, burning, and vehicular deaths, are tragically visited, apparently as a random violent act of the Universe, upon persons who are legally drunk at the time.

    During Hurricane Floyd of 1999, a medical worker in Gainesville, Florida, reported that trauma cases fell into three distinct groups. 1) Three-car pileups suffered by people racing to get out before Floyd hit. 2) Chainsaw accidents from people who weren't familiar with chainsaws or who decided to go out and chainsaw down trees leaning against their homes, sometimes after several beers. 3) Later, as the storm was passing, elderly ladies with broken hips who had decided to go out into 40 m.p.h. winds on slick, rain-covered surfaces, in bathrobes and bedroom slippers, to get the newspaper down by the mailbox. On a related note, an amazing number of men are injured while trying to kiss rattlesnakes.

Q. Isn't Aikikai hard? Ki Society too soft? Yoshinkan too stiff?
A. It depends on the practitioner.

With softness and relaxation come responsiveness.

— *Bruce Bookman, Seattle Aikikai*

In working with advanced students, who presumably represent their respective styles, the most softly effective technique I ever felt came from Aikikai, the hardest and stiffest from Ki Society, one of the most graceful and flowing from Yoshinkan. Yoshinkan is usually considered to preserve Aikido as it was up to WWII, Aikikai as it was up to O-Sensei's death. Ki Society split from Aikikai in part to emphasize relaxation and softness of technique from the very beginning, via a new teaching tool (Ki Development Exercises).These different styles offer different emphasis and different approaches to teaching and learning. Yoshinkan and Ki Society, for example, are as much or more *methods of teaching* as they are *styles* of Aikido technique. As a Ki Society practitioner, the most remarkable technical difference I have seen between the three styles is that Ki Society tends to emphasize rolls over breakfalls, and Yoshinkan techniques always move forward, never backward. Other differences are seen between individual instructors.

Meanwhile, few of us embody the pure philosophy of our particular style or chose our style strictly on that basis. Choice of *dojo* is based more on rapport with other students and on rush-hour traffic patterns.

But how different are the various styles really? In 1998, members of the international Internet Aikido-L mailing list cyberdojo resolved to meet, to compare differences and perhaps to showcase the superiority of their particular styles — only to discover that while they were all different, they were all practicing Aikido. Another happy result of this gathering is a tremendous increase in visits and exchanges between dojos and seminars.

Before, "not my style."

Now, *Aikido Friends.*

Q: Won't Seminars Be Too Confusing?
A. Seminars are valuable sources of supplemental information.

Shady martial arts schools are notorious for forbidding their students to attend seminars, read Aikido magazines or books on the grounds that it will "confuse them." Such persons are often less concerned about confusion than fearful that they will be revealed as frauds when their students realize that what they are doing bears no resemblance to real Aikido.

This is quite different from legitimate instructors feeling a tad annoyed with those who return from seminars having Seen The Light and announcing that "so-and-so does it this way and your way is wrong." Very often what they have seen are stylistic differences which can be greater between instructor and instructor than between named styles.[18] Being aware of variations can actually help to reinforce understanding of the underlying fundamentals. On the other hand, sometimes the fundamentals themselves may undergo an epiphany.

Years ago I fell in love with the Paraguayan harp. In the course of attempting to teach myself to play, I discovered that it was a true folk instrument with little or nothing actually written down. As in Aikido, the traditional course of study was to visit the teacher and memorize the lessons without written text or materials.

By wonderful coincidence, I met a Paraguayan harpist in town for the summer without her harp and willing to trade lessons for practice time. On learning that she couldn't read music, I offered to teach her. She adamantly refused for fear it would "stifle her creativity" (a common concern of play-by-ear musicians). She had another odd concern: the colors[19] of the strings and their sequence. Fortunately, mine were the "proper" configuration and so we began with the traditional beginner's piece, *La Llegada*.

"Be patient!" she urged. "Don't give up! It took me six months to learn this but stick with it and practice, practice, practice! — eventually you will get it."

And so I did. While she played the music through, I transcribed it to staff paper. Within 10 minutes I had a fairly presentable rendition of what she had needed six months to learn. It needed work, of course, but notes and timing were correct because I had the advantage of reading them off the page rather than having to memorize everything at once by rote. She was stunned and I think a bit distressed. And so was I when I realized her problem with colors of strings.

Colored strings mark the Tonic (I), Fourth (IV), and Fifth (V) (the most important notes on the scale) or a variation on those intervals. The Paraguayan harp is tuned to F (F G A B-flat C D E F) so colored strings might indicate F (First, I), B-flat (Fourth, IV), and C (Fifth, V).

She had been taught a finger position that was off by one string, hence moving the Tonic (I) from F down to E. Attempting to play in the key of E on a harp tuned to F means an extra B-flat and several missing sharps. It would sound terrible and require a massive retuning (no trivial undertaking on a harp). A comparison of good written texts (had there been any) or a few minutes with a more experienced teacher would have eliminated years of error and confusion.

Often seminars are not a matter of new information at all, but merely the opportunity to see or hear the same old things in a slightly new or different way. Sometimes slightly different words, sung to a slightly different tune makes all the difference and this is what happens on a regular basis at Aikido summer camps and seminars.

---

18. Will Reed comments on the differences in techniques between Aikikai and Ki Society which split off via Koichi Tohei. "What differences? I was at *Honbu Dojo* before the split, when Tohei was still Chief Instructor. How you did a technique depended on who happened to be teaching class that afternoon."

19. Many people are surprised to see that harp strings are colored. "Is that a Beginner Harp?" they ask. Colored strings on harps are *not* equivalent to training wheels on bicycles. They are colored to help locate a single note among so many possibilities just as the 88 keys on the piano (derived from the harp) are colored differently.

Q: Is it always so bloody frustrating?

A. Yes. No matter who you are.

Came back from class today having gotten something right maybe three attempts in two hours. I think not only have I not learned anything so far, I've actually unlearned things I may have already known (like how to do a nikyo, which I did successfully in the long ago jujutsu days, but cannot manage now). Is everybody this screwed up when they begin, or can some people just not learn it?

— *Paul Gowder, Ki Society*

Great! You're right on track! And the advanced students say the same thing. Can some people just not learn it? Only the ones who give up. Sometimes they're the natural athletes accustomed to being good at every sport they try. They just can't believe Aikido can be so alien, which may be why we tend to retain more turtles than gazelles. Former turtles are now beautiful Aikidoists because they stayed when other more athletic and coordinated types fled in frustration. The grace and beauty and rhythm and flow that you see in the senior students are from years of playing and dancing on the mat — coming back when the others didn't. You have essentially taken up Classical Ballet with a physics minor. Do not be shocked if you aren't ready to dance at Carnegie Hall after a few short months of study. Remember the old joke per the lost tourist who asks the old man on the street how to get to Carnegie hall: "Practice! Practice!"

A poster that hung on our dojo wall for many years showed a little child carefully piling a tower of his first building blocks. The caption read: "The expert in anything was once a beginner." Many times students would step off the mat, go to that picture, look long and hard, take a deep breath, turn around and go back to practice. I know because I was one.

Just keep doing and you will learn. Meanwhile, I guarantee that you have learned more than you know and right now you can help new baffled persons coming in the door. They will have questions you can answer.

[Dad] is in his early 50's and has been in Tae Kwon Do for less than a year. He used to come home from practice and tell me that he had trouble doing some of the techniques, so he told his instructor he couldn't do it because he was too old! And then he wondered why his instructor yelled at him. I was flabbergasted. The whole reason I took Aikido classes was to learn Aikido. If I already knew how to do it, I'd be teaching them! I suppose some people think that if you aren't a "natural" you can't do it, which is [nonsense] that needs to be weeded out of the collective psyche.

—*K. A. D.*

Q: If it's so simple, how come it's so hard?
A. Actually, it is very simple but it may not be easy.

They're all very simple concepts. We render them complex because we're unwilling to believe that it is really so much easier than we believe. One of my first teachers told our beginning class that on the last day of class he would reveal The Secret of Aikido. When that day arrived, he revealed to the few of us that remained that The Secret of Aikido was . . . showing up and practicing.[20]

—*Tarik J. Ghbeish, Aikikai*

I've heard Saotome Sensei refer to the Secrets of Aikido. He keeps meeting people who want to know these secrets, and he keeps telling them that The Secrets are — everything you learned in the first week of your training.

— *Jun Akiyama, Aikikai*

Q. How often should I come to class?
A. It depends.

For beginners who want to progress, we recommend three days a week. Two days a week gives you too long a time between classes but may be adequate for an experienced student. At one day a week, you will hardly remember a thing from one class to another. For most people who start off determined to come *every* day, there is a definite pattern of burnout. Three days of class throughout the week gives you training, repetition, reinforcement, and a rest in between.

Homework, however, is another matter. Consider spending at least 15 minutes to half an hour *daily* on basic exercises, even if it is only turning *tenkan* in the kitchen while waiting for the kettle to boil. Consider any or all of the exercises for individual practice in Chapter 8. Off-mat training time makes on-mat training time more efficient and rewarding.

My Aikido sucks, but every day I try to suck at a higher level.

— *Janet Rosen, Aikikai*

---

20. Garrison Keillor is a firm believer in the notion that "90 percent of life is just showing up." He attributes his success in radio to having had an alarm clock to awaken him for the early morning show. No one else wanted it.

Q. How can you say Aikido is "non-violent"? Isn't smashing an attacker into the ground a bit violent?
A. It depends — on the appropriate tool.

"Do you think," said Candide, "that mankind always massacred one another as they do now? Were they always guilty of lies, fraud, treachery, ingratitude, inconstancy, envy, ambition, and cruelty? Were they always thieves, fools, cowards, gluttons, drunkards, misers, calumniators, debauchees, fanatics, and hypocrites?"

"Do you believe," said Martin, "that hawks have always been accustomed to eat pigeons when they came in their way?"

"Doubtless," said Candide.

"Well then," replied Martin, "if hawks have always had the same nature, why should you pretend that mankind change theirs?"

"Oh," said Candide, "there is a great deal of difference; for free will . . ." and reasoning thus they arrived at Bordeaux.

— *Voltaire, Candide (1759)*

Much of the problem of "violence versus pacifism" is in the definition of what is, in the end, merely a tool.

Pacifism is not the same as *passivism* and it is not the opposite of *violence.*

Pacifism is the opposite of *belligerence.*

As *tools*, violence, pacifism, and passivism can all be *appropriate* or *inappropriate.* A peaceable man — one who prefers peace to war — may use violence where it is appropriate, just as he would use any other tool. The belligerent man is the one who uses or prefers to use violence[21] when it is appropriate — and when it is *not.*

There may also be misunderstandings of life realities, available options, morality, and focus.

Life Realities. Like it or not, there are bad people in the world. Ignoring that does not change the reality.

An instructor at a religious university proposed a conference for members who had served in some of the grimmer areas of the world and those less traveled to discuss issues of violence and self-defense. It was the untraveled ones who were certain that gentle non-resistance was the answer to everything, that murderers faced with Christ-like patience[22] would be shamed and inspired into piety and good manners. They extended this to the point of insisting that the brothers who had direct experience of a very different reality not be permitted to speak.

---

21. And note that some of the most belligerent, violent behavior may be disguised in verbal, rather than physical, violence.

22. The image of a "Gentle Jesus, meek and mild" is theologically traditional but historically incorrect. He wasn't. Not even close. Someone who tells the religious and governmental authorities of his day that they are clueless idiots, assaults the clerks and officers of the central bank with a whiplash, and arms his followers with swords when necessary to ensure that only He is taken away, fits no standard definition of "meek and mild." It is a holdover from centuries of Christianity as State Religion when a meek and mild populace was much encouraged by those who would rule it.

Available Options. The common perception is that either you a) kill, murder, or destroy or b) you lie down and play doormat. In fact there are many other options (and Aikido offers many). As Bruce Tegner noted, "there must be a full range of responses to correspond to the range of possible situations. Otherwise there is only the all-or-nothing response, which is not a choice — it is a dilemma."

Focus. One of the Hard Sayings of the New Testament is "Resist not Evil."[23] While this is often taken to mean that Evil should be allowed free-rein, that we are to drop our defenses against it, embrace it, or harmonize with it, more likely it was first, an injunction against being an automatic stimulus-response machine, and second, an issue of *focus.*

For example, I have heard Model Mugging/IMPACT Self Defense courses dismissed by some Aikidoists as "too violent" or damned with faint praise as "valuable for meeting a need some folks have for empowerment before they can move on to a more rational approach to life." Before recommending IMPACT, I took the course to evaluate it for myself. It is strongly karate-oriented because that is where it came from. I saw several situations that could be handled far more easily and efficiently with Aikido or judo techniques. But students are trained to go for an effective knockout and to get away; they are not trained to rip out lungs or eyeballs, maim or kill. Dismissing it as "too violent" dismisses useful skills while focusing a lop-sided protectiveness on the perpetrator, ignoring behavior that made defensive skills necessary in the first place, and ignoring the victim. Look at the victim.

A renowned example of focus is that of the pacifist French Huguenot village of Le Chambon. During World War II it threw itself into the work of rescuing fugitive Jews from the Nazis. Le Chambon is often cited as a triumph of pacifism over violence, but that is incorrect. Nothing done there helped to end the war. But rather than following the Resistance focus on the aggressor (with assassination, terrorism, and intelligence), Le Chambon focused on the equally hard and dangerous work of rescuing the persecuted. Nor did they work alone. Unknown to Le Chambon, the little town had its own "Schindler" in the person of German Major Julius Schmahling, the man who worked to keep Le Chambon safe to do its work. What mattered to Le Chambon — and to Schmahling — was not "death to the enemy." What mattered was *life.*

Morality. It is always right to investigate nonviolent solutions to problems. Unfortunately *pacifism* confused with *passivism* in the "do-nothing-because-it-is-more-saintly-of-me" sense is not necessarily the moral high-road, is usually unhealthy in practice and often an evolutionary dead-end. The career criminal or professional predator does not rob, rape, and kill out of desperation, but as a conscious choice of free will, convenience, or simply because it's fun and he enjoys it[24]. Therefore consider passive non-resistance to attack from the attacker's point of view: *convenient* and *contemptible.*

Sacrifice of self or others to such a perversion of right and reason is *not* a moral act.

---

23. "A *very* Hard Saying for me," says an old soldier, "for I have seen what Evil can do." So had Nietzsche, who obviously understood the problem of focus. (See page 6).

24. See Samenow, Stanton E. (1984), *Inside the Criminal Mind* for a chilling but practical dose of reality.

Ray Bradbury's classic *Fahrenheit 451*[25] is the tale of a totalitarian regime where books are systematically burned and the job of "fireman" has a whole different meaning. Former fireman Guy Montag joins a band of outlaw scholars whose means of protecting their books is to *memorize* the book, keeping the precious ideas and memories safely hidden away in mind and body until the day when they can once again be written down. Essentially the person *becomes* the book.

"I am," says Montag, "*Ecclesiastes.*"

Who are you?

You are everything you've known and done, places you've been, people you have known, skills and talents and loves and joys, creativity and points of view, tales and songs and stories, and all the things that will be lost without you.

You are an absolutely unique creation of yourself and others.

You are many books.

Treasure them and protect them.

Is it worthwhile to be the owner of so many talents, youth and strength, a cultured mind, a healthy body, and yet not even to know how to defend your life? . . . I am reminded of the story told of a certain General. One of his officers, who disagreed with him on . . . some strategic movement, had said:

"Well, General, when the time comes I will show you that I know how to die."

"Don't be a fool, Sir," replied the General. "Your duty is not to see that you get killed, but to take care that you don't."

— Baron César de Bazancourt, *Secrets of the Sword*

---

25. The title refers to the ignition point of paper. Also note that the book was *published* in 1953 at the very height of the McCarthy witch-hunt hearings.

Q. Is Aikido a Religion?
A. No. Not unless you make it one.

Founder Morihei Ueshiba was fiercely adamant that his Aikido was not a religion. Should his students become Shinto or Omote because he was Shinto or Omote? Absolutely not! He felt that Aikido should not make them anything except better Christians, Buddhists, Muslims, Jews — whatever they were already.

Unfortunately, too many people flock to worship Power or The Unknown and too many others are willing to worship or be worshipped on that basis alone.

"See my great *nikyo*? I shall, therefore, be your spiritual Master. Sign here."

"Oh yes Master!"

This is as foolish and perhaps even less sensible than Goat Worship[26] which I suspect was developed by dwellers of arid areas on observing some interesting metabolic powers of goats and desperately desiring those powers for themselves. It would be little different from persons desperately concerned with self-defense or the prestige of being a "master of mystic oriental secrets," desiring those powers for themselves and indulging in all sorts of nonsense to get them, from the simple mindlessness of herd behavior to the very worst kind of cultism.

Aikido is not a religion, however, Aikido and Ki Exercises can be used to demonstrate what all the great religions have preached. In so many ways Aikido forces us to confront secret desires of the heart, fears and hatreds, the physical effects of internal attitude and orientation. Hopefully one day, we realize that it isn't about having power over others, or about allowing others to have power over us. It isn't even about being really good at hitting people with planets.

There is a Bigger Picture.

Miss that picture and you may one day discover that all along you've been worshipping a goat.

Worship a worthy God. Then practice Aikido for the fun and the joy of it.

---

26. Horns radiate heat, regulating body temperature. When water is scarce, goats stop drinking and store water for days. To a human who lay dying of thirst beside a dry water hole, the sight of goats frolicking merrily on the rocks must have seemed nothing short of supernatural.

CHAPTER 2

Getting Started

Customs differ from one dojo to another, but here are some general guidelines of interest to beginners, from clothing and equipment to etiquette and basic skills.

Clothing

Few Aikido schools require you to have a uniform for your first class or classes. You are usually welcome to wear any comfortable sportswear. Consider, however, that jeans (if snug fitting) may restrict your motion, that you will be in positions where big balloony shorts were never intended to be viewed, and that fashionable aerobics-class gear is inappropriate.

Sweatpants provide freedom of motion and protect the knees from abrasion on a canvas mat or from sticking on a vinyl one. A long-sleeved T-shirt will protect your elbows and forearms. For attacks and grabs, however, shirts that are too stretchable or flimsy will be a problem to you and to your partner. Whatever your choice,

- Wear clean, untattered, appropriate clothing.
- Keep toenails and fingernails trimmed.
- Tie up long flowing hair for safety and comfort.[1]
- Avoid make-up, and heavy perfume or aftershave.
- Remove any jewelry. It can cut or injure you or someone else.
  Dangling wire-pierced earrings are particularly dangerous for the wearer. No watches, no barrettes, no rings.[2]

If you do decide to make a commitment to Aikido, standard practice clothing is the traditional white cotton *keikogi*[3] ("practice clothing"). Two types are used:

---

1. Long, loose, flowing hair in this manual appears under special artistic license to indicate flow and motion. In real life, long loose hair can get tangled in the course of a throw, stepped on during *ukemi* or caught under your partner's knee in a pin. In a high velocity spin it can catch a bystander in the eye. Tie it up.

2. Rings with cut stones, prongs or fancy settings can slice a partner but even the plainest of rings can be a danger to the wearer. Swelling of a finger injured by jamming or a weapon strike may make it impossible to remove a tight band just when it is most critical to do so. Pliers may work in emergency, but petroleum jelly and small flat file with toothed edge will do the least damage to ring or wearer. Both are valuable additions to the *dojo* first-aid kit which should also include chemical ice packs.

3. *Gi* is a word element that did not stand alone in Japanese. It will be used here to mean "uniform" because it is most familiar in the U. S. It is actually a *dogi* which refers to the "clothing worn while studying the way (*do*)." *Uwagi* is the jacket. See Glossary.

- **The heavy-weight judo style.**
  Helps to cushion falls and rolls. Also, those who sweat profusely during practice often tend to favor the thicker judo top because it absorbs more moisture.

- **The light-weight karate style.**[4]
  No appreciable padding, but cooler in summer, easily supplemented in winter, and easily packed for travel.

The choice between the two is usually personal[5] although the judo style is the more traditional. Always buy cotton for comfort and buy large, as cotton tends to shrink. Note that unbleached "natural" garments will shrink more than the white ones that have already been subjected to the bleaching process.

Gi

Traditionally, the jacket is put on first while you are still wearing your street pants, a tradition which addresses the possibility of an emergency such as a call to arms occurring while dressing thus avoiding being "caught with one's pants down."

1. Pull on jacket, left arm first[6].
2. Remove street pants.
3. Step into the pants (with loops in front), left leg first.
4. Snug the drawstrings through the loops and tie.

To put on judo jacket

1. Wrap right side over body.
2. Wrap left side over right side.
3. Secure with belt.

---

4. This light top was developed specifically for karate; punches and kicks under the weight of the judo jacket are quite exhausting.

5. The heavy jacket is often favored by men, especially in cold weather, because the Western men's knit undershirt is not considered good form (not a traditional Japanese garment). In hot weather they are said to absorb more perspiration but being heavier and thicker it will also make you perspire more. Feeling clumsy and uncoordinated? The heavier *gi* may actually help you learn. See why in Appendix C.

6. In the East, "left side first" is the traditional starting point for nearly all actions, so even the act of dressing mindfully and with awareness is good practice for what will happen later on the mat. In *taigi* competition, points are lost for stepping on the mat with anything but the left foot. This is opposite to Western tradition. To the Romans, especially, "starting off on the 'right foot'" meant exactly that.

To put on the karate jacket

1. Wrap right side across body.
2. Tie right front outside tie to left inside tie.
3. Wrap left side over the right.
4. Tie left front tie to right side tie.

Ladies note that jackets will gap. You will want to wear an undershirt or camisole or add some sort of fastener. A safety pin can snap open with painful consequences during hard practice; a small tie or even Velcro sewn down the inside surfaces is simple, safe, and secure. The jacket closes like a man's shirt (left over right) so that you can slip your right hand into the opening, a handy place to store a small cloth.[7]

Belt

Unlike beginning karate students who must earn the right to wear any belt, beginning Aikido students wear a belt from the very beginning.

1. Put the center of the belt at the front of your waist and wrap the ends around your body until they cross in front, right over left.
2. Pass the top (right) end around the entire belt and out again.
3. The tie that was on the right is now on the left. Pass this left-hand tie over the right to form a square knot. The "arrow" of the knot should point to the left.
4. Align the folds of the belt to conform to the knot.

The knot that is "folded" rather than forced will last longer and the weight of ends hanging down helps somewhat to keep it in place, but during hard practice it will invariably work loose and need to be tightened. Proper etiquette is to turn to the wall and make any adjustments as discreetly as possible.

7. At a time when "to be civilized" meant "to be like the Chinese," Japanese clothing styles followed Chinese clothing styles. When the Japanese court moved to Nara in 1710, it adopted dress rules based on the Tang clothing code which specifically mandated that all robes cross left side over right side just as in Chinese fashion. The Chinese (and hence the Japanese) considered right-over-left to be the sure sign of a barbarian (Dalby, 1993). For an outstanding exception, see page 55.

Hakama

The Japanese *hakama* is the traditional skirt or voluminous pants worn by the Japanese *samurai*. In theory, it hid the feet so that opponents could not use foot position to anticipate movements. This is as likely as playing soccer in a full-length evening gown to hide ball handling skills from the opposing team. In fact, in battle or bad weather, the *hakama* was worn short or hiked up to the belt so as not to encumber the feet, catch on obstacles, or drag in the mud. But, because the *hakama* can indeed conceal footwork, it is usually restricted to advanced students.

In some schools, *hakama* are worn only upon reaching black belt (first *dan*). In others, women only wear them from the beginning supposedly for the sake of modesty[8] and the tradition that a woman in *gi* pants is not dressed. In other schools, students wear *hakama* at third *kyu*.

Wearers may find that the *hakama* gives a greater feeling of stability and may improve the ability to keep One-Point. It certainly offers the definite advantage of keeping the belt firmly in place no matter how wild your practice may be. Although it may be years before a student will wear a *hakama*, it is good etiquette to offer to fold *Sensei's hakama* after class — and good practice for learning to fold one's own when the day comes.

The *hakama* may look like a skirt, but the version used in Aikido is actually the horse-back riding style of huge pleated pants. If you are in a dojo where it is worn by beginners, make sure that a first-time wearer knows this[9]. Actor and Yoshinkan practitioner Philip Akin who played in the *Highlander* TV series tells of an incident (in "Eye for an Eye") in which fellow actor Stan Kirsch ("Ritchie Ryan") was hobbled and thrown by his *hakama*.

"I was kind of showing him how to wear one while putting mine on at the same time. I only noticed that he had it wrong after we had nearly finished the shooting, so all those kendo shots to the head (which were not pulled, by the way), were all done with him in one leg.

— *Philip Akin, Aikido Yoshinkai Canada*

8. Americans may recall that in the U. S. through the 1940's and 1950's, women in pants were considered improper or downright immoral. In some areas this is still true. However, to many Aikidoists the "*hakama* for modesty" rule seems a tad odd when ladies change after class into shorts and tank tops.

9. . . . And knows which way it goes. A correspondent tells of attending an "Aikido Demonstration" at a local Martial Arts Academy. The "Aikido Black Belts" all came out wearing *hakama* backwards, *koshiita* in front. When he asked as innocently as possible what the hard thing in front was for he was seriously told that it was "to block punches." Apparently all they knew of Japanese arts was from watching Bruce Lee's *Chinese Connection;* the wicked Japanese all wear their *hakama* backwards (and their evil master is made up to resemble Toshiro Mifune). For the record, the backboard goes in *back* and like any other pair of pleated pants, pleats go in front.

Equipment

In Aikido most of what you bring is yourself. We don't use extensive pads or equipment. You may, however, want to add basic toiletries to your Aikido bag, including nail clippers and talcum powder in addition to other items below.

- **Eyewear.** There seems to be a large population of students with poor eyesight in Aikido. Many consider poor eyesight to be an advantage. Someone who cannot see well enough to focus on the hand or on details must take in the opponent as a whole and focus on his motion and direction as a whole in a way that sharper-eyed students may not. Many of course, successfully wear contacts. Sport goggles are always safe and secure. Many wear their regular street glasses if made of shatterproof safety glass and flexible frames.

- **Washcloth.** A washcloth, bandanna, or other small cloth is extremely useful during hot sweaty summer months and can be stored in the fold of the *gi* top. It also has many uses as a training tool. (See page 226).

- **Pads.** You may want to bring volleyball or skating pads for some knee exercises. Not required, but comfortable. Wear under your *gi* pants.

  Another possible use for pads is rolling practice. Students learning forward rolls almost invariably begin by falling down on the shoulder at first, yet I've never known anyone to suggest shoulder pads to beginners to get them comfortably through this beginning stage. Give it a try. Dense foam (from fabric or upholstery stores) can be stitched inside the *gi*. In an emergency, these or an equivalent, such as stray socks or a washcloth, can be taped to the shoulders.

  You might even consider learning to roll in a motorcycle jacket. (See page 83). Pads for motorcycle jackets are sold separately from the jackets and are specifically designed to protect the wearer from impact.

- **Weapons.** Most established schools will have a supply of wooden practice weapons, but you will soon want your own. They are stocked by martial arts supply houses and available mail-order.

  The wooden staff (*jo*) for beginner's practice need not be an expensive weapon handcrafted from rare tropical woods. Most students start with a broomstick or a dowel from the hardware store, but these may be weak and splintery softwood. Instead, consider a replacement handle, for a hoe or other tool, of strong and splinter-free hickory. Cut to chest (nipple or armpit) height. Check for straightness and for any splinters or uneven or weak spots where the *jo* might shatter if struck. Smooth and sand out any rough spots.

  The wooden sword (*bokken*) is best bought in person so that you can check weight and balance and only after using enough different examples at your *dojo* to have an idea of what weight and balance means.

  Note that these are *wooden* practice weapons. Don't even think of showing up at class with "Genuine Special Collector's Limited Edition 420 Stainless Steel" movie or series reproductions!

  Travel with weapons. If you are at the ticket counter about to fly off to a seminar, never ever refer to these items as "weapons." Call them "sticks" or you may miss your plane. For carry-on, try packing them in gun or golf bag (although it is said that these are subject to theft) or in a length of PVC pipe (with cover and drawstring).

Dojo Etiquette

From ancient times one dictum of budo has been: "Begin with etiquette, conclude with etiquette." The etiquette taught in aikido [is] mutual respect, consideration for others, cleanliness . . . Etiquette is an important aspect of practice for all aikido students.

— Kisshomaru Ueshiba, The Spirit of Aikido

Budo without courtesy is just a lame excuse for mutual abuse.

— Stefan Stenudd

Upon entering the *dojo*, bow to the *shomen*[10] at the front of the room. Shoes usually go on a shelf near the door, and are never worn inside or on the mat. Sandals (*zori*) may be worn inside but placed at the edge of the mat (toes facing outward) before you get on the mat.

Bowing is the traditional Japanese expression of respect, honor, and thanks.[11] The standing bow (*ritsu rei*) inclines the upper body to about 45 degrees. (The kneeling bow is described on page 41).

Bowing is polite but also practical; it helps to stretch and limber back muscles which may have tightened in the course of practice, and properly done, a bow is actually an Aikido technique, a throw, in and of itself.

1. Bow (standing) when you enter and leave the dojo.
2. Bow to the *shomen* before getting on or off the mat.
3. Bow to partners and teachers.
4. When in doubt, bow.

Protocol varies from *dojo* to *dojo*, but here are some general guidelines.

To get on the mat,

1. Remove *zori*[12].
2. Bow to *shomen* before stepping onto the mat.
3. Be seated quietly. You may wish to do some warm-up, limbering or stretching exercises before class begins. Or sit quietly in meditation. Class is about to start when the instructor steps onto the mat.

To begin class,

1. The instructor (*Sensei*) and students sit in *seiza*, the formal Japanese kneeling posture (see page 40) facing the *kamiza* at the front of the *dojo*. During this period sit in silence.[13]

---

10. This will be the focal point of the room. It may include a photograph of O'Sensei, calligraphy, flowers, or other objects.
11. It is not a religious rite. Those who are constrained from bowing by religion or principle should not bow. I have never known of a *dojo* to require bowing in order to study Aikido. It is etiquette, custom, and tradition, but not an article of faith.
12. Japanese split-toe sandals.

---

2. *Sensei* and the class bow to the *kamiza* in unison. *Sensei* then turns to face the students.

3. The class bows to *Sensei* who returns the bow.

   You may hear the phrase o-*nagai-shi-mas* ("please," usually interpreted as "please teach me"). Class now begins, usually with warm-up or stretching exercises.

To get on the mat if you are late and class is in progress,

1. Sit in *seiza* at the edge of the mat.
2. Wait for a bow from the instructor.
3. Return the bow and step onto the mat.

To work with weapons,

1. Always keep the weapon to your left when sitting.
2. Keep swords (*bokken*) or knives (*tanto*) with blade out.
3. Replace weapons in the rack with blade up.

   Blade out while sitting and blade up in weapons rack are appropriate for the martial intent of the dojo.

   In a home or in company, or in a less martial *dojo*, weapons are placed blade-side in (or down). Placing weapons blade out (or up) is considered extremely rude and threatening.

To observe a technique,

1. When *Sensei* halts practice (usually with two claps) to explain a technique, stop what you are doing at once and . . .
2. Be seated (to allow everyone a clear view) in *seiza*.

   By extension, *do not clap in the dojo during class!* Confusion will result.

To take a test when *sensei* goes around the room testing,

1. Take your test.
2. Sit down and wait for the others to finish and class to resume.

To help demonstrate a technique,

1. *Sensei* may ask you — with a bow and *dozo* ("please") — to serve as *uke* to help demonstrate a technique.
2. Return the bow, then
3. Rise and come forward.

If Sensei stops to lecture,

1. Be seated in *seiza*, facing the instructor and the side wall. Your part of the demonstration is over when *Sensei* dismisses you with a bow.
2. Return the bow and return to your place.

---

13. Different schools have differing seating protocols. Some line up strictly by rank, others do not. Some clap before or after bowing to the *shomen*, others do not.

To ask a question or work with another student

1. Indicate your request by bowing.
2. Your partner will accept by returning the bow.
3. Take turns serving as *nage* (the one doing the throw) and *uke* (the attacker). Switch partners with each technique.

   Usually, techniques are practiced 2-4 times (on right and left) by one partner, then 2-4 times by the other partner and so on. Repeat the cycle as often as possible in time allotted matching your practice to the time available.

To practice a technique,

1. Do only the technique demonstrated.
2. Be as gentle and cooperative as possible or as necessary — you're next!

To indicate discomfort or pain,

1. *Uke* slap the mat or body. If lying on free arm, slap or kick with a leg.
2. On hearing the slap,[14] *nage* must immediately release the pressure.

   Aikido techniques are designed to control while avoiding damage to the opponent, hence injuries are rare compared to many other martial arts. Nevertheless they do occur. The most common seems to be stubbed toes, often from catching toes in the seams between vinyl mats, or sore shoulders from improper rolling.

To avoid injury after a throw (as *nage*),

1. Remain upright and centered.
2. Rather than leaning over, bend knees, drop Center/One-Point.

   The beginning *nage* also forgets to step out of the way and drops *uke* on his foot or is so shocked that the technique is actually working and that *uke* is falling, that he bends over after a throw, stopping the partner's rolling toes with a chin. Do the techniques as if you were standing on ice — stay over your Center/One-Point and do not bend *over*.

To avoid injury after a throw (as *uke*),[15]

1. Go with the throw rather than attempting to counter or regain your lost balance.
2. For back rolls, put down the leg nearest *nage* and maintain contact with *nage* as long as possible.

To deal with injuries,

1. Tape any stubbed fingers or toes or tie a red cloth or bandanna[16] around an injured arm or part to signal partners to take special care.
2. Report injuries to Sensei.If you have any injury which is bleeding, get off the mat to bandage it. Do not bleed on the mat.

---

14. In a crowded class or a seminar, a slap may be hard to hear. Add the visual channel by slapping in *nage*'s sight. If he still doesn't notice, slap on *nage*'s arm, leg, or body.
15. See Bruce Bookman's excellent *ukemi* tapes (page 266).
16. As a practical example of "mind follows eyes," many students say it's better to tag the *opposite* arm. Many people are subconsciously attracted to it rather than noticing that they should stay away (the "target fixation" response).

To stop or rest,

1. If required, check with instructor before leaving the mat. Bow before leaving.
2. Bow yourself back onto the mat (or await permission) when ready to return.
3. Do not stand idle or gossiping on the mat. Practice time is limited; make the most of it. How often can you do a technique accurately in the allotted time?

To end class,

1. *Sensei* and the class will again face the *kamiza* in *seiza.*
2. All bow in unison.
3. *Sensei* will turn and bow to the students who bow to him; but this time you will hear "*Thank you, Sensei!*"
4. *Sensei* may respond with "Please thank each other!"
5. Turn and bow to everyone with whom you have practiced.

Class is now over, but . . .

To leave the mat and the dojo,

1. Bow again towards the *shomen* before stepping off the mat.
2. Assist with any mat cleaning or equipment storage following class.
3. Bow again before leaving the dojo.

Some Basic Skills

Words and Phrases

"The question is," said Alice, "whether you can make words mean different things."
"The question is," said Humpty Dumpty, "which is to be master, that is all."

— *Lewis Carroll, Alice in Wonderland*

On entering the dojo you will be hit with a barrage of new concepts and ideas, a new vocabulary and new words. Most traditional dojos use Japanese words and phrases in their classes. While this may seem intimidating at first, they are quickly learned and an opportunity to increase cultural awareness and understanding.[17] One example is the word for *Aikido* itself.

 Ai means "to fit, to be in harmony or agreement with. The lower strokes form a square which represents a mouth or opening such as that of a teapot. The upper three strokes originally formed a lid or stopper. The combination suggests two things that harmonize or fit together, such as the lid on a teapot, the cork in a bottle, the round peg in the round hole.

 Ki comes from the ancient Chinese character for *Qi*, steam, composed of elements representing sun and fire, the sources of steam. The horizontal stroke with the curved vertical line represents a boiling pot of rice with a lid and a handle. The uppermost strokes represent the rising clouds of steam. The cross within the pot represents a stalk of rice with four individual grains, the food that gives life and energy to humans.[18] Together these elements compose a symbol which came to indicate vapor, spirit, breath, or "breath power."

 Dô shows a human figure walking along, what to my eye appears to be, a paved road or path. *Dô* (equivalent to *tao* in Chinese) now means a road or path in the literal sense; by extension it can mean a course of study. There is a difference between a *jutsu* which implies a collection of "techniques," versus the *do* which implies a way of life.

Some words which you will hear from the very beginning are:

---

17. See Glossary for literal meanings and examples.
18. I once saw two elderly Korean hairdressers faced with the daunting task of hoisting a hefty customer into the chair. They succeeded. "Rice power!" they cried, exulting.

- *Sensei* — Instructor, teacher, from *sen*, before, and *sei*, living or born, literally "one who was born before you."

- *Nage* — the one who "throws" or responds to an attack. (In some styles such as Yoshinkan, this partner is known as *sh'te* (pronounced "shtey," literally the principal actor in a *Kabuki* play).

- *Uke* — the attacking partner who is thrown and performs *ukemi*, in turn, the ability to "protect" oneself while being thrown. In some styles, this partner is known as *tori*, the "attacker."

Techniques in this Japanese art are usually identified by Japanese names. Formal names for techniques are usually provided by the organization headquarters and so differ from style to style.

A string of unfamiliar sounds can be intimidating, but the advantage of the Japanese names is that once the concepts are mastered the words come apart. Most technique names describe exactly what you are going to see and do[19].

Names break down into three parts: the type of attack, the technique you will use, and directions on how to move yourself into position. For example, consider *katate-kosa-tori kokyu-nage irimi tobikomi*. Its English nickname is "Kokyu-nage Basic" but the Japanese name provides the following detailed instructions.

- **Attack**: *Katate* is "wrist," *kosa* means "cross," and *tori* is an "attack"; hence this technique deals with an attack to the opposite wrist (his right hand to your right hand). But how will you deal with this attack?

- **Technique**: With a *kokyu-nage*. *Kokyu* means "breath" (but may be interpreted as "timing"); *nage* means "throw." *Kokyu-nage* is a family of "breath-throws," techniques which depend on timing, sensitivity, and *ki* extension rather than a joint lock (such as *kote-gaeishi*).

- **Approach**: How will you move to begin the technique? *Irimi* is an "entering" motion and *tobikomi* means "jumping in." In this technique, you will move into the attacker's space (rather than around him).

Hence, loosely translated, *katate-kosa-tori kokyu-nage irimi tobikomi* means:

"An attack to the opposite wrist dealt with by entering the attacker's space, leaping into position, and performing a throw based on timing and sensitivity to the attacker's movement and position."

The same attack handled in almost the same way but with an added wristlock known as *kote-gaeishi* is called *katate-kosa-tori kote-gaeishi irimi tobikomi*, hence:

"An attack to the opposite wrist dealt with by entering the attacker's space, leaping into position, and performing a throw by unbalancing uke with a wrist-twist."

---

19. See "Teaching by the Numbers . . ." on page 168 for Guy deWolf's excellent technique for tying together names and techniques.

Seiza

Seiza ("correct-sitting") is the formal Japanese sitting or kneeling posture. To kneel and to rise, remember "left down, right up."

To go from standing to *seiza*,

1. Drop left knee to mat (right knee is up).
2. Drop right knee to mat and sit back on lower legs.
3. To sit resting, cross right big toe over left big toe. To sit in *seiza* but prepared for movement and action, stay up on toes ("live toes").
4. Rest hands lightly on thighs.

In *seiza*,

- Forehead and weight of head are over your center[19] rather than over feet.
- Lower back curves gently in.
- Knees are approximately two fists apart.
- Posture is softly erect.

When pressure is applied to the chest, *seiza* allows you to transfer the force to the tailbone which, being pushed into the mat, just makes you more stable.

It is common to lean too far forward or too far back. A partner usually provides a test for proper position, but you can easily test yourself. Proper position of torso is the point at which you can stand up without first shifting your weight forward.

You may have problems with *seiza* if your quadriceps (thigh) or other leg muscles are too tight and pull painfully on the knee. Beginners find it impossible to believe that they will ever sit comfortably in this position. You will, but meanwhile, pay attention to leg stretching exercises, especially for front thighs. Transition can also be eased by using a pillow under the hips or a *seiza* stool.

---

19. In Ki Society this is referred to as One-Point. For discussion, see page 63.

When you reach your limit of sitting *seiza* in class, first bow to the *shomen*, then relax into cross-legged sitting. Shoulders are relaxed, weight slightly forward and hands rest on knees slightly forward of ankles. Weight is properly distributed when it is difficult for a partner to lift the knee[20].

This position is inherently less stable than *seiza* because the pelvis is more rounded. For the same reason, it flows very naturally into a backwards roll.

Return to *seiza* if class is called to attention or when you need to bow.

Bowing

Unlike the traditional *karate* bow (eyes always on the opponent lest he make a sudden move), in Aikido, the kneeling bow (*zarei*) is done by lowering head and eyes to the mat, a formal gesture of courtesy, honor, and trust.

From seiza,

1. Bow forward from the One-Point by sliding both hands simultaneously from the thighs to the mat.

   Hands form a triangle and should be closed, no space showing between the fingers.

   Head is not held stiffly at top of spine, but rolls forward, like a ball rolling off a table.

   Forehead is held a few inches above the hands, parallel to the floor.

   Eyes follow direction of head.

2. Hold this position for three seconds, then rise.

Variation

Uke may test stability by:

- Pushing *nage* from side during the bowing down and the coming up.
- Standing behind, holding *nage*'s shoulders to prevent bow.

Back is rounded so that back, neck and head form a continuous curve. If you try this version of the bow with a straight flat back, you will topple forward. Instead, bow into a curve, bending and relaxing from One-Point rather than dropping from small of back.

In a more martial version of the bow[21] the left hand slides from the left thigh onto the mat, followed by the right (sword hand). The hand provides support as the torso bows forward. Back and neck can be straight[22] because the hands are already on the mat to support the weight of the torso.

---

20. For stability in *seiza*, see Tohei, 1978, pp. 40-41.See also Shifflett (1997), pp. 88-91.
21. Non-Japanese Aikido students are often heard debating the "one proper way" to bow. Actually there are many versions, depending (as always in Japan) on rank, sex, intent, and the message to be conveyed.

    Kurosawa's *samurai* adventure movie *Sanjuro* is wonderful fun on its own. But watch it again just to count and observe the many different versions of bows.
22. This bow is used in Ki Society, the tea ceremony, and Zen Buddhism.

Bowing is an act of etiquette but it is also a throwing technique in and of itself.

After a bow,

To rise from *seiza*,

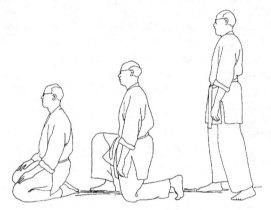

1. Bring right knee up, while bringing left toes up and forward.
2. Push off with legs (no hands!) and toes of back foot.
3. Adjust stance as necessary.

Standing, Stepping and Stance

Kamae means "posture." Linguistically it doesn't convey any particular stance. It's also used in the phrase kokoro no kamae which means "(the) heart's posture." I think that the latter of the two is perhaps as important if not more important than the physical kamae, because if you don't have the proper "heart posture," your physical posture will betray that fact.

— *Michael Hacker*

So now you're standing on the mat. You may notice that some students are standing rather differently, at an odd angle. What is this and what exactly are they doing?

Hanmi (meaning "half-body") comes from Japanese sword tradition. The precise configurations differ from style to style, but generally the front foot is pointed forward while the back foot is approaches a 90-degree angle to the front foot. *Hanmi* is a deceptively and astonishingly stable position.

In most styles, the distance between front and back foot is quite small. Stability comes from Center, not just the geometry of foot position.

Traditionally the *"samurai* walk" was a moving version of *hanmi*, an erect version of knee-walking (*shikkyo*)[23]. Although it looks and feels awkward at first, it isn't quite as alien as may first appear.

- First, it is how children make a Teddy Bear, doll, or other toy walk, pivoting from side to side.

- Second, in the Western world, this is the "Glamour Girl" walk, leading with a hip, a side, presenting at most a three-quarter view. The martial arts and women's fashion are two very different kinds of traditional warfare, but the purpose is the same — to expose the least amount of body bulk to view while sending a distinct message to the viewer.

L hanmi

R hanmi

Left *hanmi* means standing with left side of the body and left foot forward.

Right *hanmi* means standing with right side of the body and right foot forward.

Different styles of Aikido use different foot positions, but in general the forward foot is pointed directly forward or slightly out; the back foot is at an angle up to 90-degrees to the line of the front foot.

---

23. The foot moving in alignment with the arm also provides more stability under load than our more familiar way of walking. In *Samurai Trilogy II*, there is a scene of farmers dancing to celebrate the supposed arrest of the brigands. Notice the striking *hanmi* stances, the *"samurai* walk" performed by farmers who may themselves have originated it for its value in surviving hard labor. Rotating the pelvis under heavy load is one of the most common causes of chronic lower back pain.

It is said that *Daito-Ryu jujutsu* (from which Aikido was derived) used this method of walking and, therefore, the success of its techniques depend on this stance.

Hanmi looks nonthreatening, even casual and unconcerned, but offers dynamic stability and ease of motion. The classic karate stances are intended to provide a solid platform for outgoing punches and kicks, and a brace against incoming force but they are extremely unstable against lateral force.

The Aikidoist simply moves easily out of the way.

To rise into *hanmi* from *seiza*:

1. Push off with legs only (no hands!) with left knee still on mat and right knee up and foot forward. (See page 42).
2. Rise up on toes.
3. Lower heels to floor without moving weight backwards.
4. Stand comfortably, with attention at Center/One-Point.

To return to seiza from *hanmi*, the pattern is:

1. Reverse the process above putting left leg down, then
2. Right leg down.

The following stances are commonly used in all Aikido styles although names may vary from style to style. Note that Yoshinkan uses what appears to be a very pronounced forward stance which to the uninitiated eye may appear to be off-balance. In essence, the practitioner is balanced with most weight on the forward leg and less weight on the back leg which serves as a sort of outrigger and lever arm for powerful turns which come directly from the hip.[24]

Whatever the stance or style, the physical stances of Aikido emphasize balance, fluidity, ease of movement.

- **Shizentai**

  Sometimes referred to as "natural stance." Feet are aligned shoulder width apart, knees and ankles relaxed and slightly bent (see example on page 150).

  "The width of your feet limits you. It makes you strong in this forward dimension. But it makes you tremendously unstable to the side. Next time you're brushing your teeth, reading in the bookstore, look down and notice how your feet are. That's normal, natural stance, the natural way that you've evolved. That's the best thing for you. That's what we want to get to in Aikido. Then you'll be asked to bend your knees and make different kinds of adjustments from it. But the starting and returning points are always your normal natural stance." — Terry Dobson

- **Ai-Hanmi ("Harmonious" or Mutual Stance)**   R hanmi

  R hanmi

  Ai-hanmi indicates a stance in which partners legs "fit" together. That is, both *nage* and *uke* have left feet or right feet forward. Seen in *katate-kosa-tori* ("cross-hand techniques"), page 146.

---

24. See Gozo Shioda's *Total Aikido* for illustration and detailed explanation.

- **Gyaku-Hanmi (Reverse Stance)**
  In facing an opponent, *gyaku-hanmi* indicates a stance in which the legs of partners are in opposition. That is, *uke* has right foot forward, and *nage* has left foot forward. Seen in *katate-tori* or "same-side grab" techniques (see page 145).

L hanmi   R hanmi

Practice for Stance and Standing

Practice of smooth and balanced transitions between sitting, bowing, and standing has as many lessons to teach as other Aikido techniques. Observe the effect of attempting to stand with your Center/One-Point too far forward or too far back.

Note also that much of the protocol for rising, standing, and sitting, is based on traditional consideration for the sheath and sword worn on the left side and drawn by the right hand across the body.

Basic

To practice stance and standing,

1. Practice all stances with a partner calling out their names.
2. From *seiza*, standing up, sitting down then . . .
3. Cross-legged sitting to seiza to bow, and rise.

Weapons

With *bokken in obi*, combine sword practice with:

1. Standing up and sitting down,
2. Drawing sword, striking, replacing the sword in your *obi*,
3. Sitting down again.
4. Stand and sit repeatedly. Strive for balance and smoothness of motion.

Combine with *kata* (forms), with *bokken* sheathed in your *obi*,

1. From *seiza*, rise into *hanmi while* drawing sword,
2. Assume ready position with sword and go through *kata*.
3. Resheath sword in belt and
4. Return to *seiza*.

With sword or *jo* at left side placed parallel to the body,

1. Grasp weapon in center at balance point. Rise into *hanmi* drawing sword or extending *jo* into . . .
2. Ready position.
3. Return weapon to L hand.
4. Return to *seiza* and return weapon to its position on the floor.

Internal Stance

What we call "attitude" can be thought of as internal stance and what we do on the mat can be considered internally as well.

Is your internal stance rigid? Unyielding? Too far forward? Too far back? Can you evaluate which stance of so many options is the appropriate one?

An interesting features of the science-fictional *Highlander* series was the repeated demonstration of effective internal stance and the ability (and process) of evaluating the situation.

We are inspired by our animal brains and tribal roots to be suspicious and assume the worst —Bad Until Proven Good.

We are exhorted by our political system and our current perception of good to always assume the best — Innocent and Good Until Proven Guilty.

The correct stance for a warrior or any other form of survivor is neutral.

The 400-year-old Duncan McLeod demonstrates this stance again and again. He refuses to trust or assume good of someone or something until trustworthiness or good has been clearly demonstrated and validated[25]. He does not condemn for trivial reasons, he does not trust for trivial reasons.

It is an interesting contrast between the notion of "niceness"[26] which requires that the practitioner automatically assume that "everyone is just as nice as they can be and really means well" versus the notion that "everyone is malicious and dangerous and means harm."

In dangerous situations, a person subscribing to the first behavior would never survive. For the second, life would hardly be worth living.

The warrior's internal stance is neutral in the sense of no prejudgment without evidence. The key is readiness to see either black or white and act on it instantly. Philosophical gray (New Maya, "the delusion of relativism") is neutral in the sense of not believing there is any black or white, and/or believing that it is wrong or futile to judge anyone or anything. Those who subscribe to this doctrine are never ready.

— *Col. Ben H. Swett*

---

25. In contrast to our Guilty/Not Guilty, the Scottish legal system allows three possible verdicts for a trial: Guilty, Not Guilty and Not Proven.
26. Or confuse "Niceness" with goodness. "Niceness is a social strategy, a tool and possibly a weapon. See "Charm and Niceness" on page 243.

On Training

Here are some suggestions that many find useful in the journey.

- Enter the work with humility and an open mind.
- Keep a journal for your class notes, observations, memories.
- Practice with senior students, with emphasis on *ukemi* (falls and rolling).
- Work with many different skill levels and sizes of partners.
- Practice with eyes closed to pattern them via other sensory pathways; use images, feelings, or sensations to shape concepts.
- Practice at home, off the mat.
- Watch for circles and patterns, angles, triangles, lines of force.
- Break down longer techniques into component parts.
- See how softly and smoothly you can do techniques and rolls.
- Apply class concepts and principles to daily life.
- Breathe!

Dignity vs. Learning

As a beginner you will suffer a constant barrage of humbling experiences. You will feel like two left feet and the fifth wheel on a horse. You will feel like the world's greatest bumbler. We all do. Aikido is difficult if only because you are relearning how to sit, how to stand, how to walk, and even how to breathe. A big order. And that's before you even get to the throws. If you feel foolish, don't worry. We all do and you won't progress if you're more worried about dignity than about learning.

Natural and Unnatural

Although we talk about the "naturalness" of the moves, the motions and emotions which accompany them are not at all natural. That is, if someone threatens to smash you over the head with a stick, it is not natural to step into it and be delighted with the amount of force and commitment. The point is to practice until it *becomes* natural, to remove the need for conscious thinking. This can be accomplished only through endless repetition and an attitude change that makes them natural. Catching a ball is not natural either, but for how very natural it can become and the effect of that, see the demonstration for *Tekubi-Kosa Undo* on page 88.

> *Until I became a parent, I thought children just naturally knew how to catch a ball, that catching was an instinctive biological reflex that all children are born with. But it turns out that if you toss a ball to a child, the ball will just bonk off the child's body and fall to the ground. So you have to coach the child. . . .Thanks to this coaching effort, my son has advanced his game to the point where, just before the ball bonks off his body, he winces.*
>
> — *Dave Barry*

On Teaching

"Are you aware," asked one of my friends, "that these are the secrets of the sword that you are revealing to us?"
"Only," I replied, "those secrets which I happen to know."

— *Baron César de Bazancourt, Secrets of the Sword*

If you know one thing, teach one thing.

— *Koichi Tohei*

Nothing is so hard for those who abound in riches as to conceive how others can be in want.

— *Jonathan Swift*

Teaching ability is not a function or reward of rank, experience, or mat time. The minute that you know one small thing you can pass it on to another. Good teaching, however, is a learned skill like any other.

Some Basic Teaching Skills

- **Remember what it felt like to be a beginner**
  Almost the starting point. If you can remember the confusion and bafflement, the clumsiness, the feelings of stupidity and incompetence, structure your classes and your teaching materials accordingly.
  If you can't, consider signing up for a class of overwhelming complexity in which you have no experience, say, organic chemistry, perhaps. Review and re-experience the feelings of total incomprehension. Worst case you may end with a new skill.

- **Study "How to Teach"**
  Observe an experienced teacher whose classes and teaching techniques you enjoy and admire. What exactly is this person doing and how?
  What exercises were taught, demonstrations given? How were these tied to techniques? What were the time frames involved, the pacing, the timing, the proportion of lecture to exercise? How were errors corrected? What kind of feedback given or received? There is a great deal of material available on teaching techniques and styles applicable to any coursework.[27] Aikido does not exist in a vacuum.

- **Relate to the Known, then build on that foundation**
  When the student learns something, no matter how simple, then you can build on it. This may simply mean stepping through the first few steps of an exercise. When that is done, then add a few more. Only then add the hands or other details. This is how music is taught as are innumerable other skills.

---

27. For a good start, see *Instructor — Teaching the Martial Arts*, by Robert Sprackland, (1998), Appendix C, and the wonderful turn-of-the century *Secrets of the Sword*, by Baron César de Bazancourt where you will find many of today's teaching dilemmas. See also Tohei (1978), pp. 120-127.

• **Correct in the positive, avoid the negative**

Our subconscious minds simply do not recognize the verbal negative. When you repeatedly tell a student (or a child) "Do NOT do X" what the mind actually receives is repeated direction to "DO X."

Keep in view from the very first the importance of inspiring confidence in the unpracticed fencer for confidence alone implies some sort of self-possession and reacts immediately on nerve and muscle. He soon begins to feel somewhat more at ease. Some slight modifications are all that is required to correct the glaring faults that are most obviously dangerous. — Baron César de Bazancourt, *Secrets of the Sword*

• **Be aware of the learning process**

For most human beings, learning involves several distinct steps.

Experiential learning / Recognition. This is a step-by-step process in which the student must concentrate on every movement, every position. Actual learning ("saving to file") takes place when the student can say "Oh that's how you do it!" This initial stage must be reinforced by Repetition.

Repetition. The new skill or movement must be practiced until it becomes automatic, routine, reflexive. This concept was beautifully illustrated in the 1984 movie *Karate Kid*. Mr. Miyagi promises Daniel emergency training for an upcoming tournament. Daniel shows up expecting to start karate. Instead, Miyagi puts him to work polishing cars and painting miles of fence with careful instructions on the exact movements to be employed. Daniel is furious and resentful then stunned to realize that these simple movements are actually blocks[28] now made automatic through repetition.

• **Emphasize basics and drills over flourishes and frills**

Drills and repetition in Aikido are the scales and exercises of music. It's more fun to jam with the jazz band than to practice the timing, touch, rhythm and flow of scales and finger-strengthening exercises — but the basics are what make up the most advanced techniques. The notion that they are somehow separate (like *hitori-waza* from throwing techniques) is nonsense but common nonsense. In works by Bach, Beethoven, Mozart (and everyone else) you will find pages and pages of scales and arpeggios. Building blocks are important to even the most advanced students. On the other hand, so is playtime.

"We shall not cease from exploration. And the end of our exploring will be to arrive where we started and know the place for the first time." —T.S. Eliot

• **Tie the basics and drills to the actual technique**

Basics are important, but always be ready to answer the unspoken (or sometimes spoken) question: "Why do I care?"

It is always useful to show the music student that the passage that he wants to play in a beautiful sonata is actually the E-flat scale that he thinks he doesn't. It is always useful to show the Aikido student that magical throw he is yearning to do is merely the arm-dropping and spinning exercises that he thinks is merely warm-up or a waste of mat time.

• **Observe and employ the range of sensory modes**

Visual imagery is common in Aikido, highly regarded in our culture. Unfortunately, for many students, the commonly heard instruction to "visualize a glowing white light at your center" is a non-starter. Why?

---

28. This scene is the origin of the now famous phrase "wax on, wax off."

Incoming information must be processed via the sensory systems (sight, hearing, touch[30], taste, and smell). Most people have a preferred sensory system. [31]

Linguist Suzette Hayden Elgin points out: "We all know people who don't seem to do things very well unless they can see a picture, a demonstration, even read directions. Others do better if they hear information, or listen to a set of instructions. Others have to get in there and do things hands-on."

People who prefer to look use Sight ("I just don't see what you're getting at" or "Looks great to me!"). On the mat, "watch for circles!"

People who prefer to *listen* use Hearing, ("I'm just not hearing this" or "Sounds good!") On the mat, does this technique go *zip-zip*? does it go *whooooosh* or make Donald Duck noises?

People who have to *do* things use Touch ("I don't get it" or "That feels right to me!"). They may do better if encouraged to close their eyes and just *feel* the technique.

Useful information or just trivia? It turns out to be extremely important. Usually people can shift from mode to mode, but when uncomfortable or under stress they tend to lock into their preferred mode. Not only do they have difficulty expressing themselves in another sensory mode, they also have difficulty understanding.

To decrease emphasis on the visual, simply turning out the lights and practicing in the dark can change everything. Classes held during power failures have been some of our most memorable classes. Awareness of surroundings actually improves when students must rely on other senses[32].

- **Make images, feelings, and examples Real**

Is *shikko* ("knee-walking") like connecting ankles with a bungee cord?

Provide a bungee cord and try it.

Is rolling like curving over a big beach ball? Provide a ball.[33]

Is *funekogi-undo* like pushing a lawnmower? Go mow the grass.

There is a common notion that adults are familiar with all these concepts simply by virtue of being adults. Not only is that untrue, but providing physical examples and hands-on demos allows students to process information in ways that may have been missed before. Terry Dobson was notorious for using tools and toys in classes, one of the reasons his classes were so memorable. These reinforce the physical concepts.

---

30. Information processing modes are also referred to as "Visual," "Auditory," and "Tactile-Kinesthetic." Oddly enough, turning off vision can actually help apparently "visual" people. See why in Appendix C.

31. Think of the little Arkadian Prince driving his humanoid transport vehicle in the movie *Men in Black*. For more on sensory modes in teaching and communications, see "Verbal Self-Defense" on page 235.

32. Aikidoist Tim Griffiths reports on a seminar given by Nadeau Sensei. "My sensei asked him what he thought the biggest problem with aikido students was. Nadeau Sensei said "They're blind. They're deaf. And they practice what they did yesterday." Next class, *sensei* was pulling up people to perform techniques, then asking us "What did you see? What did you hear? What did you smell, or feel?"

33. See Chapter 8, "Weapons, Tools, and Toys" on page 217.

Traditional and Modern Teaching Styles

The *dojo* "too traditional" to consider these approaches should note that the very old styles *did not "teach"* as we understand it. Students were expected to watch and observe and "steal" the technique from their teachers. *Teaching* in the Western sense (via exercises, drills, and even explanation) is a very recent development. In Japanese martial arts it began in the late 1800's with educator, reformer, and Judo founder Jigoro Kano who introduced Western styles of teaching to Japan via Judo; it continued with Ki Society founder Koichi Tohei who, startled by the questions of American students in Hawaii, introduced Western teaching styles to Aikido.

Peter W. Boylan comments:

Classical Japanese budo masters are not remembered for their great teaching skills. They would demonstrate techniques, but most often they would not show you how they were doing it. Students were expected to "steal" the technique from the teacher themselves. In the classical jujutsu dojo, there really was no instruction, silent or otherwise. Kano Jigoro Shihan was the first person to actually teach techniques. He did this by mixing Western learning theory into the budo pot. One reason Judo spread throughout Japan so quickly was that students could learn the techniques so quickly. Most budo instructors in Japan now teach to a greater or lesser degree. Ueshiba was very traditional in his approach. No teach. Show. Do.

In koryu dojos today, I find the teaching atmosphere better than in most gendai dojos I have been in. There is more camaraderie, and everyone is more relaxed. The teachers are generally excited to have any students. (Kiyama Sensei was so disappointed to be losing a student when I left that he actually said something about it. This is almost unheard of in Japanese males of his generation!)

My teachers talk, but not much. The emphasis is on learning to see what you are being shown. Matsuda Sensei always looks disappointed when he shows something several times and the student (me) still has no idea what he was looking for. Then he will say a few words to help me figure out what to look at, and show me again.

Koryu budo, just like everything else in the world, changes over time. A teacher who tried to teach in the old style would have no students. What I find amusing is how many of the gendai budo insist on trying prove they are traditional by using the brutal old methods."

The Dark Side of the Course

Men you meet in the fencing room do not as a rule come there to sit at the feet of the professor, and imbibe the mystic lore of scientific theory which he expounds, but rather to be drilled and disciplined in the practical use of the sword which he holds in his hand.

— Baron César de Bazancourt, Secrets of the Sword

A poor instructor (especially if suffering from New Black Belt syndrome) can dwindle a thriving class down to nothing in a heartbeat. Some confuse mat time with stage time to show off flying spinning kicks or time to sit and drone on about Being at One with the Universe while utterly oblivious to Being at One with the flow, direction, and needs of the real live people sitting right in front of them.

It is useful to observe and analyze these classes as well. What's wrong here? Why? And how can it be done differently?

For starters, the position of Instructor must never be confused (by teacher or by students) with the right or opportunity to:

- Replay old internal parent tapes,
- Pass on an abusive past,
- Feed hunger for attention, adulation or prestige, by using a captive audience for food.

The first two behaviors appears in teaching styles heavily based on "No, no! *Don't do that, don't do this,* you're doing this *wrong* and that *wrong* and . . ." The punchline is often a gracious and beaming "There, now that's *much* better!" — but it's rarely for the student. It is more likely to be congratulations from the instructor to the instructor for having done such a fine job of instructing. It is sad to see for many reasons.

The last behavior is particularly likely in new instructors disoriented by what they see as graduation from student to instructor. They usually talk too much, practice too little. Sometimes they need to be patiently waited out. Sometimes they need to be dealt with more directly.

Those who do not recover sometimes give rise to what is known as the "Spontaneous Shihan." Those who lie about their credentials and abilities are lying to their students and are doing what they are doing for their own benefit. The student is there only for food or income[33].

Good teaching is not just "Get." Neither is it purely "Give."

Ideally it is a two-way flow.

Student is teacher. Teacher is student.

> *It is one of the most beautiful compensations of this life that no man can sincerely try to help another without helping himself.*
>
> *— Ralph Waldo Emerson*

---

33. Some hilarious examples of trolling for students or even *uchi-deshi* can be found on the Internet (and in real life). Don't rely on expansive claims, certificates, pictures on the wall, or belt-buckle size. Check with the headquarters organizations, the Aikido journals, or even feedback from the Aikido-L (see Internet Resources in Chapter 10).

Some "independent" schools are quite legitimate. Others are independent primarily because they know nothing about Aikido (consider the "Aikido Blackbelts" on page 32) but are intrigued by its current popularity and set up shop anyway.

Basically, one cannot honestly claim to be a 5th-*dan* (or whatever) Yoshinkan, Aikikai, Ki Society, Tomiki (or any other style) instructor if they do not belong and never have belonged to that organization and have only studied karate, judo, boxing, gymnastics, dance, or videotapes. All of these are valuable endeavors, but they are not Aikido.

CHAPTER 3

A Brief Ki Class

Ki was, for example, the essential principle of harmony, . . . the source of creativity expressed in the form of yin and yang (Lao-tzu) the vital fullness of life (Huainan-tzu), the courage arising from moral rectitude (Mencius), the divine force that penetrates all things (Kuan-tzu).

— *Kisshomaru Ueshiba, The Spirit of Aikido*

The hand is the cutting edge of the Mind.

— *Jacob Bronowski, The Ascent of Man*

Ki can be defined as "attention" or "mind" or "intent" although many feel that *ki* defines some sort of "magic" and since they do not believe in magic, *ergo* they cannot believe in *ki.* Those who emphasize *ki* training tend to insist that *ki* is not magic at all, that it is a culmination and a continuum of:

- **Mind** (Awareness, focus, and goal, attitude, neurology and psychology and
- **Body** (Good physics and good body mechanics).

In the Ki Society, *ki* classes address all these elements of mind and body.

Mind

In my humble opinion, "intent" would be the very best way of looking at ki, at least for starting to grasp it: The dimension and dynamics of intentions.

— *Stefan Stenudd*

In Aikido, just as in gymnastics, dance, golf, or baseball, the image is integral to the technique and the human brain differentiates very poorly between fantasy and reality. Imaging helps or allows the body to respond in ways that are quite impossible when working from the intellectual mind. Learn the feeling that the images invoke — then reproduce that feeling.

In Aikido, some ignore the laws of the physical world and hasten to attribute everything to *ki* or spiritual power. Others dismiss the effect of mind, determined to explain everything as pure physics. Likely the truth is somewhere in the middle — part mind, part body. In the real world, mind-body coordination presents itself in many ways, from blushing and stage-fright to sleep and nutrition. For example,

- **The classic experiment by Pavlov**, Russian physiologist. He rang a bell before offering food to dogs. They salivated in anticipation. Eventually merely hearing the bell ring caused salivation.

- **Visualization exercises** such as this one, heard at every "human potential" seminar. The listener is asked to imagine a tart, juicy, lemon, fresh and cold. The speaker invites you to take it from the refrigerator and hold it for a moment cool against your cheek. Feel its smoothness and texture. Now imagine taking a sharp knife, placing that lemon on a thick wooden cutting board, slicing into the smooth yellow skin. Smell the sharp, clean, fresh scent, see the spurt of juice as it is cut. Pick up a half of that lemon, heavy with juice, in your hand, and raise it to your nose. Inhale the sharp lemon smell. Put it to your mouth, sink your teeth in and take a big cold bite of that juicy lemon . . . as mouths pucker throughout the room. (And did you notice any reaction just now?)[1]

- **Ability to awaken at a specific time without an alarm clock.**[2]
  Because sleep is regulated by cycling of certain hormones, researchers measured hormone levels in sleeping volunteers who had been told they would be awakened at a specific time. About one hour before the subjects were due to be awakened, the hormone adrenocorticotropin surged indicating that anticipation, considered unique to *conscious* action, pervades *sleep* and the *unconscious* as well.

- **Food absorption.**
  It has been found to be greater if the meal is pleasurable and attractive than if the same fare is presented in an unattractive manner, say, run through a blender to make an unappetizing mush.

- **Somatopsychic responses.**
  Hypnotized subjects have developed "burns" (red and blistered skin) when told that they have been touched with a burning cigarette (but in fact touched only with a finger or an ice-cube).
  The flip side of this phenomenon is fire-walking, an expectation of coolness while strolling across hot coals. Skeptics insist that the coals can't really be all that hot, or that walkers are protected from 3,000-degree coals by insulating ash or perspiration. Unfortunately this will never be properly tested until a matching group of skeptics with no preparation but skepticism agrees to walk across the same hot bed of coals as a control group. Strangely, this does not seem to have happened, or if so, has not been widely reported. Regardless of underlying dynamics, what may be most remarkable is *willingness* to stroll barefoot through a barbecue-pit by subjects who might have been halted in their tracks by a piece of paper or a T-shirt on the mat (see page 78 and page 135).

- **Recovery and death rates.**
  Psychosomatic illness is a familiar concept but there is also "psychosomatic health" and "psychosomatic death." The well-known placebo effect and "expectation" are behind many remarkable recoveries and/or drops in death rate before birthdays or special holidays. The reverse is true in situations that do not fit a purely physical

---

1. As a similar exercise, a speaker facing an audience of skeptical and hostile fellow psychiatrists proceeded to read a selection from *Lady Chatterly's Lover* — to the growing distress of his listeners.
2. Jan Born *et al.*, *Nature, January 7,* 1999.

---

model. Cancer patients have developed and "melted" tumors based on their beliefs, hopes, and fears[3]. If, as some claim, all of these cases can be explained away as misdiagnoses, our medical system is truly in deep trouble!

Japanese clothing. The one exception to closing a garment left side over right side (see page 31) is for the dead. Health-care workers in areas with high populations of elderly Japanese are carefully trained in this tradition because of the problem of patients of good prognosis dying apparently from reading too much significance into the way that a Western nurse happened to close their garment.

How Long Can You Tread Water? During World War II, when German submarines were torpedoing British shipping, two basic groups of sailors went into the water.

1) Grizzled old salts with many years of smoking, drinking, and bad food, and

2) Strapping young men in the prime of life and peak of physical condition.

One group lived, one group died in numbers entirely beyond expectations.

Apparently the young men hit the water thinking: "Oh no! *This is the most terrible thing that has happened in my entire life!*" They were right, of course, and it seems they died of shock and terror.

Apparently the older men hit the water thinking "Oh no! Not again!" And knowing that they had survived before, they survived once again.

This pattern is not fantasy or wishful thinking. It has been observed repeatedly that persons with the tools and resources of experience (which is a power of mind), who have persons and places they love and care about have higher survival rates than those who do not, even compared to persons younger and physically healthier.

Ki Testing and Exercises

The idea behind *ki* testing is that it is impossible to test the mind directly but that the state of mind can be revealed through the body. Hence *ki* exercises and tests are essentially biofeedback exercises. You can do many of the same exercises with an electronic biofeedback monitor[4] which translates the data into a tone or light. Here the monitor is a partner and here's how to use the test equipment.

1. *Nage* (the partner to be tested) may stand or sit.

2. *Uke* (who will give the test) stands or sits perpendicular to *nage*.

3. With the palm or fingers of the hand nearest *nage's* body, *uke* applies pressure perpendicular to *nage's* chest, fingers parallel to the floor. Gradually increasing pressure is applied until *nage* begins to lose stability.

4. *Uke* observes the amount of effort required to disrupt stability.

---

3. See Becker, R. O. (1985). See Siegal, Bernie S. (1990).

4. Otherwise known as a "lie detector" or galvanic skin detector. Available from science supply houses such as Edmund's Scientific.

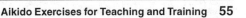

This configuration is for the beginning *nage* and for the beginning *uke* tempted to approach the exercise as a contest; it reduces mechanical advantage making it harder for *uke* to bowl over a partner.

Uke's fingers are parallel to the mat because the hand tends to follow the fingers. A test done with fingers directed upwards tends to go in that direction — a technique that makes a difficult test but an effective throw.

Testing is divided into three levels.

1. **Test One is the basic test for beginners.**

   Nage tests with gentle or gradually increasing pressure.

2. **Test Two is applied with hesitation.**

   In *nage's* sight, *uke* may bring a hand in rapidly as if to strike, stop, then proceed with the test. Or, *uke* may place a hand a few inches away from *nage's* body and wait to see if *nage* withdraws or moves toward the hand in anticipation. This is the notorious "Magnetic Hand" — *uke* holds it out; *nage* is attracted to it like magic. The cure is for *uke* to immediately test from the back.

3. **Test Three is testing with *ki*.**

   Nage must extend out so that *uke*'s *ki* never even enters *nage*'s body. Or mind.

Variations

Possibilities are endless, but the following basics test for focus, relaxation, balance and body mechanics and can be applied at any time during exercise or technique.

With *nage* in *seiza*:

- Pressing from chest and back.
- Pressing shoulder from the side.
- Lifting knee.
- Lifting hand (not up from knee, but towards shoulder).

With *nage* standing,

- Pressing from front (chest), back, and small of back.
- Pressing shoulder from the side.
- Lifting leg up from the ankle.

To test the tester,

1. Test several times to experiment with technique, feeling, and results.
2. Repeat the tests with *nage* choosing the conditions — but without telling *uke*. Verify results of *nage*'s internal choices with uke's external observations.

For example, try telling a lie.

- My name is [*right name*]
- My name is [*false name*]

From the results *uke* tries to guess which of the two *nage* was thinking.[5] *Nage* then confirms or corrects *uke*'s conclusion. This approach removes temptation for *uke* to load or skew the test in any way and provides essential reality testing for *nage*.

Tests used by the Ki Society are detailed in Book 1 of this series, Ki in Aikido — A Sampler of Ki Exercises. As these tests are unfamiliar to some styles, a persistent request has been more information on the nature and purpose of ki testing. Jan Beyen of Belgium was particularly helpful in helping to define the tests in understandable terms as you will see below.

Q. We tried ki tests once. Why didn't they work?

A. Perhaps because they were misunderstood.

Ki testing is a team sport but it is not a win/lose sport.

Many who try *ki* tests "fail" because *uke* saw himself as opponent and attacker, rather than as a teammate serving as a useful biofeedback device.

I once annoyed a new partner by failing to fall over for *kokyu-dosa*; his solution was to punch me in the ribs. I did indeed fall over, but the point of *ki testing* is not whether *nage* can miraculously survive a punch or kick "by extending *ki*." That is not a test, it is an *attack*. The point of *ki testing* is to find the points where *nage* is a little stronger, a little firmer, able to hold a little longer — and work up from there.

By analogy, suppose a friend is baking a cake and asks you to check to see if it is done. Test One for doneness in a cake is to gently tap the surface.

- Is it firm and resilient? Or,
- Is it still raw batter that gives way to the slightest touch?

Smashing the cake with a punch does nothing to help its progress. You have not "won" anything, and have been of no help at all to the friend (or the cake).

"An interesting idea," said Jan, "but I don't cook so I really don't know quite what you mean."

Or imagine that your partner has poured concrete footings for the house you are building together. You may test the footings gently with increasing pressure to see if they are strong, if they are firm, if they are set. Do you start to build your brick wall atop the footings before the concrete has developed the necessary strength to bear the load? When the weight of the overlying brick causes the half-set concrete to fail, do you say "Ha-ha! I win! My bricks beat your footings!"

The point is to test, observe, and evaluate. It is not to overwhelm, smash, or "win" by attacking any more than you "win" by smashing a half-baked pan of cake batter or a half-set form of concrete. It is a *cooperative* effort in feeling and sensing that partners can use to help each other improve.

"I have never poured concrete," said Jan.

"But I'm thinking of the first frost-weeks of winter, when the ponds start freezing over. As a kid I used to test the ice for strength (first throw a few small stones on the

---

5. These same concepts appear in the movie *House of Games* wherein a professional con-man explains these same concepts as "tells" and their usefulness and application as tools of the trade. See page 262.

ice and if it breaks, it's nowhere near strong enough). When the ice seems fairly strong, you test by placing one foot on the ice and applying increasing pressure and feeling for movement. If you do feel movement, the ice is certainly not strong enough. If you slam down hard on the ice immediately you could get very wet if it isn't as strong as you thought.

One thing that came to mind while I was looking for an example is that you also need to keep sensing subtle changes in the power that is coming towards you (or pulling away), no matter how strong it is. Some people seem to think that it's a choice between softly stroking or hard slamming (the "aiki-fruity" approach versus the "Butch-macho" approach).

When I go windsurfing (there has to be at least a force 5 wind) I have to sense the power in the sail and control it. Too little power and I'll sink, too much power and I get blown away (a catapult). On top of that there is the power of the waves that are trying to sweep away the board underneath my feet. So even with strong forces, you have to keep alert to the subtle changes in the power (and direction) to keep going. Otherwise it's a wipeout!

I guess that a ki test (on a particular exercise) would not be as easy to describe as a chemical-indicator test (think of a Breathalyzer test) where blue means STOP and green means GO (or whatever colors). But think of some kind of indicators as to what is OK and what isn't.

When you test, regardless of what happens, how much effort did it require on your part to achieve that effect? There's a big difference between knocking nage over with a fingertip versus his being so strong, so stable, so softly and immovably centered that in trying to push him over, I only knock myself off balance.

Last year I took the train for Brussels in Bruges. There's always a crowd waiting for this train, and after this stop, almost all the places are taken, so there is a (civilized) struggle to be among the first to get on the train. One morning I took my place at the edge of the crowd that was eager to get on. I stopped quite close to one guy, moving slowly along with the advancing crowd.

This guy probably felt threatened (fearing to lose his place) by my being so close to him, and started to push against my side with his arm (which hung beside him), I just stayed there, not really moving at that time (the crowd wasn't moving either). He pushed so hard that he lost his balance, and fell against the person standing on the other side of him. He then accused me of pushing him!

— Jan Beyen, Aikikai

Ki testing also has other applications. Several members of our *dojo* volunteer weekly at the local juvenile detention center and teach *ki* classes. There, little short women demonstrate Unbendable Arm with the biggest, toughest kids there. When they cannot bend it, they are astounded, aghast! "How do you do that?" "How is that possible?" *"Do you lift weights, or what?"*

They are teaching a different kind of strength. Whatever you call it, it is useful even for the children at the county detention center whose punches to the ribs or attacks to those whom they found annoying is no longer an option. Many are there because they tried that approach once too often. They've heard all the lectures. Just how well those have worked is made quite clear by their presence there.

In contrast, *ki* exercises offer up-close Real-Time proof that setting goals matters, what we focus on matters, what we think about matters, and even good posture matters — more than most of us will ever know.

The classic *ki* exercise is Unbendable Arm[6]. *Uke* tries to bend *nage's* extended arm at the elbow while *nage* keeps the arm strong but relaxed.

Unbendable Arm

This exercise demonstrates the power of a goal (extending beyond the immediate battlefield of the elbow), and the weakness of tension and fixation.

1. With one hand on *nage*'s bicep and one hand on *nage*'s wrist, *uke* attempts to bend *nage*'s arm. Test gently at first with steadily increasing challenge as *nage* learns the feel. To quantify the strength and duration,

2. Count elapsed seconds ("one-thousand-one, one-thousand-two, one-thousand-three," etc.).

Once learned, *nage* will be able to maintain Unbendable Arm, exhibiting a strength beyond all apparent physical capacity.

To help the feeling, *nage* may:

• Imagine a water pump at Center that pumps water up through the torso, through the arm and out the fingers.

• Imagine touching the opposite wall or the hand of a distant third person.

A smaller or weaker *uke* may test for Unbendable Arm by

1. Placing *nage*'s hand on his shoulder then
2. Placing his own hands on *nage*'s elbow joint and
3. Dropping weight underside.

    The taller partner may kneel or sit

Unbendable Arm can be done with just the body mechanics. But, see the difference between "extending," and "keeping *uke* from bending the arm."

Also, the test isn't just whether someone bigger and stronger or smaller and weaker can or cannot bend your arm — but how much effort is required to maintain "unbendable-ness." Compare by counting seconds.

---

6. For history and observations, see Gluck (1997), pp. 212-214, Tohei (1978), pp. 31-32, and Shifflett (1997), pp. 18, 100.

Turning from One-Point

Another example of not-stopping mind, of extension and goal setting.

1. *Uke* places hands firmly on both sides of *nage*'s hips.
2. *Nage* attempts to turn hips while:
   a) Concentrating on *uke*'s hands.
   b) Concentrating on turning around a very small point at Center/One-Point.
   c) Thinking of moving one of *uke*'s hands forward and around in a circle.

On Truth-Testing: Aikipitching

The problem with citing examples of mysterious deaths, remarkable recoveries, survivals, or fire-walking is that although they are very real, few of us know of them from direct experience. To most Americans, a topic far more near and dear — and familiar — than psychological or psychic research is sports.

"Thanks to Ki Development Exercises I feel so much more At One with the Universe" or *"My techniques feel stronger,"* is a tad vague. In contrast, baskets, goals, pitching and hitting are easily quantifiable. Either you are pitching a no-hitter, batting 0.300, winning the playoffs — or you aren't.

Basketball coach Phil Jackson[7] uses yoga, meditation, and visualization exercises in working with players, the very thing that tends to be dismissed as "fruity" or delusional in Aikido. His regular season winning percentage of .738 (545-193) is a decidedly non-fruity NBA record, and .730 playoff winning percentage (111-41) is the Number 2 all-time record. Koichi Tohei used *ki* exercises to train baseball star Oh Sadaharu and Hawaiian *sumo* champion Takamiyama.

Closer to home, professional pitching instructor John Pinkman uses *ki* training to develop pitching and hitting skills on the high-school level. Pinkman is confident that this approach creates better balance and better players, but for true effectiveness, the lines between imagination, wishful thinking, and hard reality must be clearly drawn, demonstrated, and evaluated. Does it work or doesn't it?

The only way to know is to actually quantify (measure) the results. Pinkman does exactly that. A radar gun tracks a series of 50 pitches. The results (balls, strikes, and scatter pattern) are charted on an X/Y axis under three different circumstances:

- **Under pressure.** Initially, speed and delivery for new students are erratic. When the pitcher calms, strike percentage rises.

- **Under controlled circumstances.** Students are trained in total mental control. Pitching improves.

- **In a state prepared for success.** The student is relaxed, pitching one pitch at a time, and every pitch is a whole new game. Balls are delivered at consistent speed from the same place. Balls go down, strikes go up.

---

7. See Alexander, R. (1999), "Jackson — Zen and Now" for yet another practitioner in the growing field of sports psychology and applied *ki* development.

"But for skill to *remain*," says Pinkman, "requires cognitive awareness of body control, cause and effect. To alter body mechanics or muscle memory you must *know*, you cannot only *do*. Body can only do what mind already knows. On the other hand, for efficient motion you can't take time to think, you must flow, *do*. How to coordinate mind and its body? Enter the Tao of baseball, the Zen of pitching, and *ki*. Pitching is *ki* in its purest day-to-day form."

Training begins with *ki* exercises.

1. First, we train *ki* flow "down into the ground" and ask parents to try to lift their child. After just 5 minutes of training these children are amazingly successful. Equally amazing are the expressions of Mom and Dad at their inability to lift a child who inexplicably seems to have just doubled in weight.

2. Next we train to reverse the *ki*, pulling energy from the ground up into the ball. Energy starts from the ball of the foot and flows into the ball. *Ki* begins in the foot when it comes in contact with the rubber and flows through the body and out of the hand and into the ball. At this point we teach . . .

3. A thorough understanding of the biomechanics of throwing and associated musculature. Then we introduce . . .

4. Passive, non-movement visualization, moving to . . .

5. Active visualization: throwing with eyes closed on flat ground and then on balance beams, forcing the pitcher into a state of heightened sensory awareness.[8]

"Understanding energy flow becomes much more real and easy to grasp once the student makes the sensory connection with the new experience of listening to their breathing, feeling the flowing arm motion and the path of the ball exiting their hand at a specific point in space."

"In pitching, finding the release point is an extremely critical skill and it takes players like these who are excellent players to the level of elite players. Shoulders are rotating at 2,800 degrees per second and the difference between high pitch and low pitch is only a few degrees. Finding that point involves feeling and sensitivity yet maximum energy. These repeated exercises give the pitcher the opportunity to relax, to practice and program the idea that 'I want to release the ball *here*.' But for a pitcher on the plate, doing these exercises *physically* would be considered a balk. So how to make a more relaxed, calm, and consistent pitcher in a "safe" manner? With breathing and visualization."

1. **Breathe**. Really breathe. Oxygen dilutes adrenaline and delivers energy into the whole system. Next,

2. **Visualize source**. Visualize where the pitch is *coming from*, starting from the foot, up through calf, hamstrings, shoulder, triceps. Another deep breath and . . .

3. **Visualize target**. Visualize where the pitch is *going to*.

---

8. See the rail-road track *suburi* practice described on page 225.

Most people think that a ball is thrown with hand and eyes follow. We train pitchers to close their eyes and make the throw using the flow of their energy in their body to the target. There's nothing more thrilling than throwing strikes[9] with your eyes closed.

"Pitching is physically and mentally demanding. In a typical outing a pitcher will throw 189 pitches (100 during the game, 40 in pre-game warm-up, and 49 (7 at a time) prior to each inning in a 7 inning game). During a game, exhaustion, drama and emotion interfere with *ki* flow and pitching. We drill body mechanics, but we also drill to create emotional instability, insecurity, anger, and frustration while having the pitcher throw at a very small target (for example, a softball on a batting tee). The process is this."

1. **Record** the ball's velocity and accuracy. It is always inconsistent. Rather than what most would think, anger limits ball velocity and certainly scatters the location pattern. The term "he's lost control" applies to more than the pitcher's inability to find the strike zone.

2. **Graph** the data as a learning tool. Then

3. **Lead** the player, through quiet verbal and non-verbal instruction, out of a hopeless state. We structure the pitcher's breathing, mental images, starting point of *ki*, and flow.

4. **Results**: Velocity, mental composure, and target location increase. Always.

Says Pinkman, "We need to measure and be held accountable for results. Specifically, do players improve in the game after we work with them? And does that improvement remain as consistent skill performance? It does."

"Our results-oriented training has produced an extraordinary success rate in educating pitchers. In the past two years our small program has sent 27 boys to universities to play ball. This teaching method is not for the unusual player. It is normal instruction for pitchers in our school. I have done these drills hundreds of times over the years, always with the same successful results."

"*Ki* is normal. It is daily, and it is ordinary."

"*Ki* can be used without understanding or even using the word."

"*Ki is not the product. It's the process.*"

Pinkman, like many other *ki* practitioners, believes intensely in the value of *ki* exercises. But notice that he is not relying on mind alone. A player has both mind and body. And as long as that body is on the earth, it must obey the laws of physics.

---

9. Yes, he had me do it and I did. And consider that there are thousands of blind bowlers in the U.S. who must do the same thing. See Gaines (1999).

Body

Is Aikido "mere physics?" Perhaps.

But there is nothing "mere" about good physics. The study of physics is the power and magic of the physical world and the physical body made replicable. In many ways Aikido is Remedial Physics for City Kids.

I had a useful refresher course while drying out a wet basement. The project involved digging a ditch 10 feet long, 3 feet wide and 7- to 8-feet deep to drain and repair a cracked and leaking wall and install a sump pump. A backhoe would have been awkward and damaging. I dug it by hand and I did it alone. Dirt, cinder blocks, gravel, rebar, and shoring all had to come in and out of that hole as efficiently — and as safely as possible. Good physics and good mechanics are survival tools.

When muscling 70-pound buckets of mud out of a deepening hole became impractical, up went a hoist with block and tackle. The easiest way to lift that weight? Lift feet, drop weight. Not projecting out, not pulling with arms, but dropping down, as close to ninety degrees straight down as possible, "in harmony with the laws of the universe," gravity being a major player. No need to attack a gravel pile directly when a tweak of a blade at its base will fill it with stones sliding easily downslope under gravity. *Pulling* down requires strength and effort. *Dropping* down or allowing to drop down does not.

The physical building blocks of Aikido are the same tools of lever arms, rotation, and their vectors. Some basic physics concepts often presented in specialized Aikido language are: One-Point, Weight Underside, and Relaxation.

The Concept of One-Point

"The story about the 255-pound instructor being thrown by the five-year old is about me, and took place at a Lee District kid's class. We were doing the katate-tori kokyu-nage in which nage stands beside uke, then takes a little back hop to do the throw. I was in the process of explaining the throw, when I said, "Now if Emily takes a big hop backwards right now . . . and she did. It was like having a 30-pound bowling ball hanging off the end of my arm."

"I was looking in a different direction at that moment and the throw took me totally by surprise. It was one of those moments when the ki was just right."

— Kirk Demaree

At least part of what Aikidoists call the Center, One-Point or *hara*, physicists consider to be the center of mass of the body, the point where gravity acts on the body as a whole[10] hence "center of gravity." When standing upright in a normal posture, the center of mass is approximately between the spine and the navel approximately at the level of the hip joints. From the strictly physical standpoint, One-Point is the body's center of gravity. It can also be the center point of rotation, the fulcrum of a lever. The vertical location is commonly said to be about two

---

10. In mechanics, the motion and behavior of this one point is considered to be characteristic of the entire object.

inches below the navel. In aikido, *center* at this low point is usually discussed in contrast to "weight upperside" which implies tension or mind in the torso or shoulders rather than in the abdomen[11].

In static conditions, that body is stable as long as the One-Point remains centered over its support — the feet. If center of mass moves beyond its support (the feet) the pull of gravity creates a torque that may cause that body to fall, regardless of size, weight, or muscle.

You need not be constantly over your Center to be balanced, but if off-center you will need a support (even an invisible one such as motion or inertia) or weight underside to maintain stability. A beautiful example of this appears in the movie *The Cutting Edge* which begins by comparing the very different styles of hockey and figure skating.

Weight Underside is also demonstrated in the stability of the Japanese *daruma* dolls, the Western punching clowns and balancing baby toys, and ancient engineering works from Celtic monoliths to the massive stoneworks of Peru, and the great stone giants of Easter Island.

The Easter Island statues in particular had long mystified archaeologists. How was it possible to transport 50-ton statues from their quarry to the other end of the island, many miles away? They walked — in *hanmi*. Once levered to an upright position, the bottom-heavy figures could be rotated about their stable center just like the Teddy Bears or swordsmen on page 43.

The reverse of weight underside is weight upperside. A good illustration is the person afraid of flying who sits tensely in the seat, hesitating to "put down my whole weight." It makes no difference to the airplane of course, but it makes a great difference to the person, in terms of tension and fatigue.

It also makes a difference in efficient physical power. Whether you are moving a 50-ton statue or a 50-pound *uke*, weight upperside or underside matters. It matters because it changes the dynamics, it changes the probability of the personage falling on you or *uke* falling on the mat because it changes the leverage.

And it's all just leverage, isn't it?

---

11. For more on this topic, see Shifflett (1997) p. 90, and Tohei (1978), p. 45.

"Just Leverage"

Give me a place to stand and a lever long enough and I will move the earth!
— Archimedes (287?-212 B.C.)

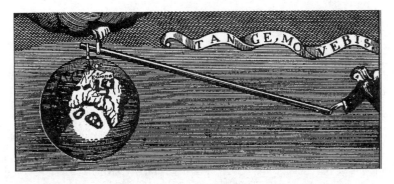

There is much popular nonsense over the pyramids of Egypt, too big, too heavy[12] to have been built by human hands. Yet those incredulous that our ancestors could move blocks of such weight and size with huge levers, massive work gangs and unlimited time and resources are strangely calm at 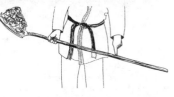 seeing a tiny woman single-handedly moving blocks of similar or greater weight and size — with the help of the relatively small lever known as a "car jack."

A shovel is a lever. It is a waste of effort to lift a load with precious energy. So much easier to lever it up around the fulcrum of an arm that (as in *funekogi-undo*) need serve only as a connector. In Aikido, similar lever arrangements allow tiny bodies to throw large bodies across the room with great ease.

Levers and Leverage

— by Dr. Joseph Toman

There are three classes of levers. three different permutations of where you can place a weight, a fulcrum, and an opposing force on a lever.

1. First-class levers have the fulcrum between the weight and the force.

   In Aikido an example is old-style *sumi-otoshi*[13]. Your shoulder under *uke*'s elbow levers them up and over. *koshi-nage* is the same action done with the hips.

---

12. The average-sized block in the Great Pyramid is about 1,200 pounds. Wow!
13. See Projection #10 ("Sumi Otoshi"), Westbrook & Ratti (1970), p. 277-281.

2. Second-class levers have the weight between the force and the fulcrum. An example is a wheelbarrow, or the *ikkyo* or *nikyo* pin, where the shoulder joint acts as a fulcrum and the musculature on the front of the shoulder wraps up onto the arm to provide the "weight" when you stretch it.

3. Third-class levers have the force between the weight and the fulcrum, like the end of a *bokken* strike where the back hand acts as the fulcrum, the front hand is the force and the *bokken* is the weight (although not a point mass).

The difference between the three is rather like choosing a gear for driving. First-class levers are low speed, high torque, if the effort arm (distance between force and fulcrum) is larger than the load arm (distance between weight and fulcrum).

Second- and third-class levers are really the same thing. Which one you have depends on the relative lengths of the load and effort arms. If you increase the length of the load arm from initially being shorter than the effort arm, you're trading how much force you apply for how quickly the load moves. With second class levers you have to move through a larger angle to get the same amount of movement of the weight, but you don't have to apply as much force. With third-class levers you move a little to get a lot of movement, but you have to exert a lot of force.

Once you have begun a technique, the reason you want to be close to your partner rather than at arm's length is efficient leverage. Standing far away puts you on the wrong end of the lever. Even "just leverage" works poorly (on your end) if you are holding *uke* at a distance.

If you're going to man-handle your *uke* you want your effort arm to be longer than your load arm, so that you have a mechanical advantage, meaning that you can trade distance for force. You want to be up close so that *uke*'s arm, that beautiful lever, is under *your* control and not *uke*'s. So now you've made *uke*'s whole arm the effort arm instead of holding *uke* at a distance and making it the load arm. It's like very static *jo-nage*. You retain mechanical advantage by always controlling more than half of the stick.

— J. Toman

The following exercise illustrates the difference in effort.

Near and Far

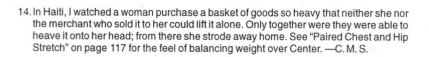

1. Hold a 10- or 20-pound (or greater) weight at arm's length (past your center). Observe the effort required to do so and how this feels while walking around.

2. Compare effort required to do the above with elbow bent. Observe the amount of effort required now that you have shortened the lever arm by a few inches.

3. Put weight on your shoulder, head. How heavy does it feel there?[14].

---

14. In Haiti, I watched a woman purchase a basket of goods so heavy that neither she nor the merchant who sold it to her could lift it alone. Only together were they able to heave it onto her head; from there she strode away home. See "Paired Chest and Hip Stretch" on page 117 for the feel of balancing weight over Center. —C. M. S.

Exhortations by your instructor to bring *uke* in close, to drop everything to your One-Point reflect this physical law. The closer you are to your center, the longer your end of the lever, the more control and power you have, the less strain and struggle. Also consider that the more stiff and hard *uke* is and the more soft and relaxed you are, the more of an advantage you have. How is this possible?

Wild Cards — Tension and Relaxation

A familiar line from various novels, war stories and murder mysteries is "the dead are heavier than the living." Actually, that would be the dead, the unconscious or drunk, and the unwilling two-year-old.

Tension improves a lever arm, relaxation degrades it. The more tense and rigid, the easier to throw. The more relaxed, the more difficult.

When you are tense, you take up all the slack in your own body, giving *uke* a direct line to your center with lots of lever arms to unbalance you. You even get tired quicker. *Uke* is trying to do this to you anyway. If you are tense, you do it for him. If you prefer not to provide this free service, relax! You will become essentially invisible to *uke* (he can no longer feel exactly where you are), and harder to manipulate. This is the source of the constant refrain: *"Don't be strong, be soft!"*[15]

I slowly came to realize that a relaxed muscle is not soft and weak, it is one that is not contracted. I might have grasped the concept more quickly if rephrased as:

> *"Tense" gives uke the gift of lever arms. "Relaxed" does not.*

"Removing slack" also allows other forces to operate that cannot otherwise. You can see this in such everyday examples as rugs and towels. To shake a rug you can:

1. Hold it with hands together, the rug or towel hanging slack and limp between. Shake it and you get no snap, only flop and flutter. For a small item, that may be enough. Or you can . . .

2. Hold snugly, hands pulling apart, slack out. Now you can snap that rug and send the dirt flying. The bigger and heavier the item, the more critical it is to take the slack out. Otherwise you have no control and won't get it moving at all.

   The locker-room rat-tail is a towel folded, rolled, and twisted to eliminate excess slack leaving a small whip-end. Inertia eliminates the rest in the course of the whipping action which can actually split skin.

Neither rugs or towels make good lever arms in their normal format, but with *slack in* and *slack out* they behave in completely different ways. So does *uke*. Who would you rather have as *uke* for demo or test? The Tinman or the Scarecrow?

---

15. And coming from karate I thought to myself: "Har! Buncha wimps!"

Rotation and Its Center

In ancient jujutsu they taught that "when pushed, pull back; when pulled, push forward." In the spherical movements of aikido, this becomes: "When pushed, pivot and go around; when pulled, enter while circling." This means that one moves in circular motion in response to the opponent and while moving spherically, one maintains his center of gravity to create the stable axis of movement. And at the same time the opponent's center is disturbed, and when he loses his center, he also loses all power. Then he is subdued swiftly and decisively.

— Kisshomaru Ueshiba, *The Spirit of Aikido*

Rotation is "just leverage" in a circle.

Observe the leverage in the following exercise. The lever is the side of the block, the back of the chair.

Cinder Blocks and Chairs

Cinder blocks are heavy to lift, easy to rotate. If you don't have a pile of spare cinder blocks in your dojo, use a chair or even a firmly packed gym bag. In real life these items become lumber, oxygen cylinders, file cabinets, or other items. Compare the effort required:

1. *To rotate* the item as opposed to that required . . .
2. *To lift* the item (especially at arm's length).

Variation

1. "Walk" the chair across the room by rotating it around its two front legs, alternating from one front leg to another. This is the same motion behind *shikkyo* (see page 106).
2. Sitting in a simple, light-weight, 4-legged chair, observe the effort required to lift yourself out of the chair compared to that required to tilt back or forward.

One of the most persistent refrains by new students who do not yet understand the power of what they are being taught is "Yes, But On The Street . . .."

"Yes, But On The Street," insists many a skeptical new student told to turn a complete 180-degrees, "you wouldn't do a *complete tenkan*."

Such responses contrasting Mat Time with Real Time usually mean that the student doesn't yet understand or trust the power of the circle in which case it is only sensible then to fall back on what has worked before (or what he imagines might work, having seen it in the movies): pure muscle power and linear energy.

There is a reason why the circle is considered the symbol of God, of holiness, of completeness, and power beyond our comprehension: rotational physics.

The only way to develop awareness and confidence in rotational physics is to demonstrate it with a Real World example. Start with a laundry bag.

Laundry-Bag Tenkan

1. Fill a laundry bag, trash bag or gym bag with old clothes or towels to make up a weight of 20-30 pounds or more.

2. *Nage* stand still at one side of mat and heave the bag as far as possible with one arm using linear energy and muscle power only. That is, no wind-up, no swinging. Keep arm and hand close to side.

3. Partner mark forward point where bag falls.

4. *Nage* turns a partial *tenkan*, releasing bag to fly across the mat. Keep arms at sides, please, to limit the size of your circle.

5. Observe the new point where the bag falls.

6. Repeat with a complete *tenkan*.

7. Compare not only the distance, but the effort required to move the bag, and the power generated in the course of doing so.

   Our *dojo* walls are lined with wood panels. I can heave a heavy bag only a few feet with a one-handed throw. A full *tenkan* will send it flying, two will fling it the entire width of the mat to hit the wood panels on the opposite side with an impressive thwack.

   Turning a partial *tenkan*, how far can you zing it?

   How far with a full turn? Two full turns?

Joseph Toman continues:

Actually, this exercise does not describe the Aikido technique. You're not really tossing *uke* like a sack of potatoes off a wall, you're guiding him around the outside of a circle in order to have more time and distance. Why? Because the perimeter of a circle is 2 times the radius of the circle times *pi* or:

$$P = 2\pi r \qquad \text{(EQ 1)}$$

In two-dimensional space, turning tenkan dissipates the initial attack over time and distance. It also encourages the attacker to over-commit to the attack by letting him think he is just about to get his balance back.

In three-dimensional space, you're also guiding him down and out beyond his One-Point ("tripping"[16]) and then back up and over ("clotheslining") once you've compromised his hip stability.

You can add a little energy in tenkan, but not a lot because then uke gets wise to what you're doing and counters by pulling back or changing the attack altogether.

— J. QT.

So, if *uke* is 3 feet away, and wants to grab you, in the linear world, the distance from *uke* to you is *r* or 3 feet. If however, you step off-line and lead him around in a circle, the distance he must travel is now 3.14 x 2 x 3 or 12.56 feet rather than a mere 3 feet — with a corresponding increase in time.

Actually, to do *tenkan* properly, you do not drive *uke* in a circle, you allow him to drive himself. The following exercise demonstrates the difference.

---

16. See "Clotheslining and Tripping" on page 178.

Rag Doll Tenkan

In *tenkan*, the competitive or contrary *uke* may pull back (rather than extending forward) while the inexperienced *nage* valiantly attempts to drag the unwilling *uke* around in a circle.This exercise allows *uke* to practice extending forward while *nage* practices accepting and aligning with the energy. In pairs,

1. *Nage* extends a wrist and stands with One-Point.
2. *Uke* takes the wrist and pushes *nage* around in a circle.
   A strange feeling? This is how it should feel.

Vectors — Deflection and Redirection

> *On reading the paper I was amazed to see how long it took him to say, "Hey! It's all vectors!"*
>
> *— Dr. Joseph Toman*

Vectors describe and analyze forces. They are represented by arrows drawn to scale, plotted on graph paper, or by trigonometric calculations. The *length* of the arrow represents the *magnitude* of the applied force. The *direction* of the arrow represents the direction of the applied force. The end result of the combined forces is the *resultant*, the single vector which would have the same net effect as all the original vectors combined.

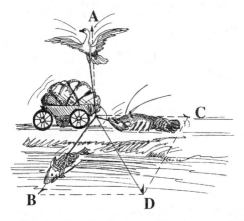

In a tale by 19th-century Russian fabulist I. A. Krilov, a swan, lobster, and a fish undertake to haul a heavy cart by pulling from three different sides.

The swan flies straight up to the sky. The fish heads for the water, and presumably the lobster trudges ahead on land.

The traditional teaching point of the fable is that without cooperation, all their best efforts cancel each other out and the cart does not move. Vector analysis, however, suggests quite a different situation.

The swan, by rising up (A) reduces friction and stability of the load.Easier to move.

Fish and lobster pull in directions B and C producing the resultant force (D).

Hence the cart *will* move, although very inefficiently. It will end up in the river, not exactly where they really wanted it to go, but it will move.

Compare this image with *sankyo zempo-nage*.

1. The *sankyo* (*swankyo*?) locks *uke*'s arm so that you control his Center/One-Point and he is rising up, possibly teetering on tip-toe. Easier to move.

2. Forward motion is provided by moving your Center, as you step forward. So far, so good. However, just as you prepare to lob *uke* across the mat . . .

3. Something fishy happens. Perhaps you pull *uke* in closer because you weren't close enough to start with. Perhaps you push *uke* slightly away because you're uncomfortable so close to the attacker. Perhaps you tense up thinking "Uh-oh, how do I do this??" *Uke* will move, but not very efficiently, and not exactly where you really wanted him to go.

The concept of "blending" is the act of aligning with the force and direction that is offered. We talk about "using *uke*'s strength and power" but tend to be a bit vague about how we do that.

In the example of the fish and the lobster, the most efficient way of moving a load is to provide pure forces in the desired direction. Fish and lobster will succeed in moving the cart, but not as efficiently as if they were directly aligned with each other, moving in the same direction. Vectors. In the illustrations below, compare the degree of "harmony," "congruence," "blending," shared goals and direction between the two partners and their arms.

Try rolling up a car window with your arm aligned with the crank, or reaching over from the side. What is the difference in efficiency and required effort?

Simply pulling in different directions distorts directions, but so does muscle tension which originates or transmits all sorts of spurious forces. Simply tightening fingers and clenching a fist and forearm almost certainly means that you are pulling back, no matter how slightly. There is a world of difference in feel and result in a *tenkan* where *nage* is leading forward, pulling back, pulling to the side, or any combination of these as opposed to a pure forward lead.

As aid to centering and direction (and also because of Aikido's sword tradition), Yoshinkan style Aikido uses a stance (*kamae*) in which hands constantly define the center line of the body and therefore direction of hips and of travel. Or, try pointing fingers into a V at waist and see how this changes perception of position, and direction, and alignment of your own body and that of others.

Certainly much of the magic and flow of the adept Aikidoist is the ability to blend perfectly with the motion offered and with the desired goal.

Jearle Walker in his classic paper "Roundabout," comments on the hefty amount of force required to actually *stop* a punch compared to the mere fraction of that needed to *redirect* it. Applying a small force at right angles to the path of a punch applies a torque to the arm which deflects the punch.

The further away you are (*ma-ai*), and the more extended *uke* is, the longer his lever arm. This puts *uke* on the short end of the lever, you on the long end, and deflection or redirection of the fist at the end of that lever takes little effort.

A remarkable example of redirection is *shomen-uchi irimi* (page 207). *Uke* attacks with a powerful overhead strike. *Nage* appears to stop *uke* in his tracks, turning him completely around in *ikkyo*. The stronger the attack, the more forcefully *uke* is spun around. But despite appearances it isn't a ferocious block. It is a simple redirection. Joseph Toman explains:

Imagine a line connecting *uke* and *nage*. *Uke* delivers an overhead strike along that line. *Nage* moves laterally off the line *omote*[17] to *uke*, making connection with *uke*'s attacking arm. The lateral distance creates a moment arm.[18] When that is combined with the force of *uke*'s attack the result is that *uke* experiences *torque*[19] around *nage*

---

17. *Omote* or *irimi* means "front, forward" or inside the line of attack.
18. From Latin *momentum*, from *movere*, to move.

and the pivot point where their arms meet. *Uke* is still going the same direction as he started out, but torque and anatomy combine to spin him around and make him travel backwards. It looks like a block because we always assume that people travel in the direction they are facing, which isn't true in this case. The two variants on this throw are adding a step forward or a step back.

- Stepping forward increases *uke*'s angular speed relative to *nage*, making the technique tighter and faster, but decreasing the energy *uke* can put into it.

- Stepping back decreases *uke*'s angular speed [20] making it a slower technique, allowing *uke* time to put more energy into it.

The following exercises demonstrate a critical Aikido skill; the ability to align with, follow, and amplify the energy that *uke* provides, rather than exhausting one's own strength. You can think of Aikido as "arm" or "body" surfing. Just like the ocean surfer, you must align and flow. Going counter to that force is commonly known as a "wipe-out." Just as you can't steer a canoe effectively unless you a moving with the current, you can't move effectively through traffic unless you match its speed and direction, you can't lead *uke* unless you align and blend.

Aiki Arm Wrestling

"Aiki arm-wrestling" is a valuable exercise for illustrating just how Aikido works and how very different it is from preconceived concepts of strength and strategy.

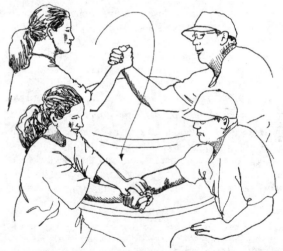

It is not collision, not resistance, not a weight and strength contest. It is aligning, accepting and following energy, until for *uke*, it's too late — and people have a very

---

19. *Torque*, from Latin *torquere*, to twist, is the tendency of a force to produce rotation around an axis, in this case, the tendency of *uke* to rotate around *nage*.
20. That is, "How big an angle will the *jo* move through in one second?" By analogy with baseball, stepping *in* requires *uke* to bunt; there is no time for a big swing of the bat and the result is a low-energy pop. Stepping *back* is equivalent to allowing *uke* time for a full swing of the bat, a line drive to center field.

hard time comprehending this simple exercise. On table or lying on mat, partners assume the classic arm-wrestling position.

1. Start by pushing arms against each other, pushing/resisting as normal.

2. At some point *nage* ceases all resistance, allowing *uke's* arm to crash to the mat. In normal arm-wrestling, this would be a "win" for *uke*. Here, *nage* uses the other hand to pins *uke's* hand. By cooperating with *uke's* strength and power, *uke* has now been "brought to the mat" and can't get up again.

The Backpacker Bounce

If you've ever been weighted down with a very heavy backpack, groceries, child or other load that makes lifting the weight straight up from a dead start difficult or impossible, try this exercise.

1. Raise up just a little bit, then . . .

2. Drop right back *down*. The natural springiness of muscles and tendons in your knees will bounce.

3. Add enough muscle and effort to amplify the "bounce" and follow it *up*.

   Parked on a slope? Rather than forcing the door closed uphill and against gravity, push it a little ways, let it fall back down where it rebounds against the spring, and follow the rebound back up to close the door.

You will see these physical principles operating throughout your study of Aikido and your study of life. A good understanding of the fundamentals of physics gives you a big advantage in Aikido and everything else. And yet it is still difficult to believe that Aikido can do what it is said to do, that is, as physicist Jearle Walker puts it: "make the strong equal to the weak." Hence, Aikido is often of special interest to women who have been carefully trained to believe for years that they cannot possibly repulse or resist an attack by A Man, meaning (in part):

Small Person cannot possibly deflect, redirect, or resist Big Person[21].

Bad guys (and many insecure Good Guys) love to hear this sort of advice offered; it does half their work for them. It is bad advice in daily life and it is great nonsense in Aikido where the stronger and more committed the attack the easier and more devastating the technique. In fact, the bigger the attacker the greater the advantage of the attacked. Don't believe it? You see this daily, in highway traffic.

---

21. A particularly absurd example of this common superstition appeared in the early 70's on a popular talk show addressing increasing assaults on women. Guests were a "Karate Expert" and an *actor* whose only apparent qualification for comment was a role in the then-current TV show "Police Surgeon." Between them they solemnly agreed that since no woman could ever resist any man, her best policy would always be "to submit." A common rationalization is that "fighting back is the worst thing you can do because it will just make him madder." (See Pinkman's comments on what happens to ball pitchers who are angry and nervous.) Situations differ, but contrary to popular fantasy and wishful thinking, police reports clearly indicate that women who fight, resist, and behave in the most unsubmissive and uncooperative manner possible are overwhelmingly likely to come out unharmed. It is the ones who are cooperative, passive, submissive, who fit an attacker's ideal fantasy victim, who allow themselves to be seen as a script, a cartoon, a fantasy scenario — something less than human — who are hurt, mutilated, murdered.

Aiki Traffic: Physics Off the Mat

— by Karl Schmidt, Virginia Ki Society

A basic law of the universe with which we must harmonize is:

$$F = ma \qquad \textbf{(EQ 2)}$$

In words this says:

Force = mass times acceleration.

As analogy to road traffic, consider:

- Small bodies/bicycles: 85 kg (~ 190 lbs)
- Medium bodies: cars: 1400 kg (~ 3,100 lbs)
- Large bodies such as fully-loaded 18-wheelers[22]: 36,000 kg (~ 80,000 lbs)

First, linear situations. To simplify, we'll assume all of our examples are elastic collisions that will ignore friction. In these linear cases, *acceleration* (*a*) is the change in velocity divided by the *time* (*t*) of that change (the duration of the impact).Change is represented by the Greek symbol delta (Δ). So, if F = ma, then

$$F = (m\Delta_v)/(\Delta_t) \qquad \textbf{(EQ 3)}$$

In words this is:

Force = mass times the change in velocity divided by change in time.

If you are sitting still on your bike and are struck by an 18-wheeler going about 40 m.p.h. (18 meters per second), the truck will continue as if nothing happened but you will be hurled forward at 2 times the truck's velocity. Assuming the impact lasts about 1 millisecond, the force you would experience would be:

F = (85 kg) (2* 18 m/s) / 0.001 second) = 3,060,000 N = 688,500 lbs $\qquad$ **(EQ 4)**

The truck on the other hand, will feel almost nothing. In some martial arts, attacks are dealt with by blocking or attacking with greater speed and force.

Suppose you as small body attack the larger body linearly? if you ride your bike at 40 m.p.h. into the 18-wheeler while it is sitting still, the truck will essentially remain motionless and unmoved but you will bounce backwards at 40 m.p.h. Force on bike and rider would be:

F = (85 kg) (18 m/s- (-18 m/s)0 / (0.001 s) = 3,060,000 N = 688,500 lbs. $\qquad$ **(EQ 5)**

Again, the truck feels little or nothing.

What about an opponent of equal size? If you drive your car at 40 m.p.h. into a stopped car of equal size, you will come to a stop while the other car will be knocked away at 40 m.p.h. The force both cars experience will be:

---

22. An 18-wheeler flat-bed trailer may weigh 32,000 pounds fueled, unloaded. Its engine alone weighs as much as a 3,000 pound Toyota pickup truck. A van will weigh more, a refrigerator truck still more.

$$F = (1400 \text{ kg}) (18\text{m/s} - 0) / (0.001 \text{ sec.}) = 25,200,000 \text{ N} = 5,670,000 \text{ lbs} \quad \textbf{(EQ 6)}$$

which is even worse! If you are smaller and dealing with oncoming linear energy, your best approach is to get off line and avoid these devastating forces entirely[23]. Otherwise, in none of these cases do you fare very well. But let's look at a circular approach. Imagine:

1. A tight circular ramp on a freeway exit.
2. The bicyclist zooming around the curve at 40 m.p.h. and the resulting forces.
3. The passenger car zooming around the curve at 40 m.p.h. and resulting forces.
4. The loaded 18-wheeler tractor trailer trying the same thing, and
5. *You* standing at the center of the circle turning around your center to watch these vehicles going by and the forces that operate on *your* action.

For a moving object to follow a circular path, it must exert a force towards the center of the circle (centripetal force), otherwise it will continue in a straight line and fly off that path, at a tangent to the circle. This centripetal force is defined as:

$$F = m\frac{v^2}{r} \qquad \textbf{(EQ 7)}$$

or in words,

Force = mass x velocity squared divided by the radius of the circle

Vehicles going around the curve of a tight exit ramp (with a radius of about 100 ft. or 30m) at 40 m.p.h. must exert an inward force through their wheels in order to maintain a curved path. For the small body (the bicycle) this force is:

$$F = (85 \text{ kg}) (18 \text{ m/sec}^2 / (30 \text{ m}) = 918 \text{ N} = 206 \text{ lbs} \qquad \textbf{(EQ 8)}$$

For the car:

$$F = (1,400 \text{ kg}) (18 \text{ m/sec.}^2 / (30 \text{ m}) = 15,120 \text{ N} = 3,402 \text{ lbs} \qquad \textbf{(EQ 9)}$$

For the 18-wheeler:

$$F = (36,000 \text{ kg}) (18 \text{ m/sec}^2 / (30 \text{ m}) = 388,800 \text{ N} = 87,480 \text{ lbs} \qquad \textbf{(EQ 10)}$$

The vehicle unable to exert the required force will go off the ramp[24].

Meanwhile, you stand at the center of the circular ramp, turning in order to watch the cars go around the ramp. Instead of your center of mass following a circular path as the vehicles above do, you are spinning about an axis which goes through your center of mass, so the forces are computed differently.

---

23. Similarly, if you are sitting in traffic and notice that the on-coming truck or car is coming too fast to stop in time, the best approach is *not* to slam your car into reverse, hoping to overcome its force with greater force. The best approach is to head for the shoulder, get off-line, don't be there, be safe, *ma-ai*.

24. . . . or suffer a blowout which may accomplish the same thing. Hence tough mylar racing tires for bikes and *steel*-belted tires for vehicles. Both are designed to deal with the enormous forces generated by speed and angular momentum.

$$F = mr\frac{\alpha}{2}$$ (EQ 11)

In words, this says:

"Tangential Force = mass x radius of cylinder x angular acceleration divided by 2"

After exerting an initial force to start, you will spin at a constant rate and therefore having no change in speed, you have no angular acceleration ($\alpha = 0$). Therefore you exert no force while spinning (except to overcome the friction between your feet and the ground). While the bike/car/truck must generate significant centripetal force to traverse the ramp, you only have to exert a minimal effort to spin and watch them.

Applying this to Aikido, *nage* stands at the center of a throw, maintaining one point and applying minimal forces. Meanwhile, *uke* is led into a circular path, in which significant energy must be expended to generate centripetal force to prevent flying off the road on a tangent.

— *K. S.*

And that is why a tiny 4'9" 80-pound Aikidoist can deflect, redirect, and throw a far larger, stronger attacker (see page 11).

If lured into a weight and strength contest, the smaller person hasn't got a chance.

Staying offline, using the tools of leverage, rotation, and the power of the circle, the smaller person has the advantage.[25]

That is the physics of Aikido.

But there is also Mind-Body Coordination.

---

25. See "The Concept of One-Point" on page 63 for the story of the 220-lb. Aikido instructor thrown by a 5-year-old girl. For the tale of the Aikidoist thrown and pinned by a one-ounce lizard, see page 12.

Mind-Body Coordination

Koichi Tohei[26] offers the following four principles for mind-body coordination.

1. **Keep One Point.** A principle of mind and body that keeps a low center of physical and mental gravity and concentrates on Center and balance, rather than on muscular strength.

2. **Relax Completely.** A principle of mind, aware but calm, and a principle of body, relaxed but alert. It gives *uke* poor leverage while increasing sensitivity to his.

3. **Keep Weight Underside.** A principle of body that embraces both heaviness and floating, that is, movement from center and allowing physical bodies and actions to flow "in harmony with gravity" as a boat floats upon the water[27].

4. **Extend Ki.** A principle of the mind that extends attention, awareness, and focus, providing a goal, a purpose, a path to follow.

It is indeed possible to dissect out the individual pieces elements but the whole point of Ki Development is "Mind-Body Coordination" — putting it all together. Like a sandwich.

Hey! you want mayo with that?

Maybe not. After all, it's "only" eggs and oil and vinegar. But cracking a raw egg over a greased pig, a head of lettuce, and a tomato will never ever be the same as the combination of processes that make it all work together.

Visualization and other internal exercises intended to develop Mind-Body Coordination are practiced by all athletes — dancers, ball players, golfers, gymnasts, skaters — and studied intently in the new and growing discipline of Sports Psychology. Physicists who study Aikido affirm (with deep regret) that they cannot do Aikido simply by running the equations in their heads. And not even the most dedicated student of Ki Development can afford to ignore the physics. They work together.

In *Aikido for Life* Gaku Homma very reasonably "debunks" a number of physics tricks as "physics tricks." Which they are. Later in the book he mentions having students roll over a piece of paper white on one side, red on the other. When the paper is laid on the mat:

- White side up, the students roll with no problem.

- Red side up — oops!

— an excellent example of mind/body coordination, where visual input and mindset affecting the physical outcomes, exactly the sort of thing that *ki* exercises are designed to observe and alter.

---

26. Koichi Tohei Sensei was strongly influenced by his studies with Tempu Nakamura, a student of yoga. The Sanskrit *yoga* means "union," (related to the English *yoke*) and implies a union of mind and body, that of the physical and that of the spirit.

27. Compare to trying to lift that boat out of the water.

Attention and Tetris

If you have problems with the possibility that attention changes the equation, consider the flip side: *inattention*.

Studies by the U. S. Department of Transportation find that using car phones is equivalent to driving with a blood-alcohol level of up to the legal limit (and possibly beyond depending on the conversation).

You can see a somewhat safer demonstration of this effect, via a computer game such as *Tetris*, which like driving, requires recognition and manipulation of geometric shapes and spaces. To evaluate,

1. Play several games to establish a skill baseline.
2. Play several games while talking on the phone or to a partner.

   Do not discuss the game itself. Rather, emphasize personal matters or topics such as taxes, or your favorite inflammatory political issue.
3. Observe what happens to your score; compare with baseline.

Attention and awareness often translate into details and action in many ways. For example, millions of spaghetti cooks around the world earnestly believe that adding a few teaspoons of salt to a pot of water will raise the boiling temperature and cook the pasta faster or better. In fact, teaspoons or tablespoons of salt added to quarts or gallons of water *do* raise the boiling temperature but only by a few thousandths of a degree. There is no possible effect on cooking *time* unless you are measuring in microseconds. On the other hand, it may effect *taste* which is a great deal of what cooking is about. And the cook or Aikidoist who pays attention to details, who is aware of processes and has a definite goal in mind will almost certainly turn out a better meal or a better technique than the one who merely threw it all together at random.

Goals matter, but they don't repeal physical law. The Ki Door exercise combines *ki* with mechanics. If a door is not available, it can also be done with *uke* standing with an arm extended.

Ki Door

1. Try to push your way through a heavy door while placing your mind *behind* you.
2. Push through the door while directing your mind *forward* and extending.
3. Repeat while extending as above, but try to push the door open from the *hinge* side.
4. Using the knife edge of your hand, heel, or thumb[28] (not an open hand), inch back along the door towards the opening edge. Where is the point where you begin to have some hope of moving the lever that is the door?

Variation

The same principle of leverage above appears in *sankyo* and other wrist locks.

Grasping the knife-edge of *uke*'s hand,

1. *Nage* place thumb near ridge of left hand and turn hand.
2. Place thumb at middle of left hand and turn hand.
3. Place thumb in line with index finger of left hand.

   Which position gives most leverage?

   What happens if you think about how strong *uke* is and how impossible it will be to turn the hand?

   What happens if you rotate the hand in your mind — but with poor mechanical advantage?

In general, our behavior is controlled by two things: what we want and what we fear. What is it that *uke* wants to do? Align with that. And consider what it is you fear (and why you are standing so far away).

Goals and intentions and the energy behind them are the vector quantities of spiritual orientation. And, as it is possible to align with physical energy, so it is also possible to align with the energy of life and human relationships.

---

28. A thumb provides a point-source of force; a hand a spread of force and leverage.

On Aikido and Music

— by Susan Chandler, Ki Society

I sit before the looming black instrument struggling for composure. The notes on the page of music have turned to hieroglyphics and my fingers to stone. At the end of my performance the other piano students smile weakly and mumble false praise. My teacher tells me to work on rhythm and timing. I flee to the practice rooms, to a small cubicle with a battered old baby grand. Alone, I sit and play the music, this time flawlessly.

To succeed at making music at the piano requires the coordinated involvement of my whole being. Ears, eyes, fingers and feet (and every part they are attached to), heart, reason and soul. All the parts must work together in time, the present, past, and future seamlessly interwoven.

How does one accomplish this? Without an audience the many parts of me come together and I succeed in making music. Under the pressure of judgement by my teacher and peers the parts scatter and the music fails.

A simple idea was introduced to me in college while I was struggling with performance anxiety at the piano. A friend described to me the process of "Keeping One-Point," something she had learned in Ki Aikido. She told me to put my mental attention at my physical center of balance in my lower abdomen. While I did this she pushed on me to test my balance. She could not budge me; I stood my ground against her force with no sense of physical effort.

Curiosity led me to try this mind/body exercise while playing the piano. To my amazement, I found that awareness of my One-Point helped me to not "fall apart" in front of an audience. The image of One-Point worked for me like a conductor coordinating the musicians in an orchestra; the many music-making parts of me came together to create music, overcoming the scattering effect of my anxiety.

The Musician's Mind/Body Coordination

One Point is one of the four basic principles in Ki Aikido for establishing mind/body coordination. Aikido, like music, is a series of events in time. Finding One-Point helps my timing, that is, the coordinated movement of all of the parts of my mind and body in a series of events in time, like playing Bach, hitting a golf ball, or doing an Aikido throw.

A symphony conductor leads the orchestra to play in time together by providing a beat that everyone follows. The relationship between a sense of timing, or feeling a beat, and mind/body coordination is circular. That is, I can establish good timing by finding my one point, and I can create mind/body coordination by feeling a beat.

A beat is a repeating cycle of build and release, like the rise and fall of a wave. When I clap my hands to express a beat, the sound of the clapping is only one moment in the life of the beat. The silent action of moving my hands apart and together again is as much the beat as the sound itself.

Effective timing involves an awareness of the entire cycle, for the Aikidoist as well as the musician. The power of rhythm and timing in Aikido movement is in riding the wave of the beat as it builds and releases and builds and releases. See this demonstrated in the *ikkyo-undo* exercise (page 101).

And the Beat Goes On . . .

1. Mark a steady beat with your feet feeling the movement throughout your body.
2. Stop the *movement*, but continue the feeling of the beat. *Uke* test.
3. Stop the *feeling* of the beat. *Uke* test.

On Zen and The Art of Motorcycles

Turn your head! Look into the turn before you turn!
No! No! Don't look down, look ahead! Mind and body follow eyes!
Look right, you'll go right. Look down, you're going down.
Relax the shoulders! Relax the arms! Breathe!
And while you're at it, smile! Have fun!

A "fruity" *ki-aikido* class?

No. A Motorcycle Safety Foundation class.

The skills, the physics, and even the instructions and imagery are uncannily similar to those heard in Aikido.

Aikido principles based on good solid physics are often ignored or disregarded by beginners because beginning speeds are too low for these forces to be readily apparent. Mat speeds at a walk-through beginning level simply do not develop the forces that will later make the same techniques so devastating. Most of us dismiss or disregard these forces at the beginning stage; better to learn and practice them as skills develop. Meanwhile, you can provide a Reality Check via similar but higher-speed activities.

Skiing, rollerblading or ice skating are most obviously similar to Aikido. In cycling (bi- or motor-) you are off the ground and on a machine, but higher speeds make the physical forces even more vividly real. Either way you will learn to harmonize with the physical laws of the universe or face the swift and terrible retribution of the physics gods.

Both Aikido and motorcycling take advantage of counterintuitive physical laws where muscular strength is not the issue. Physics is.

The Honda Goldwing is one of the largest motorcycles made. It weighs over 800 pounds alone. Add fluids, rider, passenger and gear and it will weigh much more. Off its stand, it must be over its center or supported by inertia at all times. It is simply not possible to hold a half-ton of falling bike on one leg.

On any bike it seems obvious that you steer by turning handlebars in the direction you want to go. Actually, you do not.

No matter how strong you are, at high speeds, angular momentum of the wheel makes it difficult or nearly impossible to turn the handlebars. The bigger the bike, the more difficult this is and the more critical it is to use center, hips, balance, and weight shift.

For slow, tight turns, you lean only the motorcycle while keeping your own body straight and upright. For turns at speed, you lean with the motorcycle and "countersteer," pressing the wheel *right* in order to turn *left*. Countersteering makes no more sense to the beginner than the idea that the effective way to throw *uke* "down" is to send him "up." But both are excellent physics.

Eye Direction

Eyes reveal conditions. They can also create conditions.

Most new students just can't believe that eye position (*me-tusuke*) makes a difference. Japanese martial arts consider it extremely important. To see why, experiment with proper or improper eye direction on skates.

If you try doing it wrong on a motorcycle under the watchful eye of an MSF instructor, you will hear about it. The standard instruction for turning on a motorcycle is:

Look right, go right. Mind and body follow eyes.

In MSF classes, points are deducted for not looking into the turn, or for looking down at a stop when eyes should properly be focused ahead on the horizon, on path of travel, on the goal. On rolling in class, focusing on the mat may take you directly into the mat. Instead try looking at your belt, your knee, your back leg, or where you want to go in these and other techniques.

- To do a U-turn in a MSF class, look at your own tail-light and turn. Similarly,
- To do a *tenkan*, look at *uke*'s tail light or around your circle of travel and turn.
- Try doing the opposite and compare the results.

Falls

Motorcycling requires serious protection against falls and rolls. In Aikido, if you're having trouble learning to roll or are suffering from a bruised shoulder, try rolling in a padded motorcycle jacket. Shoulders, elbows, back are protected with material that ranges from "padding" to outright "body armor" depending on manufacturer and purpose. And yes, you can roll in the helmet too. What keeps you safe on the highway will also keep you safe at mat speeds. Jacket and helmet allow you to feel the spots where you are not round enough, protect you from bruises, bangs, headaches and separated shoulders. They can ease you into proper position and keep you safe until you ready to roll unassisted.[29]

Off the mat and on the road, a standard recommendation for *ukemi* from a high speed motorcycle throw is essentially a breakfall —maximum surface area in contact with road surface, maximum braking due to friction, minimum amount of time spent travelling. In theory, you won't control a roll at 60 m.p.h. and the more time you spend rolling the more time you have to hit some other obstacle such as a tree, post or guardrail at high speed[30].

"In theory," says MSF Instructor John Garner, "but I disagree."

---

29. Caveat: It isn't reasonable to buy motorcycle equipment only to practice Aikido and potential lenders may protest, so note that pads are sold separately. These, socks, or dense foam from an upholstery store can be taped onto you or into your uniform until you are ready to solo on your own.

"Taking a breakfall at 60 m.p.h. with extended limbs (to maximize surface area) risks snagging said limbs on a pole or a tree; they may not continue on with the rest of you. I would roll. But, in fact, you should never be taking a fall that fast. If you're falling at 60 m.p.h., if you haven't already slowed and prepared, which means something has already gone terribly wrong. That something is usually awareness."

Awareness

"Motorcycling is 10 percent physical and 90 percent mental," says Garner. "A big part of the mental practice is being aware of your surroundings."

In Westbrook and Ratti's *Aikido and the Dynamic Sphere*, the process of awareness applied to self defense is broken down into:

Perception, Evaluation-Decision, and Reaction

MSF uses the acronym SIPDE meaning:

Scan, Identify, Predict, Decide, Execute.

Experienced Rider classes combine the steps to get SPA:

Search, Predict, Act

All offer a formal strategy for awareness and action and can be extended to physical exercises and techniques done in Aikido class. For the exercises in the following chapters, continue to draw the circles, extend the lines in your mind. For the same concepts that can be practiced off the mat and in daily traffic see John Garner's essay on awareness in Appendix B.

Let us not look back in anger or forward in fear, but around us in awareness.

— *James Thurber*

---

30. Bicycles may or may not reach highway speeds. On the other hand bicyclists rarely dress to survive the kind of skin contact involved in high-speed breakfalls. Rolling would seem preferable, but bicycle racers are taught to always slide out of an accident. The theory is that you lose some skin, but don't break anything. Racers are taught to "lay down" as soon as the fall starts rather than hurtling over the handlebars.

CHAPTER 4

Aikido Exercises

Aikido exercises are designed to enhance flexibility and coordination while patterning the basic motions of Aikido. The following exercises include the traditional exercises. These are presented in a non-traditional order in consideration of the difference between stretching and warming.[1]

Warming and Stretching

A supple, flexible body is as much a part of self-confidence and self-defense as are the throws.

It is easier to throw (or to injure) a stiff body than a flexible one. A flexible body can move and adjust in ways that an attacker may not anticipate. It is the difference between trying to throw a rope and trying to throw a broomstick.

Consider hamstring flexibility. Drop the hand of a flexible partner to the mat and there may be little effect since that hand can go there very comfortably; a distinct "out" or "forward" component must be added to *uke*'s Center /One-Point to make a throw. But hamstrings too tight to allow *uke* to touch toes are a different situation. If *uke* cannot bend down, his own inflexibility forces his Center forward of his feet. *Uke* essentially throws himself[2]

Flexible muscles are also stronger than tense ones because muscle power is generated by contraction over the length of available contractible muscle. Muscles already contracted due to lack of use, stress, or disease are weak. Continuous contraction without equivalent stretching or relaxation results in shortening, and loss of strength. They can also be extremely painful, producing problems from headaches and knee pain to the tingling and weakness of nerve entrapment and even dizziness while rolling.[3]

Stretch for flexibility, strength and good health but do it properly. Many schools stretch "to warm up," but stretching is *not* a warm up. Stretching cold, stiff bodies especially when combined with bouncing or overstretching tends to stretch ligaments and tendons. This form of "flexibility" is more accurately known as "joint instability" and sets the stage for chronic injury. Warm and work the muscles first, then stretch.

---

1. For a more traditional order, refer to Westbrook & Ratti (1970).
2. For a demonstration, see "The Ma-ai of Balance" on page 174.
3. Sufferers, especially if over 21, are usually told they have "arthritis." In healthy individuals, true arthritis is far less common than commonly believed; tight muscles leading to pain and dysfunction are common and largely avoidable.

For general warm-up, consider starting with the exercises which do not involve stretching, for example, most of the *hitori-waza / aiki-taiso*. Arm exercises tend to raise heart-rate and get blood moving, while those marked with * involve the large muscles of the legs which are the main target of stretching exercises and should therefore be worked and warmed before stretching. For a vivid analogy of why this matters, try stretching a frozen rubber band.

The Three-Minute Exercise incorporates many of these exercises and provides an excellent general warm-up.

1. *Three-Minute Exercise, page 87.*
2. *Tekubi-Kosa Undo* ("Wrist-Crossing Exercise") page 88.
3. **Funekogi-Undo* ("Boat-Rowing Exercise") page 90.
4. *Ude mawashi-Undo* ("Arm-Dropping Exercise") page 92.
5. *Udefuri-Undo* ("Arm-Swinging Exercise") page 93 and
6. **Udefuri-Choyaku Undo* ("Arm-Swinging-Spinning Exercise") page 94.
7. **Sayu-Undo* ("Right-Left Exercise") page 95.
8. **Tenkan-Undo* ("Turning Exercise") page 97.
9. **Ushiro-Tori Undo* ("Rear-Attack Exercise") page 98.
10. **Ushiro Tekubi-Tori-Undo* ("Rear Wrist-Attack Exercise") page 99.
11. *Ushiro Koshin-Zanshin ("Rear-Front-and-Back Exercise") page 100.
12. **Ikkyo-Undo* ("First Teaching Exercise") page 101; and Spinning Ikkyo-Undo, page 102.
13. **Zengo-Undo*, page 103 and *Happo-Undo ("Eight-Way Exercise") page 104.*
14. Wrist exercises page 108.
15. Leg stretching exercises (beginning page 113) perhaps with Supplemental stretching exercises as desired, beginning page 116.

The Three-Minute Exercise

Ki Society classes often begin with this three-minute exercise of paired movements repeated four times. Emphasize gentle stretch rather than compression. For example, in tilting the head back, think of stretching the front of the neck rather than forcing the back of your head into your shoulders. The exercise is counted in sets of 2 of 8 counts each. The count comes before the motion.[4]

1. Lateral Arm Swinging *(udefuri-undo)*
2. Bending Side to Side
3. Bending Forward and Backward
4. Shoulder-Blade Exercise
5. Tilting Head From Side-to-Side
6. Tilting Head Front to Back
7. Looking From Side To Side
8. Knee Bends And Heel Raises
9. Knee/Hamstring Stretch
10. Arm-Dropping (*ude-mawashi undo*)
11. Dropping Both Arms
12. Dropping Both Arms While Dropping Center/One-Point.
13. Wrist-Shaking Exercise (*Tekubi-Shindo*)

Variations

- In these paired exercises, *uke* test after doing the exercise once (for example, one arm swing rather than two). Repeat doing the exercise twice and compare stability.
  Why sets of two?
  For batting warmups, rather than mindless or random motions, baseball coach John Pinkman teaches players to clear the mind and focus on the ball through pre-programmed *ki* exercises. Says Pinkman:
  "We assume batting position, and visit this place twice to clue-in the body. Going there once is not enough for the body to understand what the mind wants the body to do. The mind does not already know. We have to send it a verification message. This is done by repeating the desired movement."

- Do the exercise while walking around the mat. If you do not return head (and eyes) to center you will become badly disoriented.

- Do the exercise in a motorcycle helmet. What difference does this make in your posture and balance?
  Far-fetched? Consider traditional armor, helms, and other weighty protective garb. The heavier the load, the more critical good posture becomes, surely part of the origin of the classically erect military bearing.

---

4. For Pinkman's use of *ki* development exercises in pitching and hitting, see page 60. For detailed instructions and count for the Three-Minute Exercise, see Appendix B in Shifflett, C. M. (1997).

Hitori Waza and Other Exercises

Hitori Waza is the term Koichi Tohei Sensei uses to encompass the body of exercises he teaches which are precursors to practicing technique. Funekogi-Undo, Ikkyo-Undo, and Happo-Undo are all examples of Hitori Waza. These are classic exercises of Aikido, building blocks of good technique.

— *George Simcox, Ki Society*

The following exercises are known as *hitori-waza* in the Ki Society, *aiki-taiso* in other organizations. They are the basic exercises of coordination, the fundamentals of Aikido.

Tekubi-Kosa Undo

ADS: Basic Exercise # 11, 12 ("Wrist-Crossing Exercise"), pp. 131-132; ZC p. 237.

Baffling and pointless to new eyes, *tekubi-kosa undo* is practice in relaxation while maintaining balance and proper alignment. It is also the precursor to many throws such as different versions of *kote-gaeshi*, wrist grabs and locks. Done from the back it becomes *ushiro-tekubi-tori-undo* (page 99).

With feet shoulder-width apart and arms relaxed at sides,

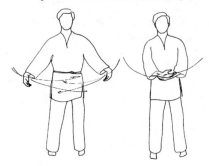

Mid-level (Joho)

1. Leading from fingertips, swing arms up to waist height, crossing wrists.
2. Drop arms to sides.
3. Repeat. Continue into . . .

Upper-Level (koho)

The tendency is to tilt backward from the waist as the arms swing up. Leading from fingertips, swing arms up to just below eye level and drop down as above.

The challenge is to emphasize relaxation of the arms, a natural swing, and proper posture. To test this,

1. Instructor calls "Stop!" at some point and directs class to:
2. Raise the left foot (balancing on right).
3. Raise the right foot (balancing on left).
4. Observe any changes in your stability when you:

a) concentrate on your hands.

b) concentrate on your foot.

c) concentrate on Center/One-Point.

d) imagine holding onto a rope from the ceiling, a pole extending up through your body, or having your Center at mat level so just your eyes are above the mat.

Tekubi-kosa undo is actually the exercise or the motion which we are trying to recreate when we tell new students faced with a wrist grab, to "look at your fingernails," or "adjust your glasses," or "scratch your nose." These familiar activities reproduce the motion while eliminating the mindblock that it can't be done merely because there's an attacker holding the wrist. The following exercise is a spectacular demonstration of the motion and the mindset. In groups of four,

1. Two partners hold *nage*'s wrists.

2. Third partner tosses a ball or bean bag straight forward to *nage*. Despite being held by the wrists, *nage will* catch it, not by struggling free of the restraining hands, but by focusing on catching the bean bag, an act even less self-conscious and more compelling than itches or glasses.

The classic martial arts exhortation, "Don't think, DO!" doesn't mean to be a mindless moron or a loose cannon. It means to catch the ball, rather than standing there thinking of all the reasons it can't be done. The first approach accomplishes great things. The second is like driving through life with your parking brake on.

Funekogi-Undo

ADS: Basic Exercise #4 ("Boat-Rowing Exercise"), pp. 123-124; KDL pp. 56-57; ZC pp. 230-232.

Funekogi-undo is the workhorse of Aikido. A committed, energetic attack is a gift of motion and energy. The more aggressive the attacker, the less work for *nage* who need only transform and redirect. But how do you deal with the static attacker who offers no energy or motion to play with? *Funekogi* gets *uke* moving with the enormous power of hips and legs and, once there is motion, almost any motion can be transformed. The pattern is:

Hips-hands — Hips-hands

Arms do not pull with muscular strength. They serve as connectors, like ropes, between the load and the hips and legs.

From left *hanmi*, with hips square, hands at waist, elbows down, knees bent,

1. Shift hips forward thrusting out arms as if pushing an oar.
2. Shift hips back, drawing arms back to waist.

To test stability, *uke* may:

- Attempt to lift hands, or push up along axis of arm,
- Push straight back from shoulders.
- Push forward from hips or small of back.
- Hips remain at about the same height, which can be checked with two partners holding a *jo*.

Variations

1. *Uke* holds *nage*'s wrists as strongly as possible.
2. *Nage* attempts to move *uke* by pulling with arms or
3. Relaxing arms and moving hips with *funekogi-undo*. Observe the effect on *uke* regardless of his size and strength.

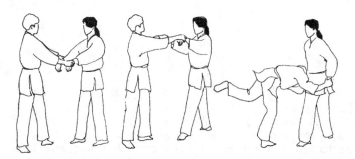

Another version of *funekogi* appears in *Ryote-tori kokyu-nage zempo-nage*, a variant[5] of *Ryote-mochi kokyu-nage zempo-nage tenkan* on page 213.

1. Leaving wrists in place, *nage* step as far to the rear as possible on the left foot, taking up slack, then
2. Turn *tenkan* to *uke*'s left side taking *uke* off balance.

   Notice that the most powerful hold can be set up for a flying *zempo-nage*.

If you do not have access to a traditional Japanese boat[6], experience a similar feeling with western oars or a rowing machine. Observe the pointlessness of muscling with or tensing the arms with these, while holding the handles of hanging plastic grocery bag, while working with a shovel.

A shovel is a lever that rotates around the fulcrum of the hand nearest the blade which need only be gripped by the hand. The shovel lifts the load when the back hand presses down on the lever of the handle. Compare the effort involved in:

* Tensing the blade arm (lifting up with muscle power) versus
* Allowing the load to simply rest at the end of the blade arm.

Apply *funekogi-undo* to mowing the lawn, repeatedly opening heavy kitchen drawers or filing cabinet drawers to get the feeling of the back-and-forth motion of hips and legs, connecting with rather than pulling with, arms.

---

5. The difference is this: in the technique on page 213, *uke* attacks with two hands to *nage*'s one hand; here *uke* grabs both of *nage*'s hands.
6. The real thing can be seen in the opening scenes of Bruce Lee's *Enter the Dragon* as a young girl sculls a boat across Tokyo harbor. It also appears in the final scenes of *Duel on Gakyu Island* (Part III of the *Samurai Trilogy*) as a boatman rows Musashi to the island for his fateful meeting with his arch-rival.

Udemawashi-Undo

"Arm-Dropping Exercise"

An exercise in raising the arm and then dropping it in alignment with gravity, using relaxation, mass and acceleration in the most effective way possible. This simple movement is the basis of many Aikido throws. It produces the "up" that makes an effective "down" in techniques such as *kokyu-nage* and *ikkyo*. The *Banzai!* position of upraised arms about to be dropped is more the "Basic Stance of Aikido" technique than anything involving mere foot position.

With feet shoulder-width apart (*shizentai* stance), *nage* will:

1. Raise arm to the highest point possible without straightening, stiffening or locking the elbow.
2. Allow the arm to drop, of its own weight, to the lowest point.
3. *Uke* test by attempting to lift straight up on the arm.

The same technique of dropping with gravity underlies sword techniques and other tools from hammers to hoes ("Gardens" on page 232). These fall of their own weight. They are not forced up or down. To do so is tiring and inefficient.

Variations

- Drop hand directly down as if the hand were sliding hand down a vertical staff.

- Working alone, raise and drop arm with a weight. After enough repetitions to begin to tire the muscle, what is the most efficient movement to raise the arm?

- In pairs, *nage* drops hand on *uke*'s out-stretched wrist. (Drop arm only; do not push or attempt to muscle or force *uke*'s arm out of the way.)
  Compare *uke*'s resulting "down" to the degree of *nage*'s starting "up."

Steve Kendall demonstrates the exercise and the application with a combination drop and step which he refers to as the *"Funky Kokyu-nage."* Drop arm while stepping to side, repeat. "To get really funky," says Steve, add an *udefuri*-choyaku (spin) in the middle and you have *Kokyu-Nage Basic*.

Udefuri-Undo

ADS: Basic Exercise #15 ("Arm Swinging Exercise"), pp. 134-136; ZC: pp. 239-240.

In class, *udefuri-undo* is usually continuous with *udefuri-choyaku-undo* (the Spinning Exercise on page 94).

Nage stands with feet shoulder-width apart, with head, eyes, and chest straight ahead. *Uke* calls the count. Count is 1-2, 1-2, 1-2, 1-2 . . . until *uke* or instructor signals the end of the series by calling a 3- 4. Notice that the torso does not turn until the final Step 4.

1. On "One," swing arms to the left, wrapping around body.
2. On "Two," swing arms to the right, wrapping around body.
3. On "Three," swing arms to left as on "One."
4. On "Four," swing arms right as you step forward with left foot.

    Uke may test for stability at this point, or *nage* may continue into *Udefuri Choyaku Undo* on count of "One."

In the movie Karate Kid II, the villagers on Okinawa had a toy drum with a handle. On two sides, a short string was attached with a lump on the end. Spinning the handle back and forth turned the drum around the handle axis, causing the strings to spin out (as in the Arm Swinging Exercise), and hit the drum with each change in direction. When the direction of the spin was changed, hit the drum, a good illustration of "turning about the center."

In the movie the little drum was mentioned as the "heart of karate."

— *George Simcox, Ki Society*

Udefuri-Choyaku Undo

ADS: Basic Exercise # 15 ("Arm-Swinging Spinning Exercise") pp. 135,136.

Remember spinning like a top when you were a child? This is the same.

This exercise develops balance, Center/One-Point, and relaxation. Keep foot motion as natural as possible, not leaping but stepping and turning naturally and comfortably. To end the motion, relax or drop into it, so there is no wobble or stumble at the end. Movement begins from the Center/One-Point, although rapid changes in direction can start from the little finger which acts like a small starter motor. Arms are not held out, they spin out due to centrifugal force; they should be so relaxed that you can feel tingling in the fingers.

Extend *ki*, that is, have a goal. Pick points on two walls to serve as reference points. From Step 4 of the "Arm Swinging Exercise" (page 93), arms wrapped to right side of body, left foot forward,

1. On "One," rotate hips 180 degrees to left. Arms spin out (they are not forced out) rising to shoulder height, then wrapping to left side of body. Draw leading foot back to close up stance into *hanmi*.

2. On "Two," reverse direction returning to original position with arms wrapped to right side of body. Draw leading foot back to close up stance into *hanmi*.

   The count is 1-2, 1-2, 1-2, 1-2 . . . until *uke* or the instructor signals the end of the series by calling a 3 - 4.

Variations

- Two spins.
- Three or more spins.

I recently heard this exercise dismissed as a newfangled and rather frivolous sort of activity of no particular value except perhaps "practice in accustoming oneself to functioning while dizzy." In fact, it is very traditional and teaches balance, coordination, focus, relaxation, and good posture all in one — no small feat. When ended with an *ude-mawashi* (page 92), it becomes *Kokyu-Nage Basic* (page 201), *Shomen-uchi ikkyo tenkan* (page 209) and many other "real throwing techniques." It is also very "real" on its own.

When I first started practicing the martial arts (in January 1951 in Ashiya, Kyushu, Japan) I was told to practice a certain exercise called ude-furi-undo, explained as a defense against a tackle. For days, we practiced this one exercise for two or more hours at a time. After four days of this, I thought "Why am I here? I am not learning anything practicing just one exercise." When I returned to class on Friday, I resolved that if the teacher had me practice it again, I would quit. Fortunately he did not, until the last 15 minutes of class, when he had me doing the same old exercise. "Well," I thought, "I can do it, it's the end of the class."

The next evening I was standing in the barracks talking to several people when one of them yelled a warning. I turned around just in time to see a guy come screaming toward me in the tackle position. I turned automatically and the guy went flying. A couple of people held him down and one went to call the medics — he'd probably been drinking and flipped out. Later, one of the guys asked me how I threw him. I didn't know, I did not realize what I had done or how I had done it. I just made a move and . . .

Then the mental light came on. Practice, practice, practice. That is what it's all about. Through practice I did a throwing technique without even thinking about it. Actually it wasn't even a technique. It was "just an exercise."

— William Thorndike, Jr.

Sayu-Undo

ADS: Basic Exercise #13 ("Left-Right Exercise"), pp. 132-134; ZC: pp. 238-239.

This exercise appears in *ude-oroshi.* (See page 211). Body is erect, not tilting or leaning but dropping Center and weight of arms from side to side. Eyes and head are forward.

Static

With feet shoulder width apart, at center position,

1. Swing left arm up to shoulder height and right arm to approximately waist height.
2. Bending left knee, shift to left side. Weight is underside, left arm settles with weight underside and right hand is at Center/One-Point.
3. Shift weight to center position as arms rise up to the right to a comfortable point.
4. Bending right knee, shift to right side, drop weight underside. Right arm settles with weight underside and left hand is at Center/One-Point.

In motion,

1. To move to left, cross outside (right) foot behind leading (left) foot while swinging arms up and to the left side.
2. Drop arms and Center/One-Point with weight underside, settling onto left foot.
3. To move to right, cross outside (left) foot behind leading (right) foot while swinging arms up and to the right side.

Uke may test either version of *sayu-undo* by:

- Testing for Unbendable Arm.
- Pushing on the shoulder from the side, eyes front vs. eyes forward.
- Attempting to lift up on the lower hand.
- Attempting to lift up on either leg.

Tenkan-Undo

ADS: Basic Exercise #10 ("Turning Exercise"), pp. 130-131; TOT: Tai no henko ichi/ni , pp. 36-39; ZC: pp. 235-236.

A *tenkan* is a "turning," a simple maneuver that is, in fact, one of the most powerful and devastating moves in Aikido. Its purpose and its power is to transform and redirect linear energy (especially a blast of fast, incoming energy) into circular energy with *nage* safe at the center, turning calmly within the eye of the hurricane.

In left *hanmi* (left foot and left hand forward)

1. Extend left hand, palm down.
2. Curl fingers back towards palm, then step or slide forward with the left foot, pivoting 180 degrees. Draw the left foot back as necessary. Left foot is still forward and right foot back (still in left *hanmi* although direction is reversed.)
3. Extend right hand, palm down then step or slide forward with the right foot, pivoting 180 degrees to original direction. Draw the left foot back as necessary.

Note that Yoshinkan style does this very differently[7] swinging the leg back directly from the hip and turning 95 degrees rather than 180. Why 95?

Yoshinkan considers 95 degrees to be the smallest angle necessary to unbalance an opponent, hence more difficult. Practicing the more difficult techniques makes others easier.

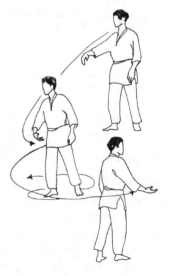

Variations

Once the motion is learned, *uke* can practice by:

- Pivoting around his own extended hand (alternating right and left hands) or around a staff
- Turning in place or
- Turning every few steps while walking.
- Turn *tenkan* in the kitchen while waiting for the kettle to boil.
  Turn *tenkan* with a teacup of water. You may find it surprisingly stable.
  \What are the motions that keep it from splashing?
  What are the motions that will cause difficulties? Compare with those required to turn *tenkan* with a balloon; with a ball and *lacrosse* stick.

---

7. See Gozo Shioda's *Total Aikido* for details of the Yoshinkan turn.

Ushiro-Tori Undo

ADS: Basic Exercise #16 ("Rear-Attack Exercise") pp. 136-137; ZC: pp. 241-242.

This exercise deals with rear attacks, specifically bear hugs and grabs to the shoulders. Facing forward in left *hanmi*,

1. Slide left foot forward while swinging arms up in semi-circle leading with little fingers and simultaneously turning wrists inward, thumbs down.
2. Sliding LF further forward, bend left knee. Rotating hips, swing forward (L) arm to right until pointing forward, rear arm (R) pointing back.

   Back arm swings around in line with the front arm. When done as a throw from a bear-hug, the back arm is actually the throwing arm; *uke* slides off the front arm.

   You will extend and bend forward from and in alignment with the extension of the back leg. The attacker rotates to the side, then slides forward and off.

   Be sure to keep hips and torso aligned with the plane of the throw. If you bend forward (that is, at an angle to the forward direction of the throw), your own hips will keep *uke* attached by blocking his forward movement.

Variation

1. *Uke* grab *nage* around shoulders.
2. *Nage* rotate wrists and arms forward as in the exercise above and
3. Walk forward.
4. *Uke* will be drawn irresistibly along.

   By attacking *nage*, *uke* has sacrificed his own One-Point.

Ushiro Tekubi-Tori-Undo

ADS: Basic Exercise #17 ("Rear Wrist-Attack Exercise"), pp. 137-138; ZC: pp. 242-243.

Here the turning wrist motion of original *tekubi-kosa-tori* exercise appears again modeling a "wrist grab from behind" and the technique for dealing with it. Step 1) below also appears in *zempo* techniques.

Step forward with left foot while curving fingertips inward, directing hands toward Center. Swing arms up to forehead level and turn fingers palm down. (The image many people mention is that of a Praying Mantis.)

1. Bend body and drop arms tracing a large circle to ground over bent left knee.
2. Step forward with right foot as in 1).
3. Bend body and drop arms over bent right knee as in (2).

    This exercise can be combined with the paired stretch on page 117 for practice of balance and stability without the throw.

    The "stooping" test prepares for and teaches stability in the final motion of this exercise and its *zanshin* version.

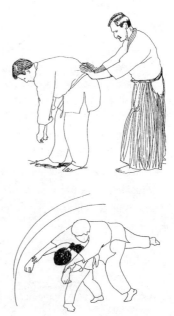

Variations

Uke may test as follows:

- Lifting up on *nage*'s wrists to see if shoulders rise or balance can be broken.
- Testing for Unbendable Arm.
- Pushing down on wrists when they are raised (a version of Unbendable Arm).
- Pushing forward from small of back.

The following demonstration shows the power of this simple movement.

In pairs, with *uke* holding *nage*'s wrists from behind and pressing down firmly, *nage* compare the effort required in attempting to:

- Raise arms by bringing them out to the sides and up, or . . .
- Raise arms by doing the exercise (bringing fingers up center).

Some styles heavily emphasize "elbow power." The basic principle is that you are mechanically weaker when your arms are held out from your body. You are stronger when they are brought in to your Center or moving along the centerline of your body. The above exercise makes this very clear. Note that if *uke* pulls your arms back well past your hips, it will be difficult to move the arms forward. Therefore, step back, moving your hips back.

In the actual throw, *nage* extends arms up and forward. Compare with dropping elbows. What is the advantage to *nage* being on the longest possible end of the literal lever arm?

Ushiro Koshin-Zanshin

ADS: Basic Exercise #18 ("Backwards with Immovable-Mind Exercise") p. 138.

This exercise is essentially the same as *ushiro tekubi-tori undo* except that it involves stepping backward (*zan-shin*).[8] It deals with a two-handed grab from the front with incoming energy.

1. Step diagonally back (off-line) with left foot while curving fingertips forward and up. Swing arms up to forehead level and turn fingers palm down.
2. Sweep right foot back, bend body from center, and drop arms tracing a large circle to ground over kneeling right knee.
3. Repeat, stepping diagonally back with right foot as in (1).
4. Bend body and drop arms over kneeling left knee as in (2).

Uke may test as follows:

- Lifting up on wrists to see if shoulders rise or balance can be broken.
- Testing for Unbendable Arm.
- Pushing down on wrists when raised (a version of Unbendable Arm).
- Pushing forward from small of back during Step 1 or Step 2.
- Pushing back from shoulders during Step 1 or Step 2.

---

8. Combined with *funekogi-undo* (page 90) to set a static *uke* in motion, it makes up the technique known as "The Ghost Throw" (or "Swan Lake" in Ki Society *taigi*.) See Projection #24 against Attack #4 on p. 312 of ADS (Westbrook & Ratti, 1970).

Ikkyo-Undo

ADS: Basic Exercise #5 ("First-Teaching Exercise"), p. 125; ZC: pp. 232-233

Ikkyo-undo is the high-flying reverse of *funekogi-undo*. It appears to be a block and in part it is, but it is more a means of aligning with *uke*'s energy, sensing and matching speed and direction of an incoming strike while rendering it harmless. In contrast to *funekogi-undo*, the pattern for *ikkyo* is:

Hips-hands Hands-hips[9]

Imagine that your thumbs are switches that allow your hips to move.

This is the exercise that brought me into Aikido. Karate students are taught to directly block the most ferocious overhead blows with forearms and so spend years with sore, injured arms. "Isn't there a better way?" they always ask. Yes. Here it is.

With *nage* in *hanmi*,

1. Hips shift forward.
2. Arms swing forward and up, fingers extended, stopping at forehead level.
3. Hips shift back.
4. Arms drop to sides, hands softly closed.

Uke can test, with *nage* static or in motion by:

- Pushing forward from the small of the back.
- Pushing into and perpendicular to the chest.
- Testing for Unbendable Arm (with *nage* standing still).

Once the rhythm is mastered, repeat the exercise while *uke*:

- Strikes *shomen-uchi* (see page 154) with hand.
- Strikes *shomen-uchi* with a plastic bat.

Staffs or swords are also used, but a plastic baseball bat is roughly equivalent to the traditional bundle of split bamboo. It's noisy when *ikkyo* is incorrect, but causes no harm (and no splinters) and *ikkyo* improves immediately.) Do not go through just the motions; with sensitivity to *nage*'s experience and skill, actually try to hit *nage* in the head with a correct *shomen-uchi*.

Rhythm and Timing

Musician Susan Chandler[10] uses this exercise to teach the rhythm and timing of *ikkyo*. Doing the *ikkyo-undo* as above,

---

9. Some styles use the "Hips-hands, Hips hands" pattern of *funekogi-undo*.
10. For commentary, see"On Aikido and Music" on page 81.

1. Have *uke* count one/two with your movement; *one* at the top of the upward swing, and *two* when your arms rest again at your sides.

2. *Nage* focus attention at the moment of the count in the *ikkyo-undo* movement. *Uke* tests by:

   Placing a hand in front of *nage*'s arm before it swings up and attempting to stop its movement.

   Placing a hand under *nage*'s arm after it has reached the top of the swing and attempting to stop the arm from moving downward.

3. *Nage* repeat the exercise, this time focusing in between the counts on the movement of arms in time, not just on their point of arrival. *Uke* test as above.

Ikkyo and Attitude

Like so many things, *ikkyo* responds to internal attitude. When doing *ikkyo* in response to a strike, there is an initial tendency towards the "Oh No!" response. Arms do not swing up, they push up. They do not reach out to greet the attack, they fend off, a far less effective approach.

Repeat the above while *nage* says or thinks the following. Which produces a more effective *ikkyo*?

- ""Oh no!" or "Oh-oh!" or
- "Stay away!" or
- "No no no!" versus "Yes yes yes!" or
- "Hi there!" or
- "Thank you!

The above shows the effect of internal orientation. It can also be changed with external tools such as a bat.

Reaching out to catch a ball also produces proper configuration of hands and arms.

Spinning Ikkyo Undo

This motion appears in many throws.

1. Do *ikkyo* exercise as above but on raising arms,

2. Spin 180 degrees.

3. Drop arms.

   Practice on a mat seam or between two markers to ensure complete 180 degree turns.

Zengo-Undo

ADS: Basic Exercise #7 ("Forward-Backwards Exercise"), p. 126.

Zengo-undo involves a series of turns, reversing direction[11]. When applied to Aikido techniques, it models a response to attacks from two or more attackers coming from opposite directions. Internally, it models the demands of two different jobs or chores that threaten to divide time and attention.

Turn completely, directing *ki*, mind, and attention, strongly forward while remaining balanced and centered. Pattern as in *ikkyo* is:

Hips-hands-Hands-hips

As in *ikkyo-undo* it is as if the thumbs are the switch that "give the hips permission" to shift. In left *hanmi*, hands lightly closed and arms hanging naturally at sides,

1. At count of "One," shift hips forward, then swing arms up, opening hands and extending fingers.

2. At count of "Two," drop arms back down to sides, closing hands softly; shift hips back. On balls of feet, pivot 180 degrees as weight shifts toward back foot.

3. At count of "Three," repeat Step 1, shifting hips forward, then swing arms up, opening hands and extending fingers.

4. At count of "Four," repeat Step 2, swinging arms back down to sides, closing hands into soft fists; shift hips back. On balls of feet, pivot 180 degrees.

Variations

Uke count aloud, calling "Stop!" at any point. Test by:

- Pushing straight back on chest.
- Pushing straight forward at upper or lower back.
- Checking for Unbendable Arm.
- Attempting to lift *nage* from ankle.

---

11. See *Shall We Dance* on page 264 for how a dance instructor might teach it.

Happo-Undo

ADS: Basic Exercise #9 ("Eight-Directions Exercise"), pp. 127-130; ZC: pp. 234-235.

Happo-undo is *ikkyo-undo* (page 101) or *zengo-undo* (page 103) done with a series of turns to model multiple attacks from "eight" different directions.

On the compass:	Or in a room:
1. North-South,	**1.** Front-back,
2. East-West,	**2.** L side-R side,
3. Southwest-Northeast,	**3.** Corner, corner,
4. Northwest-Southeast.	**4.** Corner, corner.

Footwork: L-R L-R L-R L-R or R-L-R-L-R-L-R-L

As in *zengo-undo*, the point is to turn completely, to direct *ki*, mind, and attention strongly forward while remaining balanced and centered. The temptation is to leave your mind behind, to split your attention, to be overcome by second thoughts, regrets, the accumulated weaknesses of small failures. Continuing through a series of turns, *nage* may become increasingly unstable and fall backwards in response to a soft test to the chest, having left mind and balance behind. Begin with *four* directions, continuing to eight only after getting comfortable with the first four.

In left *hanmi* (left foot or LF forward)

1. Step forward with LF.[12]
   Swing arms up into *ikkyo* then down.
2. Turn R 180 degrees stepping into R *hanmi* (RF forward).
   Swing arms up into *ikkyo* then down.
3. Turn left 90 degrees stepping into L *hanmi* (LF forward).
   Swing arms up into *ikkyo* then down.
4. Turn R 180 degrees stepping into R *hanmi* (RF forward).
   Swing arms up into *ikkyo* then down.
5. Turn left 45 degrees stepping into L *hanmi* (LF forward).
   Swing arms up into *ikkyo* then down.
6. Turn R 180 degrees stepping into R *hanmi* (RF forward).
   Swing arms up into *ikkyo* then down.
7. Turn left 90 degrees stepping into L *hanmi* (LF forward).
   Swing arms up into *ikkyo* then down.
8. Turn R 180 degrees stepping into R *hanmi* (RF forward).
   Swing arms up into *ikkyo*; hold position. *Uke* test.

---

12. LF = Left Foot. RF = Right Foot.

Variations

Step through the exercise as follows:

* Feet only, to establish direction and rhythm. When comfortable with these,
* Add the hands. When feet and arms are working together,
* Start on the R foot (rather than the left).
* Start in odd directions or with eyes closed to eliminate dependence on a particular wall or direction.
* Place a mark on the mat before beginning. Finish at that same spot.

Shikko

ADS: pp. 324-325; TOT: pp. 46-47.

Am I the only one who thinks a matfull of students in hakama doing shikko looks like a bunch of drunken penguins trying to learn ballroom dancing?

— *K.S.*

Shikko or "knee-walking" is a means of moving and maneuvering from a kneeling position. Aikido techniques done from a kneeling position are known as *suwari-waza* and require a more vivid awareness of balance, position, and energy than the same techniques done standing.[13]

Shikko is confusing to beginners because it appears to be (and is referred to as) "walking on the knees."It is not done by sliding forward on the knees (like a hands-free crawl on knee-skiies) but by pivoting from side-to-side on alternating knees as a triangle. In the diagram below, the heavy line represents the front body side of the triangle formed by two knees and feet behind.

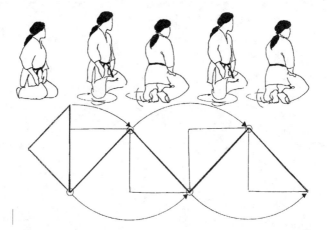

The side-to-side motion is very similar to that used in moving a chair by rotating it around its points (page 107). In *shikko*, knees make two points of the triangle base, toes the third. Stay up on toes ("live toes") with heels together at all times. From *seiza*,

1. Rise to L knee and bring RF forward.
2. Swing heel of LF to meet heel of RF.

---

13. Former students of Ueshiba Sensei (*O-Sensei*) have remarked that he scolded them for doing the techniques standing; techniques done kneeling (*suwari-waza*) are more difficult. Similarly, Yoshinkan Aikido with its emphasis on precise angles specifies 95 degrees for a *tenkan* turn because that is considered to be the minimum angle required to break balance. Training in what is more difficult will make easier approaches even easier.

3. Drop R knee to the floor.
4. Pivot on R knee, bringing LF forward.
5. Swing heel of RF to meet heel of LF.
6. Drop L knee to floor.
7. Swing heel of LF to meet heel of RF..

Variations

See the difference "live toes" makes in balance and maneuverability. The two positions differ greatly in weight shift and balance.

1. *Nage* assume a half-kneeling position with top of foot on mat.
2. *Uke* test by pressing directly forward at small of *uke*'s back.
3. *Nage* assume the same position but up on toes.
4. *Uke* test as above. Compare results.

• Walk a chair across the room. How do you move it forward, backward, in a circle?

• Many people compare the joined heels to being "tied together by a bungee cord." Get a bungee cord and give it a try.

• Do all throws on any test from *suwari-waza*.

Keep weight on shins and toes as much as possible, rather than knees. Avoid leaning forward to save ramming your knees into the floor. While knee-walking is a critical skill for *suwari-waza* techniques, the hard fact remains that knee-caps were never designed to bear body weight[14].

• Low shelves at the bookstore? Try knee-walking down the aisles.

• *Shiatzu* practitioners work on floors, not on tables. Hands remain on the client at all times, in one continuous motion from start to finish, to prevent the stress of anticipation or uncertainty for the patient. The means of moving about? *Shikkyo*. Experiment with maneuvering around and over a prone partner.

---

14. Aside from the large numbers of elder Aikidoists with bad knees, consider the findings of anthropologist Susan Sheridan who studied the bones of some 6,000 monks from the Byzantine monastery of St. Stephen c. 500 A.D. "The healthiest population I've ever studied," says Sheridan, "except in one respect — almost all the monks seem to have had arthritic knees." The monks did a great deal of kneeling and knee-walking to the point that kneecaps were rubbed smooth by impact with their thighbones. One monk wrote of descending 18 steps into a holy cave, with 100 genuflections on each step — a practice he did nightly across hard stone pavement. You, however, can wear pads and give more regard to the body. It's your only one.

Wrist Exercises

The following exercises limber and strengthen the wrists while they also pattern movements that will later be used in wristlocks. Exercises begin on the left wrist. A Common pattern is 2 sets of 5.

These are wrist exercises, not shoulder exercises. Movement starts from the tips of the fingers, not the tip of the shoulder.Because students commonly raise the shoulders first, then crank the wrist from there you will often hear instructions to:

> *"Relax the shoulders! Drop them 5 inches."*

And students are shocked.

> *"Whaddya mean 'relax the shoulders'?*
> *They ARE relaxed!"*

Sometimes it is impossible to tell the difference without outside help. *Ki* testing with a partner who serves as a bio-feedback sensor, quickly reveals the existence of tightness and tension by its side-effects. For example, see how easy it is to push over a *nage* with tense shoulders, weight upperside, and leaning back. Working in pairs, *uke* will:

- Push *nage* from side, directly into shoulder.
- Push *nage* directly from front or back.
- Lift elbow.

Nage may also practice with a mirror:

- Without raising shoulders,
- While consciously dropping them, or
- In combination with raising and tensing shoulders, arms and hands — then dropping them all together.

It is also useful to demonstrate how shoulders should feel by having the student place hands on the instructor's shoulders while to feel muscle tension or lack of it while doing an exercise or a technique.

I use the "relax your shoulders" line quite frequently since students seem to like to put strength in their shoulders when practicing technique. Sometimes I put my hand on their shoulder when they perform and they can detect that they are becoming tense. Sometimes I have them put their hands on my shoulders and perform a technique with tense shoulders and then again with relaxed shoulders. They usually get the idea and stop using tension. Most of them had no idea that they were tense. Talk is cheap. A demonstration with feeling is much better.

— *George Simcox, Ki Society*

Ikkyo-Undo

ADS: Basic Exercise # 1, Ikkyo/Ikkajo ("First-teaching exercise"), p. 121; ZC: pp. 226-230.

This exercise models the "first" Aikido technique which involves a bending of the wrist and rotation of wrist and arm forward of the body as a wristlock and throw. For actual *ikkyo* wristlock, see page 185; for technique, see page 207.

As wrist exercise,

1. Bring hands together with right palm covering knuckles and fingers of the left.
2. Raise left wrist to chest height, RH curling knuckles of the LH.
3. Drop hand and repeat.

Nikyo-Undo

This exercise models a wristlock involving painful rotation and pressure on the bones of wrist and arm. It is not done in the Ki Society which uses *Ikkyo-Undo* above, in its place, but is common in other styles, provides a stretch that *ikkyo-undo* alone does not, and illustrates the mechanics behind the *nikyo* wristlock.

As wrist exercise,

1. Grasp back of LH with palm of RH. Thumb of RH is wrapped around the knife edge of the LH.

2. Rotate fingers towards chest while dropping the elbow.

Nikyo as wristlock is described starting on page 188.

Sankyo-Undo

This exercise models the "third" Aikido technique which involves a painful inward rotation of wrist and arm as a wristlock and throw. As wrist exercise,

1. Place thumb of RH on back of LH in line with index finger.
2. Wrap other fingers around the knife edge of right hand.
3. Extend arms until they form a circle, stretching the held hand.

As *ki* exercise, extend arms into a circle. *Uke* tests by:

- Pressing into *nage*'s hands (towards chest).
- Pushing into hands and attempting to lift *nage*'s arms.
- Pushing into *nage*'s elbow toward center of circle or upward.

Nage experiment with the results of:

- Extending arms out from body.
- Pulling arms close into chest.
- Rotating wrist. (Rotation is along axis of arm so that thumb is down, then away from *nage*, then up.)

In the diagram above, arms are extended out. To see how *sankyo* would look when applied by *nage*, rotate your left forearm to vertical and press with thumb.

There is a distinct tendency for students to lean backward from the waist while doing this exercise. Watch for that and concentrate on maintaining correct upright posture.

For *sankyo* technique, see page 190.

Kote-Gaeishi

ADS: Basic Exercise #2 ("Wrist-Bend"), p. 122.

This models a throwing technique based on bending of the wrist. As exercise,

1. Grasp back of LH with palm of RH. Thumb of grasping hand is placed just below ring finger and other four fingers are wrapped around the "thigh of the thumb."

2. Bend wrist to 90-degrees and bring towards chest.

3. Drop the hand vertically down the center of the chest. For additional stretch, twist hand slightly outwards.

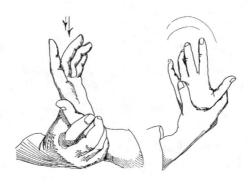

For technique, see page 196; for throw from *kote-gaeshi*, see "Mune-Tsuki Kote-Gaeshi Tenkan" on page 210.

Leg Exercises

In all exercises below, move from Center/One-Point, not from shoulders. Do not bounce and do not overstretch. Overstretching activates the body's stretch inhibitors designed to protect the muscles from damage and which may actually leave your muscles shorter and tighter than they were to start with. Proper stretching will actually increase muscular strength, and prevent physical problems such as knee and back pain related to shortened muscles.

Many of these can be done with a partner. This approach offers the fun of working with a partner, but requires even more care. In many military-style schools, a student will stand on another student's back or knees, then wonder why the partner doesn't return. Be sensitive to your partner's capabilities. Be as careful and sensitive as if working with a child.

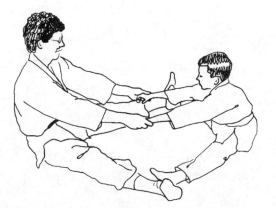

Limbering Knees and Legs

- Standing with feet together, hands on knees, rotate knees in a circle to limber and stretch. Combine with hamstring stretches and squats.

- With legs extended and toes up, bend forward from Center/One-Point (not shoulders). *Relax* into the stretch. If you cannot, you are stretching too far.
- With toes up and legs spread apart, bend forward from Center over left leg then over right leg.

Sitting Cross-Legged and Bouncing Knees

With soles of feet together and drawn into hips, bounce knees gently several times then lean forward from Center/One-Point to stretch the hip rotators. Continuing from bouncing knees above, bend forward to stretch the hip rotators.

Bending Back in Seiza

This exercise stretches the abdominal, thigh, and groin muscles. It can be hard on a bad back due to the interplay between the lumbar vertebrae and psoas muscles. For persons with lower back or knee problems, the above exercise may be done more safely by separating it into its component parts. Stretch thighs "by hand" but notice that you must stretch the muscle across both joints, hip and knee.

Supplemental Stretches

These stretches may not be traditional, but can help performance and comfort on and off the mat.

Back Stretches

A good upper back stretch. While holding onto a pillar, a post, or a doorknob,
1. Round back,
2. Drop head, and
3. Lean back pressing gently with feet.

To stretch upper back on your own,

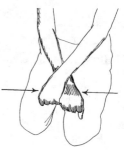

1. Extend arms to front crossing wrists at little-finger sides.
2. Make fists and press them against each other.
3. Drop shoulders.
4. Drop head or have a partner press gently on your head as you turn it side to side.

   This stretches the trapezius, the rhomboids, and other back muscles that can tighten with practice. In emergency, you can provide the head push yourself by ducking under a desk and pushing up gently.
   Hard to explain to co-workers, but a valuable stretch.

Chest and Stomach Stretches

Chest (pectoral) muscles can tighten in the course of Aikido classes, especially swordwork combined with computer work, producing chest or referred arm pain or numbness.

Chest muscles can be stretched with the help of a *jo* (staff) held behind the back. Dropping the *jo* vertically from one hand and pulling down with the other provides an excellent stretch to the triceps.

A doorway aids in stretching the chest. Stand with arms on either side of the doorway and lean through it. Changing arm position from higher to lower allows you to stretch different muscle fibers.

Tight or weakened abdominal muscles are a classic cause of chronic back pain.

1. Lying on stomach, raise straight up on arms tilting head back.
2. Turn from side to side looking over shoulders to stretch the oblique abdominal muscles.

Paired Chest and Hip Stretch

This exercise gives you a stretch through the arms, chest, stomach and hip plus all
the fun of doing it with a partner. Standing back to back, hip to hip, arms hooked,

1. First partner bends forward balancing partner 2 on hips and back.
2. Second partner bends forward balancing Partner 1 on hips and back.

Use this exercise to experiment (carefully!) with slight shifts in weight and
balance. Notice that your partner's weight seems almost negligible as long as it is
over hips and legs. Vary by combining with *ushiro-tekubi-tori-undo* on page 99.

Calf Stretch

A torn Achilles tendon is really the last gasp of a tight, inflexible calf muscles
(gastrocnemius/soleus). Runners who ignore stretching, or women who wear
extreme high heels, may have calf muscles shortened to the point that they feel
uncomfortable in bare feet or flats. Stretch by standing on the edge of a step or by
leaning against the wall.

CHAPTER 5

Rolling, Falling and Flying

Ukemi is the most practical, real-world self-defense that we teach. Few of us get into fights regularly, but all of us (in Kansas!) have to deal with ice, or stairs or curbs — we will fall and falling is dangerous. People die every day from falling down. Good idea to learn how to do it with some safety, eh?

— *Stan Haehl, Kansas Ki Society*

Did you start Aikido for self-defense? Do you see rolling practice as a waste of practice time or at best a "warm-up"? The most immediate, practical and guaranteed applicable self-defense technique is rolling and falling safely. This skill is critical to Aikido and to life, yet in many dojos and most martial arts, it receives little more than a passing nod.

Falling is basic to judo, but rarely taught in karate. When a co-worker with a son on the sport karate circuit showed me his competition videos, I could not understand why opponents did not trap the leg on the long slow kicks. It is forbidden *"because of the danger of falling."* For persons studying for safety "On The Street" I hope their opponents are so obliging! But in Real Life™ falls are a far greater daily danger than street attacks. Consider the statistics on accidental deaths.

Deaths Due To:	No. of Deaths[a]
Motor vehicles	43,300
Falls	14,100
Poisoning (solids, liquids)	9,800
Drowning	3,900
Fires & Burns	3,200
Firearms	1,400
Poison gases	600

   a. National Safety Council, *Accident Facts*, 1996 data.

Hence for accidental deaths, and despite the headlines, more people in the U.S. die each year from falls than from the far more popular media causes of drowning, carbon monoxide poisoning, fire, and firearms combined.

We have driver education classes, seat belts, child car seats, swimming and water safety lessons. We have smoke detectors, gun safety classes and carbon monoxide alarms. But who is taught to fall and roll safely?

Aikido teaches balance under extreme conditions and how to fall should you become off balance. Defense against finding oneself hurtling toward hard, unforgiving pavement is real self-defense useful on a regular basis.

The art of falling safely is *ukemi*. In performances of carefully rehearsed "movie-do" (by actors such as Chuck Norris, Steven Seagal or others) be aware that the rolls and falls by stuntmen protecting themselves from real harm, are the most real part of the performance. Similarly, there is little actual wrestling in the entertainment art known as "professional wrestling." The apparent opponents (and referee) work together as a team. Like Hollywood, the pro-wrestling circuit is total illusion. But the risk of injury is very real, and so the *ukemi* is very real.

In real life, the most common injuries "on the street" are from trying to break a fall and breaking a wrist instead. Most happen at home (one of the most dangerous places to be) on slippery floors, bathtubs, ladders or stairs, or any and all possible combinations of factors. One of our beginning students was thrown by a Sunday newspaper.

I answered the door in socks and our friend handed me the newspaper as she came in. The Sunday issue weighs several pounds and as I turned, the paper in its plastic sack hanging off one hand took me slightly off balance, my socks slipped on the tile, and I fell backwards down the stairs to the den. The den is concrete slab with carpet over it, but the automatic back roll (the only form of ukemi I'm reasonably good at) made it a non-event even though I was recovering from a detached retina and falls are on the Major No-No list. I sustained no injury, not even bruise or soreness, and don't remember any sudden impact, just a soft landing and half a roll. I'm a "Noh Kyu" and have only been practicing a few months, but the back roll ukemi has already come in handy — and was completely automatic.

— Michael Bartman, Ki Society

Ability to fall safely is one of the most valuable self-defense techniques there is. But how and why does it work? Dr. Wendy Gunther explains.

The Physics of Ukemi

— by Dr. Wendy Gunther

"Falling down" is equivalent to being hit, slugged, punched, or shot at by the ground moving at the acceleration of gravity. Whether you are hit by ground or by bullet, the wounding energy is proportional to:

mass (m) multiplied by velocity (v) squared
divided by the time (*t*) it takes for the wounding surface to contact you,
and also divided by the area (*a*) of the wounding surface.

In symbols, this is expressed as:

$$\text{Wounding energy} = mv^2 / ta \qquad \textbf{(EQ 12)}$$

Hence wounding energy decreases if we can increase time and area.

Increasing Time. If I take a bullet and touch it slowly to your skin, you aren't wounded because the marked reduction in velocity means a marked increase in *t*. During falls, you slow down the contact by rolling into it or slapping the mat with your arm like a spring. Even fractions of seconds of increase in *t* significantly reduce wounding energy.

Increasing Area. Suppose I take the same bullet and hammer it into a huge flat sheet of lead and fire it at you (in a vacuum where there's no air friction) with the same velocity (*v*) as a bullet leaving the muzzle of a gun.

The bullet will wrap itself as a flattened surface over your skin (with an area of say 720 square inches). You are extremely unlikely to be wounded simply because of the increase in area (*a*). Wounding energy is extremely low[1].

In contrast, if the area through which the kinetic energy is being transferred is reduced to the size of your chin, say 2 square inches, wounding energy is high.

To recap, the larger the mass[2] and the higher the velocity of the oncoming object, the more dangerous the situation.

The larger the area and time of contact, the safer the situation.

We usually can't change our mass or velocity, but we can increase time and the surface area of contact with the oncoming mass, mat, sidewalk, or planet.

The means of doing so are the skills of *ukemi*.

---

1. Pads and helmets work to reduce the wounding energy in the same way, by spreading the force over a larger area and by increasing time required for the force to reach you. Baseballs, punches, and planets all move much more slowly through plastic foam than through air. On *ukemi*, see ADS: pp. 139-142; TOT: pp. 48-49.

2. Because of greater mass, Big Guys, whom everyone likes to throw, are more at risk of damage on the mat than are smaller persons. Whomever you play with, play nice.

On Learning to Roll — A Course of Action

My wife is often the only woman in class and feels a bit humiliated when she can't roll in front of all the guys. Backward rolls are fine, at least pretty good. But on forward rolls, she hurts herself more when she falls on her shoulders and neck rather then going over. For me, it's frustrating because I don't know how to help her. And for her, she's getting more and more afraid.

— L. J.

Although rolling is one of the most important skills in Aikido, informal surveys of students and instructors strongly suggests that a big reason for student dropout is problems with rolling. Many students are lost due to fear of rolling and being pushed too hard too soon. Many fall by the wayside due to unnecessary pain or actual injuries from rolls. Consider then,

- How can teaching of rolling skills be made safer and more effective?
- How can we protect students until they are able to protect themselves?
- How can a student most effectively practice and develop rolling skills?

Standard procedure at many dojos is to demonstrate a beautiful roll with some basic instruction on placement of head, hands, and feet. "Here is a forward roll, a backward roll, a breakfall. Please practice." How well this works is reflected by the dropout rate due to injured shoulders and aching heads plus other considerations.

For example, in the story above, a new student starts with stage fright causing general stiffness. Meanwhile, there's no time to concentrate on the backrolls that she can do just fine or at least pretty well, because she needs to be doing something else that hurts more with every roll so that every subsequent roll whether done wrong or done right, becomes more and more painful. Talk about negative reinforcement!

Personally I favor starting adult students with rocking-chair back rolls (*koho-tento-undo*), followed by full back rolls, and only work up to forward rolls after backrolls are mastered and comfortable. If a beginner has never done rolls before, it is often counterproductive to start them off with forward rolls. There's no lack of other things to work on, too little reason to push this particular skill plus too much danger of injury and bad experience without careful and caring supervision.

Instructors often try to encourage a frustrated student by revealing that they themselves took more than a year or two to learn to roll well. This may be helpful or it may not.

- For students who are merely frustrated and who need to understand that any new skill takes time, it can be a useful reminder.
- For students who are frustrated — and hurt and injured — what you have just done is to promise them a year or two of continuing pain, headaches, bruised or separated shoulders, failure and embarassment. And the more embarassed or apprehensive the student becomes, the more tense.
- For students who are apprehensive and tense, the more injuries and pain, and panic, and the once enthusiastic new student is now lost to Aikido.

There is no need to hold back students who are familiar with rolls, pick them up quickly, or are always up for new and bigger challenges. Less confident or less experienced students should not be expected to progress at the same rate or made to feel inferior if they don't. Worst case, certain classes, groups, or techniques can be limited to a certain proficiency in *ukemi*. Meanwhile, it should be OK to stay with something that feels safe and accomplishable for awhile. If that something is back rolls, then back rolls it is. Diving back flip breakfalls can wait for another day.

This is not boot camp and it is not a contest.

Ukemi skills should be taught carefully and methodically, not just "absorbed" through random experience. For those unfamiliar or uncomfortable with rolls, consider the following progression.

1. Rocking-Chair Rolls

This simple rocking backwards and forwards roll (*koho-tento-undo,* page 125) teaches rounding and relaxation through movements that are already familiar to everyone. It allows the beginner to join in practice or someone with injured shoulder to continue practicing. *Koho-tento-undo* offers plenty of interesting dynamics for exploration. Once simple rocking-chair rolls are mastered, and the feelings and sensations associated with them are comfortable and familiar, move on to . . .

2. Full Back Rolls

Full back rolls (page 127) require attention to head position to avoid straining the neck, but they completely avoid the problem of crashing forward onto head, neck, or shoulder joint.

In Ki Society, students may often segue into full back rolls because of *taigi*[3]. Allowing the physics and inertia of *koho-tento-undo* to return *uke* to attack position may take too long to meet the time requirements. The solution is continuing over backwards into a true back roll. *Taigi* also helps because the focus is on needing to get back and attack *nage* again rather than on the rolling itself. But sooner or later you have to work on forward rolls. When you do, start them slow and gentle.

3. Small Forward Rolls with a Partner

Small forward rolls (page 131) can be presented as an exercise at first; not as actual *ukemi*, that is, as *uke* the student can "walk out" until rolls are usable; partners should allow them to do so.) Practice with partner ensures proper position and opportunity to work on patterning, to develop body memory and awareness of what a successful roll should feel like and how the body should behave.

4. Individual Small Rolls

When student is familiar with position and purpose, rolls can be done by the student alone. Combine with rolling exercises and games.

5. Standing Rolls

Front and back. By now the student should feel comfortable enough with the process to realize that the mechanics are the same, regardless of starting height.

---

3. *Taigi* are the paired *kata* developed by Koichi Tohei and practiced by the Ki Society to emphasize rhythm and flow.

6. Breakfalls

Breakfalls are rarely the first thing taught. However, forward and backward rolls need not be perfect before starting breakfalls. Furthermore, the extension required for beginning breakfalls (roll-outs) may clarify the problem that a student may be having with proper position for other rolls. For example, it is impossible to do a proper rollout with slap if the student is "pancaking."

Rolling Exercises and Games

Almost always, the best beginning exercises are those that provide some sort of distraction. A valuable tool for learning to roll is reframing the fear of falling into the love of flying via a shift in attention. The fear and tension come from the imminent but future fear of crashing into the mat. By shifting attention and concentration away from that terror and into an actual present-tense concern, we lose the fear and get on with the business at hand.

- In the Six-count rolling Exercise (page 131), it's the next roll in the series.

  The exercise provides practice in forward and backward rolls while shifting to the overall process and away from the individual pieces. The student is often astonished when all the pieces go together just fine.

- In Rolling Tag and Maximum/Minimum it's the contest.

- In 50 Rolls it's sheer exhaustion versus critical conservation of energy.

Equipment

Consider also your equipment. Obviously students will not be comfortable starting forward rolls on concrete. Nor should they.

I once taught a class where the only available space was thin industrial carpet over concrete, no pads, no mats available. Students were nearly all retirement age, except for one young overweight man (often the person most at risk on the mat) and one very athletic young man. I taught him rolls on the side, but purposely restricted class practice to back rolls, emphatically forbidding front rolls unless students came to the dojo and its mat for safe practice and individual attention.

One day when I was absent, my assistant seized the opportunity to correct what he saw as a blatant omission of a critical skill: Front rolls. On concrete.

I returned to find the entire class damaged and unable to continue, with shoulder injuries, neck injuries, bruises, broken veins and hematomas.

I have never yet gotten calm about that incident. On the other hand, teaching or learning to roll, like any other potentially risky endeavor, is for the student, a delicate balance between challenging what you don't know you're capable of versus knowing what you're not capable of quite yet no way no how. For example, many a "friend" has taken a novice out skiing and started them off at the top of the expert slope. "It's OK! It's easy!" Perhaps for him, but it is wildly inappropriate for the beginner. Both teacher and student must be aware of that.

—C. S. B.

We are accustomed to turning over control to a teacher, but part of self-defense is knowing just how far transfer of personal responsibility should go. A long-time skier may be completely unable to remember not knowing how to ski. A young man in superb physical condition may be completely unaware of the potential fragility of some 65-year old bodies.

Use proper equipment, but remember that part of that equipment is good sense and personal responsibility.

The flip side of beginning rolls on concrete is beginning rolls on a surface that is too soft. This interferes with the forward momentum and rhythm of standard rolls. The student is likely to sink to a halt (and pancake) right about the time that hips begin to go vertical and weight is concentrated down into the pad.

It is the flip side of trying to learn to pole-vault through molasses.

On the other hand, a very soft mat, a crash pad, eases beginning breakfalls.

Much easier, mentally anyway, to do what I was supposed to do than it is on the regular mat. I have a tendency to try to support myself on my arm, which is nowhere near strong enough (hey, I'm big, and I type for a living. I don't carry heavy things every day, and it shows!). When it inevitably collapses, I fall on my shoulder and it hurts, and makes me less interested in doing it again.

Knowing that I was landing on the equivalent of a feather bed let me do the little jump that is necessary to get you over the top before landing. A bit more practice like that and I may have the pattern of movement ingrained enough that I'll do it right on the regular mat too. I suggest dragging the crash mat out more often!

— Michael Bartman, Ki Society

Back Rolls

Back rolls are easiest to learn and least frightening to beginners. The motions are already perfectly familiar — identical to those used for lying down in bed or on a rug from a sitting position — with a little more tucking and a little more energy.

Backwards and Forwards

ADS #19, *Koho-tento-undo, "Rolling Backwards and Forwards"*

This is a simple rolling back and forth (*koho-tento-undo*) like a rocking chair. Sitting cross-legged with hands on thighs,

1. On count of One, roll backwards by rounding the lower back. Motion begins by rounding the lower back and dropping chin to chest. Focus on your belt knot.

2. On count of Two, roll forward to original position. Focus on a point across the room.

Respect the natural rhythm of the roll. Do not try to force yourself back up by flinging the legs forward or arching the back (which makes you concave or flat instead of round).

Variations:

Observe the positions or actions that cause the ball of your body to shift and move dynamically. That is,

- What motions will roll you backward most effectively?
- What motions will absorb excess energy?
- What motions will return you to your original upright position with the least effort from you? Try rolling backward while:
  a) Extending legs up rather than overhead.
  b) Keeping legs extended.
  c) Keeping legs tucked.
  d) Tracing an arc in the air with your toe.

For smoother rolling, imagine a:

- Goldfish bowl in your pelvis filled with water or liquid, white light. Roll and stand in such a way that you do not splash the water or disturb the fish.
- Rubber Band stretching from your Center/One-Point to the opposite wall that allows you to roll back but helps you to come forward again.

Backwards and Forwards to a Kneel

Roll back as in previous exercise, but on coming forward,

1. Tuck one leg as close to the pelvis as possible.
2. Bring other leg forward, bent at an angle of up to (but not greater than) ninety degrees. By pushing off with the tucked back leg (not with hands),
3. Rise into a kneeling position with back leg at an oblique angle to the body. (You can't roll with back leg perpendicular to the body).

   From here, it's easy to drop back to another backward roll or to rise and stand. Notice that you do not fling yourself backward. Drop Center/One-Point first, while curling into a ball. The motion is exactly like sitting down in a chair. You do not fling yourself backward into the chair, you lower your hips, *then* shift back.

What happens:

- If the near leg is not tucked?
- If the angle of the forward leg is greater than 90 degrees?
- If you concentrate on something behind you while you are rolling, especially while coming up? Compare with extending your attention forward.
  From here we will progress into full back rolls. To prepare,

1. Roll back,
2. Touch toe to mat,
3. Experiment with the most comfortable position of head and neck.

   It will not be directly down the back of your head or over the nape of your neck.

Small Full Back Rolls

A complete back roll continues the motion of the backward-forward roll but coming down from a kneeling position provides additional momentum.

To do a complete back roll,

1. Start from the kneeling position, left foot forward and left knee up, right knee and leg on the mat at an oblique angle to the body.
2. Look at your left knee. You will be "throwing" this left knee over your left shoulder.
3. Now look right, rock back and sit down beyond the mat leg while throwing your left leg over your left shoulder. Look at your right armpit. As hips go overhead, continue the motion by pushing off with left arm.
4. As you complete the roll, bring your left leg forward to the original starting position.

Variation

- Repeat small back rolls in series, two in a row, three in a row . . .
- Continue into non-stop back rolls around the mat.
- Alternate right and left sides to avoid the habit of rolling on just one side.
- Combine with *koho-tento-undo*, rising to one knee.

Back and Stand

This roll is similar to the previous back roll but ends standing. Rolling as above,

1. Tuck right leg as close to the pelvis as possible.
2. Roll back and up with leg still tucked and rise. Note that:
   The top of the right foot never touches the mat.
   Knees never touch the ground (i.e., get on your feet immediately by "kicking" the forward foot towards the ceiling.
   "Forward foot" refers to the forward foot of your starting *hanmi* position. If right *hanmi*, that will be the right foot; if left *hanmi*, it will be the left.
   Arms are used only at the end of roll to push yourself to the upright position.

Standing one-legged from this roll is an excellent exercise in coordination and balance. it is also a useful practice for new *hakama* wearers who tend to get tangled; the raised leg helps to clear the skirt while building hip and thigh strength and avoiding the dreaded "hakama toe."

Forward Rolls

The Aikido roll (unlike the tumbling roll taught in schools) does not go straight down the back, but slightly sideways down the arm, across the back to the hip. Head is tucked *away* from the rolling arm. This roll protects the nape of the neck and the spine so well that, properly done, it makes no difference whether you are rolling on a mat or on concrete as long as you are round.

Unfortunately, few new students start out round. Demonstrate a roll and they see and copy the hand on the mat, the forward motion, the head going down towards the mat and then "pancake"— fall sideways collapsing into puddle of mat-hugging confusion.

Pancaking happens when the hips fail to roll over the head and torso. Body falls or rolls to the side, rather than rolling over the head and down the line of the arm. This may be due to inadequate arm strength or simply the startling sensation of finding oneself upside down and apparently about ready to fall directly down, crashing headfirst into the mat. Panic!

It isn't necessarily significant that someone can keep Unbendable Arm when tested while standing and concentrating on the far wall. Unbendable Arm is just learning to *relax*. The real problem is learning to *apply*. We all spend years disassociating the exercise from its application. "Advanced Students" are merely those who've learned to "Do the Exercise!" and put it back together again. So, while most people can do Unbendable Arm a few minutes after walking into the dojo, they lose it completely in their first forward rolls.

There is almost always a tendency to fall down on the shoulder at first, yet I've never known anyone to suggest shoulder pads to beginners to get them safely through this stage. Why not? Motorcycle jackets and ski jackets designed for high-speed racing have padded shoulders to protect shoulders and elbows from impact while allowing freedom of movement.

Rather than emphasizing "Unbendable Arm," consider emphasizing "making the arms a circle." By definition, this means "unbendable" and means "round." It also means "arms" (not "one arm" or "no arms" as the advanced students may be doing). The student should actually grasp the right and left hands.

Instructor should be very clear on exactly where the head is supposed to be, what the student should be looking at (belt, back leg, anything but the mat). Students should review this "pre-flight checklist" before every roll until it is automatic.

Small forward rolls are a better starting point than diving breakfalls but even small rolls can involve crashing down on head or shoulder as gravity gives no quarter. The whole point of the forward roll is to translate vertical momentum (falling) into horizontal movement (rolling). In other words, don't fall or dive into the mat. Instead, imagine rolling forward along the surface of the mat.

To help with these feelings students are often told to "imagine rolling over a big beach ball." So try using a real ball.

Beachball Rolls

Aikidoist Scott Crawford (Yoshinkan) reports that the PhysioBall (about 3 feet/ ~1 meter in diameter) is a wonderful tool for teaching forward rolls to kids[4]. With partner as spotter,

1. Child lies over the ball with forward rolling arm out in front as normal. Head is turned away from the rolling hand and tucked as much as possible around the ball and away from the rolling arm.
2. Hold child from side by legs, supporting back of neck and head.
3. Slowly roll the ball forward by pushing the child's legs forward until child has rolled over. Be careful not to dump the kid onto his/her back.

The shape of the ball helps people feel what it's like to "be round" when you go over. Also, since they're basically just laying down, it may help them relax as well while helping to build body memory.

Horse Rolls

If you don't have a big enough ball or are working with full-grown adults, the following exercise helps ease the student into the position, the process and the unfamiliar sensation of being upside down in a slow and carefully controlled way. In groups of three,

1. One *uke* ("the horse") gets on hands and knees.
2. *Nage* (the rolling student) lays across the first partner's back with the intent of sliding forward and off. This provides height control and speed control.

---

4. Certainly this is applicable to adults as well. However, it is much easier to handle a 30- or 40 pound child than an adult at 3 to 10 times that weight.

3. Second *uke* checks to see that nage's arms are in a circle, that head, shoulder, and back are correctly positioned.

4. *Uke* then pulls *nage* forward by the belt towards the mat and into a roll.

Nage will,

1. Slide forward over "horse" placing hand of right Unbendable Arm on mat. (Or join hands forming arms into a large circle).

2. Tuck and turn neck and head away from the rolling arm (to the left).

3. Curving back, neck and arm into a large circle, push off with toes, move hips forward rolling along right hand and arm and across back.

4. End in a kneel or standing (*hanmi*).

One student tried this roll at her dojo but was notably unenthusiastic when I asked her how it went. "I hurt my neck again," she sighed. How? Why? Because her instructor's version was: "Take terrified student, have her dive over kneeling *uke*" — rather than moving slowly and gradually. Notice then, that the explicit purpose is slow, gentle practice in feeling roundness and correct hand, arm, and head position.

Variations:

Try the above exercise at home with a helper, rolling off a pile of sofa cushions or the edge of a low bed or couch, forward onto another cushion for safety.

Upside-Down Rolls

Much fear of rolling is the fear of being upside down. Children or very small adults may have a parent or partner who is tall enough or strong enough to simply hold them upside down by their ankles, slightly back of vertical, then lower them carefully and under complete control, to the mat.

As in Horse Rolls, the second partner checks for proper position of arms, head and neck. *Nage* curls into a roll as *uke* lowers *nage* to the mat.

Do this carefully and under control. The point is to develop confidence in the configuration of rolling and to help mind and body understand that it will not break or die merely if upside down for a few seconds. Another possibility is *jo* rolls.

Jo Rolls

Combine *jo* practice with rolling practice. Good throwing practice for nage and a wonderful aid to helping *uke* learn to roll. Here's why.

One doesn't "fall" when rolling, one provides forward, circular energy and then rolls. Many folks dive into the mat, never letting their hips raise up in the air to form the "rolling circle." Instead they dive forward onto the mat. This puts part of the circle below the surface of the mat and creates a problem.

Once I had a student who just didn't grasp the idea (as a mind thing, not a body thing) of rolling. As a last resort I had him grasp the end of a jo then I described a large, vertical circle in the air. His hand was taken upward, outward and matward. His body followed and he did one heck of a good roll. As he bounced up he said, "Is that all??"

I think he had built up in his mind that it was a very complicated, multi-muscle direction thing and he could not organize all the parts at one time. When he found that was not true he was just fine.

This can be illustrated by tying a ribbon on to the end of a jo. If the tip of the jo moves in a circle, the ribbon does too.

— George Simcox, Ki Society

Small Individual Forward Rolls

But what happened to the hurt and frustrated lady on page 122?

Brad, a new student and judo black belt, asked politely, "Have you tried these yet?" and does this tiny little judo roll where you put your shoulder on the ground and one leg forward and roll. There was silence. "Umm, do that again?!" she said.

She tried it, lived through it, and then Bob Sensei laughed and made her do 50 of them. She wasn't even in pain the next day!

—L. J.

With the foregoing preparation, *nage* should be ready to practice forward rolls individually perhaps with helper to spot and fine-tune positioning.

The student must note any rough spots. A hard thump at the small of the back or hip means the back is not round enough. Thinking of touching knee to nose or looking at the belt while rolling helps to maintain roundness. Are you rolling down the arm, or landing on the shoulder? Note and adjust.

What is the first thing that touches the mat? If standing with the rolling arm thumb down and the arm slightly curved I usually suggest that the first point of contact is the tip of the baby finger. Now you know that can't possibly hold your weight so either you "dive" into the mat (bad thing to do) or you keep your circle and roll along the curve of the arm to the shoulder and then the back with ALL points making contact.

If the arm buckles then you hit your elbow. If the arm is too straight then you hit the shoulder. But if the arm is held in the nice curve of the bokken or beach ball or unbendable and you lift through your abs then your head will be nowhere near any danger and you will smoothly go over. I like to use an image of "pumpkins falling off the back of a truck." Some will land hard and go splat while others will skitter along turning smoothly.

— Philip Akin, Aikido Yoshinkan Canada

The 6-Count Rolling Exercise

This exercise is a series of forward and backward rolls performed in a specific sequence to a count. Obviously it provides rolling practice, but it also offers the enormous advantage of *distraction*: a student striving to keep in sequence and in rhythm has less time and attention to spare anguishing over an individual roll. An excellent exercise for improving skill and flow.

A new student who was having trouble with individual rolls describes this exercise as "awesome!"

"No time to stop and think, especially no time to think of all the reasons why I can't do this. I'm too busy trying to remember the pattern, and keep the rhythm. And I'm rolling!"

Instructor may call the count and have the class roll in unison.

1. Rock back into Rocking-Chair "roll" (*koho-tento-undo*).
2. Rock forward rising to one knee and continuing into . . .
3. Forward roll then back into . . .
4. Back roll. On coming up . . .
5. Rock back (*koho-tento-undo*) . . . then
6. Rock forward to return to starting position.

Cross-Rolls

Cross-rolls (*zempo-kaiten waza*) are done as in normal forward rolls, but begin with left knee up and right arm on mat.

In the Ki Society, the first test requires three of these small rolls done in series while maintaining the same arm/leg relationships.

Why the difference? Tradition. Years ago Tohei noticed that beginners did cross-rolls naturally. He adapted the test to accommodate this roll. But beginners usually adapt so quickly to moving arm with leg that going back to the cross roll seems awkward. Nevertheless, one must learn to roll from either position. To eliminate confusion between right and left, start your practice with a sock on the "rolling" foot.

Standing Rolls

Standing rolls are essentially the same as small rolls — if you drop down first. In all cases, try to roll as quietly as possible[5].

Standing Backward Rolls

Standing backward rolls are done like small backward rolls from the kneeling position except: place the top of the foot on the mat, drop to the kneeling position and roll from there. Some styles, such as Yoshinkan, emphasize tucking the buttocks as close as possible to the heels. Try both.

Slow Standing Forward Rolls

Standing forward rolls are done in the same way as small forward rolls except that you must roll along a larger circle which extends out further from your beginning position. These should be done only after the student is comfortable with small rolls, correction position, and has demonstrated a good round circle. They should grow gradually, perhaps with the help of the kneeling partner in "Horse Rolls" on page 129.

Diving Rolls

These cover the greatest distance. Although it seems contrary to every instinct, you must extend out for maximum distance. This rounds the roll and prevents injury to your shoulder.

Why? Because when you extend, the shoulder disappears.

How you think of the roll also makes a difference.

You are not a falling rock, you are a landing airplane.
You are not falling into the mat, you are skimming over it, just passing through.

With these images in mind, aim for a specific point, extend and go there.

I dreaded rolling for years. With chronic migraine and neck problems, I was always trying to protect my head and neck, not yet realizing that what I was doing did not protect but only made stiff and tense, perpetuating the cycle.

One year while assistant-teaching, the county Adult Recreation Department class was mis-scheduled and replaced with children's Aikido classes. I dreaded them. They were like the "Toon Town" scene in Roger Rabbit with children too young and too many. But what can you do when a small child goes through the motions of a throw? — except let out a shriek and go diving across a mat crowded by little people who would be squashed flat if I hit them.

---

5. It's never wise to go to class hungry, but avoid heavy meals. Also consider that your rolls will be quieter still if you also avoid beans and cabbage.

Suddenly I was more concerned about extending out and over and through to that particular open spot right over there than I was about my head. And suddenly the rolls were smooth and soft and magical.

An amazing lesson. If concentrating on the roll or on me, it falls flat. If projecting out, concentrating on a larger circle, a larger goal, it works. Beautifully.

— C. M. S.

Rolling in the Air

You will often see an experienced *uke* tilt the head back then fling it forward to start a roll. The weight of the head adds energy to the roll before gravity kicks in and helps keep *uke* safe especially if *nage* did not provide enough energy on his own. *Uke* is rolling long before the first touch of the mat. (See "Weigh Your Head" on page 230). Eventually arms are not needed at all and become less for weight-bearing, more for simply feeling and sensing what is needed to keep their owners safe — sometimes in surprising ways.

An Aikidoist from New England Aikikai told me that she attended a seminar at Montreal one winter. It was bitter cold but well-attended, so in short order the room was steaming and wet like a sauna. When they opened the door for air, cold dry air met supersaturated hot air. Presto! Fog! — of the ground-hugging variety. Those who were thrown were landing blind, and those throwing would watch their partners disappear into the mist and re-emerge meters away.

— Janet Rosen, Aikikai

Rolling Games and Exercises

Games are not just for children, and they are valuable not just for fun but because the student's focus is diverted elsewhere.

Rolling Tag

Kids love this and although some instructors think it unseemly for adult dignity (or their own), adults have a great time too.

As in any other game of tag, choose someone to be "It" and chase the others, but only with rolls or knee walking (*shikkyo*).

Minimum/Maximum

1. Who can cover the length of the mat in the fewest rolls?
2. Who can fit the largest number of small rolls along the length of the mat?
   (Tip: cross-rolls are your best bet.)

50 Rolls

This is a series of 50 (or greater number) rolls done back and forth in alternating directions without pause. Key to success (or survival) is to not stand up between rolls. Instead, rise partway then turn and fall, rather like a figure 8. Use the falling momentum to bring you back up so that you can fall again. And breathe!

Variations:

Work as *uke* with two partners practicing *zempo* throws.

1. One partner throw *uke* towards second partner.
2. Stand, rise, and attack second partner.
3. Second partner throws uke back to first partner who throws him back.

   Uke rolls back and forth between the two. Compare 50 breakfalls.

Forward Rolling Nonstop

There is a tendency to separate motions and undertakings into individual parts. This exercise emphasizes continuous rolling. Do not stop between rolls to reset or regroup, just keep rolling. This exercise is the difference between:

1. Roll.
2. Stand.
3. Consider. . . *hmmm, perhaps I'll roll again now . . .*

and

1. Roooolllllllllllll2lllllllllllll3llllllllll. . . .

   Try this in conjunction with Obstacle Course (below).

Rolling in Pairs

Partners hold hands and roll in tandem, matching speed (and direction). They must, of course, roll on opposite arms.

Rolling With a Sword (Yokomen)

This exercise provides practice in overcoming dependency on placing the hands on the mat to roll. The oblique *yokomen* strike provides the downward beginning momentum which then flows into a roll.

Obstacle Course

An exercise in revealing and destroying mindset. Once students learn to roll, place an obstacle in the way. It may be:

- A *jo* held out by the instructor,
- A rag on the mat,
- A body or a series of bodies on hands and knees.

This exercise is also useful for observing the peculiar games your mind plays. It is amazing to see how often we panic at the supposed impediment even when it is even lower or closer than the student's roll requires. It is a perceived barrier, not a real one. The exercise is to roll anyway. Combine with Nonstop Rolls (see "Forward Rolling Nonstop" on page 135) in a circle around the mat.

Scatter more harmless laundry or bodies around the mat, use the in-between spaces for target practice. See if you notice any difference in the rolls and notice how to overcome that.

Parking Lot Rolls

If you are an experienced and seasoned upper belt and have forgotten how terrifying rolls (especially forward rolls) are to beginners, consider practicing your rolls (carefully!) on concrete or asphalt in jeans and sweatshirt.

This is useful as a demo to the performer and to the observer that "this stuff really works ("On The Street") and it isn't just a function of mats or magic clothes. Especially for circular rolls, once the techniques and dynamics of rolling have been mastered it doesn't really matter whether the "wheel" of your body rolls over a mat or over parking lot concrete or asphalt.

For more variations, nuances, and good solid information, Bruce Bookman's excellent videos on *ukemi* and advanced *ukemi* are highly recommended.

Breakfalls

A throw with enough energy and forward momentum to be a throw can be thought of as "help in getting back up." In contrast, a breakfall is intended to absorb and neutralize as much energy as possible. Rolling extends and continues energy enabling *uke* to land safely on his feet ready for the next attack. But sometimes rolling is simply not possible.

The point of a breakfall is to dissipate energy in such a way that the falling body is not injured. As much surface area as possible is in contact with the ground at one time. No one point hits the mat. Not the point of elbow, not the point of the heel, nor the point of a shoulder or chin. It is a full-body *splat* — full arm, full side, flatfoot — that spreads energy over a wide area rather than concentrating it all on an elbow, or knee, or a nose.

Exercises below offer a progression in height starting on the mat, to a couple feet, then several feet above the mat.

Some pointers: Do not cross legs with contact. Ankles may bump, bruise, or chip. Men especially may discover other painful results as the upper leg comes crashing down.

Rolling Side to Side

This very beginning exercise enables the new student to practice the feel of a breakfall and correct positioning of body, arms, and legs in the safest manner possible. In a slightly more advanced version ("fish-flops") hips and legs are lifted off the mat in the course of the movement. Because the body moves across the mat, this exercise can be used as a game or relay race for children or adults.

1. Lie on back with chin tucked to chest
2. Roll to the right, striking mat smartly with flat of right arm and right palm.
3. Roll to the left, striking mat smartly with flat of left arm and left palm.

Arm-Pull

A good beginning exercise for breakfalls. It allows *uke* to learn at his own pace, the "unfurling" action as you turn in the air is natural, and you pretty much land in the "correct" landing position. This exercise provides an actual fall but still allows a low-stress and relatively low energy check for body position and timing. Aim to land on more on your side than on your back. In a more dynamic fall, landing flat on your back will knock the wind out of you. With *nage* on hands and knees,

1. *Uke* reaches under nage's body to his opposite arm.
2. *Uke* pulls arm towards him, flipping *nage* into a breakfall.

Another exercise from the same beginning position is to unfurl not sideways but "over your head," sort of a mid-air front roll and land. It's a bit more advanced, but more what I think you should be doing in a front breakfall (instead of rolling out to the side).

There are many ways to practice ukemi techniques, just like you would "normal" aikido techniques like ikkyo. I only wish they were taught more often in the dojo...

— Jun Akiyama

Rollout

A "roll-out" begins with a standard forward roll, but ends in breakfall position. This introduces the feel of breakfall in motion, and helps develop good positioning.

Breakfall Over Partner

This step adds height but adds it safely. In groups of three with a crash-pad,

1. One partner with belt, is on hands and knees.
2. Student slides hand palm-up under kneeling partner's *obi* for stability.
3. Instructor or other partner applies *kote-gaeshi* flipping student onto crash pad.

Breakfall With Jo

"Gaining height" for breakfall is contrary to almost every natural instinct. But, it's good physics. It allows *uke* to get into position for a safe fall. You will see this demonstrated again and again in "professional wrestling" where nage helps uke vault off his back or thighs in order to come down safely into the supposedly devastating (but mostly just noisy) slam to the mat.

In a breakfall from a *kote-gaeshi* (a wrist technique) you are falling 3-4 feet. Practice from the few inches of height available from a roll means you've practiced only from a few inches of height. This exercise allows individual practice from *any* height, controlled by the position of the student's hands on the lower end of the *jo*.

- Use a T-shirt or *gi* to protect the mat from the edge of the jo.

- Use a crashpad to cushion any landings that will be higher than the student has been previously accustomed to taking.

Ukemi from Ikkyo

A slightly different technique is possible for *ikkyo* techniques in which you are diving forward to the mat, secured by one arm. *Ukemi* for this technique is a sort of modified forward breakfall.

In *ikkyo*, it is common to see *uke* flopping down to the mat with full weight on the kneecaps just prior to transferring weight to the wrist at the end of a nearly vertical arm. This may work on the mat but would have devastating results on street or sidewalk: a shattered kneecap, a broken wrist, and a straight arm that acts as a pivot point, pitching *uke* forward onto his face.

Instead, on falling forward,

1. Drop to knee and shin (not just kneecap) of inside leg.
2. Fully extend the outside leg. The extended leg provides a counterbalance which prevents your *full* weight from transferring to hand and forearm. As weight transfers forward,
3. Place entire forearm (not just the wrist) on the mat and extended forward. Arm is Unbendable and slides forward with body.

    Grasping the cuff of the *gi* before taking the fall prevents mat burns.

The following version is limited to persons whose bellies do not extend significantly beyond their thighs. Hence, it is unsuitable for pregnant women or for men of similar configuration. On falling forward,

1. Extend the outside arm with knife edge of hand towards mat (thumb up). Simultaneously,
2. Kick heels up and back as if trying to kick yourself in the fanny.

    This aligns the entire lower body so that impact is spread across the extended forearm, torso, and thighs. Kneecaps are tucked safely out of the way.

I like ikkyo because it offers the most control over an untrained uke, and uke doesn't have to know how to take a flying ukemi for me to get uke safely to the ground and pinned.

— Peter W. Boylan

On Ukemi

A very pernicious habit, which one is apt to contract in the fencing-room, and which in a duel may easily lead to a fatal issue is the habit of stopping after you have made a hit, instead of immediately recovering your guard and putting yourself out of distance. Never forget this important point; if you do, you may, after wounding your opponent, receive a mortal wound for which you will have only yourself to blame. . . The moment you think you have made a hit get back as smartly as you can, and be ready to go on fighting.

— Baron César de Bazancourt, Secrets of the Sword

What is Ukemi?

So many people think that ukemi is about falling down, how to fall down, about being thrown. Well, of course it is, but it is also about so much more.

It is about engagement, both physical and energy (which starts way before the physical and lasts way after).

It is about intent, about attack and continuation of the attack.

It is about looking for the opening to take back control after you have been unbalanced, about keeping up the attack while keeping yourself safe.

It is about sticking in there as long as possible to try to find a hole, so if nage makes some mistake you haven't bailed out and are no longer around.

It is about separating from the other person when it becomes futile to continue, so that you can live to come back and attack again.

It is constant awareness of all that is around you.

So many people just take falls. Yeah, it's fun, and some people may think it looks cool, but many times it's not ukemi. And often after the big jump the person either lies there or gets up but without awareness, so that the person who just threw uke could in fact step on or attack from behind. This awareness, this connection with your surroundings is what I find missing in most practice.

I took ukemi for a shihan at an embu recently. Afterwards, a guy told me "You never took your eyes off him!"

Of course not. I never take my eyes off the person I am engaged with. If I did, I would have a large opening and he could kill me. Sometimes it is necessary to take a breakfall or some "spectacular" ukemi like that. For those rare instances, we must practice such falls but when practicing, not get sucked into the "I wanna take cool looking falls" trap.

Uke and nage both attack each other's center, both must keep themselves safe, both must find a way to take the other's balance, to keep the connection. Always engaged, always connected. This is budo training.

— Lisa Tomoleoni, Aikido Shindo Dojo, Tokyo, Japan

On Individual Ukemi Practice

Ukemi practice as part of regular training is best, not only for safety but because there's far more to *ukemi* than just attacking and falling down. Everything can be practiced alone in some way, but rolls must be done with special care and good sense. Do not, for example, practice rolls on beds, especially not bunkbeds. Put the mattress on the floor.

> *If you do practice alone, be very careful. If you live alone and whack your head while practicing, you're in trouble! Jun is wise to do his "solo ukemi" in the dojo with other people around.*
>
> — Cady Goldfield

> *Yup. But some folks eye me warily at times, as though I'm just going to spontaneously flip up into the air during a conversation or something. (I usually provide a few seconds' warning.)*
>
> — Jun Akiyama (AKA Gumby AKA Tigger)

Or eliminate all the mats and pads and cushions or hard ground and roll in water. Roll into water at the beach or the edge of a pool. Notice the sensation of cool water moving up your neck, back and hips and notice the path it takes. You can't roll across the surface of course, but you can get the feeling of hips going over head.

> *I did breakfalls in the surf the other day. Got the kids a little too excited though. They didn't want us to stop. NB: Eliminate the slap.*
>
> — Tarik J. Ghbeish

> *Had fun with a friend from class this weekend. He practiced throws that would need breakfalls on land. I got to take them as flip/dive forward or back in the water. I am so at home in the water and it was cool not to think about how I was landing. Did lose the diagonal feel but it worked without at thought.*
>
> — N. B. R.

> *On opening night of Ringling Brothers, Barnum and Bailey Circus, a wonderful clown came out with a large newspaper, dragging a park bench. Throughout his attempts to merely sit down on the bench (without getting his hands, feet, or head stuck) he took some of the most wonderful ukemi I have ever seen.*
>
> *As the park bench "threw" him about, he took backward ukemi (as the bench tipped while he was sitting on its back), forward ukemi, and some major breakfalls. He simply threw himself forward, flipping, and landing on the ground (no mats, and the surface was not particularly giving). To the untrained eye, I know it looked phenomenal. To my semi-trained eye, I saw some wonderful ukemi, sometimes with the hand reaching back to "spot" the ground, occasionally with slapping, and one or two that might be described as "falling leaf ukemi." If you think we have it tough learning ukemi, try doing it in size 40 clown shoes!*
>
> — Scott Crawford, Yoshinkan

The story of me and aikido is basically. "Hey... this aikido stuff looks fun. Hey, you get to throw people... and not only do they not get hurt, they're not even angry? And you don't get hurt either! Sign me up!"

— *Paul Gowder, Ki Society*

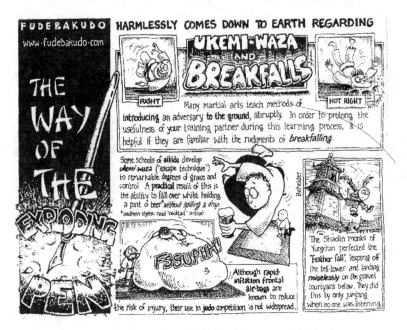

— Reproduced by kind permission of David Whitehead. See www. fudebakudo.com.

I never liked *ukemi* practice and even saw it as an annoying side-trip taking valuable class time from the "real" techniques. At least, that was so as long as I was afraid of it. Later it was flying.

Much later, when I slipped and fell in an ice storm, it probably saved my life. I went airborne, then despite tucking and slapping, hit the high curb. I ended up with a fractured skull and severe concussion. Not as bad as it could have been. A 19-year-old girl who did the same thing in the same storm died of her injuries and a classmate lost his father years ago to exactly the same thing.

At 10:00 that night the emergency room was packed, overflowing with broken arms, legs, wrists, heads, every possible combination of hurt from falling. How many of those people had ever been mugged "On The Street"? I would guess somewhere around zero to none, yet on that day, almost every one had been mugged, hit, shot at "*By* The Street."

Nowadays I tell new students that *ukemi* is the *real* self-defense portion of our program. The throwing techniques are just for fun. That isn't quite true of course.

Despite the high number of accidental injuries and deaths due to falls, the flip side is *purposeful* injuries and deaths. That is another thing entirely and it is why we have Aikido techniques.

CHAPTER 6

Grabs and Strikes

Attacks range from immediate intent to harm (strikes and punches) to restraint (to prevent the subject from drawing a weapon or harming another). In Aikido, attacks may be practiced singly or in combination.

In beginning classes, *uke* normally attacks to the forward foot, shoulder, or ribs. In general, it would be foolish to extend past the forward side and arm to attack *nage's* rear side or arm. As the Aikidoist becomes more experienced, stance becomes far less rigid but the underlying rationale remains.

Whether attacking or defending, arm moves with leg (see "Standing, Stepping and Stance" on page 43). Since Aikido assumes a right-handed attacker, *nage* usually does techniques on the left side first. Also note combinations. For example,

- *Kata-tori* is a grab to the lapel,
- *Shomen-uchi* is an overhead strike.
- *Kata-tori shomen-uchi* is a combination of these two basics (grab with strike).

Grabs are easy to break and so many martial arts do just that. In Aikido, grabs are *not* broken — they may even be secured with the other hand — to provide the starting point of techniques. Grabs tell you where *uke* is, limits his options (as breaking the hold can mean a new and different attack). And, while *uke* may be thinking "Ha! I've got you!" from *nage's* point of view, *uke* has just tied up or given away one or both or all of his weapons[1].

Basic Practice

Basic practice below is for the beginning student working as *uke* with a more experienced *nage*. Variations will provide *nage* with additional practice in response to attack. At home, the new student can also work with a "Closet *Uke*" (see page 223) or even an arm chair. For an effective drill with a partner,

1. Experienced student as *nage* calls out names of attacks.
2. New student as *uke* provides the requested stance, grab, or attack.
3. Reverse roles.

Variation

As *uke* provides the requested grab or attack, *nage* notes the direction of motion, and continues the energy and motion of the attack. *Nage* can also test effectiveness

---

1. Hence Aikido described as "The Art of 'I've Got You, I've Got You . . . Oh Nooooo!'"

of the hold by raising/lowering hand or moving it from side to side. Also apply the *hitori-waza / aiki-taiso* exercises from Chapter 4. For example, for *katate-tori*,

- For inward motion, rotate attacker's wrist inward with t*ekubi-kosa-undo* (page 88), start of many *irimi* techniques. Notice *uke*'s shoulder.

- For outward motion, duck under *uke*'s arm (start of *sankyo,* page 190).

- For incoming motion or static attack, turn *tenkan*. Notice what makes the easiest and most effective *tenkan (*page 97 and page 175), and the difference between relaxing the held arm and trying to force your way through it.

- Deflection ("wax on, wax off"). See how little effort deflects by a few degrees.

- For two handed grabs, *funekogi-undo* to start the motion, then continue motion into another exercise such as *tenkan*.

- "Standard Response." As punch or grab comes in,
  1. Sweep your opposite arm down *uke*'s attacking arm stopping at the wrist.
  2. Step back.
  3. Draw up forward foot, ending in *hanmi*.
  Observe the difference between a) brushing down incoming hand then stepping back and b) stepping back and then brushing down the incoming hand.

Focus on attacks, their names, and the exercises. Do not continue on to a throw.

Note real-life differences between attacks on men and attacks on women.

Men tend to attack *men* with punches and blows, in a pummeling, face-to-face, territorial, dominance sort of behavior. Restaurateurs and bartenders report that a common attack is what we would call a John Wayne right/left hook (*yokomen*), perhaps because it is so common in movies that many think it is the way to fight.

Men tend to attack *women* with chokes. The most common *street* attack on women is from behind, in predator/prey mode, typically with *ushiro kube-shime,* the "mugger's hold" (page 152) of one arm in a stranglehold around the target's neck, the other grasping one hand.) Another common attack, especially in domestic violence, is the choke from the front.

I recently heard two dojo-mates dismiss a botched attempt at a choke-hold technique: "Oh, well, it's not like anybody would actually attack anyone like that anyway."[2] Actually they do. For women, practice in groundwork and choke-hold techniques may be critical to training and safety.

---

2. A new student sputtered when she heard this. Contrary to popular belief, street attacks by strangers against women are rare. Attacks by abusive husbands or partners are not rare, and choke holds are common. Her estranged husband had attacked her on four separate occasions, each time with a chokehold. "But of course!" she said. "So easy when he is big and you are small. It also isn't as blatant or obvious afterwards as shooting or stabbing or breaking an arm but offers total control as you will do anything to get air." Each time, however (and with no training) she was able to turn the attack into a hip throw; he knocked himself cold on the hardwood floor. She then resolved to buy a gun to protect herself. On the way to the store, she realized that she *had* protected herself — and started Aikido instead.

Front Grabs

Judo grip or "aiki grip" or "soft grip" to a wrist starts by grabbing first with the little finger then each finger in order up to the index. This, as opposed to starting the grip with the index finger and bringing each finger into play down to the little finger. It's like holding a sword, the reverse grip of milking a cow.

— *Dennis Hooker, Aikido Schools of Ueshiba*

Katate-Tori

ADS[3]: Attack #1 ("Single-hand attack" [to same-side wrist]); TOT: Katate-mochi, pp. 58-60.

Katate-tori is the basic beginning attack in beginning Aikido.

Uke: RH and RF forward, grab *nage's* LH; fingers toward *nage* like gripping a tennis racquet, not towards self.

Nage: LH and LF forward, palm down

- Observe all the different ways that an attack can be a one-handed same-side grab but be entirely different, for example, pulling in, pushing out.

- Using different motions above, *nage* practice setting up the beginning motions for:
  Sankyo, rotating *uke's* arm *in* relative to *uke's* body (see page 190).
  Shiho-nage, rotating *uke's* arm out relative to *uke's* body (see page 194).
  Tenchi-nage, leading *uke's* arm out and down behind his body (see page 215).

- *Technique:* "Katate-Tori Kokyu-Nage Tenkan Ude-Oroshi" on page 211.

3.   References to "ADS" are to *Aikido and the Dynamic Sphere* by Westbrook and Ratti (1970); "TOT" to *Total Aikido* by Gozo Shioda (1997), "KIA" to *Ki in Aikido* by C. M. Shifflett (1997); "ZC" to *Zen Combat* by Jay Gluck (1997).
LH=Left Hand, RH=Right Hand, LF=Left Foot, RF=Right Foot.

Katate Kosa-Tori

ADS: Attack #2 ("Single-hand cross attack"); TOT: Katate-ayamochi, p. 107, for nikyo.

This "cross-handed" attack is the start of *Kokyu-nage Basic*. If "overhead" (a strike instead of a grab, with slight change in angle) it becomes *shomen-uchi* (page 154).

Uke:	RH and RF forward, grab *nage's* RH; fingers toward *nage* like gripping a tennis racquet, not towards self.
Nage:	LH and LF forward, palm up, palm down, or with hand vertical (thumb up and pinky finger down).

For palm up, rotate *uke*'s wrist inward across his body by rotating your hand thumb down. Observe behavior of shoulder and its natural lead-in to *irimi* techniques.

- As for "Katate-Tori" on page 145, practice setting up the beginning motions for *sankyo* (page 190), *shiho-nage* (page 194), and Nikyo 2 (page 189).

- *Technique*: See "Kokyu-Nage" on page 201 and "Katate-Kosa-Tori Kokyu-Nage Irimi Tobikomi" on page 202 ("Kokyu-Nage Basic").

Katate-Tori Ryote-Mochi

ADS: Attack #3 ("Attack to single hand with both hands holding")

Uke: RF forward, both hands grabbing *nage*'s LH.

R (outside) hand is above L (inside) hand on *nage*'s arm; this protects *uke* by keeping *nage*'s elbow from bending out for a strike.

Nage: LH and LF forward, palm up or down.

- *Tekubi-tori*. Combined with *tenkan* and *ude-mawashi*, generates a ferocious spin used in several *en-undo* techniques.

- As for "Katate-Tori" on page 145, practice setting up the beginning motions for *sankyo* and *shiho-nage*.

- *Technique*: See "Ryote-Mochi Kokyu-Nage Zempo-Nage Tenkan" on page 213. See also "Katate-Kosa-Tori Kokyu-Nage Irimi Tobikomi" on page 202. From Katate-tori ryote-mochi, the technique would become "*Katate-tori ryote-mochi kokyu-nage irimi tobikomi.*"

Katate-Tori Ryote-Tori

ADS: Attack #4 ("Both [single] hands grabbed by both [*uke*'s] hands"); TOT: ryote-mochi, p. 164.

Uke: RF forward, holding both of *nage*'s wrists.

Nage: LF forward, palms down.

- *Tekubi-kosa: rotate uke's* wrists by rotating yours. Observe how difficult or impossible it is for *uke* to halt this motion and what can be done with it, including conversions to *tenkan*, *irimi*, and *shiho-nage* movements. Reaching under one hand with the other, grasp knife-edge of *uke*'s hand. (See *"Kote-Gaeshi 3" on page 200*).

- *Funekogi* shifts a static *uke* into motion.

- Technique: "Katate-Tori Ryote-Mochi Kokyu-Nage Tenchi-Nage" on page 215.

Kata-Tori / Kata-Mune-Tori

ADS: Attack #5 ("Lapel-" or "shoulder-attack"); TOT: Kata-mochi, p. 63.

Uke: RF forward, seizing L lapel of *nage*'s *gi*.

Nage: LF and L shoulder forward.

- *Tenkan*. This is often combined with *shomen* or *yokomen* strik (ADS attack #17). Notice how easy it is to turn *tenkan* provided you do not freeze up and get stuck in your own clothes.

- Try stepping back into a no-hands f*unekogi*.

- For incoming motion, practice "Standard Response" (page 144) three or four hundred times, brushing down on incoming arm, stepping back, and drawing up the forward foot. (Step back first if *uke* is already holding.)

Ryo-Kata-Tori / Ryo-Munetori

ADS: Attack #6 ("Grab to both lapels/shoulders"); TOT: Kata-mochi, p. 63.

Uke: RF forward, seizing *both* lapels of *nage*'s *gi*.

Nage: LF forward, hips squared.

- *Tenkan*. Notice that this still works just as for the one-handed lapel grab.

- Experiment with a no-hands f*unekogi*.

- As for *kata-tori*, for incoming motion, practice the "Standard Response" (page 144) reaching over the near arm to brush away the outside arm with an *ude-furi* motion, or to deflect the outside arm into an *irimi* motion.

Ushiro Attacks

Ushiro ('behind") in a technique name indicates an attack from the rear.

When *nage* was armed with two swords, the safest place to be was behind them, a situation vividly portrayed in the opening scenes of *The 47 Ronin*. The point of *ushiro-tekubi-tori* ("wrist attack from behind") is to pull *nage*'s arms to the rear, rendering the target supposedly helpless while the attacker remains safely behind, shielded by *nage*'s own body. You may remember the name and the configuration of arms pulled back and seen from above as:

shiro

Ushiro-Tekubi-Tori

ADS: Attack #7, "Rear-Wrist-Attack"; TOT: Ushiro Ryote-Mochi, pp. 65-66.

Uke: Behind *nage,* pulling both wrists down and back.

Nage: *Shizentai*

- *Ushiro tekubi-kosa* and *ushiro tekubi tori*. Try raising arms out to sides then compare with doing the exercise by raising hands up center.

- Technique: "Ushiro-Tori Tekubi-Tori Ura-Gaeshi" on page 214.

- With above, flow into position for *sankyo, shiho-nage, ikkyo, kote-gaeshi*, etc.

- As an exercise in balance and stability plus a good stretch, combine with the "Paired Chest and Hip Stretch" on page 118.

Ushiro-Hiji-Tori

ADS: Attack #8, "Rear-Elbow-Attack"; TOT: Ryohiji-mochi, p. 68.

Uke: Behind *nage,* holding both elbows back.

Nage: *Shizentai*

- *Ushiro tekubi-kosa, ude-furi, funekogi,* and *tenkan.*
- With *ushiro tekubi-kosa,* flow into position for *sankyo.* With *tenkan,* flow into position for *kote-gaeshi.*
- As variation, compare with the standard schoolyard attack of one arm behind and forced upwards along the spine. It seemed like the Ultimate Attack at the time, but see what happens now if *nage* turns tenkan in the direction of *nage*'s elbow.

Ushiro Kata-Tori

ADS: Attack #9, "Rear-Shoulder-Attack"; TOT: Ushiro ryokata-mochi, p. 67.

Uke: Behind *nage,* holding both shoulders of *gi.*

Nage: *Shizentai*

- *Ude-furi choyaku, funekogi, tenkan* and bowing. See illustration on page 42, a *zempo-nage* which can be also be applied to a standing bow.
- *Uke*'s intent is to unbalance *nage* to the rear by moving shoulders behind hips. What happens if you move your own hips backward? Consider the difference in difficulty between tilting a standard chair backward and attempting to do the same thing to a chair on casters.

Ushiro Kubi-Shime

ADS: Attack #10/#16, "Rear-Neck-Attack"; TOT: pp. 188-189

This is commonly known as "The Mugger's Grab." It is the most common street attack on women[4].

Uke: Behind *nage,* R arm around nage's neck, LH grabbing *nage*'s L wrist.

Nage: *Shizentai*

- *Ushiro-tekubi-tori* (page 99): As L wrist rises (preparatory for *sankyo, zempo-nage*), combine with *sankyo* and see what happens to *uke*'s neck grab.

- Press the arm holding your neck *into* your chest. Observe the difference between holding the arm in place and attempting to pull it away.

- What are the positions of neck and head where you will choke yourself against *uke*'s arm? What are the positions which will give you breathing room? Note that the best option is *not* pressing your neck into *uke*'s forearm in an attempt to "get away."

- Observe also, how little control *uke* has over your hips.

Ushiro-Tori

ADS: Attack #11/12, "Rear-Attack"

Uke: Behind *nage,* a bear hug with both arms around *nage*'s shoulders or waist, pinning arms.

Nage: *Shizentai*

- *Ushiro-tori-undo* (page 98). Observe what happens to *uke*'s stability when you rotate or do not rotate thumbs down or raise arms.

- On moving into throwing position, observe what happens to *uke* (and how successful the eventual throw would be) if you bend forward from the waist versus rotating and bending from sideways with knee, hips, shoulders, and arms in the same plane. The throw is actually from the rear arm (triceps) out the forward finger. Experiment with feeling the connection between the two.

---

4. According to studies by IMPACT Self-Defense.

The venerable *Aikido and the Dynamic Sphere,* by Westbrook and Ratti, is almost The Standard Aikido Textbook. Its numbering system for attacks and techniques (such as Projection #3 Against Attack #1) is a neat solution to the problem of different terminology between styles. However, it can be difficult to decipher, especially for beginning students. The following chart is organized by attack number and name, keyed to the "Immobilization" (Imm.) or "Projection" (Proj.) and referenced to the page number in *Aikido and the Dynamic Sphere* on which the combination appears. Practice the attacks moving into the set-ups for different energy and options which result in the different techniques.

Attack	Attack Name	Defense Name	Defense	Page
#1	Katate-tori	Nikyo	Imm. #2	180
		Sankyo	Imm. #3	192
		Kokyu-nage	Proj. #1	227
		Ude-oroshi	Proj. #2	244
		Kaiten-nage	Proj. #3	252/332
		Tenchi-nage	Proj. #9	272
		Sumi-otoshi	Proj. #10	278
		Shiho-nage	Imm. #6	330
#2	Katate-kosa-tori	Sankyo	Imm. #3	193
		Kokyu-nage	Proj. #1	230
#3	Katate-tori-ryote-mochi	Ikkyo	Imm. #1	168
		Nikyo	Imm. #2	182
		Kote-gaeshi	Imm. #7	219
		Kokyu-nage	Proj. #1	232
		Sumi-otoshi	Proj. #10	280
#4	Ryote-mochi	Shiho-nage	Imm. #6	209
		Kokyu-nage	Proj. #1	236
		Koshi-nage	Proj. #4	257
		Tenchi-nage	Proj. #9	274
		Ghost-throw	Proj. #23	332

#5	Kata-tori	Ikkyo	Imm. #1	169
		Sankyo	Imm. #3	194
		Yonkyo	Imm. #4	200
		Shiho-nage	Imm. #6	210
		Ude-oroshi	Proj. #2	246
		Aiki-otoshi	Proj. #5	260
		Ude-kiri	Proj. #7	269/332
		Tenchi-nage	Proj. #9	276
		Sumi-otoshi	Proj. #10	281
#6	Ryo-kata-tori	Kokyu-nage	Proj. #1	237
		Ude-oroshi	Proj. #2	247
#7	Ushiro tekubi-tori	Ikkyo	Imm. #1	170
		Nikyo	Imm. #2	184
		Shiho-nage	Imm. #6	211
		Kokyu-nage	Proj. #1	238
		Ude-oroshi	Proj. #2	248
		Koshi-nage	Proj. #4	259
#8	Ushiro-hiji-tori	Kote-gaeshi	Imm. #7	220
		Kokyu-nage	Proj. #1	239
#9	Ushiro-katate-tori	Yonkyo	Imm. #4	201
		Kokyu-nage	Proj. #1	240
		Ude-oroshi	Proj. #2	249
		Aiki-otoshi	Proj. #5	264
#10	Ushiro-kubi-shime	Ojigi-nage	Proj. #15	294
#11/12	Ushiro-tori	Zempo-nage	Proj. #13	292

Strikes

Beginning Aikido deals with three basic strikes, two of which (*shomen-uchi* and *yokomen-uchi*) are derived from the Japanese sword tradition.

Shomen-Uchi

ADS: Attack #13, "Front-Strike"; TOT: pp. 50-51.

To differentiate this $traight-up-and-down $trike from *yokomen*, think of it as:

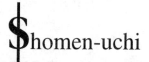

$homen-uchi

Uke:	LF forward, raise RH overhead, then drop strike straight down to *nage*'s head while stepping forward onto RF.
Nage:	LH and LF forward.

Initial set-up and stance vary between styles and schools. At the Virginia Ki Society, shomen-uchi is essentially a *katate-kosa-tori* ("cross-hand-attack" page 146), targeting head rather than wrist. *Uke* starts in a stance opposite to where he will end to allow a step into the strike. This is often explained as "attack the back foot." As George Simcox teaches, "Attack *nage's* forward right foot with your right hand," that is:

- *Uke* starts on LF simply to move into the attack, just like throwing a ball.

- Step forward onto RF, striking down with your RH.

    This configuration allowed two persons to pass, back to back, if the fight was not entered into. The aim was to expose as little of yourself to the opponent as possible.

    — *George Simcox, Ki Society*

- *Uke* practice striking; *nage* step off-line and extend with *ikkyo-undo* (see exercises starting on page 101) letting *uke* slide by. Notice how little time and effort are required do avoid or deflect the strike.

- Techniques: "Shomen-Uchi Ikkyo Irimi" on page 207 and "Shomen-Uchi Ikkyo Tenkan" on page 209.

Yokomen-Uchi

ADS: Attack #14, "Side-head-strike"; TOT: p. 53.

To differentiate *yokomen* and *$homen-uchi,* observe the diagonal stroke of the *Y* in:

Yokomen-uchi is an oblique sword cut[5]. Raise the arm and/or weapon straight up just as for *shomen,* but cut down diagonally while rotating the hips. As in *shomen-uchi,* raising the sword overhead allows you to blend with the force of gravity for maximum power.

Uke: LF forward, RH overhead, striking diagonally to *nage*'s neck while turning hips and stepping into R *hanmi.*

Nage: LH and LF forward.

- *Uke* observe power generated by starting the strike from side; from overhead.
- As *uke* strikes *yokomen, nage* observe the path of the arm. This is the path of travel, the vectors, that you must blend with.
- *Ikkyo. Nage* practice "blocking" — actually feeling, flowing with, redirecting — the strike. How softly can you do this? By aligning and blending, how invisible can you become to *uke*?
- Techniques: "Yokomen-Uchi Shiho-Nage Irimi" on page 204 and "Yokomen-Uchi Shiho-Nage Tenkan" on page 206.

---

5. *Samurai* armor had a tiny gap where the helmet neck piece and shoulder armor met. *Yokomen* strikes attempted to exploit that gap.

Mune-Tsuki

ADS: Attack #15, "Middle-punch"; TOT: *Shomen-tsuki*, p. 56

Uke:	L *hanmi*, draw back RH in fist; stepping into R *hanmi*, punch forward to the solar plexus or belt knot.
	Practice: Same punch to a punching bag or makiwara to check form and effectiveness.
Nage:	LH and LF forward.

Mune-tsuki ("middle-punch") or "punch to chest" is done in different ways, but in traditional Eastern styles it tends to be an uppercut punch to the solar plexus.

Students often hesitate to offer a real punch for fear of injuring their partners (see page 164) or simply because they have no idea how to punch. Either option deprives the partner of practice with real punches, real energy, and real commitment behind them. This is important because although Aikido doesn't emphasize punches, other martial arts do.

- *Tenkan:* As a form of "fisty dodge-ball," observe that it doesn't matter how hard *uke* hits — if you aren't there.

- *Ude-furi:* In combination with *tenkan*, sweep same-side arm down *uke*'s arm preparatory for *kote-gaeshi,* especially for a curled wrist with uppercut. (See "Finding the Wrist" on page 198.)

- *For beginning uke:* Aim for the knot of *nage*'s belt. This provides a specific target especially for the *uke* who "punches" by waving his arm in a vaguely forward direction often completely outside *nage*'s body, often due to fear of harming nage. Aiming at the knot gives partners the opportunity to know that the block or *tenkan* was effective or ineffective, while protecting *nage* from harm.

  Meanwhile, practice with a pillow, punching bag, *makiwara*, to learn the actual dynamics behind effective punching.

  For the *nage* working with a beginning *uke* who may not realize that he's not really punching, work on *ma-ai*, backing up across the mat to force forward movement and commitment.

- For beginning *nage*: *Uke* start slowly with a punching *motion*, gradually increase force and speed to a fast and powerful "real" punch.

Other Techniques

Kicks

Kicks are rarely used in Aikido, but are common in other styles and appear in various Ki Society *Taigi* (notably *Taigi* #7.) They are always of interest to new incoming karate students, but avoid them unless an instructor is present. If unbalancing *uke* is too successful, the consequences from a kick are far worse than from a punch and karate students rarely have experience in falling. Kicks include:

- *Choku-Geri* ("straight-kick" or front snap kick),
- *Mawashi-Geri* ("round-kick" or roundhouse kick),
- *Yoko-Geri* ("side-kick")

Atemi

Atemi is a "strike" or blow, which in Aikido is used to distract, startle, or in general, to disrupt an attacker's focus and rhythm. It is not usually intended to physically smash or injure; it operates more on the level of psychological warfare. It may take the form of a punch, a kick, or even more subtle motions: a palm whizzing by the face, a *Stooge-ido* poke towards the eyes which startles, surprises, unbalances. An attacker may be fully prepared to take on the most ferocious blows, but a soft unexpected flick to the tip of the nose diverts brain cells to dealing with the problem of *"What was that?!?"*

Some insist that there are no punches in Aikido[6] but this is not the case.

> I can safely say that there is atemi in Ki Society Aikido. Taigi 13 (third technique is called "yokomen-uchi kokyu-nage atemi" and is done with a ki-ai on the atemi). Taigi 19 Mune-Tsuki, has only one technique that does not include atemi. My favorite is called simply mune-tsuki kokyu-nage shomen-uchi; the shomen-uchi is the response to the attack. There are others that are in the test requirements, such as the katate-tori tenchi-nage that used to be in our 5th kyu test.
>
> — Brian Kelley, Ki Society

> I don't know from Ki Society, but a fairly high ranked student of Chiba Sensei once told me that he doesn't teach atemi to beginners, not because it isn't important, but because everyone thinks they know how to hit people. If you include the atemi when teaching new students, they tend to focus on what they think is familiar to them, and end up pounding on each other instead of learning good body mechanics.
>
> — J. Toman

---

6. A quote attributed to a high-ranking USAF-West (Aikikai) sensei is this: "He said there were no strikes in Aikido so I hit him again."

Breathing

Breathing is the most obvious of self-defense techniques. (Stop it and you die rather immediately). Breathing can also be used as an attack. The Ki Society emphasizes breathing practice, but does not emphasize strict rules for breathing[7] or the idea that breathing *in* makes you weak. Nevertheless, when aware of breath (your own and that of others), it is possible to disrupt an opponent's attack through disruption of his rhythm breathing. Attacking or closing *ma-ai* when the opponent is breathing out is not so much an issue of "being weak when exhaling" as it is an issue of not having yet inhaled the oxygen needed for further physical effort.

The principles of breathing and also using your opponent's breathing to your own advantage are contained in all martial art practices that I have encountered in 45 years of practice. Control of your own breath should be included at fundamental levels of study. It is built into all kata and some teachers don't make a big deal out of it at basic levels, but I believe it is very important. Using your own breath and then your opponent's breath as strategy is part of all techniques. As we become more sensitive to timing and rhythm we will find that breathing ties everything together.

— Chuck Clark, Jiyushinkai Aikibudo

Ki-Ai

Ki-ai is a powerful shout or cry, "with *ki*." For *nage*, *ki-ai* concentrates and focuses mind and body. It is fundamental to karate and to other styles including IMPACT Self Defense training (which is heavily based on karate). Nowadays *ki-ai* seems rarely taught in Aikido although it was clearly important to Ueshiba.

For *nage*, a spirited *ki-ai* is invigorating if only because it requires *breathing* rather than holding the breath. For the attacker, an unexpected *ki-ai* can also be more — for man or beast. And if you're ever attacked by a moose . . . .

In 1997, Associated Press[8] reported the adventure of a Norwegian politician who was hunting rabbits when he was charged by a moose protecting her calf. Rather than trying to fend off a half-ton of angry mother moose with a rabbit gun, he decided to use his best weapon — his voice.

"I unleashed a tremendous shout . . . The moose instantly collapsed onto the ground, a meter from me."

As corroborated by witnesses, the stunned moose lay there for several seconds before staggering to its feet and wobbling quietly away.

In the same year, the sudden frenzy and collapse of an Okapi, a rare antelope, was attributed to a rehearsal of Wagner's opera "Tannhauser" in a park some 300 yards from the Copenhagen zoo, perhaps similar to epilepsy induced in humans by certain frequencies and rhythms of sound. A shocking sensory overload may be the mundane explanation of many seemingly mystical "no-touch throws."

Nothing more, but nothing less.

---

7. Breathing *out* when falling is learned very quickly after being winded by a breakfall.
8. Associated Press, Jan. 2., 1997

Nage and Uke — Partners in the Dance

In the partnered practice that is Aikido,

- *Uke* offers the raw material of the attack then "receives" the technique.
- Nage "throws" or performs a technique appropriate to *uke*'s attack.

New students are often disturbed by the notion of cooperation and teamwork between *nage* and *uke* which must make it "faked" or "staged" or "phony." Aikido is indeed cooperative, but it isn't *uke* who's cooperating, it's actually *nage* who cooperates with *uke* by following, aligning with, and blending with *uke*'s attack.

In the performance art known as "Pro-Wrestling" you will see excellent gymnastics and superb *ukemi*. No one is supposed to get hurt, but it works only because of careful cooperation[9] between the players.

For example, in the breakfall technique known as a "Body Slam," *uke* vaults off *nage*'s thighs or shoulders to gain height. *Nage* helps by delaying any downward force until *uke* has head tucked and is fully horizontal in order to obtain the greatest degree of surface area in contact with the mat. In the "Flying Body Break," the "attacker" leaps from the ropes to land on his quarry. Or so it seems. In reality, the "victim" is the "catcher" or "spotter" there to help the "attacker" land safely. Each is protected by his *ukemi* skills and by his partner. Yes, it's comic book, yes, it's staged — but the physics are real, the risk of devastating injury is real, and the *ukemi* is real. The cooperation between *nage* and *uke* is real and keeps both parties safe so that they can come back and play another day. In Aikido practice we must do no less.

How to Be Nage

- See *uke* as your partner and teacher (page 159),
- Match speed and direction of the attack (page 160),
- Continue the motion (page 160),
- Don't muscle the technique (page 161),
- When *uke* counters, stop and ask for correct energy (page 161),
- Respect *uke*'s ability to take a fall — and let go (page 162).

See Uke as Partner and Teacher

Uke is *not* your enemy. *Uke* is a partner who has loaned you a physical body for a time so that you may learn Aikido skills. Treat that gift with gratitude and respect. In Aikido and *ki* exercises, *uke* serves as the biofeedback monitor that makes the exercises real.

Are you off-balance or not? Is there a throw or not? Is your technique effective or not? You can dance through the motions forever on your own. Only *uke* can tell you if they are truly effective.

---

9. See *Exposed! Pro-Wrestling's Greatest Secrets*, page 261.

Match Speed and Direction of the Attack

My eyes, his eyes. My feet, his feet. For the enemy, that agreement is the one thing they can't handle. It doesn't have to be long but it does have to be total. Opposition they can handle, but when instead of presenting them with more opposition, you present them with agreement, it's absolutely devastating. And it's the soul of the art.

— Terry Dobson

In matching *uke*'s speed and direction, staying just barely out of reach, *nage* actually blends, vanishes, disappears, into the attack. This matching and blending is a form of camouflage, a weapon in and of itself. Blend into the attacker's own power and direction and he will feel only himself and be unable to counter. It is extremely disconcerting to attack, to be aware that something astonishing is happening, but to feel nothing at all.

Notice that a tense tight grip by *nage* adds new and different directions of force. Notice that trying to speed through the technique faster than the attack is itself an attack. There should be only one attacker.

Learning to blend in Aikido is very much like a two-year-old learning to pet a cat. It is the same balance and sensitivity required to drive an automatic transmission, to pull a weed effectively with root, to "stick to *uke* like white on rice," to turn touch into music[10].

As pianist and piano teacher, it's interesting to note that while we're pressing down what is basically a block of wood against a string that some have a good 'touch' while others just play. It's the touch, the blending with the block of wood that makes all the difference. — Margarete Brandenburg, Kokon Ryu Renmei Aikido

Continue the Motion

Continuing the motion continues the preceding principle of matching speed and direction. Many martial arts styles respond to an incoming punch or kick with an opposing block of greater force or inertia. In Aikido, an arm may appear to be blocking a strike but is not. It is more a *feeler* to sense the speed and position of the oncoming attack. The apparent block may deflect the incoming energy, but the purpose is never to block it with opposing force.

Cattle herders needing to slow or stop a stampede did not gallop headlong into an oncoming wall of longhorns. They matched speed and direction with the leaders, deflecting and turning the mass into a large roiling circle.

When the Highway Patrol needs to slow or stop high-speed traffic, they do not block oncoming cars by driving at greater force and inertia into oncoming traffic. Neither do they throw up a stationary roadblock to bring vehicles to a sudden slamming stop. Instead, they employ a rolling roadblock. Troopers driving in each lane of the roadway match the speed and direction of traffic, then gradually decrease speed as necessary.

In Aikido, the attacker's incoming energy is your raw material for unbalancing *uke* and allowing a throw to happen.

---

10. Neuroscientist, artificial intelligence researcher and musician Manfred Clynes proposes that emotion and touch have measurable and repeatable waveforms. See Smith, T. M. (1991).

What if you don't get a real attack? What if you only get uncommitted strikes and punches and there is no motion or energy to continue?

New students often simply don't know how to punch or strike, or may fear causing harm and aim so far off line that it provides no threat and no energy to work with.

If *uke* is punching or striking offline, not moving at all makes it clear what is happening. If *uke* is unfamiliar with the whole concept of striking, it also helps to provide a specific target. Have *uke* aim for the knot in your belt, a specific target that is also padded should they fear connecting and harming you.

Nage can also compel a committed attack by repositioning. For example, if *uke* is stopping short with a punch or a strike, keep backing up across the mat just out of range. It is useful practice of *ma-ai*, and it will eventually produce a genuine committed forward motion. If *uke* doesn't realize what he's doing, this will help to clarify the situation. It is far more effective than complaining that "there's no energy there."

> *For a weak overhead strike (shomen-uchi) I step back and place my hands so that they would catch the strike with palms up if it were to be in the correct place. The miss is obvious and the uke usually doesn't need any more correction. If they do I have them practice striking into my hands (usually held at waist level) a time or two and then, without telling uke, fail to step back and execute the throw instead. Works about 90+% of the time.*

> — *George Simcox, Ki Society*

Don't Muscle the Techniques

Purely physical strength is limited by the physical body. There will always be someone bigger and stronger, if not now, then tomorrow or 20 years from now.

Aikido allows you to use *uke*'s strength, rather than exhausting your own. Aikido gives you a tremendous advantage over a larger, heavier, stronger opponent *provided you avoid a weight and strength contest*. To use his size, strength and energy, you must blend; align with it, stay with it, go in the direction that it is going.

The more you struggle and strain, the less likely you are to be doing Aikido.

The more you feel you have done nothing, the more likely you are to have done the technique correctly.

> *I have a mentor in the psychotherapy field, Stephen Gilligan, a psychologist in San Diego and an experienced Aikidoka. One of the many things he has written that stays with me is the way uke and nage relate:*
>
> *Heart to heart*
> *Mind to mind.*
> *Center to center.*
> *As Steve says, in psychotherapy, if you do that, the rest is easy.*

> — *Leonard Bohanon*

When Uke Counters . . .

1. Stop and ask for the correct energy or
2. Use the counter- attack energy.

Every technique will seem to work about twice when an *uke* who does not understand his real role begins to counter. Beginners who counter to avoid being thrown or to make a point, are frustrating and confusing for the beginning *nage*. *Tenkan* techniques are designed to deal with incoming energy. If *uke* pulls back, the *tenkan* technique won't work, but he sets himself up for an *irimi*.

Both partners must understand the energy the technique is intended to deal with. If *uke* is providing the wrong attack for the technique being practiced, tell him so. Do not, however, be too quick to blame failure of technique on *uke* "giving the wrong energy." Be sure that you are doing the technique correctly and then if the energy is incorrect, correct it. If there is any doubt, ask *Sensei* for help. At higher levels (and respecting *uke*'s ability) match the technique to the energy and attack presented. Two things will happen.

1. The technique will work.

2. The aggrieved *uke* (completely unprepared for being thrown across the mat when he thought he was countering so very well) will protest:

   "But that's not the technique we're supposed to be doing!"

   The answer to *uke*'s astute observation is:

   "Yes! — but that is the energy that was given. Why don't we try it again with [the correct energy]."

   A useful lesson for both partners.

There is a tale told of nearly every master Aikidoist who has just performed some fascinating technique.

> *"Amazing!" cries the student. "Please do that one again!"*
> *Sensei agrees and the student attacks again. But Sensei does an entirely different technique. Then another. And another.*
> *"Why don't you do the same technique as before?" cries the student."*
> *"Because you haven't given the same attack as before," says the Sensei.*

Respect Uke's Ability to Fall

When you throw, respect your partner's ability to take a fall. Letting go protects both the thrown and the thrower.

Beginners are often so shocked to see that a throw actually works, so startled at the sight of *uke* falling to the mat that they hold on with the idea of helping *uke* down. This is kindly meant, but can be dangerous. *Uke* must be free to roll or, for a brand-new beginner, to walk out of a throw.

The flip side is the danger to *nage*. Bending *over* to help *uke* can mean being kicked in the face by flying feet. If you wish to drop down to the mat,

- Bend at the knees and ankles.
- Drop *down* from the One-Point/Center.
- Imagine that you are doing these techniques on ice.
- Always, always keep One-Point/Center.

How to Be Uke

- Give the correct energy and follow through (page 163).
- Match the speed and energy of your attack to *nage*'s ability to protect you and your own ability to take a fall (page 163).
- Do not counter (page 164).
- Learn the technique well enough to "throw yourself" (page 165).

Do you see throwing as winning and falling as losing?

Uke is the most important person on the mat, *nage*'s teacher, the one who attacks and rolls so that *nage* can learn Aikido.

Give the Correct Energy and Follow Through

We practice specific techniques to practice dealing with specific types of energy and motion. If *uke* does not supply the energy or motion for which the technique was designed, the technique may be forced, but it will not flow. It is like trying to sailboard or windsurf in a dead calm. Both partners need to understand the energy the technique is intended to deal with. If you are unsure of the correct energy, ask *Sensei* for help.

Tenkan techniques, for example, are intended for an attacker who is moving, pushing, shoving, punching forward. *Nage* turns (*tenkan*) and leads *uke* into a circle, at a speed that keeps the hand almost — but not quite — within grasp. *Uke* is kept reaching forward for the hand that is just a split second, just a hair, beyond his control[11].

You may attack slowly, but continue the motion — don't stop short. The raw material for many throws is the momentum, inertia, and change in balance of the follow-through. These increase with increasing speed and decrease or vanish with decreasing speed.

Walking slowly through a technique which relies on speed and momentum will not "work" in the sense of Uke Falls Down; it will "work" in the sense of establishing the individual steps — the notes — of the technique. Once these are learned, increasing speed teaches rhythm and flow but there must be power and commitment behind the attack in order for a technique to work.

Aikidoist Jan Beyen compares this to the windpower needed for sailboarding. Sailboarding simply "does not work" without windspeeds of around 15 knots.

Match Speed and Energy of Attack to Nage's Ability

Respect your partner's ability, never holding harder or attacking faster than *nage* can handle. The first few times through a new technique, move as easily and gently as you would through a new dance step. When your partner begins to feel the pattern and flow of the movements, you may give more of a challenge but always give the appropriate attack, especially when working with beginners — for their sake and yours. Too fierce an attack may be more than *nage* can handle and can result in injury. Part of *nage*'s technique and practice is to protect *uke*. If the attack is beyond *nage*'s ability to do so and the results are beyond your skill to take *ukemi*, you may be injured.

---

11. For what it should feel like, see the "Rag Doll Tenkan" on page 70.

Q: I'm willing to make it an on-target strike, but I'm not willing to make it a "real" strike...one that I can't stop easily prior to contact. So am I screwing up their training or protecting them?

A.: You are describing what a considerate, caring students would do: determine what the level of training your opponent can handle and then "challenge" them a bit so they can grow. This has two purposes:

You don't unnecessarily hurt a practice partner and you don't suffer the natural consequences of attacking with more force than you can handle when the appropriate technique is applied and you are sent flying

I have seen more people hurt because they worked beyond their ukemi than because they were harshly attacked with more force than they could handle. I've seen pulled muscles, scrapes and one serious broken bone. All were a result of ukemi that didn't do what it was supposed to do, but I've never yet seen anyone get punched out.

— George Simcox, Ki Society

Do Not Counter

As *uke* you are there to help and challenge your partner, not to engage in a contest.

Any Aikido technique can be countered. While it is very tempting to do so, that isn't the point of beginning practice. The point of practice is *practice*. Specific attacks involving specific energy are dealt with via specific techniques. Attacks are staged in class in order to practice a specific response, a particular placement of hands and feet, a specific point of rotation, even a particular mindset. An attack inappropriate to the material to be practiced will not work.

For example, *tenkan* techniques, designed to dissipate and redirect fast incoming energy by continuing the motion *forward*, do not work if *uke* pulls *back*. *Nage* may succeed in dragging *uke* around in a circle, but that is a pointless exercise which may lead you to the false conclusion that Aikido isn't "real" or that *nage* is fooling himself. In reality, the source of the problem is *uke* who may then add insult to injury by staging an elaborate imitation fall.

Countering is typical of the *uke* who does not understand his real role as helper and teacher or who does not understand or want to admit that changes in energy and direction are actually different attacks. If the exercise is to practice *tenkan*, and you counter with a hold appropriate for some other technique, it will be difficult, painful, or confusing for *nage* and your own learning will be impaired.

Or, you may learn more than you expected. A counter sets you up for another technique. While you are thinking of the motion you are blocking rather than the new energy you are presenting, the counter to your counter tends to have more devastating consequences. As you go flying through the air you will be experiencing "Real Aikido."

The accomplished Aikidoist may actually provides an opportunity then wait for *uke* to counter in order to take advantage of that specific energy. For example, in *Kokyu-Nage Basic nage* leads *uke* down then waits for him to counter by attempting to come up. *Nage* does not force *uke* up. Instead he waits for him to come up, then helps him to come up, adding just a little extra energy to *uke*'s energy so that the final up is more than *uke* was expecting — or can deal with[12].

---

12. For the same strategy applied to verbal techniques, see "Typecasting" on page 244.

On the other hand, don't collapse just because *nage* appears to have completed the technique so now it must be time to fall down. While this can give *nage* a false sense of security, it can also give a *false insecurity* if your partner feels that you are merely collapsing on cue.

Never see your partner as competition; don't resist falling with the notion that if your partner succeeds in throwing you, you have somehow "lost."

If you are *afraid* to fall, learn to fall, a critically valuable self-defense technique in and of itself. We also practice falling in order to help others learn.

If you are *unwilling* to fall, examine your motives — you may find such hidden devils as fear, false pride, dignity, and the delusion of winning versus losing.

"Win" by being an effective teacher.

Learn the Technique Well Enough to Throw Yourself

The test of good *ukemi* is not whether you can counter *nage* ("Ha ha! you can't throw me!") but whether you understand the technique well enough to provide the correct energy and to guide an inexperienced *nage* through the technique and the throw. The ability to do so is not "tanking" and does not make the technique "phony" — it is a teaching technique, and once again, *uke* is the teacher.

On the other hand, beginners are often told not to fall unless they are actually thrown. This is because they don't know enough yet to be able to guide the throw and to avoid the habit of "tanking" even in response to bad technique.

It is also because beginners often take terrible falls on their own. They may launch themselves into a mass of other students, or land in a way that risks injury.

But there's another side to the issue.

> *Senior students tend to go ahead and roll as soon as a junior student gets the technique even a little bit right, with the definition of "right" becoming more stringent as nage becomes more skilled. For complete beginners, it's real progress deserving of positive feedback if they move their feet and hips at all, even if they're still mostly using arm strength.*
>
> *Meanwhile, beginners don't yet have the awareness to protect uke and often don't realize that "Making Uke Fall" is not necessarily the same as "Good Aikido." I'm therefore likely to be much more protective of my joints and much more aware of my "landing zone" when I'm working with beginners. I might roll when I otherwise wouldn't in order to avoid getting damaged.*
>
> — *Katherine Derbyshire, Aikido Schools of Ueshiba*

Yet another side of the issue is this: The flip side of teaching the throw from *ukemi* is learning the throw from *ukemi*. Beginners are often distressed that many advanced students seem unwilling to work with them. This is sometimes true, and often for all the wrong reasons, but most often because the newer student (who has not yet learned how to protect his partner) wants to concentrate on throwing the senior student who in turn needs time to work on other skills. Traditionally, beginners learned by taking years of *ukemi* for advanced students before studying the throws themselves. If you concentrate on *ukemi* skills and volunteer to *uke* for advanced students you will learn and you will never lack practice partners.

CHAPTER 7

Locks & Throws

The secret behind the throws? Physical principles based on gravity and movement from Center. Internal principles based on focus, calmness and relaxation. And Koichi Tohei's basic principles for the practice of Ki-Aikido.

1. **Extend Ki.** Extending awareness, attention, focus, intent, and goal.

2. **Know your opponent's mind (intent).**
   What exactly is it that *uke* wants to do? We are controlled by what we want . . .

3. **Respect your opponent's *ki* (energy/inertia/intent).**
   Per the physics of Aikido, practice being aware of and sensitive to speed, force, and direction in order to blend with it. Focus on these rather than on the attacker.
   Is the attack circular? Is it coming straight at you? Is it down? Up? Fast? Slow?

4. **Put yourself in your opponent's place.**
   Move into the position where *uke* would be stable, but can't because you and your center are there. In *tenkan* it is the middle of the circle. In throws, it is the position where *uke* is supported, where supported only by you, or not supported at all.[1]

5. **Perform with confidence.**
   . . . and we are controlled by what we fear. Having confidence in your techniques requires that you have *done* them, *practiced* them, *experienced* them often enough that they are no longer a hopeful leap of faith into the void, but a confident use of known and trusted tools of mind and body.

Aikido techniques range from simple to complex, with infinite variation and nuance, but the basic techniques (*waza*) are divided into *katame-waza* ("immobilization techniques") and *nage-waza* ("throwing techniques").

Katame-waza are commonly known as "wristlocks" or "armlocks." Wrist, elbow, and shoulder joints are manipulated to control the attacker's balance and body.

Nage-waza are the actual "throws." The two categories overlap, but many *nage-waza* are based solely on redirection of weight, speed, and momentum.

There are innumerable techniques in Aikido and every beginner wonders how they will ever keep them straight. Instructors are fond of saying that they are just different expressions of the same basic principles, but while teaching principles, it is also useful to provide a way to organize these different expressions. Sensei Guy DeWolf offers a useful framework.

---

1. Always look for the invisible third leg that would keep *uke* from falling if only it were there and he could lean on it but it isn't and he can't.

Teaching by the Numbers . . .

— By Guy DeWolf, Ki Society

One of the biggest problems facing new Aikido students is learning the Japanese terminology. Those of us who have been around longer forget how many Japanese words we know and how baffling the exotic terms we use so casually among ourselves can be to novices. Back when I first started studying Aikido, our group met in a building with a parking problem. People were constantly coming in from outside and asking us to move our cars so they could get out.

"Please move the Honda."

"Somebody move the Mustang."

"We need somebody to move the white van!"

One evening when requests for vehicles to be moved had been particularly frequent, my sensei said to me, "Get into your *hanmi*."

"Oh no, Sensei," I said. "I drive the Thunderbird."

Now that I am an instructor, I want to spare my students similar embarrassing moments. When new students come into the *dojo*, I like to expose them to some of the terminology of Aikido and at the same time give them an overview of the structure of our art. I choose one of the regular students to act as my uke and do a brief presentation that I call . . .

The 9 Basic Attacks, 9 Basic Throws, and 2 Basic Moves of Aikido

Before I begin, I reassure the new students that I don't expect them to memorize the terms as I go. The idea is not to make them feel pressured to learn everything immediately, but to expose students to the terminology of Aikido in the beginning to make it more familiar when they hear it again later.

9 Attacks

I categorize the nine attacks into 6 grabs:

1. Katate-tori ("wrist-attack")
2. *Katate-kosa tori* ("cross-wrist attack")
3. *Katate-tori ryote-mochi* ("wrist-attack with both" hands on one of *nage*'s wrists"
4. *Katate- tori ryote-tori* ("wrist-grab with both" hands grabbing both of *nage*'s wrists")
5. *Kata-tori* ("lapel attack")
6. *Ushiro tekubi-tori* ("attack to *nage*'s wrists from behind") and:

3 strikes

1. *Shomen-uchi* ("front-head strike")
2. *Yokomen-uchi* ("side-head strike")
3. *Mune-tsuki* ("mid-level-punch")

I give the English translation for each of these terms, explaining that *kata-te* means "wrist," *tori* means "attack" and so on.

The 9 Basic Techniques

I do the same thing with the 9 basic techniques. I demonstrate:

1. *Ikkyo,*

2. *Nikyo,*
3. *Sankyo,*
4. *Yonkyo,* (explaining that these exotic terms simply mean the "first-," "second-," "third-," and "fourth- technique.") Then I move to
5. *Kokyu-nage* ("Breath-throw"),
6. *Shiho-nage* ("Four-direction throw"),
7. *Ude-oroshi* ("Arm-drop"),
8. *Kote-gaeshi* ("wrist-bend"), and
9. *Zempo-nage* ("forward-direction throw")

    explaining that each technique can be performed in response to a variety of attacks and that these combinations of attack and response make up the body of Aikido.

Two Basic Movements

My journey through the basics of Aikido is completed by demonstrating the "Two Basic Movements" of:

1. *Tenkan* ("turning") and
2. *Irimi* ("entering").

I show the students pairs of techniques that differ only in the method, as for example *shomen-uchi irimi* versus *shomen-uchi tenkan*. Seeing these presented in pairs makes Aikido terminology meaningful in the students' minds. Finally I explain how techniques are called out:

1. The attack,
2. The response, and
3. The technique.

I demonstrate some of the techniques whose names follow the rule but also point out names that *don't* follow this rule. The term *kokyu-nage*, in particular, requires additional explanation. I tell students that, unless some other throw is also given as a part of the technique name, it will be a *kokyu-nage*, a "breath" or "timing throw."

Presenting attacks and techniques in terms of families and explaining the rationale behind the technique names gives students a structure or mental framework where they can hang their new knowledge as they acquire it. Educational theorists refer to these mental frameworks as *schema* and many believe that *schema*, either constructed by students themselves or supplied to them by their teachers, are vitally important in learning.

Ultimately, Aikido students must construct their knowledge of the art for themselves as they progress, but we instructors can give them a head start. When I spend part of an evening categorizing techniques and then teaching by the numbers, I'm giving my students not only a lesson in Japanese terms but also the beginning of a personal understanding of the art that we all study together.

—G. D.

Nage slipping away
Almost got 'em this time, ha!
Mat greets me loudly.
    —Kevin Beck

Movements — Ma-ai, Tenkan and Irimi

Ma-ai, tenkan and *irimi* are the most basic tools of Aikido. The differences between them can be thought of in terms of "danger zones." Most hostile humans are most dangerous in front, in the direction of the eyes. In general,

- *Irimi* is "entering" and turning *uke*'s danger zone away.
- *Tenkan* is "turning" *yourself* around and away from *uke*'s danger zone.
- *Ma-ai* is simply not being there, or being out of reach or out of the danger zone.

Ma-ai

> *I cannot begin to tell you the number of dumb looks I've seen by simply leaning back and letting a guy's fist fly past my face. Of all the reactions the dude was expecting, me getting out of the way wasn't one of them.*
>
> — *Marc MacYoung, Watch My Back*

The turn-of-the-century classic, *Secrets of the Sword,* by Baron *César* de Bazancourt, is a sort of Socratic dialogue on the most basic essentials of the sword and self-defense. In the course of 11 evenings, the Baron proposes to strip away the techniques, the daunting foreign terminology (French), and reduce years of study to the most basic, root essential of swordsmanship. The essential that the Baron presents is *ma-ai*.

Literally *ma-ai* is "harmonious-distance," the natural or proper space maintained between bodies. *Ma-ai* is your first line of defense, the most important technique in your toolbox. It is space and time, rhythm, and flow.

- In traffic it is safe following distance between cars.
- In social encounters it is the distance that indicates neither cold distance nor inappropriate intimacy.
- In conversation, it is rhythm and timing and degree of familiarity.

The Ma-ai of Space

Proper space is the distance required for safety from collision, reaction time in case of attack,[2] the position which requires a complete step and body commitment on the part of an attacker. If the attacker can connect with a strike without a step, you are much too close.

In Aikido, *ma-ai* is commonly thought of as the distance between two standing partners when they touch the fingertips of their outstretched arms but this distance is not absolute; it is constantly modified by the situation.

For armed partners, the distance is greater as sword or staff increase effective reach by several feet. Proper distance between partners using swords is with just the tips of the swords crossed. Closer means that a single step could result in a killing blow.

Ma-ai is different even for two partners of different size and reach. A short partner who cannot reach a long-armed partner may still be standing too close.

For *taigi* (paired exercises of choreographed attack and defense as practiced in the Ki Society) the proper starting distance between partners seated in *seiza* for the initial or final bow, is about 12 feet, or the distance of two *tatami* mats.

Ma-ai can also be thought of as the distance that allows you to see and take in a potential attacker's entire body, from head to foot. This is not only for time to react to an incoming punch or kick. It is to observe body language.

The human brain is exquisitely attuned to body language and the intent that underlies it. Don't believe it? If you are a commuter, consider that you may be negotiating the highway equivalent of Han Solo's trip through the asteroid field in the Millennium Falcon on a daily basis, half awake and even before you've had your coffee. How do you know who is going to dart out of the next lane? Fail to stop? Wander across four lanes of traffic?

How do you *know*?

You *know* because a tiny tilt of head, a drop of a shoulder is enough to tell you.

The same tiny motions are critical in martial arts and self defense. The more of them you can see, the better. Hence emphasis on full body view (rather than simple horizontal distance), to receive information — and to send it. De Becker (1997) explains a common violation of this type of *ma-ai* in both information gathering and the message conveyed.

> *". . . Many do not use the full resources of their vision; they are reluctant to look squarely at strangers who concern them. Believing she is being followed, a woman might take just a tentative look, hoping to see if someone is visible in her peripheral vision. It is better to turn completely, take in everything, and look squarely at someone who concerns you.*

2. Observe the use of *ma-ai* in computer games such as *Tetris*. As a rain of geometric blocks fall from the sky, the player must form a complete row. The program works to reduce *ma-ai* which in turn reduces available maneuvering space. With few incomplete rows on the screen, there is plenty of space to anticipate and maneuver. With a full screen of incomplete rows, the player's speed and reaction time must increase exponentially, while maneuverability decreases.

This not only gives you information, but it communicates to him that you are not a tentative frightened victim-in-waiting. You are an animal of nature, fully endowed with hearing, sight, intellect, and dangerous defenses. You are not easy prey, so don't act like you are.

Personal Space

People who have difficulty with the idea of self-defense are often those who have difficulty with or have been carefully trained out of the idea of their own right to personal space. They may roar into action when someone else is endangered but have extreme difficulty responding when they themselves are the target of hostile behavior. The following exercise tests and demonstrates personal boundaries.

At a table and in casual relaxed circumstances (and very carefully!):

1. Push a glass of water, mug of beer, towards the table edge and "*nage*'s" lap.

2. Observe the point at which *nage* takes action to prevent a spill.

   How long and how far does *nage* continue to ponder or rationalize intentions. For example, *"What in his background would make him act in this manner?"*

   "Why would she being doing this? She's really A Very Nice Person."

   Nage must simply deal with the situation before it lands in a lap. The point at which the unwitting subject does deal is a good rough guide to the limit of personal space, useful for a beginning point of awareness and assumptions.

Light-Bubble

1. Imagine you are standing in a bubble of light, with the consistency of thick honey or Neoprene, which extends at least to the palms of your extended hands, above your head and just below your feet, in front, to the sides and in back.

2. Drop arms to sides and with a partner approaching and backing away, practice maintaining the same distance throughout class time and throughout the day.

Variation

- On The Street, minimum size of your bubble of awareness should be four seconds in front of you, increasing and elongating forward with increasing speed. If you can't see four seconds of travel ahead, say in an area of curves and hills, you are going too fast. At 60 miles per hour your bubble of awareness should be as far ahead as you can see.

- Practice counting and timing your speed, spacing, and awareness of others, planning ahead for problems rather than cutting in and out at the last minute. And see Appendix B.

Ma-ai Jo

With a partner, place a *jo* between you. At the beginning stages, place it just above the belt; with practice, place it below the belt.

1. Take turns backing up, moving forward, and stepping side to side, moving in a circle maintaining distance so that the *jo* does not fall to the ground.

   (Additional practice is gained by not letting the *jo* attack your toes).

2. Move slowly at first increasing speed only with success at keeping the *jo* in its position.

The Ma-ai of Time

Time is God's way of keeping everything from happening at once.

— Anon.

Time is an essential of Aikido and of life and yet consider common comments about violence.

"It came out of the blue!"
"There was absolutely no warning!"
"Must have just snapped!"

This is rarely true, whether the attack is by natural disaster, serial killers, the IRS, or a *dojo* partner.

Part of blending is matching the speed — timing — of an attack with awareness of its beginning. No attack ever began at point of impact. Nevertheless, we often do techniques as if the attack had no beginning, no past, and no course of travel. Observe this in the following exercise.

Timing Belt

With *uke* sitting in *seiza* and armed with a *gi* belt doubled in his right hand,

1. *Nage* walks or jogs past *uke*'s left side.
2. *Uke* whips the belt from right to left, parallel to mat, attempting to catch *nage*'s ankles while *nage* attempts to hop over the moving belt.

   Even experienced students will often wait until they see the belt at their ankles. By then it is too late. The attack begins when *uke* begins to move and possibly sooner. The *nage* who hops at that point avoids the belt. On the other hand, students often run through this exercise repeatedly without understanding why they continue to get smacked. Musicians may understand it as the downbeat of the conductor's baton. Others perhaps, do not.

The defense against the overhead strike of *shomen-uchi* is *ikkyo-undo* in which *nage* swings arms up to meet and blend with the incoming strike. We often wait until the strike arrives, then try to rely on lightning reflexes and power despite little room to maneuver. Like the belt strike, *shomen-uchi* does not begin with the strike and it certainly does not begin at impact. It begins with the intent and certainly no later than the upward motion. The beginning of effective defense is not at the impact, but at its birth and development; "Doing the exercise" of *ikkyo-undo* as *uke*'s arms rise allows blending before the downward motion can even begin.

Time Blending

1. *Uke* strike *shomen-uchi*.
2. *Nage* wait to respond until strike is on the way down.
3. Observe ease or difficulty of performing technique.

Variation

1. *Uke* swing arm repeatedly up overhead as if to strike *shomen-uchi*. Do not strike; just drop arm and repeat. *Nage* swing arms up (*ikkyo-undo*) matching *uke*'s speed and direction.

2. *Uke* strike with a complete *shomen-uchi*. *Nage* swing arms up (*ikkyo-undo*) matching *uke*'s speed, direction. Complete the motion with a technique.

3. Compare the ease of motion and control between the two approaches.

The Ma-ai of Balance

Balance, center, and body mechanics effect *ma-ai* in ways completely unrelated to actual distance. By controlling center it is possible to put *uke* at an angle where he cannot strike. *Uke* can see *nage*, close by, within easy reach, but any attempt at *atemi* destroys balance causes *uke* to throw himself. To demonstrate this principle:

1. Stand with your back to the wall.
2. Attempt to touch your toes.

   You *can* touch your toes [3] while falling forward, but do you really *want* to?

A few degrees of rotation also makes a big difference in vulnerability. For example, *tekubi-kosa-undo* can be applied in many ways to many grabs. Rotating the wrist while leading *uke*'s arm inward will cause the shoulder to drop. *Uke* may not realize it yet, but he's now off balance while his own arm and shoulder blocks his other arm and shields you. Likewise, rotating the wrist which rotates the arm and shoulder may cause the hip to shift as well so that *uke* is no longer over Center and is off-balance.

As in *shiho-nage*, experiment with degrees of wrist rotation, and degrees of inward lead, also known as *irimi*. "Not being there" commonly appears as *tenkan*.

---

3. . . . if that's something you can do normally, of course. Note the parallel between this and lack of flexibility. A stiff *uke* with extremely tight hamstrings who can't decrease hip angle and maintain balance by shifting weight backward also throws himself if his hand is led downward.

Tenkan

Seeing me before him, the enemy attacks,
But by that time I am already standing safely behind him.

— Morihei Ueshiba

Tenkan is a means of rearranging yourself in space.[4] So is almost anything else, but *tenkan*, a simple turn, simultaneously removes you from immediate danger zone and makes you the center of a rotating circle.

In left *hanmi* (L foot and L hand forward)

1. *Nage* extends L hand, palm down.
2. *Uke* enfolds *nage*'s L wrist with the R hand.

   Grasp gently at first to provide a pivot point and a point of reference rather than an exercise in dealing with a "death grip."
3. *Nage* curls fingers back towards palm, then steps or slides forward with LF foot, bringing RF around to rear, pivoting hips 180 degrees to end approximately shoulder to shoulder with *uke* or slightly behind. Draw the L F back as necessary.

   L F is still forward and R F back (still in L *hanmi*); lead is forward.

Power Test Tenkan

In *tenkan* techniques beginners commonly back up instead of moving forward. A *nage* extending *ki* and moving forward is the center of the circle. *Uke*, rotating around the outside, is at a disadvantage.

Moving backward makes *uke* the center of the circle and puts *nage*, rotating around *uke*, at the disadvantage. The following exercise shows the difference. *Uke* grabbing *nage*'s wrist and with eyes closed,

1. *Nage* performs an incorrect *tenkan*, by pointedly backing up.[5]
2. *Nage* performs a correct *tenkan*, motion and lead correctly forward.
3. *Uke* compare. Which one is more compelling?

Floating-Foot Tenkan

When doing a *tenkan*, *nage* commonly slides forward with the same-side (forward) foot, then turns. With a resistant *uke*, there may be collision. Instead of sliding directly forward, *nage* can,

1. Lift the front foot, then
2. Enter and turn 180 degrees (as for standard *tenkan*).

---

4. For more *tenkan* exercises (Balloon Tenkan, Weighted Tenkan, Rollerblade or Bicycle Tenkan, and Verbal Tenkan) see Shifflett (1997).
5. This is a highly instructive exercise but remarkably difficult to demonstrate — everyone who sees you doing it invariably bounds across the mat to inform you that "you are backing up!"

> The momentary balancing on one foot makes *nage*, like a balloon, sensitive to the slightest force or energy from *uke*. *Nage* naturally goes around and collision is avoided.

Starting and ending attacks, techniques, and rolls on one foot develops balance, timing, and a greater awareness of the energy involved[6].

Dead Arm Tenkan

The flip side of a floating foot is a floating arm. Sensei Jim Baker (Aikikai) describes the relaxation of the arm in these terms: "Let the forward arm die."

Water Tenkan

It is often difficult for a student to realize when he is backing up, when he has left his circle, when the energy has changed from rotational to linear. Practicing small, tight turns in water encourages circular motion as linear motions are resisted by the water[7].

Tiny Tenkan

We often tend towards the large, swooping, *tenkan* during warm-up exercises. Practice small, quick, turns as well.

The late Don Lyons (Iwama style) used the image of attempting to "stab yourself in the stomach" with your own hand. Turn *tenkan* just before the hand can connect.

Snowboard Tenkan

There is nothing like being totally locked onto a single piece of board, tearing down a mountain to realize the importance of shifting vertical posture around a well-balanced center. I credit the lessons of my many tenkans for having survived the adventure.

— Michael Speece, Ki Society

---

6. It also protects against the dreaded "Hakama Toe," toes tangled in the folds of the skirt worn by advanced students.
7. For other advantages of "Poolkido" and practicing in water see page 13 and page 141.

Irimi

In Tom Clancy's thriller, *Hunt for Red October*, a Soviet submarine fires a torpedo to destroy the *Red October* before its officers can defect. To the shock of the crew, the captain's apparently suicidal response is to order full speed directly towards the oncoming torpedo — which impacts harmlessly against the hull. When the expected distance between source and target was abruptly closed, the torpedo had no time to arm itself. A nautical *irimi*.

In Aikido, certain *irimi* movements by *nage* appear to be nothing more than a direct frontal clash with *uke*. They are in fact, a redirecting of energy in a way that *uke* did not intend or expect by:

- Pre-empting an attack before *uke*'s full energy can be developed,
- Following motion in which *uke* is pulling in, rather than extending out.
- Changing (redirecting) the motion or direction of the attack.

Pre-empting and redirecting energy and motion is especially clear in *shomen-uchi irimi*. In this technique,

1. *Uke* attacks with an overhead strike. *Nage* appears to simply block the incoming strike — no blending may be apparent at all.
2. *Uke* then appears to bounce violently off of his intended target, for no apparent reason, and is thrown.

It appears to be a full frontal clash of force against force. It is not. In part, *nage* preempts *uke*'s attack before the strike can develop its full potential[8] and the energy that is left is dealt with off-line and redirected.

Following the motion, energy or direction of attack will be familiar to those who have ever picked blackberries or other forms of roses armed with vicious thorns. If you pull directly away from the fierce, recurved thorns you will be ripped and torn. The best technique is *irimi*, entering and following the direction of the thorns just long enough to deflect, *redirect*, and disengage them.

---

8. See "Shomen-Uchi Ikkyo Irimi" on page 207.
   Irimi is nicely described in TOT p. 18 and 60.

Clotheslining and Tripping

If you ever rode your bicycle through backyards filled with laundry and caught a clothesline across throat or chest while the bottom half of your body kept on moving, you know what clotheslining is. Kokyu-nage Basic and its variations are "clotheslining" techniques.

In "tripping" techniques, the body hurtles forward while the legs remain behind. Examples are zempo-nage, ikkyo-irimi and any of their variations.

— George Simcox, Ki Society

Tenkan and *irimi* address the *horizontal* plane of movement. *Clotheslining* and *tripping* address the *vertical* plane of movement. While these terms or concepts do not appear to have official names in any style they are useful for categorizing throws and pre-empting common problems.

To new eyes, it appears obvious that the best way to get *uke* down to the mat is to push *uke* down, but this isn't the case. Understanding the underlying rationale helps to get the beginner past this point.

"Clotheslining" techniques involve leading *up*, allowing *space* and *time* for *uke's* hips and legs to move forward of his torso. The best way to get *uke* down is not to push down, but to *lead uke* down then *lead up*. In Kokyu-Nage Basic, the final motion is *up;* as *uke* can't stay there, the "clothesline" that he trips on is thin air. In *tenchi-nage*, shown here, the clothesline is more readily visible: it is *nage's* arm which *uke* has just run into.

In either technique, *nage's* hand may follow *uke* to the mat, but it is a *follow* not a *force*. Attempting to force *uke down* neutralizes and defeats the spacial mechanics of *up* that these techniques are based on.

Another common mistake is trying to throw *uke* too soon, not allowing sufficient *time* for *uke*'s hips to pass his shoulders. This defeats the time mechanics of the throw, by actually helping uke regain balance and control.

"Tripping techniques" require leading *down*, moving *uke*'s upper body forward with legs and hips behind.

"Insufficient down" (often due to trying to throw *out*) defeats the mechanics of this particular technique. The advice to "drop *uke*'s hand down *through* the mat" as in *irimi* and *zempo-nage* reflects this issue.

Katame-Waza

Our sensei says that it's all very nice to cause pain, but not very useful if your attacker says "OWW!" and then bashes you because you hurt him which he could do because you were busy causing pain instead of controlling their center.

— Dex Sinister, Aikikai

Katame-Waza ("Immobilizations") are commonly referred to as wrist-locks. These are:

- *Ikkyo* ("first-teaching"),

- *Nikyo* ("second-teaching"),

- *Sankyo* ("third-teaching"),

- *Yonkyo* ("fourth-teaching"), and

- Gokyo ("fifth-teaching").

Wristlocks are rarely an end in themselves; they are the first or intermediate step to a throw ("projection") such as *zempo-nage*, or a final pin (a modified wristlock). Wrist-locks can be exquisitely painful, especially to new students with tight inflexible wrists. Pain, however, is not the ultimate goal. All locks aim to control the shoulder, by way of the fingers, hand, wrist, and elbow joints. The lock may produce control and immobilization, sometimes via an implied threat of pain or discomfort — but the ultimate goal is control of *uke*'s center. Once that control is obtained, *nage* proceeds with a throw or a pin. In practice, the wrist-lock is applied until *uke* moves as intended or taps out.

Consider studying wristlocks in series[9] to clarify the relationships between them. *Ikkyo* becomes *nikyo* becomes *sankyo* becomes *yonkyo* becomes *ikkyo* and so on. Combine with *shiho-nage* and *kote-gaeishi* to observe the patterns of entry, setup and application. Also consider practicing wristlocks in *seiza* during the initial presentation. This isolates muscles, bones, and balance. It also focuses the student on the mechanics of the wristlock and away from the notion that "success" means Putting Uke On The Mat — *uke* is already there. For beginners, differentiating the name or starting motions of one technique from another is tough enough without added inputs of technique and foot position.

This approach can be a big relief for beginners. I have seen advanced students spend years in confusion because they were afraid to ask at first, later afraid to admit that they were still hazy on the mechanics and application.

A common problem is poor understanding of physiology. All martial arts books seem to agree that "a thorough understanding of the underlying anatomy is critical to effectiveness" but they usually stop there and solid information has been rare. Physiologist and Aikidoist Greg Olson (Aikikai) actually looked and studied the internal anatomy of shoulders, arms, and wrists.

---

9. See "The Cycle of Katame-Waza (Wrist Locks)" on page 184.

On Osae-Waza and Katame-Waza

— by Dr. Greg Olson[10]

Osae Waza ("Securing/Holding Technique") is a classification of Aikido with the purpose of immobilizing *uke* with "securing" or "joint-locking" techniques[11]. Although these techniques manipulate *uke*'s skeletal system and/or painfully stimulate the tissues of the arm, the primary purpose is to safely secure and exert control. These techniques are divided into five primary classifications: *Ikkyo*, Nikyo, *Sankyo, Yonkyo*, and *Gokyo*. Key points in all techniques are:

1. Controlling *uke* through balance (taking the center).
2. Grasping the elbow itself before and during the pin.
3. Rotation of *uke*'s arm.

Common mistakes in all techniques are:

1. Failure to unbalance *uke*. Trying to "throw" *uke* quickly, rather than control of *uke*'s balance or center is always a temptation.
2. Taking *uke*'s arm to the mat before *uke*'s balance is taken or torso is in place on the mat.
3. Grasping the arm above the elbow before and during the final pinning phase.
4. Trying to secure the *uke* with muscular strength rather than through technique.
5. Not having the knees next to *uke*'s arm and body.
6. Not having the feet in the "toes up position" (*kiza*).

Ikkyo

The ikkyo pin is done with several variations. In one, a mechanical method, *uke* is pinned by direct pressure on the elbow joint itself. The elbow and, therefore, arm and body are pinned to the mat by mechanically holding the elbow in the extended position and pinning it to the mat with the weight of the *tori*'s upper torso.

Another method stimulates the ulnar nerve on the medial side of the arm. The ulnar nerve[12], within its connective tissue, crosses over the humerus at a location medial to the epicondyle of the humerus, at a point where it is relatively unprotected by muscle, tendons, or ligaments. Pressure applied with a back and forth motion of *tori*'s knuckle pinches, rolls then releases the ulnar nerve.

---

10. Dr. Olson's articles on Aikido wristlocks are listed in Chapter 10. For article reprints and related materials, contact Dr. Olson at golson@montana.edu.

11. Note terminology of *tori* = *nage*. "Securing" techniques are *osae waza;* "joint locking techniques" are *kansetsu* waza. *Omote* pertains to the "front" version of the technique, *ura* to the "rear" version.

    In medical terminology, *medial* pertains to the "middle" and *distal* to the "far" (as in "distant") end of a structure. As you look at the back of your own hand, *hyper-extended* (as in *sankyo*) refers to a position with the wrist bent towards you, nails up. *Flexed* refers to a position with the wrist bent away from you, nails down.

12. Although slightly distal (towards the forearm) to this location, the ulnar nerve is the same nerve that gets your attention when you hit your "funny bone" (an ancient pun on the "humerus" bone of the forearm).

Nikyo

It is often said that the purpose of the techniques is not to cause pain; nonetheless, pain is produced either by stretching of the tendons and muscular tissue of the forearm or by compression of several of the bones of the wrist. If *uke* does not have stretched musculature and related tissue, pain may come from a stretching of muscular tissue. If *uke* is an accomplished practitioner of Aikido then pain may be from compression of the periosteum[13] of two bones in the wrist.

While applying this technique, *tori* must grasp the hand of *uke* completely so that there is no space between tori's palm and the back of *uke*'s hand and **tori**'s thumb must be pressed firmly against the second knuckle of *uke*'s thumb.

Common mistakes are:

1. Not grasping the hand of *uke* completely.

2. Grasping with the thumb and index finger rather than thumb and little finger.

Sankyo

Compared with other wristlocks, *sankyo* is less focused on compressing nerves or stretching any one particular muscle. Sankyo has a more diffuse and generalized effect on *uke*'s anatomy. Pain is caused by the stretching and manipulation of the entire mass of extensor muscles at their origins [near the elbow].

Tori grasps *uke*'s hand in such a way that *uke's* arm forms an arc controlling *uke*'s balance. Grasping *uke*'s fingers adds a particular ease in accomplishing the technique. *Uke*'s wrist and fingers should be hyper-extended (bent back) rather than flexed (bent forward). Once the structure of the *sankyo* form is understood the technique can be accomplished with very minimal effort.

Yonkyo

Yonkyo is a particularly difficult but effective securing technique with several different variations. The *omote* ("front") and *ura* ("rear") variants vary in their effect on the anatomy of the arm.

Yonkyo Omote. In the *omote* version of *yonkyo*, *tori* unbalances *uke* to the front. Grasp *uke*'s wrist using your thumb and little finger. Medium back and forth pressure to the tendons of the *uke*'s forearm with the large knuckle of the index finger produces intense wrist pain. Turning *tenkan* to add energy creates even more pain and causes compliance in *uke*. Common mistakes are:

1. Not grasping *uke*'s wrist using the thumb and little finger and thereby not allowing for the correct application of pressure with *tori*'s index finger knuckle.

2. Trying to apply too much pressure and therefore not being able to manipulate the tendons of the forearm.

Yonkyo Ura. In the *ura* variation[14] of *yonkyo*, *tori* unbalances *uke* by stepping off-line towards the rear, then applies pressure to the periosteum of the radial bone of *uke*'s forearm. Using the knuckle of the index finger as a fulcrum while turning *tenkan* to create energy produces intense pain in *uke's* forearm.

---

13. Human bones are covered with a nerve-rich layer of tissue, the *periosteum*, or tissue "around the bone" which produces "exquisite pain" when manipulated in ways that the body was not designed to handle.

14. The *ura* ("rear") version of *yonkyo* is slightly different from the *omote* versions. In *ikkyo*, *nikyo*, *sankyo* techniques, anatomical considerations are the same for both *omote* and *ura* versions.

Exact grasping technique is very important to apply the correct pressure and have the technique unfold with the correct form. Energy for this technique is derived directly from the *tenkan* and *tentai*[15] turning techniques.

Common mistakes include:

1. Not grasping with thumb and little finger.

2. Tying to force your knuckle into the radial bone of the *uke* rather than fully grasping the wrist and then, applying knuckle pressure to the radial bone (via the hips) with the *tentai* and *tenkan* turn.

---

15. *Tentai* pertains to "turning" in place rather than by changing position as in *tenkan*.

The Cycle of Katame-Waza (Wrist Locks)

The four basic *katame-waza*[16] form a cycle of techniques. The choice of technique is based, as always, on the energy that *uke* offers. Every technique can be countered, but the motion necessary to do so sets *uke* up for the next lock in the series. Practice the complete series slowly, as an exercise in placement, transition, and ultimately, effectiveness. Note that the cycle can go in either direction.

Ikkyo	Uses a 90-degree wrist bend and is applied to *uke*'s relatively straight arm. Using the bent wrist as a crank, *nage* rotates arm and shoulder forward to the mat. *Uke* may counter by bending the arm and leading back with elbow, setting up for *nikyo*.
Nikyo	Uses the N or Z bend in the arm that *uke* used to counter *ikkyo*. Works via compression and rotation of the wrist joint; hand is held in place or rotated up while elbow is rotated down or dropped. *Uke* may counter by raising the elbow or by straightening the wrist, setting up for *sankyo*.
Sankyo	If *uke* attempts to reverse the wrist-out *nikyo* bend, *nage* can ease it into a palm-out bend (seizing knife-edge, or *tegatana*[a] of same-side hand). As *uke* raises the elbow, *nage* helps it to come up to 90 degrees with the forearm, rotating the vertical plane of the forearm towards the body. Rotation coupled with upward motion should send *uke* up on toes. *Uke* may counter by dropping the shoulder forward and turning away from *uke*, setting up for *yonkyo*.
Yonkyo	Combines downward rotation of the forearm and elbow with compression of the median nerve (on thumb side of forearm) or periosteum. Ideally, the palm-side knuckle of *nage*'s forefinger is in contact with sensitive tissue; *uke*'s attempt to turn away presses bone and nerve into the side of *nage*'s joint. *Uke* may counter by bending wrist (wrist-out) in attempt to shorten the forearm muscles and protect nerve or bone, setting up for *ikkyo*. And the cycle repeats . . . .

a. Knife-edge of the hand.

16. *Gokyo* is the "fifth technique" but there is no reasonable way to counter it that will return you to *ikkyo*. Some styles include a *ryokyo*. A correspondent who begs to remain nameless claims that it is merely an arm bar and that elevation to "Sixth Technique" status is like the amplifier that goes up to 11 in Rob Reiner's rock-band spoof, *This is Spinal Tap*. "What does 11 get you?" "Well it's one louder, isn't it?"

Ikkyo

ADS: Immobilization #1 ("First Teaching") p. 166; TOT: Ikkajo, pp. 82-83.

I rather like ikkyo. As uke, if I get tired I can just stay down and take a nap.

— *George Simcox, Ki Society*

Ikkyo is the first of the wrist locks. It is usually applied to a straight arm and elbow in combination with a 90-degree bend of the wrist. To differentiate from other techniques, you may wish to remember it as:

Ikkyo is a relatively painless but effective technique which controls the shoulder (hence disrupting *uke*'s balance) by rolling it forward via fingers, wrist, and elbow. If *uke* is holding your left hand with his right, to apply *ikkyo*:

Technique

1. As *uke* reaches for your left shoulder with his right hand, brush down on *uke*'s attacking hand with your right hand so that your fingers wrap over the knife edge of *uke*'s hand. Your thumb is aligned with *uke*'s thumb and index finger.

2. Step to the rear with LF.
3. Draw back the forward foot.
4. Rotating *uke*'s wrist, thumb down and to a 90-degree bend, lead *uke*'s arm up and over his L shoulder in a circular path. Reinforce this circular motion with your other hand, coming up under *uke's* elbow or upper arm and *rolling* (not pushing) the arm over while . . .
5. Stepping / skipping / sliding straight forward with outside (R) leg.
6. Rotate your hips so they are square and forward, dropping *uke* straight down to your arm's length, his shoulder lower than his hand.
7. Moving forward as necessary with your outside leg, bring *uke* down to the mat.

Pin

1. Extend *uke*'s arm at 90 degrees or more to his trunk. *Nage* faces in the same direction as *uke* with knee in armpit and *uke*'s other knee firmly secured against uke's arm. *Nage*'s inside hand covers *uke*'s elbow, outside hand grasps *uke*'s wrist. Wrist is bent at 90 degrees or more.

2. With *uke*'s fingers form a triangle with fingers of *nage*'s other hand, directing them to a point at the tip of the triangle and about 6 inches below the mat. Release pressure immediately when *uke* slaps (taps out).

Variation:

• With inside knee in *uke*'s armpit, *uke*'s arm secured against your knees, experiment with holding down the elbow only.

• Try the "Gi Hold-down" in which *nage* places a knee on *uke*'s *gi* in armpit to assist in pinning shoulder to the mat. This is sometimes presented as the "Power of *Ki* Hold-down" but that is a spelling error.

The 90-degree wrist bend is an important part of the technique especially in response to a grab, and most especially if the attacker is much bigger and stronger[17]. See why with the OK Test.

The OK Test

1. *Nage* touch thumb and forefinger in a circle. Try to hold the two fingers together while *uke* attempts to pull them apart.

2. *Nage* bend the wrist at 90 degrees. *Uke* compare the forces necessary to pull the fingers apart. *Nage* compare the amount of effort required to keep them together.

Finger strength is extremely poor when the wrist is sharply bent. This anatomical point applies directly to *ikkyo*[18] as follows.

The Ikkyo Elbow Pivot

1. *Uke* grab *nage*'s wrist.

2. *Nage*, with Unbendable Arm and leaving hand in place, pivot elbow down, hand up, catching *uke*'s wrist in the V of thumb and forefinger.

3. Nage notice *uke*'s wrist bend. Touch *uke*'s hand with your other hand and compare the degree of strength or effort required to remove the hand; by *uke* to keep it there.

4. Compare the effort required by *nage* to bend *uke*'s wrist at the hand *without* dropping the elbow or the ease or difficulty of removing *uke*'s hand.

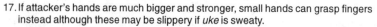

17. If attacker's hands are much bigger and stronger, small hands can grasp fingers instead although these may be slippery if *uke* is sweaty.
18. It also applies to daily life. Opening a jar? Attempting to do so with wrist bent and fingers extended is an extremely weak position and can strain the hand. Drop wrist, a far stronger position.

Back and Forth

Practice *ikkyo* (*irimi*) as a back and forth exercise to practice position and lead.

1. *Partner 1* start by attacking with RH to Partner 2's left shoulder.
2. Partner 2 moves into *ikkyo irimi*, bending Partner 1 down to the mat, but before the throw,
3. Partner 1 rises, turning Partner 2 and applying ikkyo, bending Partner 2 down to the mat, but before the throw . . . .
4. And the cycle repeats.

Errors and Counters

Experiment with all of these, slowly. Compare to results obtained with good form.

In technique:

- Stepping forward with inside leg; *uke* may be able to grab it.
- Failure to drop *uke* far enough down. Think of first dropping him directly down *through* the mat and only then coming up to the proper position.
- Dropping *uke* down but with shoulder higher than hand. *Uke* can easily rise and turn the tables on *nage* (an action known as "conversion").
- Not maintaining your Center / One-Point; allowing *uke* to regain Center.

In pin:

- Floating hips," that is, leaning forward over *uke*'s arm. A wiley and flexible *uke* — or a testing instructor — may unbalance and throw *nage* forward.
- Allowing *uke* to regain control of elbow.

Although *nikyo*, *sankyo*, *yonkyo*, and *gokyo* are techniques in their own right, they are often thought of as the "second," "third," or "fourth" resort if *ikkyo* fails. *Uke*'s counter provides *nage* with the energy to flow into the next.

For example, if *uke* realizes that *nage* is moving into the basic *ikkyo irimi* described here, he might counter by tensing and blocking the forward movement of his arm. *Nage*'s counter to *uke*'s counter is to flow immediately into *ikkyo tenkan*[19] which uses the new force and energy being offered by *uke*.

---

19. This technique is one of several popularly known as "Airplane." See page 209.

Nikyo

ADS: Immobilization #2 ("Second-Teaching"), pp. 174-177; TOT: Nikajo, pp. 96-97.

Nikyo is the "Second Technique." *Uke* can counter by moving into *nage* and bending the elbow. Since the wrist is already bent in, this counter produces the **N**-shape ideal for *Nikyo*. To differentiate this lock from the others, remember:

Nikyo is a painful rotation and pressure on wrist bones and nerves. It can be done in numerous ways, but key is relative motion of hand rotating up and forearm rotating down with compression of wrist and/or arm bones.Two versions of *nikyo* are presented here. For the configuration and an idea of what it should feel like for *uke,* see "Nikyo-Undo" on page 110. Apply the lock carefully, slowly, and release *immediately* upon hearing *uke*'s slap.

Nikyo 1

This is the first version of *nikyo* usually taught to beginners. The hand-on-chest position aids the beginner in keeping the attacking hand absolutely still, or perhaps "steel." As Chuck Gordon explains it, "the one hand is *steel*, the other is a *feather*." Many of us spend years allowing *uke*'s hand to rotate down with the elbow and wondering why the lock doesn't work. Because it isn't locked, that's why. For effective *nikyo*, watch for this tendency and eliminate it.

1. Place *uke*'s RH hand in the hollow of your L shoulder, *uke*'s fingers turned towards your armpit and hand (*tegatana*) vertical. *Uke*'s elbow should be bent into the "N" position.

2. Maintaining the bent-wrist *nikyo* position, move your other arm over *uke*'s arm until your fingers can pass over *uke*'s. This puts your elbow into position for moving downward onto *uke*'s arm.

3. Facing *uke* directly and imagining that the index finger of the holding hand is a sword, with a soft bow, slice *uke* from head to toe, down centerline of the body.

Variations

Consider the geologist's view of relative motion. In designating movement along fault blocks of an earthquake, it doesn't matter if the left block went up and the right block stayed still, or if the right block went down and the left block stayed still. The relationships along the fault line (note the arrows) are the same and will be marked with the same symbols.

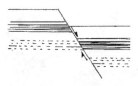

In *nikyo*, the hand may remain still while forearm rotates *down*, or hand may rotate *up* if the forearm remains still. Either way, relative relationships must be present

Nikyo 2

Nage applies *nikyo* to *uke*'s same-side grab (LH grabbed by *uke*'s RH). *As nage,*

1. Rest your RH atop *uke*'s hand to keep it in place.
2. Rotate your left wrist around to top of *uke*'s wrist, emphasizing the N or Z configuration in *uke*'s arm (wrist and elbow bent).
3. Cut down with palm of hand, imagining that the middle finger of your holding hand is a sword, slicing *uke* from head to toe, straight down the centerline of the body.

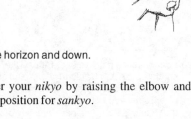

For the cut, nage must *really* cut. Instead of squooshing *uke*'s wrist (as happens when *nage* focuses on "causing pain"),

1. Mentally raise sword hand high, then
2. Slice down, cutting the sky in two, to the horizon and down.

Didn't make it that far? *Uke* may counter your *nikyo* by raising the elbow and rolling the shoulder forward — the perfect position for *sankyo.*

Sankyo

ADS: Immobilization #3 (""Third-Teaching"), pp. 187-191; TOT: Sankajo, pp. 108-109.

Sankyo is the "third" wrist lock. To differentiate it from others, remember:

Sankyo and oyknaZ

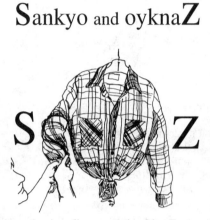

Sankyo locks the joints of wrist, elbow, and shoulder. For maximum effectiveness all must be stretched to their limit. Several motions are involved in taking up slack, all of which add another small part to the whole

As *uke* seizes your hand (same-side or cross):.

1. Touch lightly to keep the hand in place.
2. Enter, passing under his arm and rotating it.

    If you are applying *sankyo* on the left side (from your point of view) you will be moving around and ducking under *uke*'s right arm in a counterclockwise direction. If you are applying *sankyo* on your right side (his left arm) you will be ducking under *uke*'s arm and turning so that you face in the same direction as *uke*. This rotates *uke*'s arm towards his body. For *uke*, it is the same motion of turning the hands inward as in "Ushiro-Tori Undo" on page 98[20]. See also "Swankyo" on page 71.

    Nage's upper hand controls *uke*'s wrist, thumb, and four fingers above the wrist, palm of the hand on *uke*'s knuckles. Keep slack out of *uke*'s wrist, elbow, and shoulder by applying torque with hands and hips. Point your own index finger at *uke*'s armpit.

---

20. For a practice partner, see "Closet Uke" on page 223. In a plaid shirt, the S or Z configuration can be clearly seen. But how is a Z of "Zankyo" different from the N of *nikyo*? *Nikyo*'s N is more horizontal, *sankyo*'s Z more vertical and primarily a direction of twist that you will see in the muscles and skin, as when you wring out a towel. Note that *S* and *Z* also designate direction of twist in vines in botany, of fibers in textile arts.

Nage's lower hand (outer hand) lightly holds *uke*'s fingers, keeping them slightly hyper-extended (bent back) below the forearm. Your hand applies torque on *uke*'s hand; the axis of rotation is *uke*'s middle finger.

3. Bring *uke* up on his toes.

   Any throw from *sankyo* should be done from this tip-toe position. Once *uke* is on his toes (and probably slapping)

4. Cut straight down.

   Traditionally, this is a sword cut. In more modern terms, imagine tapping home plate with your baseball bat. For either situation, the motion is to rotate the tip of the sword or the bat down, not the handle.

   The tiny interval between the beginning of the cut and the actual throw gives *uke* the momentary illusion of relief and he will come down to earth. Continue this motion by flowing into the actual throw.

   Taking *uke* up on his toes, then allowing him to come down, then starting the throw (three separate moves) is not nearly as effective as using *uke*'s natural downward movement in one continuous downward flowing motion.

Variations

- Because beginners often confuse the approaches to *shiho-nage* and *sankyo*, practice going back and forth between these two. Observe that *shiho-nage* rotates the arm *outward* away from the body; *sankyo* rotates the arm *inward* towards the body. If you are practicing with a shirt, you might consider a masking tape label showing direction of movement.

- *Sankyo* requires rotation and locking of all three joints so count them 1-2-3. Wrist, elbow (forearm), and shoulder.

- Practice moving smoothly from *up* to *down* into throw.

- Establish *nage*'s correct ending point; *nage* point at *uke*'s armpit with extended index finger.

If you do not have all the slack out, or if the fingers can flex, *uke* can spin in the direction of his free shoulder, seize your wrist, converting it to a *kote-gaeishi*, and you to a flying *uke*. *Uke* may also counter *sankyo* by pushing away and straightening the arm, but this is the position for *yonkyo*.

Yonkyo

ADS: Immobilization #4 ("Fourth-Teaching"), pp. 198-199; TOT: Yonkajo, pp. 118-119.

> *"Last night I tried to explain that the point of yonkyo is not to crush a nerve but to control uke's center through the elbow. The language I used obviously failed to get the point across. Can anyone translate this?"*
>
> *"Certainly. It's something like . . ."*
>
> *"No, that's not quite right, let me show you, OK? Now you do it . . . No, you're still just squashing the wrist, do it like this, OK? Come on, get up, it doesn't hurt that bad, try again . . . No, cut through the elbow like this . . tell you what, why don't you practice with Big Earl (the one with wrists thicker than a kindergartner and nerves, if he has any, buried so deep you'd probably strike oil before you found them)?"*
>
> *After about six years they start getting it right . . .*
>
> — Tim Griffiths, Iwama

Yonkyo is an extremely effective technique but also difficult to do correctly. It involves painful compression of the periosteum of the bone and of nerves in the arm (usually the radial nerve, but others are possible) whose location and accessibility may vary with individual and musculature. Further it is not as commonly practiced in formal class as other techniques, because when successful it is so exquisitely painful for *uke*. Do it well and *uke* may not be able to use his hands for several minutes and once recovered may be sore for several days. Hence *nage*s of kind heart are reluctant to impose on their friends, while persons of fiercer nature must remember that *nage* inevitably becomes *uke*.

To differentiate yonkyo from the other wristlocks, observe the upside-down **Y** position of thumb and forefinger.

The knuckle or joint used in *yonkyo* is the base of the index finger on the palm side. If you drive a car with a manual shift, you can practice the feeling of pressing with this joint by moving the gearshift with this point instead of pulling with the fingers.

Part of the difficulty of *yonkyo* is transition from the sankyo to *yonkyo* position. The transition of hand positions can be practiced at first without going into the actual nerve-numbing technique.

From *sankyo*, when *uke* counters by straightening the elbow/arm,

1. Leaving lower hand on *uke*'s hand, *nage* slides upper hand up to catch *uke's* forearm in V of thumb and index finger.

2. To apply *yonkyo*, rather than focusing on trying to compress nerves or purposely cause pain, focus on rotating *uke*'s elbow down to the mat. The feeling is like tapping a baseball bat on home plate.

3. Rotate from hips so that the motion presses the base joint of *nage*'s index finger into *uke*'s arm.

Yonkyo is effective when *uke* has a straight arm with fingers extending straight out. If you allow slack, *uke* may counter by bending the wrist, shortening the flexor muscles of the forearm, protecting the radial nerve. But the resulting straight arm with bent wrist is the ideal position for *nage* to counter the counter by returning to *ikkyo*. And the cycle repeats . . . .

Shiho-Nage

ADS: Immobilization #6 ("Four Direction Throw"), pp. 206-208; TOT: p. 71.

Shiho-nage is considered to be one of the most fundamental techniques in the Aikido repertoire.

It doesn't require the precise attention to anatomy seen in the previous wristlock techniques. However, one of the most common problems is maintaining the lead which tends to evaporate at the "top" of the technique. The other common problem is damaging *uke* by cranking the arm out to the side, usually because *nage* doesn't really know quite where *uke* really is. The following exercise addresses the problem of lead. See technique and a "position" exercise on page 204.

The Barbarella Lead

Alan Drysdale offers this exercise[21] "to teach *shihonage* in a way that does *not* require *uke* to choose between jumping over his own arm or getting a broken elbow.")

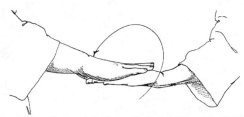

1. Stand in *ai-hanmi* (both *uke* and *nage* with their RF feet and RH forward). *Nage* offers RH palm up; *uke* lays hand palm down on *nage*'s hand.

   Uke's job is to maintain light palm-to-palm pressure and not let the hands separate. *Nage* will move through *shiho-nage*, pressing lightly against *uke*'s hand also, and moving so that the pressure is maintained. To start the movement,

2. *Nage* turns hand over, easing *uke*'s hand down and out into position for *shiho-nage*.

3. *Nage* steps in, maintaining pressure, leading hand up and over.

   This is where most people lose the contact, and resort to grabbing *uke*'s fingers.

---

21. Alan notes that he "stole it from Chuck Clark."

    For why it's named after "Barbarella," rent the movie. You might also think of it as Alan's *Rocky Horror Picture Show Shiho-Nage*. "The Palm-to-Palm thing reminded me of RiffRaff and Columbia getting ready to do "The Time Warp." — Eric Tilles

4. Nage leads *uke*'s hand out behind shoulder.. . .

5. . . . Then down back and towards the mat.

Kote-Gaeshi

ADS: Immobilization #7 ("Wrist-Bend"), pp. 216-218; TOT: pp. 144-145.

I remember getting certified for Two-person CPR and water rescue. In one lesson, we were learning how to deal with a drowning victim trying to pull you down. I kote-gaeshi-ed him. I passed.

— *David C. Pan*

*Grizzly crunching sound
Like tigers eating marrow
Oh! was that your wrist?*

— *Joel Zimba*

Kote-gaeshi ("wrist-bend") is usually considered a wristlock although it doesn't fit well into the basic foursome of *Katame-Waza*. It also differs from these in that it is an actual throw, rather than an intermediary technique on the way to the throw.

It is similar in another unfortunate respect. Because of dynamic forces leading up to the technique, a student can muddle through it for years without ever quite understanding what makes it work or why it went wrong. This is especially true if emphasis is on Making Uke Fall Down rather than on learning effective technique. Consider therefore, practicing the mechanics from *seiza* and eliminating the throw while learning what works, what doesn't, and why.

Kote-Gaeshi 1

1. Holding *uke*'s right wrist with your left hand....
2. Take up the slack.
3. Roll/rotate wrist and fingers, especially the index finger, toward the forearm.
4. Lead *uke*'s hand towards your center and down leaving room for him to fall.

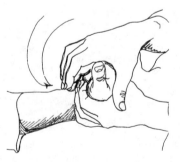

Variations

This version of *kote-gaeshi* is a natural for an uppercut punch or any other situation where the wrist is already bent. By removing slack, and controlling *uke*'s index finger, *kote-gaeshi* becomes a one-finger throw. This is because of two muscles controlling the index finger (the extensor digitorum and extensor indicis) and associated tendons.

The longer extensor digitorum) begins above the elbow and ends at the tip of the index finger. Hence it crosses four joints: the elbow, the wrist, the knuckle of the hand, and the two joints of the index finger.

Kote-gaeshi 1 isn't just a matter of curling "the fingers" but of curling the index finger specifically. The outer three fingers share flexor tendons (which are necessarily relatively loose and floppy). The index finger has its own dedicated tendon. Not only is this tighter then the others, but the more joints it must flex over, the tighter it becomes.

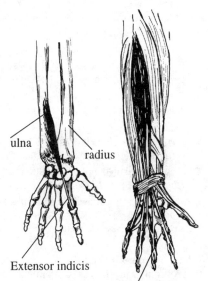

ulna

radius

Extensor indicis

Extensor digitorum

To feel the difference,

1. Bend your wrist to 90 degrees or as sharply as you can. Notice the natural position of your fingers: index finger more extended, last three digits more relaxed. Try touching your palm with each finger in turn. Which is easiest? Which more difficult?

2. Push the large knuckle of the index finger towards your forearm in the direction of your palm; see how far it goes without discomfort.

3. Repeat with the middle, ring and little fingers and compare; you will be able to bend them much farther with no discomfort.

4. Repeat the above curling one or two finger joints versus curling all three.

5. Repeat the above with wrist held straight (no bend).

To see the difference (what is actually happening inside),

1. Lay two pieces of tape on your arm in positions of the two tendons.

2. Repeat the exercises above.

3. Notice what happens when you bend your wrist, the knuckles. What happens when you add twist?

Most beginners see *kote-gaeshi* and interpret it as wrenching the elbow out to the side in an attempt to haul *uke* off his feet. It seems logical that this would be most effective. In fact, it's dangerous to *uke* (you can snap the elbow, the ancient version of this technique). And, it is actually a less effective throw.

To compare "wrenching" versus "curling,"

With partners in *seiza*, *uke* with arm extended.

1. *Nage* slowly applies *kote-gaeshi* by curling up *uke*'s hand with attention to the index finger while bringing *uke*'s hand towards own Center or One-Point.
2. *Uke* observe and report the point at which he begins to feel discomfort and the point at which he begins to fall.
3. For the *uke* who refuses to acknowledge discomfort, *nage* may simply observe the point at which the shoulder begins to drop and *uke* begins to lose balance.
4. Repeat by slowly twisting *uke*'s elbow out to the side (the "common sense" *kote-gaeishi*). Observe the point at which the shoulder begins to drop and *uke* begins to lose balance.
5. Repeat both of the above while "giving the slack back" to *uke*; that is, *nage*'s arms are extended, *uke*'s arms are close in to the body.
6. Compare relative motion and effort required to unbalance *uke* in all cases. Compare with *Kote-Gaeshi* 2 and 3.

   To actually do the throw from *seiza* (making it a *suwari-waza* technique) *nage must move, pivoting on the knee opposite the kote-gaeshi to allow room to keep uke's arm extended and space for uke to fall.*

Generally you will find that properly done, proper application of *Kote-Gaeshi* involves only a few inches of lateral motion and little effort.

Finding the Wrist

Targeting the wrist and grabbing for it is far less reliable than targeting the entire arm. An arm, after all, is much larger and leads directly to wrist. Start the motion like an open-handed block, then allow the hand to soften and cup *uke*'s arm, sliding towards *uke*'s wrist. Uke's hand will stop nage's motion in exactly the proper position, much like a knot at the end of a rope. In pairs,

1. *Uke* attack with a slow *mune-tsuki punch.*
2. *Nage* turn *tenkan* and experiment with:
   a) Grabbing directly for *uke*'s wrist versus ("catch the wrist").
   b) Sliding arm down *uke*'s arm from upper arm to wrist. To be really sporting,
3. Repeat *with eyes closed* at different speeds.

Giving Back Slack

Rolling arm, wrist and hand back towards *uke* "gives back slack." With slack in the arm, wrist, and fingers, the throw won't work. Or, it will offer the opportunity of a reversal; that is, enable *uke* to flow into another technique such as Kokyu-Nage Basic to throw the now extended and off-balance *nage*.

Think of *kote-gaeshi* like going fishing. Rolling the wrist, hand, and fingers is like rolling up the reel on a fishing rod.

- You are weaker and *uke* stronger when you are reaching out to *uke*'s Center.
- *Uke* is weaker and you are stronger when you draw *uke* in to *your* Center.
- Do you go to the fish? Or do you bring the fish to you?
- Try both approaches. See which works better and why.

Hips and Legs

Landing the fish is made still more effective by adding hips and legs.

1. Imagine that *uke*'s hand is linked to your same-side forward foot.
2. As you curl wrist and fingers, bring them to your Center while sweeping your same-side foot and hip back; with them flow your arms and hands as if attached to the foot. You can practice this motion alone. With a partner, be sure to allow space for *uke* to fall safely and to protect your own toes.

   The "hand linked to foot" motion is the vertical version of the motion (horizontal) used to make a toy walk. (See "Standing, Stepping and Stance" on page 43.

Kote-Gaeshi 2

TOT: pp. 144-145.

This version of *kote-gaeshi*[22] is similar to Kote-Gaeshi 1, except that it is actually a wrist turnout. Instead of rolling up the index finger,

1. *Nage* curls *uke*'s little finger outward and towards the foot that is swooping back, leading *uke*'s straight but locked arm forward and down towards what is now the back foot.
2. Note again that arm is *extended*, not wrenched to the side.

---

22. Some of us in the Ki Society refer to this as the *August Kote-Gaeshi* because very sweaty hands can render the finger-curl of *Kote-Gaeshi 1* very slippery when hands are wet with sweat. A more secure grip is provided by *Kote-Gaeshi 2* and by *Kote-Gaeshi 3*.

Kote-Gaeshi 3

This version of *kote-gaeshi* is based on *tekubi-kosa undo*, the wrist-crossing exercise (see page 88).

As *uke* holds *nage*'s left hand with right hand,

1. *Nage* curl fingers, rotate and cross wrists,
2. Reach under *nage*'s hand to grasp *tegatana* of *nage*'s hand.
3. With other hand, make a "hand-sandwich," *uke*'s hand enclosed in yours.
4. Like cutting down with a sword, bring *uke*'s hand to your Center while stepping back, hand coordinated with foot as described in "Hips and Legs" above.

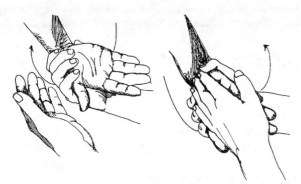

Aikido Throws (Nage-Waza)

One does not do Aikido to someone, one does Aikido with someone. [You can't do] Aikido to people as if it were a definable technique. Technique has form, form has function, the content of the function is Aikido. Not the Form or its Function but the "content" defines the art. Don't react but interact, don't do things to someone but with someone. Using the opponent's strength...

— Dennis Hooker, Aikido Schools of Ueshiba

The following basic throws are presented primarily as an overview to relate to the Hitori-Waza exercises presented in Chapter 4 and the training exercises presented here. Directions are generalized descriptions of Ki Society style (because that is what I am most familiar with) and in no way intended to serve as the definitive description of any technique. This set of techniques makes up the 5th *kyu* (first adult level) test at the Virginia Ki Society.

You, your instructor, or your individual style may emphasize other points, processes, or procedures. Adapt as necessary.

Kokyu-Nage

ADS: Projection #1 ("Breath Throw"), pp. 224-226.

Kokyu-nage comprises a family of "breath-throws," or "timing-throws." There are many different applications of this concept. but the underlying principle is that the attacker is thrown by manipulation of timing and balance rather than by a wrist lock or immobilization.

In *kokyu-nage* the attacker holds *nage*. *Nage* does not hold the attacker. In fact, *nage* does so little to the attacker that if the attacker were to let go — cease his attack — he could simply walk away without consequence. This issue must be clearly understood by the student. Otherwise beginners tend to devolve into a "This would never work because I could just..."

"Just what? Let go? Walk away? Yes. Exactly."

In several styles, Kokyu-Nage Basic (*katate kosa-tori kokyu-nage irimi tobikomi*) is the first technique at the beginning of every test during the course of your Aikido career. This "20-year technique" is a "breath-throw" applied to a "grab to the opposite hand." Note that pins are never used with *kokyu-nage* techniques.

Kokyu-nage techniques tend to be "clotheslining" throws, based on a lead *up*. Take care not to not rush the *up* motion. *Uke*, not nage, decides when to come up. Trying to force *uke* up when *uke* is still going down conflicts with (opposes) *uke*'s energy and counteracts the throw; forcing *uke* up before hips (center) have moved forward of Center actually helps *uke* to regain Center and balance.

Katate-Kosa-Tori Kokyu-Nage Irimi Tobikomi[23]

ADS: Projection #2 ("Cross-hand attack, dealt with by entering and jumping in") also known as "Kokyu-nage Basic," p. 230.

Uke:	L *hanmi*, grabs *nage*'s LH with his LH, reaching forward throughout technique.
Nage:	L *hanmi*, presents LH, little-finger-side down.
Mechanics:	*Nage* redirects incoming energy around then *up* (a place where *uke* cannot stay for long). Torso goes up, legs continue forward ("clotheslining," page 178).
Hitori waza:	*Ude-mawashi-undo, ude-furi undo.*

You may think of this technique as "The Hello Hug and A Tour of the Dojo. (*See our nice walls, nice mat? nice ceiling? Oops!)*

1. As *uke* grabs *nage*'s L wrist, *nage* leaves the seized hand in place and moves straight in (*irimi*) until resistance is felt in *uke*'s arm.

2. With RF step behind *uke*; RH thumb and index finger cradle base of *uke*'s head, a soft, effective but barely noticeable hug, not a jerk or torque to the chin or neck.

3. Leading and circling to the L (extending forward, never backing up) seized arm drops straight down, rises up, then follows *uke* downward with weight underside.

4. When *uke* attempts to stand up, *nage* "helps" by leading arm to a point on the ceiling while simultaneously dropping R arm with weight underside on *uke*'s R shoulder. *Uke*'s upper body follows the "up" while his legs continue forward, moving out from under him.

5. As *uke* falls, invert R hand, following *uke* down to the mat with the little finger.

---

23. Sensei Jim Baker (Aikikai) describes this as "The French Waiter Irimi-Nage." "Greetings Madame! Let me lead you to your table. What? No tip? You fall down!"

Variations

- *Placement. Nage* repeatedly step into position, leaving seized hand in place with Unbendable arm.

  a) Uke note whether *nage*, in the course of turning, pulls back.

  b) Work to eliminate any tugging and make the move as smooth as possible.

- *Attack and Lead. Uke* feel difference in lead between:

  a) Extending forward (correct) or

  b) Pulling sideways or back. *Uke* let *nage* know if the lead changes to anything but forward. A string or cord (rather than a wrist grab) makes direction of force visible. Note that a forward lead is easier if you are looking in the direction that you are going.

- *Up and Down.* "Down" to a 6-footer may be "up" to a 5-footer. Tall *nage* with short *uke* must check to see that lead has actually dropped down below *uke*'s center. If you and your partner are a "Mutt and Jeff":

  a) Standing shoulder to shoulder, where are your hands?

  b) How far down does the taller person have to reach to be "down" to the shorter one?

  c) How far down does the shorter one have to bring *uke* to have an effective "up"?

  d) What happens if the tall *nage* drops to his knees?

  e) Try technique from *suwari-waza.*

Shiho-Nage

ADS: Immobilization #6 ("Four Direction Throw"), pp. 206-208; TOT: p. 71.

Pivoting of the hips, complete redirection of attacking energy, and the unusual fact that it can be applied to almost any attack, from energetic to static, make *shiho-nage*[24] one of the most fundamental Aikido techniques.

Yokomen-Uchi Shiho-Nage Irimi

ADS: ("Diagonal-strike to head with entering four-direction throw") pp. 214-215; TOT: pp. 76-77.

Uke:	L *hanmi*, stepping into R *hanmi* striking *yokomen* with RH.
Nage:	L *hanmi*, pivoting back into R *hanmi* to avoid strike.
Mechanics:	*Nage* continues incoming motion and by changing direction, guides strike to *uke's* rear where *nage* is stable but *uke* is not.
Hitori waza:	*Ikkyo-undo, tenkan*

This throw is sometimes referred to as "London Bridge" as mnemonic for ducking under the arm during the turn.

1. *Nage* step back, arms rising into *ikkyo undo*, guiding striking arm down.
2. Touching *uke's* wrist with your RH and switch to R *hanmi*; rotate *uke's* wrist by turning your LH hand palm up. Step toward *uke* with RF crossing his body, turning it. (Remember, in *irimi*, *nage* turns *uke*. In *tenkan*, *nage* turns himself).
3. Lead *uke's* arm up and around, turning under your arm so that *uke's* hand and forearm are curled over *uke's* own shoulder, palm down.
4. *Nage* rotates hips to the R while dropping Center; end looking into *uke's* ear.
5. Drop *uke's* arm over *uke's* same-side shoulder, down *uke's* back and straight down to mat.

---

24. The name is usually interpreted as "four-direction throw," but in Japanese culture, *shiho* suggests "around the world in all directions" as we might refer to the "four corners of the earth" but mean "around the whole circle or globe of the earth." From *shiho* came *shippo*, a symbol composed of interlocking circles and representing expansiveness.

Variations

In practicing the above *shiho-nage* technique, you are continuing the lead. But first note where the lead should go.

Yokomen Only

1. *Uke* strike *yokomen* several times.
2. *Nage* observe the path of *uke*'s arm and hand.

This is the path that *nage* should follow.

Feeler Shiho-Nage

It is common (and dangerous) to force *uke*'s arm out to the side during the turn or the throw but this occurs when *nage* is unsure where *uke* actually is. Practice with eyes closed. Keeping in constant contact with *uke*, roll around *uke*'s arm and shoulder, feeling *nage*'s position constantly.

1. Repeat the Barbarella Lead exercise (page 194) with eyes closed.
2. Feel the lead, and feel the *contact* as you roll around *nage*'s arm and shoulder.

   This exercise removes dependence on eyes, activates sense of touch. You will know, because you *must* know, *exactly* where *uke* is.

Yokomen-Uchi Shiho-Nage Tenkan

ADS: ("Diagonal-strike to head, four-direction throw with turn"), pp. 214--215; TOT: p. 75.

Uke:	L *hanmi*, stepping into R *hanmi* and striking *yokomen* with RH.
Nage:	L *hanmi*, pivoting back into R *hanmi*.
Mechanics:	*Nage* turns *tenkan* around striking arm, and guides it to rear where *nage* is stable but *uke* is not.
Hitori waza:	*Ikkyo-undo, tenkan-undo.*

Like the *irimi* version, this throw is sometimes referred to as "London Bridge."

1. Begin as in *yokomen-uchi shiho-nage irimi* above, but turn *tenkan* around *uke*'s hand.
2. Lead *uke*'s arm up and around, turning under it so that hand and forearm are curled over his shoulder, palm down.
3. Step through, leading hand over *uke*'s shoulder and down back to mat.

Shiho-nage irimi is a natural for the *yokomen* motion as it simply continues and wraps *uke*'s arm up in its own motion. The *tenkan* version appears to clash with this motion but actually extends and deflects the *yokomen* strike into *tenkan* rather than suddenly reversing direction.

Experiment with *extending* the strike into a tenkan, as compared to stopping it to reverse and *do* a *tenkan*.

Ikkyo

ADS: Immobilization #1 ("First Teaching") pp. 166-167; TOT: Ikkajo, pp. 82-83.

Ikkyo is one of the most fundamental of Aikido techniques, the first of the cycle of wrist-locks.

Shomen-Uchi Ikkyo Irimi

ADS: ("Front-strike to head, first wrist-lock technique done by entering") pp. 171-172; TOT: shomen-uchi ikkajo osae ichi, pp. 84-85.

Uke:	L *hanmi*, stepping forward into R *hanmi* to strike *nage*'s head.
Nage:	R *hanmi*.
Mechanics:	Reversal of *uke*'s incoming strike.
Hitori waza:	*Ikkyo-undo*

1. Swing arms up into *ikkyo undo*, not blocking, but extending in the direction of *uke*'s fingertips. Make contact with *uke*'s arm before forearm has passed vertical, deflecting it in direction of *uke*'s fingertips.

2. Circle *uke*'s arm up in front of his face and body then forward and down; your LH around uke's upper arm stabilizes and rolls his shoulder forward.

   Uke should pivot off center around a new point of rotation — the shoulder.

3. Stepping or skipping forward with RF (outside foot), lead *uke* down to the mat.

Variations

See comments by physicist Joseph Toman on page 72. This technique and its results tend to be mystifying because we tend to assume that attacks are linear. That is not the case here. This is clarified by striking with a *jo*. Notice that:

- The lines of force are circular.

- The most powerful (and dangerous) point is tip of hand or *jo*, not the upper arm.

- At time of contact with the arm, the *jo* is not yet a danger.

Perhaps the best way to understand *ikkyo-irimi* is to first do it wrong.

1. Partners assume a static position.
2. N*age* push directly in against *uke*'s power.

   Observe that this approach accomplishes nothing. Where is the way out?
3. Notice the direction of *uke*'s fingers; lead in *that* direction instead.

   Observe results.

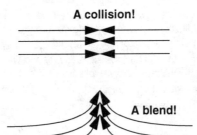

A collision!

A blend!

Shomen-Uchi Ikkyo Tenkan

ADS: ("Front-strike to head, first wrist-lock technique done with turning") pp. 166-167. Commonly known as "Airplane."; TOT: shomen-uchi ikkajo osae ni, pp. 86-87.

Uke:	L *hanmi* stepping forward into R *hanmi* to strike *nage*'s head.
Nage:	R *hanmi.*
Mechanics:	A counter to *uke*'s attempt to counter *ikkyo-irimi.* Redirects the resisting forward energy into a *tenkan* spin.
Hitori waza:	*Ikkyo-undo, tenkan-undo*

1. Begin as in with *ikkyo-irimi,* but as *uke*'s arm reaches highest point of the circle, step forward with LF to stand just behind *uke*'s shoulder.
2. Swing RF back and around (*tenkan*) rotating the hips; simultaneously . . .
3. Drop *uke*'s arm 90 degrees down to mat. (Try for a 180-degree turn).

Variations

This technique can be done on its own, but it is often used as a counter to a counter to *ikkyo-irimi. Uke* knows what's about to happen and blocks by pushing forward to resist *nage*'s attempt to send his arm over his shoulder in *nage*'s forward direction. Practice the following:

- *Uke* strike *shomen-uchi* then hold arm firmly pushing forward.
  Uke practice the feel of directing that energy forward and around into a tenkan.

- Experiment with *nage*'s ending position. What happens if you end your *tenkan:*
  a) Standing in front of *uke*?
  b) Even with *uke*?
  c) Slightly behind *uke*?

Kote-Gaeshi

ADS: Immobilization #7 ("Wrist-Bend") pp. 216-218; TOT: p. 57.

Mune-Tsuki Kote-Gaeshi Tenkan

ADS: ("Mid-level punch with wrist-bend and turn") p. 223; TOT: Shomen-tsuki kote-gaeshi ("Front-punch with wrist-bend") pp. 146-147.

Uke:	From L *hanmi*, *uke* steps forward into R *hanmi*, and punches to midsection with RH.
Nage:	L *hanmi*.
Mechanics:	*Nage* leads incoming energy around in a circle, redirecting it into a wristlock forward of *uke*'s center ("Tripping," page 178).
Hitori waza:	*Kote-gaeshi-undo, ude-furi-undo, tenkan-undo*

1. As *uke* punches, *nage* sweeps hand down *uke*'s arm to wrist and turns *tenkan*, hand at hip.

2. *Nage* absorbs energy of punch, leading in circle until *uke* is felt to be unstable and directed strongly forward.

3. Applying *kote-gaeshi*, *nage* reverses direction, such that *uke* walks into the wristlock at the same time that *nage* sweeps back the same-side leg, unbalancing *uke* while simultaneously opening up a place for *uke* to fall.

Variation

It common to grab for the hand, a small target, easily missed.

• Practice sweeping your hand down *uke*'s arm while grasping lightly. Think of making a "U" with thumb and forefinger. The bottleneck of the wrist will stop your hand in exactly the right position.

• Now try the above with your eyes closed.

Ude-Oroshi

ADS: Projection #2 ("Arm-Drop") p. 244.

One of the family of "clotheslining" throws, *ude-oroshi* ("arm-drop") uses the same motions seen in the *sayu-undo* exercise. No beginner ever believes that this technique could "really" work (especially "On The Street.") It requires effective dynamic *tenkan* and precise timing but is devastatingly effective. Students commonly try to push *uke* over with an arm but the arm should merely lead.

Aikidoist Dan Henry likens the arm to the bowsprit on a ship, "it leads, it extends, but it's the vessel itself (the Center) that does the real work."

Katate-Tori Kokyu-Nage Tenkan Ude-Oroshi

ADS: ("Same-side grab, breath-throw, with turn and arm-drop"), also known as "Emperor's Clothes," pp. 244-245)

Uke:	L *hanmi*, seizing nage's R wrist, energy forward.
Nage:	R *hanmi*, RH palm down.
Mechanics:	Incoming energy is deflected and redirected in a circle which leads to "Clotheslining."
Hitori waza:	*Tenkan-undo, sayu-undo*

1. *Uke* grabs *nage*'s R wrist with his LH.

2. Pivoting on RF, *nage* turns palm up turning *tenkan* around the seized hand ending shoulder to shoulder with *uke*.

3. With fingertips extended forward forming a V with Center (as if carrying a stack of laundry or a basketball) *nage* leads *uke* around Center until *uke* is in dynamic motion.

4. Stepping out of circle, *nage* bends knees dropping One-Point and leading *uke* down and forward of his Center. The motion is very similar to that of bowling.

5. As *uke*, descending towards the mat, begins to attempt to rise to regain his balance, *nage* swings both arms upward as for *ude-mawashi*.

6. End in *sayu-undo*, weight and One-Point dropping down onto RF.

Variations

- *Nage*'s body must be in full contact with *uke*'s body so that weight of *nage*'s body and arm are dropped onto *uke*'s unbalanced upper torso when the knee is bent in *sayu-undo*. Lacking this contact, *nage* ends up trying to force *uke* down with a one-arm push. Experiment with trying to do the technique at a distance and compare with close contact.

  Philip Akin (Yoshinkan) comments: "I can use strength and push down with my arm or I can let me knee go soft and bend." Notice that in *sayu-undo*, arms are not forced down, they drop down with a drop of Center and a bend of the knee. Do the exercise!

- Arms do not act alone. They rise in coordination with upward thrust of legs, rise of One-Point. They descend with downward drop of One-Point and body weight. If *tenkan* and downward lead have been done well, the upward lead will leave *uke's* upper body off-balance to the rear while legs continue hurtling forward. Experiment with isolating arms, exaggerating upward lead, eliminating upward lead, combining with upward thrust of legs.

- Notice that *tenkan* proceeds in a horizontal circle to develop momentum. Once *uke* is moving, *nage* steps out, transforming the horizontal circle into a vertical circle. *Uke* is laid down in a sliding fall perpendicular to *nage*.

  Do the technique on the seam of a mat or a chalk or tape line to check positioning. What happens to *uke* if you do the entire throw while continuing to turn *tenkan*? What happens to *uke* if you step out of the circle as described above? Which approach offers more control of *uke*?

Zempo-Nage

ADS: Projection #22 ("Forward-Throw"), p. 308.

This is a large family of "forward throws." In the Ki Society, they are done not by hurling *uke* forward like pitching a baseball into the outfield, but by moving your own center forward then simply dropping the leading arm (*ude-mawashi-undo*) 90 degrees down to the mat. *Zempo-nage* are common as final techniques in *Taigi* (Ki Society) so that *nage* can help return *uke* to his proper position for the final bow.

Ryote-Mochi Kokyu-Nage Zempo-Nage Tenkan

ADS: ("Both-hands grab, breath-throw, throwing forward-throw with a turn") pp. 308-309.

Uke:	R *hanmi*, seizing both of *nage*'s wrists, energy forward.
Nage:	L *hanmi*.
Mechanics:	A "tripping" throw. *Uke*'s Center is lead up, forward, and then down ahead of his supporting feet.
Hitori waza:	*Tekubi-kosa undo, tenkan-undo, udemawashi-undo, funekogi-undo.*

1. Nage turn with full *tenkan* to *uke*'s R side.
2. Moving Center/One-Point forward, raise *uke*'s hands, then drop leading hand 90 degrees down to mat. But not that this is not a throw *down*; *uke* slides off the arm carried by his forward momentum just as rapidly moving water thundering over a 90-degree cliff does not fall straight down, but flows forward and down.

Ushiro-Nage

ADS: Projection #16 ("Rear-Throw") p. 295.

Ushiro does not refer to any particular technique but any number of throws done in response to attacks from "behind." The wrist grab from behind was intended to disarm or neutralize an attacker armed with swords or knives. Techniques usually begin by bringing the attacker forward, then flow into any number of other possibilities from *ikkyo*, to *kote-geshi*, to *kokyu-nage* to *zempo*. The following is a static grab which is converted into the *sankyo* wristlock.

Ushiro-Tori Tekubi-Tori Ura-Gaeshi

ADS: ("Rear-attack to wrists, with a turning to the rear") p. 295.

Uke:	Behind *nage*, holding both wrists, pulling down
Nage:	*Shizentai*
Mechanics:	Rotation of *uke* around *nage*'s "earth" hand.
Hitori waza:	*Tekubi-kosa-undo, ushiro tekubi-kosa-undo*

1. *Nage* extend LH straight down, forming center of *uke*'s rotation.
2. Leading from fingertips, bring RH to Center/One-Point then lead up centerline of body, fingers pointing up.
3. As hand leads over *uke*'s head, pivot on LF to your L side.
4. Step to *uke*'s rear (*ura*), turning him "inside out."
5. Extend both arms out and drop One-Point 90 degrees to mat.

Tenchi-Nage

ADS: Projection #9 ("Heaven-and-Earth Throw"), p. 274.

A basic exercise in weight upperside, weight underside, and unbalancing.

Katate-Tori Ryote-Mochi Kokyu-Nage Tenchi-Nage

ADS: ("Both-hands grab, heaven-and-earth breath-throw") pp. 274-275; TOT: pp. 164-165.

Uke:	L *hanmi*, seizing both of *nage*'s hands, energy neutral or back and down.
Nage:	R *hanmi*.
Mechanics:	"Clotheslining" by moving *uke*'s torso backward of feet.
Hitori waza:	*Udemawashi-undo*

1. *Nage* drops L elbow, Center/One-Point,
2. With LH *atemi* motion to *uke*'s One-Point (to draw *uke*'s attention), *nage* leads LH up, RH down and forward
3. *Nage* slides past *uke's* forward *LF* with RF continuing LH upward in an "S" pattern as if throwing *ki* (or a pizza) up and over *uke*'s shoulder.
4. Step through and up with LF then drop Center/One-Point down to the earth.

Variation

- There is often confusion about which is the throwing hand. It is actually the "earth" hand. The "heaven" hand leads *uke* "upperside" making *uke* easier to move (see "swankyo" on page 71) while the "earth hand" moves *uke*'s torso forward of his stable center.
  This is also known as the "pizza and dollar bill" throw. Most beginners try to knock *uke* over with the "heaven" hand. To return focus to the "earth" hand, imagine — or place — a dollar bill on the mat for *nage* to pick up. Live pizza is optional.

- Students often attempt to force their way through *uke*. To prevent this, and return focus to unbalancing and dynamics, *nage* offer two fingers to *uke*. Fingers aren't as strong as wrists: trying to muscle through a technique risks a sprained finger. Start with index fingers. With practice, go to pinky fingers.

Zagi Kokyu-Dosa

Not a wrestling match, but an exercise in relaxation, expansion, balance and control.

ADS: ("Seated Breath-movement") pp. 109-111; TOT: Kokyu-ho, pp. 168-173.

Uke:	In *seiza*, seizing outside of both of *nage*'s wrists.
Nage:	In *seiza*, offering arms to *uke*.
Mechanics:	Variable. Can be done as *tenchi-nage* or via many other forms of unbalancing.

1. Extending through fingertips, *nage* moves Center/One-Point forward unbalancing *uke* to one side or the other.
   Do not throw straight back in *seiza;* it is awkward and painful for *uke*.

2. As *uke* falls, follow his motion with whole body, ending in *seiza* with your R knee in his R armpit.

3. Hold-down: In *seiza* on toes with back erect, gently press *uke*'s L wrist and R shoulder with knife-edges of your hands (if on *uke's* right side; reverse for L side).

Variations

- Try this exercise with *nage* and *uke* clasping hands around a basketball.
- To see the steering-wheel motion, try the exercise with a hula-hoop.
- Experiment with consciously sending every push or thrust of energy down to your Center or to the center of the earth.
- What happens if you imagine that you are bigger, larger, and sitting deeper under the mat than *uke*? Imagine only your eyes peering over the top of the mat.

Taigi #5

Taigi 5 combines five of the above techniques (or their variations).

1. *Shomen-uchi kokyu-nage*
2. *Yokomen-uchi shiho-nage irimi*
3. *Mune-tsuki kote-gaeshi tenkan* (with turnover and hold-down)
4. *Kata-tori-ikkyo irimi*
5. *Kokyu-Dosa*

CHAPTER 8

Weapons, Tools, and Toys

Weapons

The techniques you learn in Aikido are not weapons. They are tools which can be used to save a life. If you use them as weapons, you will get cut by them. You will hurt somebody or get hurt. If you use them with virtuous intention, you will go right through the opposition.

I stole this theory from 150 Japanese sword teachers.

— Terry Dobson, *It's a Lot Like Dancing*

Aikido offers training in the traditional Japanese weapons — sword (*katana* or *bokken*) and staff (*jo*, similar to the Old English quarter-staff of Robin Hood and Little John)[1]. Sword and staff are a tad archaic as "weapons" but as tools they teach the concepts of extension, alignment, rotation, leverage and *ma-ai* more effectively than empty hand techniques alone. They are also the original source of many Aikido techniques in which the empty hand emulates the rise and fall of a sword. They also emulate Real Life better than the empty hand. There is nothing quite like a whack across exposed knuckles to teach proper position or make its reasons more luminously clear.

Kata are choreographed exercises designed for individual practice of flow, balance, and timing, and often contrast the control of rapid motion with the calm relaxation of the beginning and the end. When practicing individually, visualize an opponent. Practice with a real opponent will raise your forms from a purely theoretical art to an artfully applied science.

Note that the count is not a count as we usually think of it. Numbers serve as guidelines to what more than to when. Follow the natural rhythm of the *kata* and do not try to force it into rigid time constraints.

Ideally, *kata* begin and end at the same point. Practice this by dropping a marker at your starting point; see how close you can come to finishing at the same point — with your eyes closed.

In learning a *kata*, divide practice into stages.

---

1. Aikido includes knife techniques, but they aren't as heavily emphasized. Peter W. Boylan notes: "Traditionally, the knife wasn't even considered a serious weapon in Japan. Recall that until the 1870s, Japan was a country where part of the population was required by their social position to walk around with two long, sharp pieces of steel in their belts. Anything shorter than about 1.5 ft. (40 cm) would have gotten a big grin, and then the person holding it would have been bisected."

   In modern Japan, the knife is the Number 1 murder weapon; for Number 2 and why defenses against swords aren't so archaic after all, see "Bokken" on page 218.

1. Begin in a group of four or more experienced people so that no matter which way you turn there will be someone to follow.

2. Practice on your own, without relying on someone else's motions. Split the steps into sections (such as 1-5, 5-10, 10-15, 15-20, or any natural combination of motions) then recombine the small sections into larger segments and practice these.

3. After you have the sequence under control, practice with your eyes closed. This removes the visual clues (i.e. "when facing the door, I poke . . .") on which you may be unconsciously relying.

4. Practice in opposition with a partner.

   Now your motions are opposite, time and space must be perfectly coordinated.

In the documentary that Kubrick did, they just pick up the thigh bone and start doing shomen strikes, no counting or nuthin'. I guess they're Aikikai. In the next scene we see they get immediate martial effectiveness, but they're by a puddle, so it might be a misogi thing too.

It's nice when these things can come together.

— *J. Toman, Aikikai*

Bokken

Practicing against sword attacks is actually useful, even f not for defending against swords. One of the most common weapons around is the baseball bat (in Japan, the second most common murder weapon behind kitchen knives). The basic strike with a bat is usually a wild helicopter men cut.

— *Peter W. Boylan*

Principles for Sword Training

1. Hold the sword softly with LH at base of the hilt; put your RH at the top of the hilt to steady it. Power comes from the base hand.

2. Keep the tip calm and steady.

3. Use the weight of the sword and gravity to cut. Do not force the blade down — unbalanced forces will tilt the blade and tension in your arm will slow it.

4. Raise sword overhead whether you intend to strike *shomen* or *yokomen*.

5. Maintain attention and focus.

6. Cut first with the mind, then with the sword.

Yokomen Strikes and Tenkan

1. Starting in L *hanmi* (N) step R, strike L/R *yokomen*.[2]

   You will end up in R *hanmi* facing (S).

2. In R *hanmi* (S) step L, striking L\R *yokomen*.

---

2. A *yokomen* starting on the R side and striking to the L. A R/L *yokomen* will start on the L and strike to the R. Letters are for directions. N=North, S=South, E=East, W=West.

You will end up in L *hanmi* facing (N).

3. Repeat.

4. Repeat the above practicing in pairs.

   The result is a series of alternating clockwise and counterclockwise turns. Practice on a mat seam, a chalk line or a piece of tape to control direction.

Yokomen Strikes and Blocks

In pairs,

1. Strike *yokomen* and block across the mat.

2. *Nage* alternates R and L *yokomen* while *uke* blocks.

3. Switch then return in the opposite direction.

   It is helpful to work down a mat seam or other marker such as tape or a chalk line.

Be sure that the sword goes over the head for a *yokomen* strike, not from the side as in baseball.

Live Blade

No matter how often I had been instructed to "put my mind at the tip" and "extend *ki*" and gone through the motions, the sword was just a hunk of wood until the day I had occasion to chop down a tree with a machete. The blade cut into the wood with ease when I simply let it go; with difficulty the more I tried to force it. Suddenly those lessons became luminously clear. With a machete (from Army surplus or outdoor stores) and a log[3]:

1. Strike target with the middle of the blade.

2. Strike target with the tip of the blade.

3. Repeat while forcing blade down or allowing it to drop.

4. Compare effort and effectiveness.

Happo Undo for Sword

Happo Undo ("Eight-Way Exercise") is done on the eight points of the compass. For basic exercise, see page 104).

The first set of four positions (A) may be thought of as facing the four square walls and is characterized by sword thrusts or pokes. During thrusts, the "blade" faces away from the forward foot.

The next set of four (B) on the diagonal, consists of sword strikes done in immediate succession.

From *seiza*, with sword at left side, blade out, *nage* bows, draws sword, rises into R *hanmi*.

---

3. You can also make a target of a tire (see "Tires" on page 226) to replace the log. Provide vertical support for practice cutting lengths of bamboo with a *tameshigiri dai* (see *"PVC Tubing" on page 225*).

(A) On the Square,

1. From R *hanmi* ready position, strike *shomen*; step forward with LF and poke (blade faces R.)
   Note: the full step is done this time only).
2. *Zengo* to R *hanmi* while raising sword; strike *shomen*; slide forward with RF and poke (blade faces L).
3. Step into L *hanmi* while raising sword; slide LF forward and poke (blade faces R).
4. *Zengo* to R *hanmi* while raising sword; slide RF forward and poke (blade faces L).
   Zengo to L *hanmi* while raising sword.

(B) On the diagonal,

5. In L *hanmi*, strike *shomen*. *Zengo* to R *hanmi* while raising sword.
6. In R *hanmi*, strike *shomen*. *Zengo* to L hanmi while raising sword.
7. In L hanmi, strike *shomen*. *Zengo* to R *hanmi* while raising sword.
8. In R *hanmi*, strike *shomen*. To end, with sword in R hand only, fully extended and parallel to the mat,

- Turn 360 degrees to starting position ending in L *hanmi* but sweeping sword back with RF.
- Step back into L *hanmi*, ready position, and
- Return to *seiza*.

Variation:

Do the entire exercise with *uke* testing every step, from

- Attempting to block the forward bow to
- Holding the blade throughout the cuts and swings of the exercise.
  Rough on *uke*, but an excellent exercise in efficiency of motion.

Wooden Staff (Jo)

Principles for Jo Training

1. Hold the *jo* lightly.
2. Control the *jo* with the rear hand.
3. Move the *jo* freely.
4. The line traced by the *jo* is never broken.

The previous exercises listed for *bokken* can also be done with the *jo*. Before starting techniques, Steve Wolf suggests a simple movement, swooping the *jo* through the path of a figure 8, changing from hand to hand.

The purpose is to get comfortable with the weapon, develop balance, sure-handedness, and familiarity with the center of the jo and its relationship to your center before adding other human beings or movements to it. Principles for *jo* training are very similar to those for *bokken*. Variations on the *jo* allow the user to focus on principles rather than on the characteristics of a particular weapon. The materials below vary from steel bars, to wood, to PVC piping.

Heavy Jo

Weight requires efficiency of motion, but again, use good sense. Mr. Diesch hastens to point out that while this seemed like good weight training at the time, it was eventually halted due to a rash of muscles sprains and tears.

> *Many years ago we practiced jo kata with the steel bar from a set of weights. It weighed 10 Kg by itself. We used to repeat the kata and pass the metal one up the line one place till it got to the end, and then pass it back down again. There was always a scramble to be at either end of the line, because then you only had to have the heavy jo once or twice. We once made a lead jo by filling one-inch copper pipe with molten shot, but someone "accidentally" lost it.*

— *Jonathan Diesch*

The Fluid Dynamic Jo

Fill a length of 1-1/2 PVC with water and sand, cap it, and seal it. The weight and fluid motion of the interior require large circles, nicely curved tenkan and irimi. If you do sharp or bumpy movements, it will jump out of your hands like a live thing.

The 1/8" Dowel Jo

For an interesting switch on the weighted workout of the heavier designs above, try working with a delicate 1/8" dowel.

The Silk Scarf Jo

To watch circles and flow, attach a silk ribbon or scarf to the each end of the *jo*. Flowing, circular motions are clear. Short-cut or chopping motions are quickly revealed.

Tools and Toys

This homely game of life we play, covers, under what seem foolish details, principles that astonish. The child amidst his baubles, is learning the action of light, motion, gravity, muscular force.

— Ralph Waldo Emerson

Effective teaching commonly draws analogies between the topic and already-familiar objects and situations. The following items are useful for demonstrating basic concepts of Aikido. Items in sight and in hand makes them still more real.

- **Balancing Baby / Tightrope Walker**

    A classic science toy for demonstration of weight underside. See what happens if you flip the model over and attempt to balance it on its head with weight clearly upperside. See also "Daruma" on page 223.

- **Balloons**

    A balloon senses what you cannot. Excellent tool for practicing alignment of forces in tenkan. Try turning *tenkan* around a balloon cupped (not held) in your hand. The feeling is like holding the ball in a lacrosse stick or scooping fish in a net. Also useful for breathing practice.

- **Balls**

    Useful for illustrating the "roundness of motion" Very large exercise balls such as the "Physioball" are also useful for teaching rolling. Rather than merely instructing the apprehensive new student to make himself "round like a ball," let him actually feel it. See also "Hula Hoop" in this listing, and Chapter 5 on rolling.

    To demonstrate roundness of motion in *kokyu-dosa nage* holds the ball while *uke* grasp wrists. Smaller balls can be used to demonstrate circularity of *sankyo*, *nikyo*, *shiho-nage* and other exercises. See also: http://onlinesports.com/pages/I,OLY-BA364P-3.html

    Small balls or bean bags can also be used for dodge ball to teach another useful Aikido lesson: it doesn't matter how hard an opponent hits if you aren't there.

- **Bean Bag**

    Use for "catch" in the partnered *tekubi-tori*-with-beanbag exercise on page 88, an act even less self-conscious and more psychologically compelling than "fix glasses" or "scratch head." One night we had great fun trying to throw the bean bag into the air, roll, and catch. We didn't succeed, but great exercise for timing and focus.

- **Bio-Feedback Sensors**

    Available from various sources at widely varying prices. Edmund Scientific has a wide range. An illuminating illustration of the differences between tension and relaxation and their impact on stability, balance, and technique.

- **Bonsai**

    In Aikido and other arts, a classic exercise is expansion/contraction. The Japanese art of *bonsai* is a different form of the same exercise. Through root pruning, adult trees centuries old, complete in every way, are mere inches tall. Tradition has it that this art was taught by Buddhist monks to demonstrate change in point of view.

A similar concept in the West is the gazing ball. I'd seen them for years but never understand the point of sticking a shiny ball on a post in the yard. Garden catalogs explained the mystery: a different point of view, a wide-angle reflection of the garden itself blooming in miniature in the depths of a mirrored glass. See also Escher's classic etching of a fish in a pond. Expand, contract, choose your focus.

"My plan, probably four or five mornings out of seven, is this: Morning readings. About ten minutes zazen, that's short, but works for me. In apartment with (kid's sized) bokken shomen, shomen-tsuki, yokomen, and kote cuts are in order of 25 each with two sets. Do kote-men-do next and then the Tohei iaido katas, ten each. On weekends go to a outdoor sport park in town and add the jo kata and jo and bokken techniques from our aikido waza. Outside I can use my regular sized bokken. If I miss a morning I often head to the park after work and do 30-45 minutes before coming home. It makes my day seem smoother somehow. Somehow the more comfortable I am handling the bokken and jo solo doing waza or kata the easier the waza becomes empty-handed with partners." — N. B. R.

- **Breakfall Pole**

Tony Fitts uses a ceiling support pole in the *dojo* for *ukemi* practice. Padded and covered with carpet, it allows individual practice of "clothesline" breakfalls or sliding falls as from *tenchi-nage* and *tenkan ude-oroshi*. This is a similar idea to the traditional Japanese makiwara, a straw-padded target for various types of practice (from *maku* "to wrap" and *wara* "hay." The "classic" makiwara for punching and kicking were made by wrapping hay around something (a tree, a pillar) but can be anything from layers of cloth or leather or other padding tacked to a wall or wrapped around a board. See Punching Bags on page 225.

- **Daruma/Boxing Clown /**

For demonstration of Center and Weight Underside. The weighted bottoms of the classic children's toys, boxing clown or balancing baby, return them to the upright position after being knocked over.

The Japanese *Daruma* doll is the same idea; a rounded figure made of paper maché with a weighted bottom. When knocked over, it rolls around then returns to upright, representing triumph over adversity.

- **Closet Uke**

Stuff a shirt with rags or crumpled newspapers; add a head of paper bag, pillow, or balloon if desired. Hang on a cord or a hanger to swivel from a door frame and you have your own live-in *uke* to practice positioning and procedure. If you aren't yet at the point of being able to visualize and dance through the techniques on your own, this provides valuable feedback. Keep him around for garden or Halloween.

You might also consider adding directions with masking tape. Can't remember the difference between *sankyo* and *shiho-nage*? Why not tape directions on the sleeve? Sankyo, turn arm in; *shiho-nage*, turn arm out.

- **Cord / String**

  For jump rope, either a great warm-up and aerobic exercise, or for practicing leads and direction. For example, the lead on a *tenkan* should be forward. When cord is stretched out to the side, the problem becomes clearly visible. Also useful for the "Timing Belt" exercise (see page 173) although a *gi* belt can also be used.

- **Gyroscope / Top**

  A vivid demonstration of the stability of motion.

- **Hula Hoop**

  Great for diving rolls or illustrating circles of motion such as the "steering wheel" motion of *en-undo* throws and others. (See also exercises illustrating rotation and center in Chapter 3). If nothing else, use it as it was intended perhaps while singing Monica's Song[4] which can't help but increase awareness of hips.

- **Masking Tape/Chalk**

  Use to mark starting and ending points, lines of travel or other guidelines on the mat where a permanent mark is not desired. It's often useful to work along the seam of a mat to establish direction and position, to demonstrate whether you're moving forward or backing up. A large canvas mat may have seams in only one direction; smaller joined mat sections may catch toes in their multiple seams.

  Tape and chalk work very nicely to provide guidelines. See Shioda's *Total Aikido;* positions and movements are greatly clarified by photographing figures and partners from different angles and overhead against a quadrant of masking tape.

  By extension, consider the Sword Dances found in many cultures. In Scotland (and elsewhere), the dancer performs intricate steps over two swords crossed on the ground. The romantic tale is that a victorious Scottish Chieftain threw down his enemy's sword, topped it with his claymore, and danced around them in victory. But where did he learn that dance, eh? It seems to me that an excellent approach to teaching position, direction, and the center of a circle in a pre-masking tape society might be simply to throw down crossed swords. (The danger to bare toes might also develop an awareness similar to that developed by intersecting vinyl mats.)

- **Mirrors**

  Mirrors are always valuable for observing body position on your own or in contrast to an instructor. If long expanses of mirrors are impossible, two mirrors on adjacent walls in a corner allows side and front views. Use as tool, not a crutch, that is, translate what you *see* in the mirror into what you can *feel* in your body on your own.

- **Paper Towels**

  A twisted paper towel is useful for practicing leads. Lacking the strength of a washcloth or a cord, even when twisted, it helps to inspire cooperation between nage and *uke*. If *nage* yanks forward it will break. If *uke* pulls back it will break.

- **Plastic Bats**

  Extremely useful for teaching *ikkyo*. The plastic bats produce an impressive THWACK! but no harm is done aside from a slight sting, enough to encourage the student to do the exercise even better. This is the same idea as traditional Japanese bound bamboo slats but cheaper and splinter-free.

---

4. See *It's in Your Hips, Appendix A.*

- **Punching Bags**

  A heavy bag or the traditional Japanese *makiwara* (a padded target for punching and striking) are both useful for teaching students how to actually punch with power and focus. Although Aikido doesn't usually use punches in its defensive techniques, other martial arts do. Before *nage* can effectively practice a defense against a punch *uke* must be able to produce one. See also **Tires**.

- **PVC Tubing**

  A length of PVC tubing filled with water and sand, capped and sealed, gives a whole new feel for the flow and movement of *jo kata*. If you shortcut motions, the *jo* will practically leap out of your hands. For visual input, a silk scarf or ribbon at each end will highlight movements that are circular and those that are not.

  Larger diameters of sturdy PVC pipe are useful as carriers to protect weapons and swords in iffy situations such as airline luggage.

  It can also make a utilitarian *tameshigiri dai* for sword practice. Stand a length of PVC in the center of a large bucket. Check with a level to make it perfectly vertical. Fill the bucket with angular gravel such as bluestone, or pour in concrete to secure the pipe and weight the bucket. A length of bamboo or other material standing in the tube provides a vertical target for sword practice.

  Railroad Tracks.

  Excellent for practicing strikes, *kata*, and other exercises with *bokken* or *jo* on a permanent balance beam, with balance and awareness."[5]

  Fred Younger, who laments the scarcity of Iwama-style training partners in northern Iowa, reports: "I do all 7 sword suburi, paying particular attention to 5-7 as I feel they are the most challenging. I have also gotten a lot out of doing a *shomen* cut, pivoting 180 degrees, *shomen* cut, pivoting again, I start in migi hanmi, usually 8 pivots and cuts, then repeat in *hidari hanmi*. Keep in mind that when working in this situation you aren't working to perfect your forms. You are working on maintaining your center on difficult footing. I also like to do jo kata and suburi on steep hillsides (close to 45 degrees) from different starting positions; uphill, downhill, and parallel to the hill. It adds a different facet to your training. "

- **Rubber Knives**

  Mechanically it matters little what the training tool looks like. Psychologically and emotionally it matters a great deal. It is one thing to practice knife techniques with a block of wood, quite another to face sharp steel.

---

5. Compare this to Aiki-Pitching training methods with balance beam on page page 61. Sensei Jim Baker (Aikikai) reports that Saotome Sensei has a similar structure, a balance beam, for training built in his *dojo*.

Sensei Tony Fitts has students bring in all the real knives they can find, the scarier the better, just for the emotional shock value. "When you're faced with a real knife, you're going to be shocked. Do it here. Get over it. Get on with practice." Rubber knives from theatrical supply shops are serve as an intermediate step between the visually unreal and the visually very real.

- **Skates, Skiies, and Bicycles**

  Great "cross-training" of basic physical concepts and sensations. Using appropriate care, try turning or riding in a circle while testing the effects of eye direction, attention, extension and focus.

- **Swings**

  Rope, tire, or bag swings with small children can always use a push. Fred Younger suggests striking the rope or chain with a *jo*. Great practice for focus and extension and great fun for the kids.

- **Tires**

  For thwacking with *jo* and *bokken*. A frame-mounted or hanging tire (weighted to dampen swings) will serve nicely. Wrap tire with a cloth to prevent black marks on weapons.

- **Wash Cloth**

  A wash cloth tucked in the *gi* has myriad uses. Most obvious is patting away sweat when hot and drippy but it is also a teaching tool. Harry Eto of Hawaii constantly uses a washcloth to illustrate the relaxed, 90-degree drop down (rather than a forward hurl)) that makes *zempo-nage*. An *uke* with small hands may be unable to hold on to large wrists but both partners can hold the ends of a cloth. In *tenkan* techniques done this way, the washcloth also gives immediate visual feedback if *nage* is backing up rather than moving forward.

- **Water**

  Support for persons who cannot practice easily on land. Possible uses range from providing support for people with bad knees or heavy weight (see "Poolkido" on page 13) to checking balance and position. For example, if you do an exercise off-balance in water you will drift. Water is also a wonderful way to practice rolls and breakfalls without the consequences of landfalls.

CHAPTER 9

Off the Mat, in Real Life

Practicing Alone

I didn't have anyone to practice with.
My first partner in Aikido wasn't even human. It was a tree.

— *Terry Dobson, It's a Lot Like Dancing*

There's more to Aikido than mat time. Practically speaking, there will never be enough time on the mat to practice all that needs to be practiced and outside practice is critical. Practicing rolls, balance, breathing, the physics and internal attitudes of Aikido should be a continuous and meaningful part of daily life. Consider too, the practice of harmonizing and blending applied to social skills and verbal self-defense. Sometimes for individual practice we have the notion that we need special equipment, special exercises to make the practice worthwhile. Actually not. Why rely on mat time to practice *tenkan-undo* or *funekogi-undo* when you can do them in the kitchen or with a lawnmower? Peter Rehse points out:

Kenji Tomiki was imprisoned for three years[1] after W. W. II, apparently for his position as Professor at the University of Manchuria, possibly for teaching aikido to senior army officers. He spent most of that time in solitary confinement, in a cell 3 meters square. There he developed the unsoku and tegatana exercises. It boggles the mind to think of the number of times he performed these but I think they are perfect for the average hotel room. You develop tai sabaki, fluidity and a good sweat (be aware of rug burns on your feet).Repetitive tenkan and irimi exercises would serve just as well. Since all of the above exercises are considered basic, traveling is a good opportunity to work on something that many don't emphasize during regular training (i.e., "let's get to the waza").

— *Peter Rehse, Shodokan Aikido*

Travelling? Working? Shopping? or home? Consider the following.

- **Breathing**
  Some say breathing is the most important part of Aikido practice, that anything less than several hours a day is inadequate, indicating a less-than-serious student. Whatever your opinion of appropriate time, it probably won't happen on the mat. Outside self-practice required. For a wealth of information on how to breathe from a world-

---

1. He had taught Aikido to senior army officers, but was apparently imprisoned due to his position as Professor at the Manchuria Kenkoku University lecturing in *Bugaku* ("martial studies"). "Possibly," says Rehse, "the Russians distinguished this from English lit."

renowned voice teacher, see Lessac (1960 and 1978)[2]. Breathing is not something you do 20 minutes a day when you remember, but something you do 24 hours a day every day that you're alive. Instead of a few minutes of breathing practice in class, practice all through class and throughout the day.

- **Stretching**

  You don't need extreme flexibility to do Aikido but the more limber you are, the easier it is to blend and flow. The stiffer you are, the easier to throw and easier to damage. Yet stretching cold muscles can be counterproductive and dangerous. Better done following a brisk walk or combined with hot-tub sitting.

- **Rolling**

  You can practice all kinds of rolls on your own — forward and backward, rolling break-falls — on grass, soft carpet, or even hard floor. I began on industrial carpet over a concrete floor. Not the best for flying forward rolls, but excellent for back rolls and learning how to round and tuck. The "thump-thump" that indicates poor rounding may be absorbed by a more forgiving mat or mattress. Do not roll on a bed. Put the mattress on the floor. See Chapter 5 for comments on rolling alone.

- **Sword Cuts and Strikes**

  Consider 100 sword strikes or a series of staff exercises as a regular daily exercise. Be sure you're doing them properly, however.

  Practice doesn't necessarily make perfect — it makes permanent.

- **"Dancing" the Techniques**

  Practice techniques by visualizing an attacker and stepping through the motions. If you need a more visual support, a stuffed shirt on a hanger will help you practice the the names and positions of various attacks, the difference in approach between *shiho-nage* and *sankyo*, between *irimi* and *tenkan*.

  You can also "dance" the attacker's part. Why would you want to do that?

  Because *uke* (the attacker) is the teacher. Especially when dealing with a beginning *nage*, the test of good *ukemi* is not ability to block a technique. The test is:

  Do you understand a technique well enough to guide an unfamiliar *nage* through the technique and the throw —without the visual and physical support of a partner?

  Find out by visualizing or dancing the attack, seeing and blending with the incoming energy, performing the technique and the hold down.

- **Mind Dancing**

  Can't sleep? Go through a list of techniques mentally, from the attack through the technique to the hold down. Work up to an entire test without losing concentration.

- **Surfing the Subway**

  Subway or bus is a great opportunity to practicing balancing and blending. Observe the difference in balance between a stiff-legged stance, or standing with tension in your shoulders versus bent knees and dropped weight. Notice how you can transform the forward inertia of hard braking into an "up" or a "down." For safety, of course, do these exercises with control, a stable support at hand and in situations where you will not alarm other passengers.

2.See also Tohei (1978) pp. 61-69, and Shifflett (1997), pp. 141-148. For breathing linked to emotion, see Snyder, B. J. (1998).

- **Funekogi Mower**

  Funekogi-undo is the "rowing exercise" and can be applied to rowing machines at the gym or setting heavy equipment other than boats in motion. Walking lawn mowers are an excellent tool for making the difference between pushing with arms and moving with One-Point luminously clear. Equally applicable to opening heavy doors, heavy file drawers, and dealing with other obstacles.

- **Dogs and Cats**

  Try turning *tenkan* with your dog, keeping the hand, the stick, the ball, just ahead of him. The dog will love it and you get good practice in judging distances and *ma-ai*.

  I first came to really understood *tenkan* the day a free-running German shepherd attacked my puppy on his leash. Puppy with shorter wheel base, less mass, and a leash to hold him in, could stay ahead of the larger dog but I found myself standing in the center turning slowly as a furious cyclone of activity swirled around me.

  Bigger now, this would-be sled-dog has given me a clear lesson in the difference between depending on arms and depending on center. Control with upper body can be tiring; with leash wrapped around hips it's easy. Feel the difference. And note that the first touch of the leash on your thigh is signal to practice *tenkan*.

- **. . . And Horses**

  "Any experienced horseman/woman uses *aiki*," says Cady Goldfield. Although a measure of "equine psychology" is part of the mix, a large part of horsemanship is to "become one" with the horse. Meaning that your body becomes exquisitely sensitive to the horse's every move, every intended move and every behavior. Likewise, the horse feels and senses his rider's body, weight shifts and signals, however subtle."

- **Groceries . . .**

  Groceries and the resulting bags of trash can be heavy awkward loads. In many areas, paper bags which must be held in the arms are giving way to plastic sacks that can hang from the hands by their handles, their weight completely "underside" in perfect alignment with gravity. As in *funekogi-undo* (see page 90) the arms need serve no purpose other than connection between body and load. Compare the weight and bulk of groceries that you can carry hanging to what you can hold in paper bags. Compare the effort required to do so.

- **. . . and Garbage**

  Lifting heavy bags into a tall bin may be beyond the capabilities of a small person of moderate strength — if statically lifted directly up against gravity. If a moving load is *directed* up rather than *lifted* up, the situation changes. Notice that almost any movement (even that of dropping) to get the bag moving and then *redirecting* that motion, makes the bag easier to lift up. With care (strong bag, non-messy load, and easy target, to avoid disaster) experiment with turning *tenkan* to get the bag moving, direct it upwards and into the can. Feel the difference between muscling a heavy load and a one-handed flick of the wrist.

  Compare a full *tenkan* to a partial turn. This is the power behind karate's spinning kicks and of Aikido *tenkan* techniques.

- **Jaywalking**

  Some view it as the ultimate exercise of awareness, blending, and flowing. The point is not only to cross the street safely, but to do so without disturbing the consciousness or flow of oncoming drivers or policemen.

- **Chess and Go**

  The Japanese game of *Go* and the worldwide game of chess both teach strategy. Both were popular with the military classes of their respective cultures. Garri Kasparov, the 13th world chess champion, simplifies it to "chess is war." Or as someone said, "A young warrior learns tactics; an old warrior has learned *strategy*" (a word which comes from the Greek for "general.") An interesting detail of the *Highlander* television series was the emphasis on strategy rather than the standard super-hero frontal assault — and a chess-board visible in nearly every episode.

- **Focus and the Tupperware™ Randori**

  Pick a practice or a point, and focus.

  Can you drive a nail with one blow? Pick a single voice out of a choir? Follow a presentation from beginning to end without diverging to daydreams? A useful skill on and off the mat.

  Aikido training shows up in many subtle ways. Awareness of space and position, balance and direction. When an attack is not an attack, when it is, and what its component parts may be.

  At my house, we store plastic containers atop the refrigerator. Every so often there is a *shomen-uchi* attack of avalanching containers. A few years ago I realized that I no longer saw it as a chaotic avalanche of things; I saw it as: a bowl, a cover, a cap of definite speed and direction.

- **Weigh Your Head**

  How much does your head weigh? Locate an equivalent weight and consider how this feels when held in any position other than directly atop neck and center. A motorcycle helmet may weigh only 3-4 pounds, yet notice how off-balance and disoriented you may feel if you try to do a technique with anything other than good posture. Consider, then, the importance of good posture on balance and energy efficiency.

- **Taping the Test**

  If concerned with an upcoming test, consider videotaping or tape-recording the test of a senior student. Follow through all the test requirements, dancing the techniques, concentrating on timing and flow.

  Instructors may wish to make such tapes available to their students. Consider a complete callout of the test (the dress-rehearsal) on one side, explanations of the test techniques and what you are looking for on the flip side (training side).

  If you are helping a fellow student prepare for the test, go through the entire test, from start to finish, from presentation to return to place in line. For beginners, the terror of the first test is often less a matter of the actual techniques than stage fright and uncertainty about the procedure itself — where to stand, when to bow, and what to do when finished. More new students have dropped out of Aikido due to terror of the unknown, than boredom or disinterest. Help them any way you can.

- **Meditations and Changing Point of View**

  What is the value of a different point of view? For example,

  Observe the difference between professional and home movies. How many cameras? How many seconds, on the average, do you think the standard scene (point of view) lasts in a professional movie? Watch a movie and see. The standard number of cameras in professional work is three (and there may be more). Individual shots last only about 3 to 5 seconds before switching cameras and point of view[3]. Shots in commercials last about one second. The viewer is constantly given new information or insight that would be impossible with just one camera from a single viewpoint.

In techniques and exercises, try placing point of view overhead or to the side then "watching" yourself as if moving through water complete with bubble trail.

Pick a topic and argue it from both sides.

Practice looking at other possibilities. "The 'flip-side' is . . . ." A classic example: stop lights. Parents are forever telling children annoyed because they were stopped by a traffic light, "It's OK — we'll be first in line next time." The most hot-tempered person I know still says that to every red light he meets and I have never seen him lose his temper in that one situation.

- **Short and Tall**

  Tall *uke* / Short *nage* and reverse will always have different points of view. You may carry this concept off the mat and home, for example:

  Tall husband carries short wife around the house so that she can see what he sees: the top of the refrigerator, the difficulty of reaching lower cabinets.

  Short wife leads tall husband around the house as he stoops to see things from her point of view: the difficulty of reaching high cabinets, the names of books on the lower shelves.

- **D-Days**

  What are the 20 things you want to do before you die? Plan now.

---

3. Scenes in older movies, closer to the live-stage tradition, tend to last much longer.

Gardens

I learned more about economics from one South Dakota dust storm than I did in all my years in college.

— Hubert Humphrey

In one of his Drenai Saga books, David Gemmell's character "Druss the Legend" says that he would rather be a warrior than a farmer because he felt he lacked the courage to be a farmer.

— Neil McKellar

"Farming is *budo*," said O-Sensei, and for the enormous amount of emphasis he put on farming and gardening, there is surprisingly little commentary on his reasons or his thoughts in that area.

Armies and farmers have always been linked. The first formal armies were in Sumer, their role was the design, upkeep and maintenance of the life giving system of canals. Subsequently, most wars have been fought over who gets to keep the food the farmers grow. In Greco-Roman mythology, Ares/Mars, the god of war, was originally a god of agriculture. The practical need to protect the crops and life is also the root of the Japanese *samurai* and martial arts from other lands.

Gardening and farming are also acts of creation. For northerners, February is the worst of months when we let our minds stop at the dark and cold. It is the gardener who sees the buds, observes that the sun has been coming back for well over a month now, that we are leaving the dark and turning again towards the light. Knowing that, February becomes the most fervent time for dreaming and planning. When everyone else is still huddled inside, the gardener is out in the cold and damp planting the seeds of what will one day be the colors and shapes and smells of the coming spring. It is creation and dedication — and often brutally hard work. Ken Speed noted:

The "farming" O-Sensei was talking about and the "farming" that is done now (even on a small scale) are very different. I know nothing about 19th century Japanese farming techniques, but I know quite a bit about 19th century American farming techniques. I learned them from my great uncle and my grandfather and they are hideously, viciously, exhaustingly labor intensive. That huge labor element may be one of the things O-Sensei was referring to inasmuch as when you are doing things that are laborious and repetitive you learn to use your body in the most efficient way possible. When my grandfather replaced fence posts, driving them into the ground with a sledgehammer, he'd swing the hammer in an arc and pull it into his center at the very end of the swing, just before he hit the post. It is exactly the same motion we use when we swing a bokken, then draw it in towards our center at the end of the swing. When my great uncle finished milking he'd carry four milk cans from the cow barn to the pump house to immerse them in well water to keep them cold. They must have weighed around one hundred or more pounds apiece. He simply learned how to use his body efficiently.

Musician Ross Robertson wrote:

I'm no farmer, nor historian of Japanese culture, but I think it's reasonable to assume that O-Sensei had an agenda of unifying the class hierarchy somewhat. It's my understanding that the warrior class and the farm folk did not historically mix well. I'm speculating, of course, but my take on it is that it would have a good deal to do with his vision of a world family."

We know from his writings and personal anecdotes that his budo became increasingly oriented toward nurturing and cultivation, attempting to revolutionize the old view of budo as a means of destruction. While farmers must also plow, uproot, weed out, clear the land, the ultimate aim is to engender life."

Although not a gardener myself, as a musician and composer I find thinking of "growing" songs more productive than trying to "write" or "construct" them. Much of what would not work is thrown on the "compost heap" and later on something may grow out of it. So agriculture can be a very useful metaphor for many endeavors.

A common remark on weapons work: "Ha! He looks like he's using a hoe!"— in turn suggests that neither knows how to use a hoe properly. Give it a try. Proper use of a hoe is amazingly similar to proper use of sword.

Bob Burns of San Diego Aikikai comments on forks, and hoes, and swords:

In 1987 I began to train with Chiba Sensei. In 1989 I suffered an injury that kept me from working. Being raised on a farm as a boy I got back into the soil where being an organic farmer allows one to be uke for Mother Earth. One must be very alert, watching those little critters who tell you what needs addressing in the garden, much the same as listening to our bodies while we train Aikido.

I began a small garden working in it four hours a day. I noticed when I went to training, that my body, after being in the garden, was more supple and flexible. When I did not garden, my body was more stiff. I am sixty years old, and have to pay close attention to what my body tells me.

It also felt that the tenchi (heaven-and-earth) dynamic of gardening was directly related to my training. I utilize the Jeavons French double digging technique (John Jeavons is my garden Sensei) and I began to make the tip of the fork, shovel, or hoe alive. I sent my body energy through it, feeling the earth from the tip. Bending my front leg, keeping my spine straight while digging, I found I could double-dig all morning non-stop, with a rhythm, breathing as we do when we train.

It was then that I realized that farming and Aikido are the same thing. The life force was identical.I got this information from my own eyes, ears, nose, and body. I then felt the connection between the Aikido and the farm.I also sit zazen, and at the same time felt this life force in my sits as well.It is a subtle indescribable hands-on real force that can be found only by letting go, and becoming whatever we do. It is this life force I am sure that O-Sensei is guiding us towards via out art in Aikido.

Ironically, my weapons work changed.

Chiba had told me that I could not do weapons. His reason was that it seemed that I wanted to kill my mate during practice. I went one year without touching jo, bokken, or katana.Thus my feeling for the hoe, shovel, and fork became tender, loving and sensitive. It also became more powerful and efficient. When I came back to weapons they felt light and beautiful. I was able to strike fast, but be soft at the same time.This sense went back to the garden tools.

The excitement and the bond between the garden and Aikido is so dynamic.My dream is to one day open a dojo where students farm as part of the training, to feel the life force that comes from the earth and that feeds us.

Voltaire's wickedly hilarious lampoon of the idealistic philosopher Rousseau, gallops from class prejudice, war and murder, treachery and deceit, to syphilis, the

Church and heretics, piracy, shipwreck, slavery, the Lisbon earthquake and cannibalism. Beneath the wild plot twists and fast action there is an underlying motif of gardens. Candide spends a brief time in a classical Utopian paradise, but for love of Miss Cunegund, cannot stay. Many trials and adventures later, the tale ends in Voltaire's more modest vision of earthly paradise, another garden which involves far more than gardening. All members of the little group help and contribute, not just in gardening but by sharing their own individual talents of baking, textiles, carpentry, and husbandry. As another hint that New Age isn't so new, Dr. Pangloss (despite a faith badly shaken) used to say now and then to Candide:

There is a concatenation of all events in this best of possible worlds; for, in short, had you not been kicked out of a fine castle for the love of Miss Cunegund; had you not been put into the Inquisition; had you not traveled over America on foot; had you not run the Baron through the body; and had you not lost all your sheep, which you brought from the good country of El Dorado, you would not have been here to eat preserved citrons and pistachio nuts."

"Excellently observed," answered Candide; "but let us cultivate our garden."

And so they do. It is a miniature model of the world — with a clear contrast drawn between those who bloody the earth and those who cultivate it. And meanwhile, is everything for the best? Do murder and hatred, gain and loss all happen for a reason and come to the best possible end?

Perhaps.

Perhaps not.

Nevertheless, says Voltaire, we must cultivate our garden.

Another passionate gardener, the late, great Henry Mitchell, offered the garden as another parable for life. "How often in great gardens," wrote Mitchell . . .

". . . do we see some inspired grouping of plants that only the highest art could have placed just so; that only the most informed and delicate taste could have arranged in just that combination of texture, color, bulk.

And almost always it turns out it was not specifically planned that way at all. Usually the original planter had included a revolting assortment of this and that (all of which has died or been chopped down because of desperate overcrowding) and the thing we admire, in the great garden is not some glorious composition come at last to maturity. Instead it is merely the feeble survivor of all that had once been intended, but which never worked out at all.

In this respect the garden is very like life itself. The coherence, the pattern, the glory even, is rarely planned and steadily approached, but is instead merely what at last is seen from the rubble of false starts, absurd ambitions and clumsy efforts.

Verbal Self-Defense

Voice and speech are first lines of defense and our chief weapons of offense.
                                                    — Arthur Lessac, Voice Coach

When I was first dating Jim I had to gather my courage in both hands to tell him that I was angry at him. I don't remember the issue, but I remember working myself up to mentioning it for the better part of a week. Naturally when I finally got it out, it came out with much more force and anger than was actually needed. I said fiercely to Jim:

"I really HATE IT when you do [X]!" (whatever it was).

And Jim said thoughtfully, "Yes, Hal doesn't like it when I do that either."

He didn't offer submission. He didn't meet anger with anger. He didn't block. He didn't apologize.

He came from 90 degrees and redirected the anger. I remember the sensation of floating, as if in a void — unable to attack any further.

                                                    — Wendy Gunther

We often think of language as we think of a fan — a frivolous sort of accessory for wafting hot air about. Pretty, decorative, pleasant, but largely insignificant.

The *samurai* fan (*tessen*[4]) however, was something more. Much more. Beautiful and elegant, under its cover of painted silk and shining black lacquer were ribs and spines of sword steel. The outer ribs were heavy enough to fend off strikes from a sword. The thin inner ribs, hidden under the thin silk covering, ended in sharp points that could stab and slash when opened. Closed, it served as a bludgeon or billy to jab at vital points. It was an efficient and deadly weapon in its own right, replacing more overtly offensive weapons in situations where swords and knives were strictly forbidden.

Language is a similar tool in many ways. It can be the most vicious of attack weapons. It can also be an enormously effective defense. Like the deceptively delicate *tessen* in trained hands, verbal self-defense skills are appropriate in situations where swords, knives, and other physical solutions are wildly inappropriate or simply do not work.

The truth is that verbal and emotional attacks are far more common than mere physical attack, usually precede physical attack when physical attacks actually occur, and are often far more difficult to deal with as training is so rare. The phrase "On the Street" as commonly heard and interpreted in martial arts classes is mostly nonsense — the real battlegrounds are in the shop, the office, the boardroom, the kitchen, the bedroom, the bar, the beltway. The weapons are words, and their underlying messages.

Consider verbal skills as a critical part of martial arts training. You had better, because Bad Guys use them too, even On The Street.

---

4. For use of the *tessen*, see Mizukoshi, Hiro, *Aiki Tessenjutsu*, on page 254.

Much of the desperate "shopping for a Black Belt" is certainly because the prized Black Belt is seen as a status symbol but it may also be seen as the solution to problems that are verbal in origin. That is, "When I am a Black Belt people will respect me and won't bother me anymore."

It doesn't work of course, because physical solutions don't address the non-physical origins of the problem and can (and often do) make the problem even worse. Verbal problems require verbal solutions, yet training in effective verbal skills is rare. Linguist Suzette Elgin notes:

> *We're not taught about language as a system at all but as a vague sort of thing hanging out in the air somewhere. We have the feeling that only the highly trained expert, the trial lawyer, or those with "the gift of gab," "the silver tongue" can know anything about language.*
>
> *This is a shame because you are by definition an expert in your language, simply because you speak it. You just need a little more information, terms, principles, concepts that will let you put to use information that is not currently available at the level of conscious awareness.*

Elgin considers verbal skills to be so critical to self-defense that their study qualifies as a martial art in its own right. Compare the linguistic concept of matching Sensory and Satir modes (see page 240) with the Aikido concept of matching speed and direction, blending with the partner or attacker before actual execution of a technique. Here Dr. Elgin presents a brief overview of "The Gentle Art of Verbal Self Defense."

The Martial Art of Verbal Self-Defense

— by Suzette Haden Elgin, Ph.D., Ozark Center for Language Studies

You're in a bar with friends, enjoying a pleasant evening. Suddenly a man in a booth near you shoves his date roughly against the wall and pulls back his hand as if to smack her hard across the face. You move fast. Before he can even begin to follow through on the threat, you're standing over him. "That's enough!" you say, quietly but firmly. But it's not enough for this joker. First he whirls around and tells you to mind your own business, and then — when you shake your head and say, "Sorry, I can't do that" — he comes roaring up out of the booth and goes for you. This is a serious mistake on his part; in ten seconds you have him down and begging for mercy, and you aren't even sweating. You hold him there while his date gets up to go call a cab and head safely for home. When she tries to thank you, you smile and shake your head. "No thanks required," you tell her.

This is what martial arts are for, right? This is walking the warrior walk, following the bushido path, doing the *tao/do*. With quiet confidence in your skills, you can go anywhere and know that when violence comes your way you'll be able to deal with it efficiently, effectively, and honorably. You're ready for anything. Right?

Maybe. Let's consider a different scenario.

You're in a business meeting, working through a new sales plan your boss has put together. And the boss keeps picking on one of your colleagues — making sarcastic remarks, interrupting her, ridiculing everything she says, doing his best to make her look foolish and stupid in front of everybody at the table. The woman looks at you, hurt and fear in her eyes, and her message is clear — she's asking for your help. Now what? Well, you could of course move fast and have your boss down and begging for mercy in ten seconds. You could hold him there on the floor, saying (quietly but firmly), "All right — apologize!" and not let him up until he did as you told him. And then when the woman he'd targeted tried to thank you, you could smile and shake your head. "No thanks required," you would tell her.

Ridiculous? Absolutely! You might feel that what I've just described is exactly what you'd like to do in such a situation. But you know it's out of the question.

And that's the problem, of course. Unless you're someone who spends all your time in physically permissive environments such as bars and mean streets, most of the situations of conflict you run into in modern life are going to be like the second scenario. They're going to be situations in which the use of physical force — no matter how skilled, no matter how controlled and restrained, no matter how classical and respected a set of moves it may include — won't be appropriate. They're going to be situations in which using your martial arts skills is more likely to get you fired or arrested, or both, than to win you honor and respect. Situations in which what's needed is not physical skills but verbal ones. What does that mean for you as a martial artist?

All too often, in my experience, it means that in the majority of conflict situations in your life you will either do nothing at all or you will do something that makes matters *worse* and none of your hard-earned martial arts skills will be of any use to you.

Physical violence, the most visible and obvious chunk of this problem, almost always begins with verbal violence — with arguments, and hostile language. It's more efficient and enormously cheaper to deal with violence while it is still verbal.

Among the classical martial arts there are some which are intended specifically as systems of combat; their goal is to subdue enemies by the use of physical force. Other martial arts, however, are supposed to be different. Their core principle is that real victory means never needing to use physical force, because you are (as Joe Hyams puts it in *Zen In The Martial Arts*) "so strong inside that you don't have any need to demonstrate your power."

In these systems, the best outcome for encounters of potential conflict is an *honorable* resolution without using any of the physical techniques of that particular martial art. Notice, please, that I stress "honorable." Avoiding the use of physical force by running away, or by lying, or by toadying, is not honorable, and none of those actions is an acceptable choice except in the rarest of life-or-death situations.

We have many excellent schools and teachers of these arts in the Western world today. But I see two problems in the way that their students are being prepared for life.

- First: Most of the students don't appear to be learning that core principle. So far as anyone can tell by observing their behavior, their primary goal is to win in combat, whether real or staged, just as if their chosen discipline were one of the killing arts.

- Second: Even when the principle is remembered and learned the students are not being taught what to do instead of using physical moves[5]. Just saying, *"Don't use physical force until you've tried talking and that has failed,"* is accurate, but is not enough. No one would tell a student, "Just keep using some kind of effective physical force until the opponent is subdued," and consider that enough. Making it up as you go along is not a martial art.

Terry Dobson and Victor Miller[6] wrote that "What we need is a new definition of conflict, a new way of looking at it, a new way of experiencing it, and a new way of

---

5. For example, consider Sun-Tzu's famous statement that "the highest skill is not winning one hundred victories in battle but subduing the enemy without fighting."

6. See Introduction in Dobson (1987).

responding to it." They were absolutely right — except in one small detail. It's not so much that we need new ways; not yet. That is not the most economical solution to the problem. What we need is to re-learn some very old ways of looking at, experiencing, and responding to conflict, ways that are new to us now only because we have forgotten about them. We need to re-learn the principles and strategies and tactics that make up the neglected martial art of verbal self-defense.

"The Gentle Art of Verbal Self-Defense" is a precise system like any other martial art. Its foundations are in those very old ways that I've been referring to, combined with the adjustments that are necessary to make them work in today's world. Its goals are to teach just two things:

- How to establish and maintain a language environment in which verbal violence almost never happens. (That is, to have such personal "presence" — such *sai*— that people around you would not even think of trying verbal violence there.)

- How, in those rare situations when verbal violence cannot be avoided, to deal with it efficiently, effectively, and honorably — with no loss of face on either side of the conflict.

Yes — with no loss of face on either side. That may strike you as a strange idea. Dobson and Miller put it very well:

You've bought into an imaginary, arbitrary system where everything's a contest and there are no ties — just sudden-death play-offs and a long walk to the showers.

The idea that every difference of opinion, no matter how trivial, has to end with a clear Winner and a clear Loser, is imaginary, arbitrary, and really is "something new." Although it may seem as natural to you as the air you breathe and as inevitable, this is in fact an idea that we have invented for ourselves, only recently and it has brought us nothing but trouble and misery. It's time to admit that it's an idea whose time has come — and gone — and that it has been a failure. We've been there, we've done that, and it was a mistake; time to move on.

Verbal self-defense has an advantage that no physical martial art is blessed with: Its core tactics and techniques and strategies, even its principles, are already known by the students. They are included in the grammar of the students' language, already stored in the students' long-term memories. They don't have to be learned the way kicks and holds and throws must be learned. All the students have to learn is new ways of indexing and organizing those elements — plus the strategy of making conscious decisions in verbal conflict just as they would in physical conflict. The basic principles of verbal self defense are identical to the basic principles used in physical self-defense and in Aikido.

1. Know that you are under attack.
2. Know what kind of attack you're facing.
3. Know how to make your defense fit the attack.
4. Know how to follow through.
5. Know that anything you feed will grow.

But wouldn't you *know* if you were under attack? Not necessarily. The attacker may not fit your image of an attacker: a small child, a frail elderly relative, or someone who is ill. The attacker is often someone that you are in a close relationship with.

As on the mat, you must judge intensity, strength, the degree of violence that you are actually facing in order to adapt your defense to use just enough force, no more and no less, in response to the attack. Don't go after butterflies with a machine gun.

Just as there is an English grammar for questions and commands, there's a grammar for verbal attacks. In English they are not so much in the words as in the music. If you hear language with the abnormal stresses indicated below, you are under attack.

What's an attack?

It isn't the shouting, curses, or epithets people usually think of. Yelling of garbage is just part of a bigger physical abuse pattern. Verbal Abusers are more subtle.

Attack Patterns

The English verbal attack has a two-part pattern.

1. **Bait**, the part that gets your attention, the part you're expected to fall for (equivalent to a feint or *atemi* in Aikido), and

2. **Presupposition**, something that a native speaker knows is part of the meaning of a sequence of words, even if it isn't there on the surface. For example:

> Even JOHN could pass THAT class.

As a native speaker of English you already know that two other sentences are included here. You know that John is no great shakes and that the class isn't worth much either. You don't have to say that "even John whom everybody knows can hardly reason his way out of a paper bag . . ."

The pattern alone says there's something wrong with both John and the class.[7]

A common example of *bait* is the phrase: "If you REALLY loved me . . . ."

For example:

> If you REALLY loved me, you wouldn't waste MONey the way you do.

*   **Bait**: "Wasting money."

*   **Presupposition**: "You don't love me."

*   **Response**: Ignore the bait. Respond to the presupposition rather than to the bait as the attacker intends and expects you to do.

    Here's what happens when you do take the bait and feed the pattern . . .

SPEAKER 1:	Whaddya MEAN, waste MONey? I'm very CAREFUL with our money!
SPEAKER 2:	OH, YEAH? Well how come it's only THURSday and we're BROKE?.
Speaker 1:	It's not MY fault you can't make a decent living!

---

7. If you doubt the significance of tone in English, find a copy of the classic audio skit "John and Marsha" by humorist Stan Freberg.

    "John," says the female voice. "Marsha," says the male voice.

    These two words only are repeated throughout the recording. On the written page this "dialogue" conveys nothing. To a listener, messages conveyed by timing, tone, pitch, and emphasis are so very clear that the skit was widely banned. — C. M. S.

There's going to be a fight, a row, and it's not going to be pretty.

To deal with a physical attack, the Aikidoist matches speed and direction and chooses an appropriate technique. How is it possible to match a verbal attack? By matching the Sensory Mode being used by the attacker and choosing an appropriate Satir Mode.

Sensory Modes

People who prefer sight, hearing, taste/smell, or touch will use language that reflects that mode.

People can and do shift between modes when relaxed. Under stress, they will not only lock into a preferred mode, they will even have difficulty expressing themselves or understanding language coming at them in another sensory mode. For example,

---

SPEAKER 1:	This looks bad.
SPEAKER 2:	"I don't feel that this is a problem.

Speaker 1 has used SIGHT Mode. Speaker 2 has *mismatched* with TOUCH Mode. Mismatch destroys rapport. On the other hand,

---

SPEAKER 1:	This looks bad.
SPEAKER 2:	"I don't see this as a problem.".

Speaker 2 has *matched* with SIGHT Mode. Matching builds rapport by blending with incoming language. Remember that anything you feed will grow. If you don't know what to do, don't use any sensory mode language at all, but if you can, match.

Satir Modes

The second tool classifies language into Satir Modes.[8]

- **Blaming.** "Why don't you EVER . . . ," "Why do you ALWAYS. . . ?" complete with fist-shaking, jabbing, threatening body language to match.

- **Placating.** "Oh I don't care, you know me, whatever you want, it's OK," with cringing, squirming body language to match.

- **Computing.** Third-person and vague generalizations avoiding words like *I, Me, Mine, You, Yours.* "There is undoubtedly good reason for this delay. No reasonable person could . . ." "Many people find that. . . " Body language is the absolute minimum, very Mr. Spock.

- **Distracting.** Cycles through all of the other Modes and their respective body languages. It is verbal panic.

- **Leveling.** Simple truth expressed as faithfully as possible for the speaker. Lacks the word emphasis of other Modes.

---

8. These classify language, *not* personality type.

People can cycle through Satir modes or lock into one under stress just as they do for Sensory modes. Do you match Satir Modes as you match Sensory Modes? Not necessarily. Once you've recognized the Satir Mode coming at you, decide "Do I want this to grow?

If you *do* want it to grow, match that mode.

If you *do not* want it to grow, *do not* match. Here's what happens if you *do* match.

* BLAMING at a blamer will always lead to a scene, a fight.
* Two placators PLACATING at each other will starve to death before they decide on a restaurant.
* Two computers COMPUTING introduce dignified delay. (Typical of committee meetings which is why so little gets done.)
* Two distractors DISTRACTING build a feedback loop of panic feeding panic.
* Two levelers LEVELING have simple truth going in both directions. It will grow.

What does it mean to say that something involving only language — no kicks, no jumps, no punches, nothing of that kind — is a martial art? Please look at the following dialogue, which takes place at a hospital "checkout counter." Try to hear the language in your head as you read with emphasis to sections in capital letters. The speakers are the angry wife of a hospitalized patient, and a hospital clerk.

Wife:	"How can you POSSibly ask me for money when my husband is lying in there in AGony??! DON'T you have any human feelings at ALL??"
Clerk:	"Now, wait just a minute! I don't make the rules around here, and I don't set the fees! I'm ONly doing my JOB!"
Wife:	"Oh, sure! SURE you are! And you're getting a big KICK out of it, TOO! My husband and I aren't human beings to you, we're just NUMbers! Just a couple of staTIStics, THAT'S all we are! And YOU . . . ."
Clerk:	"LISten! I don't have to take that kind of talk from you!! Who do you think you ARE, ANYway???"

The hospital staffer in this dialogue is under attack, but would be in big trouble if he responded by leaping over the counter and immobilizing the furious attacker with a choice move or two. However, responding the way he has — by what we call "giving as good as he gets" — isn't working either. It's undignified, it wastes valuable time, it throws fuel on the fire and makes things worse, and it's likely to end with the wife suing the clerk, the hospital, or both. There has to be a better way — and there is.

The type of language behavior used by both of these people is Blaming. We know what happens when a Blaming attack gets a Blaming response, as in the dialogue: That sets up a Blaming Loop. It feeds on itself, and it guarantees combat. Let's do something else instead, as in this revision.

| Wife: | "How can you POSSibly ask me for money when my husband is lying in there in AGony??! DON'T you have any human feelings at ALL??" |
| Clerk: | "People have a very hard time thinking about money when someone they love is in pain." |

Wife:	(Sighs.) Yes. They do. And that's what's wrong with me right now. I'm sorry I took your head off like that."
Clerk:	"That's all right. No problem."

The wife has opened this language interaction with Blaming, as in the original dialogue. But rather than blaming back, the clerk has chosen to use a response of a very different kind: Computing.

The result is also very different. The next two utterances in the dialogue, instead of being yet more Blaming, are Leveling — the plain unadorned truth, going both directions. They show us two people who are now talking to one another, successfully, rather than fighting.

This example is familiar to almost everyone and a perfect demonstration of one of the most common patterns of verbal self-defense. It looks like this:

SPEAKER 1:	Opens with a Blaming utterance.
SPEAKER 2:	Responds with a Computing utterance.
Speaker 1:	Switches to a Leveling utterance.
Speaker 2:	Responds with a Leveling utterance.

Everyone uses these tools. They're part of the grammar of English. But there are three ways to use them.

- One is just to wing it — do whatever feels right to you at the time and depend on blind luck. That's not safe, and it's not smart.

- The second option is to pick one tool and use it all the time, no matter what the situation — any martial artist knows where that is sure to get you.

- The third way — the way that works — is *to make deliberate systematic and strategic choices* among the modes, based on your knowledge of the situation, your skills, and your experience. That's how it supposed to be done.

When you have mastered both a physical martial art and the martial art of verbal self defense, you are no longer at a loss in the multitude of conflict situations in which physical moves are inappropriate or forbidden. Now, it's true: With quiet confidence in your skills, you can go anywhere and know that when violence of any kind comes your way you'll be able to deal with it efficiently, effectively, and honorably. You truly are ready for anything.

—S. E.

. . . . Except perhaps, for dealing with Bad Guys who use exactly the same verbal skills as a means of interviewing, building rapport with, and setting up a victim.

Is violence random?

Did an attack just "come out of the blue"?

Probably not.

Why? Because first (as is common in street attacks) you may be interviewed.

The Interview Language of Physical Attack

As Billy walked away down the aisle, I asked the girl [a young teenager traveling alone] if I could talk to her for a moment, and she hesitantly said yes. It speaks to the power of predatory strategies that she was glad to talk to Billy but a bit wary of the passenger (me) who asked permission to speak with her. "He is going to offer you a ride from the airport," I told her, "and he's not a good guy."

— Gavin de Becker, The Gift of Fear

The patterns presented by Dr. Elgin above are used in verbal attacks perpetrated *in place of* (although they may escalate to) physical violence.

The language of the predator who is fishing, evaluating, preparing to reel in a potential victim is a bit different. The patterns below are an interview, a feint, a trap, a snare, *as preparation for* planned physical violence. They may use exactly the same Sensory and Satir Modes so useful for blending and establishing rapport, to please and to charm. Unlike the verbal patterns of every-day social encounters, these are played as prelude to physical violence, mugging, murder. Counselors who work with criminals must be constantly aware of their attempts to control the conversation — and by extension, the counselor — through verbal attack. Remember Dr. Elgin's Number One rule of verbal self-defense:

Know that you are under attack.

In a situation with a hidden goal of physical attack, there is often a definite pattern and protocol which may rely heavily on language. The following list is based on information in Gavin de Becker's *The Gift of Fear*[9]. The common verbal patterns of a "pre-attack interview" are as follows.

- **Forced Teaming**. Blending and intentional development of rapport for ill purpose. "*We're* in the same boat," "*we* need to," "*we* are," "*we* will"... when it is premature and inappropriate, and sometimes where it might not seem to be.

  In the film *House of Games*, a psychologist is led or allowed by a skilled professional con man to believe that in studying con games together, the two are a "we." The tool he uses is primarily language.

  In Aikido, "teaming" appears in blending with the partner, matching speed, direction and the apparent goal.[10]

- **Charm and "Niceness."** Think of *charm* as a verb rather than a noun, and then consider what the verb "to charm" really means. As de Becker notes:

  "He was so nice" is a comment I often hear from people describing the man who, moments or months after his niceness, attacked them."

---

9. I cannot recommend this book too highly. The title refers to the intuitive sense of fear, foreboding, or foreknowledge that something is wrong or about to happen, so often trained out of us on the basis of good manners, "political correctness," false knowledge, or dismissed on the basis that "feelings" are not "logical." Indeed, they can be a phenomenally accurate reading of intent via body language and verbal patterns. Meanwhile, for those who see "good manners" as equivalent to "doormat," see anything by the formidable Miss Manners (Judith Martin).

Charm is a behavior *choice*, a social *strategy*. It is not *personality*, it is not an indicator of good intent. It is not the same as *goodness*. In Aikido it is perfectly possible to throw *uke* with a gentle smile, great maliciousness of heart and intent to do terrible harm. It is possible in many other situations as well.

- **Too Many Details.** Telling the truth? The teller won't feel doubted. Lying? The teller knows it. Even if it sounds believable to you, it doesn't sound believable to him because he knows better, so he continues to throw in additional details, explanations, and self-justifications, many designed to appeal to emotion.

  There may be more than a touch of Satir's Distractor Mode thrown in to keep the interviewee off-balance, less able to focus on the situation at hand.

  In Aikido it might be an *atemi* and *ki-ai*, plus the three other things that are always going on in almost any Aikido technique. Combined, these produce sensory overload and confusion.

- **Typecasting**. Typecasting involves a slight insult or faintly derogatory remark to which you are expected to respond in such a way as to prove it untrue. "You're probably too young, too old, too stuck up, anal, bitchy, inhibited, too [x] to do [y]." This statement invites you to "prove" that you aren't [x] by doing exactly what the perpetrator hopes you will do which is [y].

  Exactly equivalent to the Aikido strategy of providing a move to counter, for example, dropping a leading arm *down*, then waiting for *uke* to counter by coming *up*. *Nage* adds just enough energy that the final *up* is more than *uke* was expecting — or can deal with.

- **Loan Sharking**. Unsolicited psychic debt. The classic example from the dating world is the fellow who offers dinner; when his date does not deliver on his intended but previously unstated ulterior motive, she is reminded that he "paid for dinner." It attempts to exploit via the target's sense of obligation, no matter how wildly inappropriate that sense of obligation may be.

- **Unsolicited Promises**. One of the most reliable signals of questionable motives. It ties in with lying ("too many details") mentioned above. The predator knows he's not reliable, he's just trying to convince *you* that he is. As Elgin directs, "respond to the presupposition."

  Here, the presupposition is: "You Don't Trust Me." Do not respond to a presupposition as something that must be proven wrong (as in "typecasting") in order for you to be approved as "nice" (by a potential attacker with an agenda). Instead, consider that this person has noticed that you do not trust him. Why is that? You may have good reason not to. When someone says "I promise," consider the presupposed distrust to

---

10. I have long thought of this as "the printer *zempo-nage*." On approaching a graphics house as a first-time walk-in customer, I asked whether payment was due up front or after 30 days or so. Instead of replying directly, the owner looked at me searchingly and asked when the project was due. "Three weeks," I replied. He brightened and immediately extended credit on a thousand-dollar job to a total stranger. Why?

    "Because," he said, "people who give you lead time, are working from a schedule, and behave calmly are rarely out to stiff you. The ones who come in with 'emergency' jobs, short-turn around times, and who work to pull you into a sense of urgency that keeps you up all night working on their projects are the ones who disappear, never to be seen again."

which you are supposed to respond and then consider that your distrust may be exactly the correct response.

- **Discounting "No."** Refusal to hear and to accept "No" is a blatant violation of ma-ai, an attempt to gain control or unwillingness to give it up. In the victim selection interview, it is an active attempt to find the person whose ma-ai, personal space and autonomy can be violated, the easier the better (and the safer and more efficient for the perpetrator).

  In Aikido, violation of ma-ai is time for technique, whether it is simply moving out of that space (in a direction that does not qualify as "effective herding" from the attacker's point of view") and re-establishing ma-ai, or forceful physical action.

The interview is over.

Is violence random and unpredictable? It is actually quite predictable. Oddly enough, it often comes back to etiquette, the standards of proper behavior for a society and life.

Life Etiquette

No matter how many mean things you say or do to someone, they still aren't going to like you for it.

— J. E.

The etiquette taught in aikido [is] mutual respect, consideration for others.

— Kisshomaru Ueshiba

The Way of a Warrior, The Art of Politics, is to stop trouble before it starts. The Way of a Warrior is to establish harmony.

— Morihei Ueshiba

The future is neither ahead nor behind, on one side or another. Nor is it dark or light. It is contained within ourselves; it is drawn from ourselves; its evil and its good are perpetually within us. The future that we seek from oracles, whether it be war or peace, starvation or plenty, disaster or happiness, is not forward to be come upon. Rather its gestation is now, and from the confrontation of that terrible immediacy we turn away . . . as though the future were fixed, unmalleable to the human will, and to be come upon only as a 17th century voyager might descry, through his spyglass, smoke rising from a distant isle.

— Loren Eiseley, The Night Country

So now you have added the power of verbal skills to your weapons bag. How will you practice these tools? In real life as in the dojo, ma-ai and etiquette — good manners and responsibility — are your first line of defense and a powerful tool.

Rudeness in the office causes anxiety, depression, and illness. Managers who dismiss the discomfort of their employees should consider that it also hurts the bottom line via a clear pattern of decreased work time, work hours, effort, and commitment to the company. Rudeness at the home company leads to the same patterns of distrust, despair, and divorce.

Rudeness on the road has led to tragic accidents and deaths, most of which were easily avoidable and just as easily triggered. Studies have shown that persons waiting to turn at a left-turn signal light linger just a wee bit longer if there are cars behind them; that people who know someone is waiting for their parking space take a distinctly longer time to pull out than those who have no one to keep waiting. Although they are small breaches of etiquette, small subtle attacks, the recipients recognize them for what they are, if not consciously, at least at the gut level.

A common plea following violent verbal or physical confrontation is "But I just couldn't let him get away with it!" If an escalating situation leaves you or others dead, injured, or facing legal fees and lost time for no reason other than raging ego and hurt pride, he *has* gotten away with it. More accurately, everyone loses. The discipline of good manners and good sense is part of the toolbox.

This weekend I drove into a crowded parking lot and pulled into a space. When I got out this guy in a car was livid. I had taken his space and didn't I see that he was waiting for it.

I walked over to his car and my first reaction was to tell him to get lost. It then came to me in a flash like Saul of Tarsus on the road to Damascus that maybe I was in the wrong and not him.

"Gee," I said, "I'm sorry. I didn't see you waiting. I'll just move my car and find another space."

"What did you say?" he asked.

"I'll move my car," I said again, "and I'm very sorry."

"Oh," he said. "Look, never mind."

"No I insist. . . It was my fault. I'll move my car."

"No man it's okay!" And he drove away looking perplexed — but mellow.

— Philip Akin, Aikido Yoshinkai Canada

The Timeframe of Violence

Medical conditions are lumped into two categories, "acute" and "chronic." An *acute* condition (from Gr. *ake*, a point; L. *acutus*, something sharp) is one of sudden onset at a given point in time. A *chronic* condition is one that occurs over "time" (from Gr. *kronos*). An aspirin is good for the acute condition known as a "headache." For long-term migraine or cancer, a broken heart or a broken mind, other treatments are needed.

As there is a time frame of physical ills, there is also a time frame of violence.

Martial arts students in particular love to see themselves as noble warriors, waging heroic battles against *Eeviil* with thrilling action-hero derring-do. Yet every great strategist, from Sun-Tzu to Musashi to O-Sensei, has insisted that the greatest art is stopping trouble *before* it starts, either by nipping problems in the bud, or by dealing with the long-term view of the situation. The violently explosive, adrenalin-charged, heroic remedies we imagine are fantasy. Brain candy. Even when applicable they are too often mere band-aid remedies, too little, too late, applied to acute situations years after the chronic problem began its long, slow march through time. As in the "Timing Belt" exercise (page 173), it is equivalent to ignoring the origin and waiting until the blow meets its target.

Suppose you are attacked "On The Street," but succeed in disarming and controlling your attacker. He is tried, convicted, and sent to jail for a very long time. Case closed? Think again. The assault is only the contact point. As in every other attack, there is a time-line. Consider the time-line in both directions.

Consider the future.

Every year, we spend more resources on violence and its consequences. The U.S. has more people in prison (and more people per capita in prison) than any other Western industrialized nation. In 1997, we spent $28.9 billion on 1.2 million prisoners. That is approximately $24,000 a year per prisoner — more than a year of tuition and fees at Harvard University. The tab for an elderly prisoner in poor health is still higher, some $65,000 a year. You will pay that in tax money to support the attacker and his fellow inmates, perhaps while struggling to cover your own rent, food, and tuition or expense for your children. Meanwhile, lives are disrupted or lost on both sides of the equation.

Consider the past.

The attack, the crime, the hatred and anger and fear or exploitation behind it did not appear out of nowhere. Profilers and counselors say that 100 percent — as in *all* — serial killers have a history of being abused as children. If we follow the time line back, we find that these children were not snatched from the street to be damaged by evil perverted strangers. The vast majority of abused children are abused by their families, with the quiet consent of neighbors, friends, and others who see but refuse to see, and so allow the cycle of abuse to continue.

The murderous Cain demanded of God, "Am I my brother's keeper"?

And the response through the ages, through the laws of worthy men and worthy gods has always been: *"Well yes, actually, you are."*

The same is true of that brother's children and all the other lives, souls, and futures that hang in the balance.

It is often said that defending a spouse or child from a violent and abusive partner or parent is a no-win game as the defended will turn on the defender. Why? Because that person has come to confuse abuse with love. The cycle will continue with the next generation.

You must defend against attack, destruction, and murder, but you need not wait until the point of contact. Stopping trouble before it starts, turning the situation from the Dark Side towards the Light is the higher art. Helping and caring for the lost ones and for those who will be lost without help requires more dedication, more caring, more hard work than mere punches, *kata* and kicks.

Aikido is supposed to be great for this. However, despite much idealistic wishful thinking, Aikido doesn't automatically make you wise or kind or noble. It doesn't make you Yoda or Obi-Wan.

It doesn't make you morally superior to karate students, judo players, politicians, or even the local gymnastics team.

Aikido is a tool.

It teaches lessons to those who are paying attention and, like Garrison Keillor's Powder Milk Biscuits, can give shy persons the courage to get up and do what must be done but cannot be done when afraid to speak out, afraid to move, afraid of being battered and broken, afraid of dying.

Innumerable martial artists who began their studies through fear of abuse or a need to "prove" their toughness or manliness have remarked that after acquiring their skills, they no longer needed to use them. Simply knowing that they were in the toolbox was enough.

Aikido gives you tools for war, for peace, for building and beautifying lives, or just for mowing the grass.

And besides all that it's great fun.

Come play!

CHAPTER 10

Resources

Magazines

Aikido Journal
Aiki News, 50-B Peninsula Center Dr. #317, Rolling Hills Estates, CA 90724.
Phone/FAX: (310) 265-0351. Website: http://www.aikidojournal.com e-mail:
ajmag@earthlink.net.

Aikido Today Magazine
Areté Press, P.O. Box #1060, Claremont, CA 91711-1060. Phone: (909) 624-7770,
FAX: (909) 398-1840. Website at: http://www.aiki.com/ATM.

Furyu: The Budo Journal
Tengu Press, P. O. Box 61637, Honolulu, HI 96839 USA. For back issues, editorials,
online order information and forms, animated GIF files, and links to other Japanese
cultural and martial arts sites see: http://www.furyu.com.

Journal of Asian Martial Arts
Via Media Publishing Co., 821 W 24th St., Erie, PA 16502 USA, (800) 455-9517 /
FAX (814) 838-7811. An academic and historical approach to martial arts history
and practice. E-mail: info@goviamedia.com.

Journal of Japanese Sword Arts
JJSA is a monthly (sometimes bimonthly) publication dealing with all aspects of the
Japanese Sword Arts. It developed from *The Iaido Newsletter* which began
publication in 1987. Available by subscription only, from Sei Do Kai:

http://www.uoguelph.ca/~iaido/

Shambhala Publications, Inc.
Horticultural Hall, 300 Massachusetts Avenue, Boston, MA 02115-4544. Order
Line: (800) 726-0600. Website at http://www.shambhala.com

Books, Websites, Organizations

Alexander, Rachel (1999), "Jackson — zen and now": *The Washington Post*, Nov. 9, D-1.
Shaquille O'Neal in the lotus position? A profile of basketball coach Phil Jackson,
brought on to revitalize the ailing Los Angeles Lakers via yoga, zen, and meditation.
A far-out approach? It worked for Michael Jordan and the Bulls. Coach Jackson's
regular season winning percentage is an NBA record.

American Women's Self-Defense Association.
See website at: www.awsda.org.

Anderson, Bob (1980), *Stretching*. Random House.
Probably the most comprehensive manual on stretching to be found.

Associated Press (1999), "Angry moose brought to its knees by politician's oratory":
Jan. 2, 1997.
On the adventures of the deputy mayor of Songdalen, Norway, who encountered an
angry moose while armed only with a rabbit gun and a *ki-ai*.

Bandler, R. and Grinder, J. (1982), *Reframing*. Real People Press.
On changing point of view and the amazing connections between mind, body, and
language.

___ (1979), *Frogs Into Princes*: Real People Press, Moab, UT 84532.
Effective tools for learning and for changing point of view.

Bazancourt, Baron César (1862/1998), *Secrets of the Sword*: Laureate Press.
"A sharp point [is a reality that] makes short work of illusions."

Proposing to share his views of fencing with several acquaintances, some experienced, some novice, the author presents a Socratic dialogue concerning the sword over 11 evenings of instruction. Topics range through fencing, the hard realities of armed combat, and life itself. At the end, the Comte de C. exclaims on the value of the wonderful advice.

"If one could only think of it all at the critical moment, one would be well provided."

"Think of only half of it," answers the Baron, *"and you will not do so badly — there are so many men who cannot think at all."*

Becker, Robert O., (1985) *The Body Electric*: William Morrow & Co.
A thrilling account of Becker's research on regeneration of nerves and limbs, previously believed impossible in any animal higher than salamanders. This is not New-Age fluff or wishful thinking but hard-nosed cutting-edge Real Science. Becker proposes (as have many others) that the healing process, *ki*, *ch'i*, faith healing, spontaneous remissions, placebo effect, all have an underlying common connection — bioelectrical field phenomena. He supports his theories with hard, practical, and revolutionary data which spelled the first hope for spinal cord and other severe injuries.

Berger, K. T., (1988) *Zen Driving:* Ballantine Books.
An update to the traditional Zen walking meditation.

Born, Jan et al. (1999), *Nature*: January 7.
A study from the University of Lubeck in Germany per the ability of certain people to wake up at a designated time without setting an alarm clock, a distinct example of mind-body coordination. As sleep is regulated by the cycling of certain hormones, Born measured hormone levels in 15 sleeping volunteers who had been told they would be awakened at a specific time. About one hour before the subjects were due to be awakened, the hormone adrenocorticotropin surged indicating "that anticipation, which is generally considered to be a unique characteristic of the regulation of conscious action, pervades sleep."

Dalby, Lisa (1993), *Kimono — Fashioning Culture:* Yale University Press.
The history, aesthetics, and meaning of Japanese clothing, from its Chinese inspiration to present-day.

David, Catherine (1996), *The Beauty of Gesture — The Invisible Keyboard of Piano and Tai Chi*: North Atlantic Books.
A lyrical and haunting essay blending *Tai Chi* (or other martial arts) and music.

De Becker, Gavin (1997) *The Gift of Fear*: Dell Publishing.
"The human violence we abhor and fear the most, that which we call 'random' and 'senseless,' is neither . . . We want to believe that human violence is somehow beyond our understanding, because as long as it remains a mystery, we have no duty to avoid it, explore it, or anticipate it. We need feel no responsibility for failing to read signals if there are none to read. We can tell ourselves that violence just happens without warning, and usually to others, but in service of these comfortable myths, victims suffer and criminals prosper."

I cannot say enough about this book. Get it, for yourself, for your loved ones, for your children, for your world. Profound insight into the marvels of the human body, mind, and soul. Is violence random and unpredictable? No. A thorough discussion of the patterns, profiles, protocols, and even the myths of violence. From verbal tools and forms used by Bad Guys to perceptions of time and risk to the making and makeup of "monsters" — why "they" are us and how we create them. Profoundly insightful, wise, compassionate, and practical.

Dobson, Terry, and Miller, Victor (1987) Aikido in Everyday Life — Giving in To Get Your Way: North Atlantic Books.
Translates aggression and defense into the visible realm through the geometry of and symbolism of Aikido's triangle, circle, square. See the movie *Grand Canyon* for an outstanding example of the triangle, circle, square defense.

Drysdale, Alan E., 1996, *Doing Aikido*: Spitz Publishing.
Drysdale wrote his book for "students who are neither total beginners nor advanced *yudansha*" assumes one has some familiarity but is not adept. Emphasis on critical key principles such as extension, leading, and taking of Center. See Alan's exercise for leading in *shiho-nage* ("The Barbarella Lead" on page 194).

Elgin, Suzette Haden (1980), *The Gentle Art of Verbal Self-Defense*: Barnes & Noble Books.
On the mat we learn to recognize a physical attack for what it is and respond appropriately. Here is Aikido applied to verbal and emotional attacks which are far more common than mere physical attack and far more difficult to deal with as training is so rare. The phrase "on the street" as commonly heard and interpreted in martial arts classes is usually nonsense — the real battlegrounds are in the shop, the office, the kitchen, the bedroom, the bar, the beltway. The weapons are words and attitudes. (For business, see Fungaroli, 1996.)

Elgin provides rare and valuable training in the tools and the ethics of language. Compare the linguistic concept of "matching Satir modes" with the Aikido concept of matching speed and direction, blending with the partner or attacker before actual execution of a technique. There are many more books in this series, all excellent and uniquely valuable. She talks Virginia Satir and family relationships but you may hear Lady Jessica and the Bene Gesserit training of *Dune*.

In the real world, self-defense seldom involves physical techniques and throws. A Hard Truth: Because most attacks and assaults are non-physical, physical responses (throws and blows to the overbearing boss or annoying co-worker) are options only in the realm of fantasy. Here's how to deal with Real Life. And yes, "On the Street" because Bad Guys use these techniques too. See de Becker (1997).

Additional seminar materials including the two following publications, are available only via mail-order. Contact: Ozark Center for Language Studies (OCLS), P. O. Box 1137-R, Huntsville, AR 72740 or call (501) 559-2273. E-mail: ocls@madisoncounty.net or http://www.sfwa.org/members/elgin

Language in Emergency Medicine: On dealing with patients or family members who are hurt, hysterical, and abusive.

Language in Law Enforcement: It is always disturbing to meet frightened beginners who think they need killing techniques for "on the street." Police and others actually on the street know that "99% of the job is verbal." And no one gets more or worse verbal abuse than these folks. A fascinating manual on verbal *tenkan*, redirecting, and neutralization, for those who are really "on the street" as opposed to fearing or fantasizing about it.

___ (1997) *Try to Feel It My Way*: John Wiley & Sons.
Some students deal best with written visual input, while some need to hear. Others are "feelers" for whom "visualizing" is a non-starter. No they can't "see" it. They "don't get it" partly because they are operating in another mode entirely. These are touch dominants, people who have to "get their hands on things" in order to "grasp" new material. Rephrasing visual images to a different sensory set such as "feel a warm weight at your center" will help get the point across as will having students go through technique with eyes closed. The mother-lode of information on "TD's."

Fudebakudo. For the world's greatest Aikido cartoons, see www.fudebakudo.com.

Fungaroli, Carole S., 1996, *The Slam and Scream*: The Noonday Press.
Think of this as: *The Irimi/Tenkan and Ki-Ai* in business life. Punches, kicks, and throws do not transfer well from the mat to the business world. The inner techniques and basic concepts do — and may be critical to your survival. This is "Self-Defense

9-5" written especially for secretaries, admin assistants, and clerks who are mugged on a daily basis by unrealistic pay scales, power games, retaliatory firings, society's stereotypes and their own perceptions of work and available life goals. Hilariously entertaining, wickedly accurate, and packed with practical information. See Elgin for the language skills critical to actually applying the above.

Gaines, Patrice (1999), "Hitting the Head Pin — Blind Bowlers Ready to Make a Mark": The Washington Post, Saturday, November 13, B-1.
An article on blind bowlers who must and do extend and target with the mind's eye.

Glassner, Barry (1999), *The Culture of Fear — Why Americans are Afraid of the Wrong Things*: Basic Books.
Crime, drugs, minorities, teen moms, killer kids, mutant microbes, plane crashes, road rage, and so much more. See this and a current almanac for the real statistics behind what they tell you on the news at 11 and what they don't. In many ways an update of Cantril's classic psychological study of panic over the Halloween 1939 Orson Welles' radio presentation of *War of the Worlds*.

Gluck, Jay (1996), *Zen Combat:* Personally Oriented.
Jay Gluck is the author of "Masters of the Bare Hand Kill," the 1957 *True* magazine article that introduced karate to America. The article expanded to become the karate chapter of the original (1962) edition of *Zen Combat*. He was asked to photograph Ueshiba for a similar article on Aikido, but when editors saw the resulting photos of American military police, karate blackbelts, and sword-wielding *kendoka*, all "looking everywhere but at the little old target," they rejected the photos as "posed" or "rigged." "Modern Zen Fools" details an encounter between Morihei Ueshiba and the cartoonist/engineer Rube Goldberg. Like Terry Dobson's "A Kind Word Turneth Away Wrath," a rare glimpse at the real spirit behind "real Aikido."

Grayson, Betty and Stein, Morris (1981), "Attracting assault — victims' nonverbal cues": *Journal of Communication:* Winter, vol. 31, n. 1, p. 68.
How do muggers select their victims on the street? It is fast (about 7 seconds), unconscious, but heavily based on posture and body movement. Also reviewed in the August 1980 Psychology Today: "Body Language that Speaks to Muggers."

Grinder, J. and Bandler, R. (1981), *Trance-formations — Neuro-Linguistic Programming and the Structure of Hypnosis*: Real People Press.
More on Mind-Body Coordination from the psychological side.

Hall, Edward T. (1973), *The Silent Language*: Anchor Books.
The classic work on something that every culture defines differently and every culture takes for granted: time and space: *ma-ai*. See also de Becker (1997) for the protocols of attack in crime and violence.

Hallie, Philip (1997), *Tales of Good and Evil, Help and Harm*: HarperCollins.
The best work I have ever seen on the dilemma of violence versus pacifism, of good versus evil, the creation of good and light out of chaos. It ranges from the story of Le Chambon in Vichy France to Joshua Hull, who founded the beginnings of the U. S. Coast Guard at a time when luring ships and their passengers to death and destruction were a viable economic base for many seaside towns.

Heckler, Richard Strozzi (1990), *In Search of the Warrior Spirit*: North Atlantic Books.
A chronicle of Heckler's teaching of awareness disciplines to the Green Berets, and what he learned from them. A superb work in many ways. Particularly remarkable for the recurring themes of Us versus Them, the myth of the belligerent professional killer versus the peaceful and morally superior martial artist or civilian, and our cultural identities of strong versus weak. A thoughtful exploration of the nature of a true warrior versus the fantasy version.

Homma, Gaku (1993), *Children and the Martial Arts — An Aikido Point of View*: North Atlantic Books.
An excellent manual on the pros and cons of martial arts for children and for those who care about them on and off the mat.

Homma, Gaku (1990), *Aikido for Life*: North Atlantic Books.
On beginning Aikido, from the point of view of the new student and the instructor. Succinct, insightful, and wise.

Impact Personal Safety and PREPARE, Inc.
This program comprises several programs including that formerly known as Model Mugging. For programs in your area, call 1-800-345-5425 or visit their web page at: http://www.PREPAREINC.com. For children, see safety@kidpower.org.

Highly recommended for intensive and practical self-defense. This approach is particularly suitable for women based on the observation that most martial arts such as karate and boxing were designed by and for men and rely on upper body strength. Like Aikido, Impact Personal Safety relies more on hips, legs, and center.

Like Gracie jujutsu, it emphasizes going to and applying techniques on the ground. Unlike all of these, it acknowledges specific differences between attacks on men and attacks on women. Men attacking men? Face-to-face and territorial. Men attacking women? The predator approaching from behind with a grab and a strangling chokehold. *Ushiro.*

Internet and World Wide Web Addresses and Resources.
Web addresses and pages for Aikido information on the Internet.

http://www.aikiweb.com is Jun Akiyama's Aikido Web, the most popular Aikido site on the web. To find a dojo, see http://www.aikisearch.com. See also:

http://www.aikido-l.org

for information on the Aikido-L, a high-volume mailing list on all topics of Aikido. maintained by Kjartan Clausen of Norway, and by Jun Akiyama in the U. S. A. For Kjartan's superb Aikido FAQ pages, see (and please read before posting):

http://www.ii.uib.no/~kjartan/aikidofaq/

Aikikai Hombu Dojo offers information (including addresses and phone numbers) on *shihan* sent abroad (currently 9 to the United States). See their webpage at:

http://www.aikikai.org/about/dojo_e.html

For the Virginia Ki Society in Merrifield, Virginia, see: http://vakisociety.org or (703) 573-8843 (*dojo*) or Chief Instructor George Simcox at kimas@erols.com. The Official Ki Society Web Page with dojo addresses and information is at:

http://pw1.netcom.com/~aikidoki/Directory.html

The "Unofficial Ki Society Web Page" includes essays, commentary, and links at:

http://unofficial.ki-society.org

See Aikido Yoshinkai website for an extensive multimedia gallery of video clips at:

www.aikido-yoshinkai.org

For updates on the above addresses and other information contained in this book,

http://Round-Earth.com

If Aikido just isn't for you, consider a new and terrible martial art (and just look at the tests for black belt!)

http://www.geocities.com/Colosseum/Stadium/2477/index2.htm

Kernan, Michael (1989), "The durable wit of Stan Freberg — a humorist's memoir of the gag life": *The Washington Post*, Sunday, February 5, p. F-1.
On building worlds in the mind.

Lessac, Arthur (1960), *The Use and Training of the Human Voice —A Bio-Dynamic Approach to Vocal Life*: Mayfield Publishing Company.

____ (1978), *Body Wisdom*: Lessac Research, 20 Vermont Ave., White Plains NY.
Lessac is one of the most famous voice coaches in the theatre and acting world.

He taught voice by teaching Unbendable Arm many years ago. Many of his lessons on "floating" took place in a pool to actually experience the feeling followed by "recreate the feeling" on land and in air. He talked of "radiating energy" (we would talk of "extending ki") and of buoyant energy (where we would talk of "weight underside") explained as "Gravity down, but air up."

MacYoung, Marc (1993), *Ending Violence Quickly — How Bouncers, Bodyguards, and Other Security Professionals Handle Ugly Situations*: Paladin Press.
Grim but informative reading by a professional bouncer, prison and security guard. Although he mentions the verbal skills needed to defuse impending violence his commentary is largely on recognizing the verbal signals of impending aggression. For real verbal skills, see Elgin. For information on the futility of being logical with drunks and what to do instead, plus street smarts and how not to be a target, see this.

Marshall, John (1988), *Make Your Own Japanese Clothes*: Lark Books.
Anyone can make a plain *gi* and belt (plus many other garments) quickly and easily. Here's how. Does not include *hakama*; for that see order form in back of this book.

Mauldin, Bill (1945), *Up Front With Bill Mauldin*: Henry Holt and Co., Inc. Facsimile edition published by W. W. Norton & Co., 1995.
A 50th anniversary re-issue of the WWII classic. A review of real (as opposed to imaginary) martial art in real life, starring Mauldin's Everysoldier dogfaces, infantry riflemen Willie and Joe. Reading the accompanying essay and text in 1999 is even more poignant now than I ever remember it being when I read it years ago.

Mizukoshi, Hiro (1997), *Aiki Tessenjutsu*: Airyudo, Tokyo, Japan.
A book of instructions on using the *tessen* (iron fan) as a weapon. In Japanese with excellent pictures. Book and fans available from Mugendo Budogu (see "Supplies" on page 267) or visit http://www.budogu.com

Model Mugging. See Impact Personal Safety.

Morgan, Forrest E. (1992), *Living the Martial Way*: Barricade Books.
A valuable overview of martial arts with clear and practical viewpoints on what it means to be a martial artist. To this career military officer, it isn't a sport or game and it certainly isn't a fashion show. Addresses many common concerns, from evaluating a *dojo*, avoiding scams and cults, bowing vs. religion, training goals and procedures. Remarkable for its chapter on the meaning of "honor" as opposed to "pride" or "face" with an actual checklist for evaluating the underlying motives for revenge or suicide. Don't laugh: this list would quickly reveal most such undertakings for what they actually are in Real Life or the cinema substitute.

Moss, Riki and Watson, Jan E. (1993) *It's a Lot Like Dancing*: Frog, Ltd.
A memoir by and of the late Terry Dobson as he went about the exercise of dying. Good sense, salty wisdom and the luminous photographic art of Jan Watson.

Nagrin, Daniel (1988), *How to Dance Forever*: William Morrow and Co.
"We practiced our dance numbers for eight hours a day for six weeks prior to principal photography," — Ginger Rogers
Is Aikido "a lot like dancing?" Not exactly. Dancing is much harder. If you're having problems with fatigue or injury with a heavy practice schedule of say, 10-12 hours per week, consider the professional dancer who may now practice for 10-12 hours per day for weeks or months on end. Nagrin began his distinguished solo performance career in 1957 at age 40, which popular wisdom considers retirement age for dancers and other athletes. Practical and pithy advice from the trenches on what works, what doesn't, why and how to keep you dancing — on the stage or on the mat — forever.

National Highway Traffic Safety Administration (1999), *An investigation of the Safety Implications of Wireless Communications in Vehicles*: U. S. Department of Transportation (DOT).
If you have trouble believing the benefits of focus, consider the flip side: the consequences of distraction. Researches concluded that talking on the phone while driving was equivalent to blood alcohol levels of at least the legal limit.
See: http://www.nhtsa.dot.gov/people/injury/research/wireless/

Olson, Gregory D., Seitz, Frank C., and Guldbrandsen, Frank (1996), "An inquiry into application of gokyo (Aikido's fifth teaching) on human anatomy" in: *Perceptual & Motor Skills*, vol. 82, pp. 1299-1303.
An anatomical investigation of *gokyo* to determine the source of pain involving manipulation of the wrist joint and associated ligaments. See also Seitz, F. C.

___ and Seitz, Frank C. (1994) "What's causing the pain?— a re-examination of the Aikido nikyo technique" in: *Perceptual & Motor Skills*, vol. 79, pp. 1585-1586.
Presents the conclusions of two separate investigations (one being Olson and Seitz' 1993 paper) of *nikyo* and the possible reasons for discrepancies in their results.

___ and Seitz, Frank C., and Guldbrandsen, Frank (1994) "An anatomical analysis of Aikido's Third teaching — An investigation of sankyo" in: Perceptual & Motor Skills, vol. 78 pp.1347-1352.
An anatomical study of the muscles, tendons, and ligaments involved in *sankyo*.

___ and Seitz, F. C. (1993), "An anatomical analysis of Aikido's second teaching — an investigation of nikyo" in: *Perceptual & Motor Skills*, Vol. 77, pp. 123-131.
A careful anatomical analysis of the cause of the pain produced by *nikyo*.

___ (1990), "An examination of Aikido's fourth teaching — an anatomical study of the tissues of the forearm" in: *Perceptual & Motor Skills*, vol. 71, pp. 1059-1066.
The anatomy of Aikido's "fourth teaching" (*yonkyo* or *tekubi-osae*).

O'Connor, Greg (1993), *The Aikido Student Handbook*: Frog, Ltd.
An excellent basic introduction to Aikido for beginners in the United States Aikido Federation (USAF).

Pipher, Mary (1994), *Reviving Ophelia*: Ballantine Books.
A gritty look at the very real consequences of our media-soaked society, what our glorification and marketing of sex and violence is doing to our children, and case histories of those who are paying the consequences. Pipher calls for a "new form of self-defense" with a new definition of *freedom*: not the liberty to blow here and there with the voices of friends, the media, or the winds of the day, but "effective setting of goals and sailing toward your dreams." The author is also remarkable for the ability to appreciate a client for who and what she is at the time, then build on that. Perhaps all counselors are trained to do so, but here it is striking.

While this work focuses on young girls, the consequences have been just as bad or worse for boys, in so many ways the more fragile sex. Boys represent three out of every four children identified as learning disabled and four of every five juvenile court cases involving crimes. They commit 95 percent of juvenile homicides, and are far more likely than girls to have drug and alcohol problems.

In the wake of the Littleton, Colorado, shootings clinical psychologist Patricia Dalton noted that "boys have more problems than girls in virtually every category you can think of with the exception of eating disorders." For those of us who feel that this is someone else's problem, Dalton warns: "While girls tend to internalize problems, taking their unhappiness out on themselves, boys externalize them, taking their unhappiness out on others." Girls or boys. Boys or girls. Our children. Our future.

Pinkman Pitching
A professional pitching coach who like many practitioners in the growing field of sports psychology, uses *ki* exercises to improve physical performance. See: www.pinkmanpitching.com.

Prudden, Bonnie (1985), *Myotherapy*: Ballantine Books.
Aikido is easier on your body than almost any of the other martial arts but you may nevertheless develop occasional muscular aches and pains. *Kiatsu* ("pressing with *ki*") uses pressure and *ki* for healing. I was trained in myotherapy which uses pressure only but I quickly found that purely mechanical pressure is far less effective than a combination. On the other hand, energy running along seemingly mysterious "meridians" is disturbing to many Westerners. There is, however, a better than 90 percent correlation between the acupuncture, *shiatzu*, or *kiatsu* lines based on

meridians and the myotherapy lines based on muscle attachments — no mysterious new organs or "*ki* glands" required.

In my opinion, "lines" in the different pressure techniques are a short-cut method of following anatomy. You can refer to "Line A and B" or you can refer to "the medial and lateral aspect of the erector spinae." A&B is easier, but the other is extremely descriptive (once you learn the terms) and introduces you to the universal language of medicine. Per myotherapy, see note in Nagrin (1988). For a more scientific approach, see Travell (1983).

Ravizza, Ken, 1995), *Heads-Up Baseball — Playing the Game One Pitch at a Time*: Spalding Sports Library.
The internal game of baseball.

Salzman, Mark (1995), *Lost in Place — Growing Up Absurd in Suburbia*: Vintage Books.
  "When I was thirteen years old I saw my first kung fu movie, and before it ended I decided that the life of a wandering Zen monk was the life for me. I announced my willingness to leave East Ridge Junior High School immediately and give up all material things, but my parents did not share my enthusiasm. They made it clear that I was not to become a wandering Zen monk until I had finished high school. In the meantime I could practice kung fu and meditate down in the basement. So I immersed myself in the study of Chinese boxing and philosophy with the kind of dedication that is possible only when you don't yet have to make a living, when you are too young to drive and when you don't have a girlfriend."

A charming and hilarious account of growing up in the 70's while seeking enlightenment through martial arts, sidetrips through astronomy and cello practice and an excellent answer to the eternal question: "Why bother?"

Samenow, Stanton E. (1984), *Inside the Criminal Mind:* Times Books.
Chilling insight into the criminal mind. It is, interestingly enough, practically a blow-by-blow parallel of Scott Peck's *People of the Lie* writ secular. Peck emphasizes the first step of breaking through The Pretense. Samenow presents people who actively choose to steal, assault, rape, and kill not out of desperation but because it is convenient or because they simply *enjoy* doing these things.

Rather than emphasizing vocational training for convicts as the solution to all ills (because "what you get is a criminal with a new skill") he works only with those who genuinely want to "get clean." This approach[1] skews the group from the start, but is the only true starting point. From there comes a program of strict responsibility and honesty. Does it work? For these clients, Samenow's program is renowned for having beaten the statistics on recidivism. Invaluable insight on criminal choices and behavior, its origin in children, and an opportunity for we, the supposedly "Good People," to take a long, hard look in the mirror at our own hearts and minds.

Saotome, Mitsugi (1993), *Aikido and the Harmony of Nature*: Shambhala Publications.
History and anecdotes of Aikido founder Morihei Ueshiba by a former live-in students (*uchi-deshi*). Ranges from the ideals of honor and service in the *samurai* tradition, to the elements of "reality," wave-forms, gravity, and spirituality woven into the descriptions of individual Aikido techniques.

___ (1989), *The Principles of Aikido*: Shambhala Publications.
Aikido philosophy and techniques. Particularly remarkable for the chapters on "The Sword" and "Ukemi." If you are caught in the common beginners' delusion of *nage* as "winner" and *uke* as "loser," this will help you see *ukemi* (giving attacks and taking falls) as discipline and art in its own right.

---

1. It has much in common with that of an ancient Jewish rabbi renowned for his healing abilities whose opening question was: "Do you *want* to get better?"

Seitz, Frank C., Olson, Gregory D., and Stenzel, Thomas E. (1991), "A martial arts exploration of elbow anatomy — ikkyo (Aikido's first teaching)" *in: Perceptual & Motor Skills*, Vol. 73, pp. 1227-1234.
An examination of the nerves, bones, muscles and mechanics affected by *ikkyo*.

Siegal, Bernie (1990) *Love, Medicine, and Miracles*: Harperperrenial Library.
The value and even the reality of the link between mind and body is often considered somewhere in the realm of theoretical. (If all those remarkable recoveries are due to "misdiagnosis" as some claim we have other problems!) Here the link is shown to be very real indeed and of immense value to those who beat all the odds, bypassed all the statistics, overcame standard medical wisdom and defeated cancer and other deadly conditions of body and soul.

Shifflett, C. M. (1997), *Ki in Aikido — A Sampler of Ki Exercises*: Round Earth Publishing.
Exercises used in the Ki Society for stability, balance, and relaxation, and for the patterning of Aikido techniques. Includes instructions for the test technique and step-by-step exercises. Fully illustrated with detailed line drawings.

Shioda, Gozo (1968) [Trans.: Geoffrey Hamilton], *Dynamic Aikido*: Kodansha.
Aikido Yoshinkan style, with clear, close-up photographs. Especially valuable for notations of lines of force. Some consider this to be "Aikido Lite" compared to Shioda's subsequent *Total Aikido*. Both are valuable. *Dynamic Aikido* has one clear advantage over *Total Aikido* — larger pictures. *Total Aikido* has more illustrations but these had to be reduced to fit available space and the photographs do not include the lines of force and direction shown in *Dynamic Aikido* drawings. Consider including both in your Aikido library.

___(1996) [Trans. David Rubens] *Total Aikido — The Master Course*: Kodansha.
Excellent enlargement of the Yoshinkan style *Dynamic Aikido*. The photos do not have the close-up detail of the first book but this is because so much more material is presented. Many techniques are shot from overhead against a grid; text emphasizes important points and common mistakes. One problem: in some pictures, the point the picture is trying to make is about half a second later than the snapshot. Especially useful for the notes on how not to do it. A valuable resource for all styles. For a remarkably irreverent commentary, see Twigger (1997).

Smith, Timothy K. (1991), "Manfred Clynes sees a pattern in love — he's got the printouts": *The Wall Street Journal,* Tuesday Sept. 24, 1991, A-1.
On neuroscientist Clynes and his work on "sentics," the waveforms of touch, emotion, and music. See http://www.superconductor.com/clynes/WSJ_art.htm.

Snyder, Brian Joseph (1998) "From fear to love — the simple steps" *in: The Rebirthing Newsletter*, vol. 10, n. 1.
A New Age commentary on *breathing* per Manfred Clynes' waveforms of emotion. See: http://www.netreach.net/people/waterboy/seminars/text/tolove.htm. "Aikido is love," said Ueshiba. If the waveform of love is a sine wave . . . .

Sprackland, Robert (1998), *Instructor — Teaching the Martial Arts*: Young Forest Co.
Short and to the point. Teaching styles, teaching myths, and teaching. Rank does not mean ability to teach. Teaching is an entirely separate learned skill and here is a good place to start. Includes basic but critical information on setting up a *dojo* or training program. Sensible and valuable for both instructors and students.

Stevens, John (1984), *Aikido — The Way of Harmony*: Shambhala Publications.
Biographies of the Founder of Aikido, Morihei Ueshiba, and of Shirata Rinjiro, the author's instructor. Detailed analysis of Aikido philosophy and techniques with such basics as proper bowing, sitting, standing, breathing. Extensive photographs.

Sullivan, Edward F. (1993), *Necessary and Reasonable Force*: Modern Bu-jutsu.
Consider the common notion that "On The Mat" a technique is done one way, but "On The Street" you can and should beat the stuffing out of an attacker. The people who are *really* "On The Street" — police officers and emergency personnel — know very well that this popular fantasy is just that — fantasy. Here a veteran Chicago police officer discusses the legal meaning of "necessary and reasonable force" and

liability. Techniques for de-escalating situations without resorting to force (with anecdotes of rookies who didn't, apparently due to watching too many cop shows). Take-away's and controls for the times when physical techniques are necessary. Notice the emphasis on *ma-ai,* stepping off-line, and again, the affirmation that some 95 percent of the job is verbal.

Talbot, Michael (1991), *The Holographic Universe*: HarperPerennial.
An astonishing new view of reality: the Universe as an immense hologram. A unified field theory of consciousness and matter.

Tanner, Ogden (1989), "Bonsai —- a way of looking at trees with different eyes" in *Smithsonian Magazine*, Vol. 20, n. 7 (October).
The history and some unusual applications of the art of *bonsai.*

Thompson, Geoff (1994), *Watch My Back — A Bouncer's Story*: Paladin Press.
Physical violence of the bar-bully type is almost always preceded by distinct verbal and postural rituals, presented here in great detail.

Tohei, Koichi (1978), *Ki in Daily Life*: Ki No Kenkyukai H.Q., Tokyo, Japan.
I was pleased to have read this book just for the commentary on the Japanese phrase *suisei-mushi*, meaning "to be born drunk and to die while still dreaming." Koichi Tohei was student, *uchi-deshi, and designated Chief instructor* for Aikido founder Morihei Ueshiba. He is the founder of *Shin-shin Toitsu Aikido* (Aikido with Mind-Body Coordination).Here are standard Aikido exercises linked to daily living.

___ (1976), *Book of Ki — Coordinating Mind and Body in Daily Life*: Japan Publications.
From training body, mind, and soul to raising a golf handicap. Contains exercises and an introduction to *kiatzu*, a method of healing with *ki*.

Travell, Janet G., M.D., and Simons, David G., M.D. (1983), *Myofascial Pain and Dysfunction — The Trigger Point Manual, Vol. 1*: Williams & Wilkins.

___ (1992), *Myofascial Pain and Dysfunction — The Lower Extremities, Vol. 2*: Williams and Wilkins.
The late Dr. Travell was Professor Emeritus of Clinical Medicine at The George Washington University School of Medicine, and these are the landmark book on muscular pain and dysfunction. "Paradoxical Breathing" (Vol. 1) explains the importance of correct breathing and the consequences of improper breathing. If unfamiliar with medical terminology, the superb pictures alone are adequate for understanding why too many *kote-gaeishi* will produce sore muscles or numb hands; why you may be dizzy while rolling — and how to fix it.

Text emphasizes injections of a muscle relaxant, a non-option for non-physicians and not even necessary as pressure techniques such as myotherapy or *kiatsu* may be equally effective while avoiding the post treatment pain that follows injections. See Prudden (1984) for a non-medical version based on muscle origins and attachments in lay terms plus a description of the basic pressure technique; see Tohei (1978, 1983) for the same concepts based on meridians; see Zi (1996) for breathing exercises; see Nagrin (1988) for these and other approaches which an athlete in a sport that looks a *lot* like dancing has found most helpful.

Twigger, Robert (1997), *Angry White Pyjamas* — An Oxford Poet Trains with the Tokyo Riot Police: Indigo, London.
Sara thought martial arts were pretty silly. To a trendy young Japanese, aikido was about as sexy as morris dancing.

Twigger combines insight, inanity, history, hilarity and commentary on traditional and modern Japanese culture. Many Yoshinkan practitioners have been outraged by its apparently myopic point of view, while others have privately giggled over some all-too-accurate descriptions. Whatever your conclusions, it's a highly entertaining read centering around a brutally demanding course "where any ascetic motivation soon comes up against blood-stained dogis and fractured collarbones." Surely the only Aikido book combining goldfish, Mike Tyson, roaches, mildew, and martial arts all in one. Reviewed by BBC (Jan 99) as one of the best books of the year.

Sequel: *Big Snake*, in which the irrepressible Twigger, while surfing the Internet, discovers that the Roosevelt Prize of $50,000 for the live capture of a snake over 30 feet long is still unclaimed and, with a brilliant leap of logic (apparently due to "between engagement and marriage" jitters and despite the fact that snakes rarely grow over 30 feet), decides he is the obvious man for the job. Much the way he decided to enter the Riot Police training program after only six months in Aikido.

Ueshiba, Kisshomaru (1987), *The Spirit of Aikido*: Kodansha.
The late Kisshomaru Ueshiba was the son of Morihei Ueshiba, Founder of Aikido, and the head of Aikikai. Presents a detailed review of the underlying philosophy of Aikido and its pre-WWII history.

U. S. Dept. of Transportation, An Investigation of the Safety Implications of Wireless Communications in Vehicles: National Highway Traffic Safety Administration.
See http://www.nhtsa.dot.gov/people/injury/research/wireless/ for electronic version. Cell-phones and their distractions to driving, and compared to equivalent impairment by high blood-alcohol levels.

Voltaire, *Candide* (1759).
A wry and witty look at human nature. This 18th-century masterpiece is as sparkling today as it was then. Available on the Internet at: http://www.litrix.com/candide.

Yoshikawa, Eiji (1935/1981), *Musashi*: Kodansha.
This epic tale of Japan's legendary swordsman Musashi Miyamoto is often compared to James Clavell's highly fictionalized *Shogun*. Clavell ends with Lord Toranaga (the actual historical Tokugawa Ieyesu) preparing for the fateful battle of Sekigahara. Yoshikawa's story begins with the young Takezo going to war in hopes of honor and glory only to end among the dead and dying on that same battlefield. Ieyasu's bloody victory ended generations of relentless warfare under rival lords competing for power and control. Hence while Yoshikawa's novel offers plenty of thrills and adventure, it is also the tale of a warrior learning to live in a strange new world where peace was unexpectedly broken out.

Not even the phenomenally clunky English translation[2] can ruin the swashbuckling tale or the wonderful images of a long-vanished world: a band of honorable *samurai* who support themselves by weaving horseshoes of straw rather than turning to brigandry, the Rent-a-Cow transportation system with in-flight meals, lords and ladies, a wise priest, and a lesson on rigidity and relaxation learned from a lute.

Walker, Jearl (1985), "Roundabout — The Physics of Rotation in the Everyday World" [Readings from "The Amateur Scientist" in *Scientific American*]: W. H. Freeman & Co.
The physics (lever arms and centers of rotation) behind the techniques. Aikidoist Walker discusses the physics of *yokomen-uchi*, *ushiro-nage*, the judo hip-throw, and why as a Small Person he gave up karate for Aikido. How we do what we do on the purely mechanical level.

Westbrook, A., and Ratti, O. (1970), *Aikido and the Dynamic Sphere:* Charles E. Tuttle Co.
The classic Aikido textbook, written when Koichi Tohei was Chief Instructor at Honbu *dojo* in Tokyo. Invaluable for the superb line-drawings which emphasize the circular motions and for its presence on the bookshelves of Aikido students worldwide. Also consider: if you're trying to describe a technique over the Internet to a fellow practitioner using a different set of terms, a good bet is to reference the page and technique via this book.

---

2. So tin-eared, so awkward that it is painfully reminiscent of Mark Twain's essay on "James Fenimore Cooper's Literary Offenses" and even P. D. Q. Bach — and *still* a great story. The book appeared on a *Highlander* PR trailer, apparently only because the cover features a sword. The writers apparently knew nothing of it. A pity.

Yausa, Yasuo (1993), *The Body, Self-Cultivation and Ki-Energy.* State University of New York Press.
An examination of *ki* in history, martial arts, healing, and daily life.

Zi, Nancy (1986), *The Art of Breathing.* Vivi Co.
Exercises with visualizations for improved breathing by a professional singer and voice coach. In Aikido, as in yoga and other arts, breathing is a discipline in and of itself. The idea is this: If you can't control your own breathing, you control nothing. Order from Vivi Co., P. O. Box 750, Glendale, CA 91209-0750 / 1-818-500-8084. http://theartofbreathing.com.

Movies and Videos

I am Hieronimo, I am Tamberlin,
I am Faustus, Barabbas, the Jew of Malta, and . . .
Oh yes, Shakespeare. . .
I am Henry VI.

—*Actor Ned Alleyn, Shakespeare in Love*

Many an actor has noted that acting is a form of reincarnation. It gives you the opportunity to experience and understand hundreds of lifetimes in addition to your own. While most movies and videos presented here are fictional, the ideas behind them and the people who choose to convey these particular ideas are real or may become real. Observe purpose and intent.

Bad Day at Black Rock (Director: John Sturges, 1954)
Classic tale by John Sturges, director of *The Great Escape* and *The Magnificent Seven.* Merely by appearing unannounced and unexpected, a mild-mannered stranger (Spencer Tracey) sends a small town with a dark secret into a frenzy of suspicion and fear. A story of choices: the shame and guilt of having made the wrong ones, the terror and opportunity of a second chance. Includes a short scene of karate versus the classic Western Bully filmed in 1954 when karate was still a rare and exotic oriental art. See Gluck (1996).

Clean and Sober (Director: Glenn Gordon Caron, 1988)
Facing drug and murder charges, real-estate hotshot Daryl Poynter (Michael Keaton) decides that a drug clinic, with its guarantee of complete anonymity, would be the perfect hideout — and is in for a big surprise.

While this appears to be a movie about *drug* addiction, it is actually about *addiction* in its endless variety, whether to external sources or internal ones, whether material goods, alcohol, sex, food, self-image or the desire to prey on or to control others to hide one's own lack of self-control. Morgan Freeman as a drug counselor and M. Emmet Walsh as an Alcoholics Anonymous counselor can't be fooled because they've been there themselves and already know all the lies. Notice the two different images of car headlights presented at the beginning of the film and at the very end.

Enter the Dragon (Director: Robert Clouse, 1973)
At the beginning of this movie there is a brief shot of a young girl sculling a boat in the harbor, a brief but excellent demonstration of *funekogi-undo*, the "rowing exercise." The classic spoof on this classic Bruce Lee film is Kentucky Fried Movie, "feature attraction" of "Fistful of Yen." See also Bruce Lee's *Chinese Connection* (1972) in which actors portraying Japanese wear their *hakama* backwards and their evil master is made up to bear a remarkable resemblance to Toshiro Mifune.

Exposed! Pro-Wrestling's Greatest Secrets (Don Wiener, 1998)
A fascinating review of the circus act known as "pro-wrestling." Between the hype, the shills, the cartoon costumes, and the scripted wins and losses, it's easy to say that "it's all fake." Well it isn't. It is real, industrial-strength *ukemi*. No one is supposed to get hurt, but should anything go wrong, the risk of accidental injury is very real. The physics are real. The *ukemi* is real. These men are real athletes and this is one really tough way to make a living. Available from www.NBC.com (1-800-NBC-4144). Fascinating viewed in tandem with Bruce Bookman's *Ukemi* tapes.

The Firm (Director: Sydney Pollack, 1993)
One of the few modern movies, including martial arts and others, where the protagonist uses his head rather than just punching or running. A mysterious law firm spins a web of easy money and material things. No one has ever escaped and lived until neophyte lawyer Mitch McDeere (Tom Cruise) finds a way out with a small but powerful weapon of the law and negotiation. The FBI investigator, wanting something a bit more dramatic is incredulous, yet "it's more than you had on Al Capone!" retorts McDeere. Dramatic and bombastic not necessary — just what works. An excellent performance by Gene Hackman as a lonely man who wishes he had done better — and does.

In Dan Millman's *Peaceable Warrior*, Socrates proclaimed gymnastics to be "a warrior's art." Observe its use in contrast to more standard weaponry in McDeere's campaign for life, law, and freedom. Consider the *tenkan* of his announcement of contact by the FBI, and the stunning *irimi* of negotiation with a deadly client.

Grand Canyon (Director: Lawrence Kasdan, 1992)
A strange and beautiful look at violence, real and imaginary, the interrelationships between lives and the things that actually matter. In the beginning moments of this film you will see a great Aikido Master working as a towtruck driver (Danny Glover). Watch what he does and how he does it then compare his actions with Terry Dobson's diagrams for attack and defense. (See Dobson, 1987.) Another haunting scene follows Steve Martin's portrayal of a movie maker exploiting the lucrative genre of make-believe violence; after a real mugging he sees the light — then chooses to walk back into the darkness.

The Great Escape (Director: John Sturges, 1963)
Based on a true story of Allied prisoners of war who tunnelled out of a German prison camp in 1944. Of the 75 escapees, those who got into gun battles at the rail stations, punched out guards, stole aircraft and other dramatic and highly visible solutions to the problem, never made it. This is the source of the famous scene (and poster) of Steve McQueen fruitlessly attempting to elude Nazi pursuers via State Fair motorcycle stunts. (Legend has it that he refused to make the movie unless allowed to film this bravura sequence.)

Who actually escaped? Only three: two who posed as harmless fishermen and one on a bicycle, all with a firm goal but who moved so calmly and gently that they never aroused the suspicions of watching soldiers. Also notice the character and behavior of the camp commandant and those under his command in contrast to more modern portrayals of German troops. The original book by inmate Paul Brickhill is still in print, superb, and well worth reading. Strategy, feint, technique, and teaming.

Groundhog Day (Director: Harold Ramis, 1993)
A charming remake of the legend of the Flying Dutchman of folklore with a kinder, gentler, wiser ending. The profoundly unlovable and unloving Bill Murray is trapped within the same day, apparently doomed to live it over and over — forever.

What would you do if you could live forever? What would you do if no one knew? How long before money, manipulation, and preying on others becomes very very boring? What counts? What's next?

Hidden Fortress (Director: Akira Kurosawa, 1958)
George Lucas' 1977 movie *Star Wars* is the most popular American movie ever made (if one counts the book spin-offs inspired by story and characters). This 1958

Japanese film by Akira Kurosawa was the inspiration. Lucas saw it in film school and never forgot it. Toshiro Mifune is general Rokurota Makabe, who in *Star Wars* becomes Obi-wan Kenobi and Han Solo. Princess Yukihime becomes Princess Leia Organa, and the two hapless wandering foot soldiers who come to the aid of the disguised princess become C3PO and R2D2. The Source of the Force.

C3PO and R2D2 are big improvements on the two bickering gold-hungry (hence "Goldie" in *Star Wars?*) foot soldiers. Note Kurosawa's title in Japanese: "Three Bad Men in a Hidden Fortress." We know the two nasty foot soldiers are bad, but why the noble and loyal Toshiro Mifune? The princess knows — and I think that is why her sly little smile on Kurosawa's seemingly odd choice of cover.

Many reviewers have referred to the "deadpan expressions." Actually those are "masklike expressions" which come (with much of the movie's symbolism) from *Noh* theater tradition.

Highlander (Producers: Panzer and Davis)

The more experienced you are in any martial art, whether taiji or Tae Kwon Do or Aikido, the more it becomes like a game of chess. This is a universal combat principle. And, when you get to the high levels of any art, you see that aggression is replaced with pure strategy. — Cady Goldfield

"It isn't about fighting," says immortal Duncan McLeod, while training for a coming battle. "It's about strategy." He's often outclassed and outnumbered but what comes up again and again is strategy, awareness, and a chessboard that shows up somewhere in almost every episode.

The *Highlander* TV series was a long-running version of *Groundhog Day:* What would you do if you could live forever? How long before money, manipulation, and preying on others becomes very very boring? The science-fictional premise of a race of eternal beings engaged in a long-running game of sudden-death elimination offers a different and valuable point of view. How many centuries do you hold a grudge? How long do you hate? How do you behave when you can kill or not kill and nobody knows? Who and what are you? — and why?

The series was renowned for its emphasis on ethics and moral issues, learning and growing, in the world of an eternal warrior who must nevertheless deal with the everyday griefs and joys of mortal life. Not your standard TV superhero. For those who long for "real" swordplay, see *The Princess Bride*.

House of Games (Director: David Mamet, 1987)

He said "Son I've made a life out of watching people's faces. knowing what the cards are by the way they hold their eyes . . . .— Kenny Rogers, The Gambler

A psychologist is drawn into a game of sleight-of-hand, treachery and deceit in the belief that she is studying the art and psychology of the con game. It is, in fact, observing, evaluating, and studying her. Superb illustrations of de Becker's summary of the verbal and psychological tools of the con, from "forced teaming," "tells" and body language, to our sad tendency to see and hear only what we want to.

Ikiru (Director: Akira Kurosawa, 1952)

Watching the same actors appearing repeatedly throughout Kurosawa's films gives the feeling of repeated lifetimes, new lessons learned. Takashi Shimura starred in Kurosawa's *Seven Samurai* as a compassionate warrior weary of killing, of never winning. In *Ikiru* he is a different kind of killer, head of an army of bureaucrats whose work has become the mindless murder of creativity, innovation, and effectiveness. Again he is tired of killing, tired of never having won. Distraught on learning that he has cancer, he is even more horrified to realize that he actually died years ago of loneliness and boredom. He has long since forgotten how to live. An initial foray into drunken debauchery turns to a quiet, persistent resolve to make a difference in life — and the dawning discovery of what life really is.

It's a Wonderful Life (Director: Frank Capra, 1946)
Success and failure are issues of time. This movie is so familiar and (now having gone out of copyright) is played so constantly that it is sometimes difficult to remember how very good it is.

In terrible despair and on the brink of suicide, George Baker (Jimmy Stewart) is allowed to see life as it could have been had he never lived. The differences are immense and all due to what appeared at the time to be small insignificant choices, tiny turning points in the road, the ones we make every day.

Karate Kid (Director: John G. Avildson, 1984)
Famous for the training scene in which Daniel thinks he's there to become a lean mean fighting machine and learn esoteric martial secrets. Miyagi (Pat Morita) puts him to work painting fences and waxing cars. Source of the "wax on, wax off" line now heard at some point in every martial arts school. The scene of attempting to catch flies with chopsticks comes from *Musashi* (see Yoshikawa's novel on page 259). "Cobra Kai" has also entered the martial arts language to describe a *dojo* where abuse is mistaken for discipline, bullying and treachery for martial fervor.

Kentucky Fried Movie (Director: John Landis, 1979)
Raunchy and definitely R-rated, but a hilarious send-up of various American cultural icons. It helps if you remember 1970's TV commercials. Feature Attraction: "Fistful of Yen," a good-natured spoof of Bruce Lee's classic *Enter the Dragon*, James Bond movies, spaghetti westerns, Disneyland and *The Wizard of Oz*.

Still timely for its commentary on martial arts movies that feature the now-obligatory "Really Spiritual Martial Arts Guy" segment — it's been done. In "Cleopatra Schwartz" ("She's 6 feet of fighting fury! He's a short Hassidic Jew!") this formula was intended to be completely absurd. And was.

The Mask of Zorro (Director: Martin Campbell, 1998)
I saw some great Aikido in the video my spouse just bought home, The Mask of Zorro. You know, where a drunken Antonio Banderas is hurling himself at Tony Hopkins? I feel a lot like that with my sensei. — Aikido Student

A far-fetched but entertaining remake of the classic tale. Listen especially for Hopkins' advice on strategy, the critical importance of the tool and weapon of etiquette, presentation and manners. Observe the training circle which also appears in the *Highlander* episode "Duende."

The Piano (Director: Jane Campion, 1996)
This strange and haunting movie is remarkable for its different points of view. A ship's hull seen from below. The frame of a hoop skirt as shelter for mother and child. A teacup seen from above. A stage performance of the tale of the murderous Blackbeard seen by the British as light entertainment, by the horrified Maori as a deadly emergency. The language of lips and tongue versus the language of music. And relationships made and broken based on who can see — and hear and understand — in new and different ways.

Powers of Ten (Directors: Charles & Ray Eames, 1968)
A breathtaking change in point of view. A man dozes on a picnic blanket in lake-side Chicago. Every ten seconds we are ten times further out from our starting point until our galaxy is only a distant glimmer of light. The viewpoint then returns to the man's hand at the rate of 10 times more magnification every ten seconds, ending within a proton of a carbon atom. *The Films of Charles & Ray Eames*, Vol. 1. A history of the Eames team appeared in the May 9, 1999 issue of *Smithsonian Magazine* with shots of the film making.

The Princess Bride (Director: Rob Reiner, 1987)
At the *dojo*, whenever the subject of Martial Arts movies arises, we have the karate kids, the Jackie Chans, Bruce Lees and Steven Seagals, *Lethal Weapons* 1 . . . n, but someone always seems to say, somewhat blushingly, "Well, actually, my favorite is *The Princess Bride*." There are immediate howls of laughter, a blast of quotes, scenic re-enactments, listings of anachronisms, and Shrieking Eel noises by persons

Resources

who are also not left-handed nor The Dread Pirate Roberts. Great fun with superb fencing scenes as opposed to sword waving.

Red Beard (Director: Akira Kurosawa, 1964)

All Kurosawa films are about learning and growing. Here the late Toshiro Mifune, as a gruffly compassionate doctor, teaches a vain and arrogant young man profound lessons on the meaning and opportunities of life. Interesting for its emphasis on the many different ways that he fights for his patients. In one scene the weapon is a blast of *jujutsu*, in others it is faithfulness and determination.

Royal Wedding (Director: Stanley Donen, 1951)

Thin plot, but the source of the famous scene in which Fred Astair dances with a hatrack. As always he makes his partner look very very good. No clash. Only blending and flowing. Consider this in dealing with *uke*. Consider experimenting at home with the same partner or try the exercise with a *jo*.

Sanjuro (Director: Akira Kurosawa, 1962)

A rollicking tale of feudal Japan. In this sequel to *Yojimbo*, a gruff and rough wandering *samurai* (Toshiro Mifune) comes to the aid of a band of naive and hopelessly idealistic young noblemen. The young men see only yes and no, black and white. In their impatience they are determined to deal with every situation in a haste which results in death and destruction.

Mifune highlights the contrast between explosive action and relaxation, appropriate action and appropriate inaction, the dangers of seeing everything in black or white, judging by surface appearances, and how insistence on Action Hero Solutions lead to tragic ends. Notice how Sanjuro deals with (or attempts to deal with) his former foe in the final scene.

When enemy soldiers come to ambush the Boy Scout *samurai* where they have met at a secluded shrine, Mifune drives them down the steps, surely the inspiration for a strikingly similar picture in Westbrook and Ratti's *Aikido and the Dynamic Sphere*. The scene of the young men emerging from under the floorboards reappears in Lucas' *Star Wars* when Han Solo, Obi-Wan Kenobi, and Luke Skywalker emerge from under the floorboards of the *Millenium Falcon*, following almost identical advice from a seasoned warrior that there are many ways to fight. Note also the trademark screen wipes which Lucas (an enthusiastic Kurosawa fan) used in *Star Wars*, in turn inspired by Kurosawa's *Hidden Fortress*.

Seven Samurai (Director: Akira Kurosawa, 1954)

In this classic film by Akira Kurosawa a village hires *samurai* (with a young Toshiro Mifune as a young *wannabe*) for protection against the annual harvest-time raiders. In the candidates' test, observe who is selected and why.

This movie inspired Hollywood's *Magnificent Seven* cast as a western in which director John Sturges seems to have carefully matched the faces and personalities of the original Japanese actors. (For example, the fierce and dark Toshiro Mifune becomes the fierce and scowling Charles Bronson; Takashi Shimura who shaved his head to pose as a priest becomes Yul Brynner with trademark shaved head.)

The leader of the Seven, the compassionate Takashi Shimura, has made a career of killing but is tired of killing, tired of never winning. "We did not win here," he says at the end of their successful but costly campaign. "The farmers won." In *Ikiru*, also starring Shimura, we begin to understand why and how.

Shall We Dance (Director: Masayuki Suo, 1997)

"In Japan," announces the opening lines, "ballroom dance is regarded with much suspicion." This leader was probably added by the distributor for the benefit of Western viewers who consider waltz and foxtrot hopelessly dull and old-fashioned. Not so in Japan where a proper Japanese salaryman does the unthinkable: takes up ballroom dancing lessons. Besides insight into Japanese culture, this charming tale offers unexpected insight into Aikido (leading, blending, and protecting one's partner), the actual meaning of *sensei* (often misunderstood in the West), teaching (*zengo*, *ma-ai*, and other basic steps), and attitude towards others. Consider the

264 Aikido Exercises for Teaching and Training

images of the men practicing individually, moving through the steps of the "techniques" alone to practice flow, sequence and balance before working with *uke*. Watch how carefully Tamako *Sensei* guides and protects her students' development with twinkly grace, wisdom, and compassion.

Shawshank Redemption (Director: Frank Darabout, 1994)

To redeem is defined in part as: "To recover ownership of something through payment of a sum, to fulfill a pledge, set free, rescue or ransom."

A financial planner (Tim Robbins) is wrongly condemned for life to Shawshank Prison for murdering his wife. The experienced inmates bet that this quiet man will crack the first night. Not only does he not crack, ever, but in the course of a secret 20-year goal he starts a library, education program, and groundwork in his campaign to rescue the prison from the control of a sadistic warden. While this movie appears at first to be about surviving the rigors of prison, it is actually about goals, and soft, gentle, persistent progress towards those goals, blooming where you're planted, and life — any life — as an act of creation.

Side Kicks (Director: Aaron Norris, 1993)

An asthmatic youth lost in a fantasy world is taken in hand by the canny and kindly Mr. Lee (Mako) who leads him out of the trap of fantasy into the world of real competence, true confidence, and genuine self-control. All the elements of the standard martial arts movie are here: good guy, bad guy, the opportunity to "take revenge" on one's opponent by beating him to a pulp — and they are all slyly lampooned and redirected. Who is the enemy? It isn't really the class bully; it is asthma. The karate competition is won not by trashing an adversary but by "breaking," an exercise in concentration and self-control. The beautiful girl is not the prize won by defeat of a rival; she already liked him anyway — for himself. And "don't need karate *gi*," points out Mr. Lee (racing from kitchen to competition in an apron) "to break blocks."

Chuck Norris' all-time best movie pokes gentle fun at all his others. While it suggests the value of hero-worship for setting direction and goals (the boy in the final scene gave me goose bumps), emphasis is firmly placed on the need to move beyond. For a sly commentary on "movie-*do*," watch the restaurant brawl scene carefully to see Chuck Norris made up in beard and black leather doubling as Biker Bad Guy.

The *Star Wars* Trilogy and Prequels

George Lucas' world of *Star Wars* has long been enormously popular with Aikidoists, inspiring many to begin training. Mle on the Aikido-L commented, per the 1999 Star Wars trailer:

Mle: I know, I know, "it's just a movie."

And Michael H. expostulated: BLASPHEMY!!!!"

And mle replied: Chill, skirt-boy. I've been a rabid, slavering fan since I was 9. Star Wars primed me to be the MA junkie that I am now. I am merely trying to be understanding of the non-Jedi[3] on the List.

And Krystal Locke tells this tale:

A local radio station did a ticket giveaway for the re-releases. To win you had to convince them you deserved one. Many people told sob stories, some pitiful, some funny, and won tickets. Typical. Then a 10-year-old girl called up, and when the disc jockey asked her why she deserved a free ticket, she told him very calmly "Because I am studying to be a Jedi."

"Oh really!" he laughed. "And just how are you doing that? Where did you get your light saber?" with just a hint of scorn.

---

3. The noble "Jedi" Knight appears to be a sly derivative of the Japanese term *Jidai Geki* ("spaghetti Samurai Cowboy Flicks").

"Well," she replied, "for the last 3 years, I've been working hard in school, and I get straight A's. I go see the old people at Linda Vista and talk to them every week. I've been taking karate for 2 years, and will be testing for my green belt next month. My Mom said if I do all these things, I will be a Jedi knight."

I was laughing and crying, and cheered when the guy gave her (with some embarrassment) four tickets for her whole family.

The Force is with her.

Episode I: The Phantom Menace (Director: George Lucas, 1999)

A special-effects extravaganza designed to set the scene for the "following" *Star Wars* trilogy. The story of Anakin, the good-hearted young boy who will one day become the evil Darth Vader. Lucas suggests that Evil is not an intrinsic part of an evil person, but the result of choices made, especially those made through fear.

Star Wars (Director: George Lucas, 1977)

Many of the concepts attributed to "The Force" come directly from Aikido. Darth Vader's hissing breath is a wonderful parody of *ki* breathing; his helmet is the traditional *samurai* helmet and bamboo armor reinterpreted in black plastic. (See the movie *Teenage Mutant Ninja Turtles* for an example of the almost-real thing worn by the wicked Shredder.) Observe Ben Kenobi's calm and impartial graciousness to all, even the despised 'droids, in contrast to the generally spiteful and frenetic behavior of almost all other main characters. (This same character of calm graciousness is displayed by Master Splinter, the *ninja* rat in *Teenage Mutant Ninja Turtles*.) Note also the horizontal wipes, a signature technique by the late Akira Kurosawa whose 1958 film *Hidden Fortress* inspired *Star Wars*.

The Empire Strikes Back (Director: Irvin Kershner, 1980)

Who has Luke destroyed when he strikes down his enemy in the cave? The inspiration for Yoda is believed to be modelled on Misao Shoji of Gardena, California. A superb Aikidoist, he is also renowned for his pixilated sense of humor. His favorite song, "Found A Peanut," is sure to be sung several times in the course of any workshop where he is present.

Return of the Jedi (Director: Richard Marquand, 1983)

On video and in slow motion, watch the clash between Vader and Emperor. Lucas went to great effort to compose scenes largely invisible at normal film speed. Compare with Saotome's (1993) account of experience as Ueshiba's *uke*.

Ukemi: The Art of Falling: Bruce Bookman

Falls are a leading cause of accidental death and injury yet safe falling is rarely taught. Even in Aikido where it is a critical technique and teaching skill, it is rarely taught in a systematic manner. Bruce Bookman corrects that lack with two well-done videotapes.

Volume 1: Basic Ukemi progresses from simple rocking chair rolls to breakfalls. Includes strategies for improving *ukemi* by effective blending with your partner.

Volume 2: Advanced Ukemi continues to high-flying breakfalls and flips.

Watch these then compare with the falls seen in "pro-wrestling."

Yojimbo (Director: Akira Kurosawa, 1961)

Gang warfare in Japan of 1860 with an American Western frontier motif. This classic tale starring Toshiro Mifune was inspired by Dashiell Hammet's *Red Harvest* and re-made as Sergio Leone's *Fistful of Dollars* with Clint Eastwood and (badly) as *Last Man Standing* with Bruce Willis.

Two rival merchants fight for control of the town, importing more thugs daily to swell their ranks and power. In wanders Yojimbo, a *samurai*, sworn to uphold the law [the New Sheriff in Town persona] but a *ronin* seen as willing to do anything for money. Mifune flits back and forth pretending to be holding out for the highest bidder. He carefully pits the two gangs against each other based on what they want and what they fear. A fascinating study of honor, morality, psychology and strategy.

Supplies

Aikido and Ki
  66 Spruce Street
  Cambridge, Ontario
  Canada, N1R 4K3
  http://angelfire.com/biz/aikidoki
  Voice: 519-623-300
  Handcrafted *jo, bokken*, and *tanto*, of indigenous Canadian woods, primarily
  Golden Oak and White Ash. Traditional and custom designs.

BudoBear Patterns
  P. O. Box 3855
  Merrifield, VA 22116
  Voice: 703-641-9169
  FAX: 888-542-4543
  patterns@round-earth.com
  Patterns and books for Japanese clothing. *Hakama, hapi, haori, tabi, kimono,*
  Japanese textile arts, martial arts, and more. Free brochure.

Bugei Trading Company
1070 commerce Street, Suite i
San Marcos, CA 92069
Voice: 760-736-4785
Toll-free: 800-437-0125
FAX: 760-736-9225
www.bugei.com
Catalog: $5.00
  Enormous selection of books, videos, prints, clothing, weapons, and equipment in
  the Japanese *samurai* tradition.

Bu Jin Design
2430 30th Street
Boulder, CO 80301
Voice: 303-444-7663
FAX: 303-444-1137
www.bujindesign.com
Free catalog.
  Well-made, long-lasting uniforms, *hakama*, weapons bags, and more. Also features
  Ikeda *Shihan*'s Aikido and weapons videos.

Edmund Scientific
  101 East Gloucester Pike
  Barrington, NJ 08007-1380
  Toll-free: 800-728-6999
  www.scientificsonline.com
  Biofeedback devices and science tools and toys.

Kiyota Company, Inc.
  2326 N Charles Street,
  Baltimore, MD 21218
  Toll-free: 800-783-2232
  Voice: 410-366-8275
  Uniforms, *hakama*, weapons and books and general martial arts equipment. Their prices are much lower if you order 5 or 6 weapons at a time.

Mugendo Budogu LLC
  6025 South Division Avenue
  Grand Rapids, MI 49548
  Voice: 616-534-9800
  FAX: 616-534-7576
  http://www.budogu.com
  Excellent quality equipment and clothing imported from Japan. Mugendo can also supply high-quality Japanese steel swords made in the traditional manner.

Sei Do Kai Supplies
  Kim Taylor
  44 Inkerman St.
  Guelph Ontario
  Canada N1H 3C5
  Voice: 519-836-4357
  FAX: 519-836-9873
  kataylor@uoguelph.ca
  See catalogue at: http://www.uoguelph.ca/~kataylor/catalog.htm
  Custom individually produced wooden weapons for martial arts. Also *iaito* from Fujiwara Kanefusa in Japan.

CHAPTER 11

Glossary

— by Chizuko Suzuki

Notes on pronunciation[1]:

Japanese has five short vowels; [a] art, [i] ink, [u] wood, [e] egg, [o] dog, and five long vowels; **a**, **i**, **u**, **e**, **o** which should be pronounced as a continuous sound, equal in value to two identical short vowels such as *shomen*, document) and *shomen*, front) with a long "o" sound.

Double consonants: **kk**, **pp**, **ss**, and **tt** indicate a slight pause before them as in *ikkyo*, *bokken*, and *happo* (eight directions).

In Japanese, Chinese characters, *kanji*, can be read in two ways.

	Left	Right	Hand	Sword	Body	Technique
Chinese way	sa	yu	shu	to	shin	gi
Japanese way	hidari	migi	te	katana	mi	waza

Single Chinese characters are often read in the Japanese way; combinations may be read either way. For example, "left hand" and "right hand" are read in the Japanese way as *hidari-te*, and as *migi-te*, but the the "left-right" exercise can be read as *sayu* in the Chinese way.

Sound changes occur when two Japanese readings are compounded: **k** becomes **g**, **s** becomes **z**, **t** becomes **d**, **h** becomes **b** or **p.** For example, *te*, hand + *katana*, sword = *te-gatana* or *tegatana*.

Japanese is rife with homonyms having the same sound but different concepts written with different Chinese characters. Hence, *Shin-Shin Toitsu Aikido* is "Aikido with Mind-Body Coordination" as *shin* can mean mind and also body.

ai n.— from *au*, to fit, suit, harmonize, agree, accord. Harmony, integration, unification. a coming together. In the context of Aikido, it is used to signify the spirit of harmony and accord, hence Aikido is "the Way of Harmony."

ai pre. — each other. *Ai-te, from* " + *te*, hand, a companion, a partner, an opponent. *Ai-hanmi* indicates *nage* with right foot forward and *uke* with right foot forward. See **gyaku** and **hanmi.**

ai n.—love, affection. *O-Sensei* said, "*Aiki* (harmony spirit) is *aiki* (love spirit) ."

Aikido n.—'the way of harmony, from *ai*, harmony + *ki*, spirit + *do*, way.

ashi n.— leg or foot.

atemi n.— a strike, from *ate*, strike, hit + *mi*, body. In Aikido, the strike is ideally a feint, not intended to injure but to distract, startle, and lead *uke's* mind.

---

1. **a.= adjective adv. = adverb n.= noun v.= verb pref. = prefix suf. = suffix**

bokken n.— wooden sword, from *boku*, wood + *ken*, sword. Originally *bokken* was a practice sword used to avoid damage by or to the razor-sharp and costly *katana*. Eventually it came to be considered as a weapon in its own right.

Different schools use different styles for practice; some (such as the *suburito*) are extremely heavy; movement with tension or weight upperside is readily revealed by exhaustion and painfully sore muscles. See **shinken** (real sword).

budo n.— martial arts, from *bu*, power, bravery, military affairs + *do*, way.

budo n.— a warrior, from *bu*, power, bravery, military affairs + *shi*, warrior, leader, scholar, noble people. See **samurai**.

bujin n.— a warrior, from *bu*, power, bravery, military affairs + *jin*, person. See **samurai**.

-dachi n.— variant of *tachi*, from *tatsu*, to stand. See **tachi**.

dan n.— a level, a step. A rank above *kyu*. *Shodan* is first level; *nidan* the second, *sandan* the third, *yondan* the fourth.

do[1] n.— way, path, discipline, study with physical and spiritual implications. In the literal sense, a road or path; by extension, a course of study or a way of life but certainly not limited to martial arts.

Aikido is The Way of Harmony.

Kendo is The Way of the Sword.

Kyudo is The Way of the Bow (archery).

Kado is the Way of Flower [arranging].

Chado or *Sado* is the Way of the Tea [ceremony].

do[2] n.— rib area, from waist to shoulders. This term appears in Kendo and other sword arts as a target area for cuts.

dohai n. — equals, from *do*, same + *hai*, fellow. Typically refers to one's school mates or those entering a company in the same year. See **senpai** and **kohai**.

-dori n.— variant of *tori*, from *toru*, to grab. See **tori**.

dojo n.— place of practice, training hall, from *do*, way + *jo*, place. A *dojo* is a place which offers training in the way, *do*. *Dogi* or *dojogi* refers to the uniform or dress worn while practicing a given discipline.

Dojo, "the place of enlightenment," is a word derived from the Sanskrit bodhimanda, the place where the ego self undergoes transformation into the egoless self. — Taitetsu Unn

dojo-sukui n.— *dojo* , loach + *sukui*, scooping. Appears in Taigi 8.

dosa n.— action, movement, from *do*, movement + *sa*, creation. Although sometimes mistaken for a wrestling contest, *kokyu dosa* is actually an exercise in breath movement and *ki* extension.

en n.— circle. *En-undo* describes a circular motion. *Kokyu-nage en-undo* and *kote-gaeshi en-undo* are named for their pronounced circular motion.

fudo-shin n.— the immovable-mind, from *fu*, not + *do*, moving + *shin*, mind, not in the sense of stubbornness or rigidity, but in the sense of calm, stability, and imperturbability. It is the calm and stability of a spinning top. While the mind cannot be tested directly, it can be tested through the body, as we do with various *ki* tests. Hence *fudo-tai* (immovable body) is considered to indicate the condition of *fudo-shin*.

fune-kogi n.— a boat rowing motion, from *fune*, boat + *kogi*, rowing, but very different from western-style rowing. Japanese boats were equipped with one oar which was sculled back and forth and also served as the rudder.

-gaeshi n. — variant of *kaeshi*, from *kaesu*, to turn out. See **kaeshi**.

gedan n.— lower level, from *ge*, low + *dan*, level. On the body, the area below the waist.

gi n.— *clothes*, but note that in Japanese this element does not stand alone; the use of *gi* to indicate practice uniform is an English usage. It is often used specifically like *Judo-gi*, *Karate-gi* or *Kendo-gi*. The uniform worn in class is *keikogi*, "practice clothes" or *dogi*, the clothing worn while you are practicing the "way."

gi n. — a technique. *Gi* [the Chinese reading], equivalent to **waza** [Japanese reading]. *Ken-gi* are sword techniques, *jo-gi* are stick techniques, *tai-gi* are body, or "no-weapon" techniques.

-giri n. — variant of *kiri*, from *kiru*, to cut. *Happo giri* is a sword *kata* involving "cutting in eight directions." See **kiri**.

go n. — back, rear. [Chinese reading] See **ushiro** [Japanese reading]. Contrast with *zen*.

go-kyo n. — "fifth teaching," a painful pinning or immobilization technique.

gyaku n. — reverse; opposite. *Gyaku-hanmi* describes *nage* standing with right foot forward, *uke* with left foot forward. See **ai** and **hanmi**.

hachi-no-ji n. — figure eight, from *hachi*, eight + *no*, of, possessive particle + *ji*, figure or letter.

hagai-jime n. — pinion, from *hagai,* a part where feathers cross + *jime*, from *shime*, strangling.

hai adv. — yes. Pronounced in one sharp breath, not *hái-eee*, as in the English short form of hello.

hakama n. — the voluminous pleated pants or divided skirt worn over the *gi*. In Ki Society, it is worn by students ranking 3rd *kyu* and above.

hakucho-no-mizu'umi n. — *hakucho*, swan + *no*, of, possessive particle + *mizu'umi*, lake. Also known as the "Ghost Throw."

han n. — half, pertaining to physical position. *Zagi han-dachi* from *za*, seated + *gi*, techniques + *han*, half + *dachi* from *tachi*, standing, describes techniques in in which a standing *uke* attacks a *nage* seated in *seiza*. *Nage* may rise to one knee, a half-standing position.

hanmi n. — *han*, half + *mi*, body is the basic Aikido stance in which the feet are placed to form two sides of a triangle, exposing only half the body to the attacker. Commonly garbled in English as "hamni." See **ai** and **gyaku**.

hantai n. — opposite, from *han*, reverse + *tai*, confront. In techniques involving a *hantai-tenkan*, *nage* reverses direction and turns.

happo-undo n. — The "eight direction exercise." Combines *zengo-undo* with *ikkyo-undo* to practice correct extension of *ki* and attention.

hara n. — the Center (One-Point) in the lower abdomen, thought of as physical and spiritual center of the body. *Hara kiri* (garbled into English as "harry-karry") was Japanese ritual suicide, involving a knife cut, *kiri* to the *hara*.

honbu n. — headquarters, from *hon*, base + *bu*, section, group. Garbled into English as "hombu."

hiji n. — elbow. *Ushiro hiji-tori* describes "elbows grabbed from the rear."

hikoki-nage n. — *hikoki*, airplane + *nage*, throw. Appears in Taigi 18.

hitori-waza n. — *hitori,* one person + *waza*, techniques. In Aikido, these are unpartnered single-person exercises to develop balance and coordination, and to pattern the basic movements of Aikido techniques. See **kumi-waza**.

ikkyo n. — first immobilization technique, from *ichi*, one, first + *kyo*, teaching. Also called *ikkajyo* or *ude osae* in different styles. See **katame**.

irimi n. — *iri*, from *ireru*, to put inside + *mi*, body. In Aikido, *irimi* is an entering motion, a stepping *inside* the line of attack. In Ki Society, *irimi* techniques are the equivalent of techniques designated as *omote* in other styles. Compare with **tenkan**.

jo n. — a wooden staff, stick. *Jo-nage* ("stick-throws") are techniques in which *nage* has the *jo* and uses it to throw an attacker. *Jo-tori*, ("*jo*-grabs") are the set of techniques used to disarm an attacker with a *jo*.

joho n. — upwards, from *jo*, up + *ho*, direction. See **kaho**, downwards.

juji n. — letter ten, from *ju*, ten + *ji*, letter. Appears in Taigi 13.

ju-jutsu n. — *ju*, soft, pliant + *jutsu*, art, craft, skill or discipline. An art of pliancy or strength through yielding, a Japanese form of unarmed combat which uses joint locks and throwing techniques.

-kaeshi suf.—from *kaesu*, to turn out, a change, reversal. (The suffixed *-kaeshi* often becomes *-gaeshi* in compound such as *kote-gaeshi*.) *Kote-gaeshi* describes "*turning the inside facing wrist, kote, to the outside.*" *Kiri-kaeshi* ("cut and reverse") involves a complete reversal (180 degrees) of *uke's* motion. *Ura* ("back or reverse") + *gaeshi* turns him inside out, facing the other way just before falling.

kaho n. —downwards, from *ka*, down + *ho*, direction. See **joho**, upwards.

kaiten n.— revolving, rotating, from *kai*, turn, revolve + *ten*, roll. *Kaiten-nage* is a spinning throw; *uke's* body will revolve once before he is led down to the mat. In *zenpo-kaiten-nage*, *uke* falls forward like a wheel.

kamae n. — posture, stance.

kata n.— shoulder. *Kata-tori* is a shoulder grab.

kata- pre. — one side, single. *Katate-tori* is a single-hand grab. See **ryo-**, both.

kata n. — form; hence a *jo kata* is a form done with the staff, intended to demonstrate flow and rhythm, an awareness of space and placement while perfecting technique.

katame n.— an immobilization, from *katameru*, to lock, to pin, or to harden. *Katame-waza* are immobilization techniques and include *ikkyo*, *nikyo*, *sankyo*, *yonkyo* and *gokyo* which mean "first," "second," "third," "fourth," and "fifth" techniques, respectively.

katana n. — a Japanese steel sword, slightly curved and single-edged. *Katana* is the Japanese reading. The Chinese reading is *to*. The wooden sword is a *bokken* (see **ken**). *Te-gatana*, hand-sword, refers to the use of the edge of the hand as if it were a blade or knife edge, a technique common in Karate.

kazu n. — number.

one — *Ichi*	Six — *roku*
two — *ni*	Seven — *shichi* / *nana*
three — *san*	Eight — *hachi*
four — *shi* / *yon*	Nine — *kyu* / *ku*
Five — *go*	ten — *ju*

keiko n.— practice, training, study, lessons, from *kei*, to think + *ko*, old. *Keiko-suru* (v.) originally meant "to think of old things," later to "to learn or study old things such as arts, skills, and techniques." Learning these things requires *training*. Thus, nowadays *keiko* means *training*. *Keiko-gi* are "training clothes."

ken n.— a straight, two-edged sword. *Ken* is the Chinese reading. [The Japanese reading is *trurugi*.] *Kendo* is the "Way of the Sword" and its practitioners are known as *kendoka*. *Shinken* is a real sword. See **shinken** and **katana**.

kesa-gake n.— a diagonal cut from shoulder from *kesa*, surplice, part of monk's costume hanging from shoulder + *gake*, from *kake*, hanging, laying, putting over. Appears in Taigi 26.

ki n.— the universal spirit; life energy. In Japanese, *ki* appears in many contexts such as *gen-ki*, a spirit of health, *byo-ki*, a spirit of sickness, *ai-ki*, a spirit of harmony.

ki-ai n.— a piercing shout with *ki*, from *ki*, spirit + *ai*, harmony. The concept is that of an outpouring of *ki* energy from the One-Point, unifying body and spirit. In modern Japanese, it also refers to vigor. To put *ki-ai* into something (*kiai wo ireru*) means "to work at something with vigor."

kiri n.— from *kiru*, to cut. *Tekubi-kiri* is a cut to the wrist; *ude-kiri* is a cut to the arm. The American phrase *harry-karry* is a garbled version of *hara kiri*, a ritual cut to the *hara*, or Center (One-Point). This word also appears as *giri*, hence *happo-giri*, a sword *kata* involving "cutting in eight directions."

kohai n.— [one's] junior, from *ko*, back, later + *hai*, fellow. See **dohai**, equals, and **senpai**, senior.

koho n.— back; backwards, from *ko*, back + *ho*, direction. *Koho-tento undo* is the rolling backwards exercise. See **zenpo**.

kokyu n.— breath, from *ko*, exhale, call + *kyu*, inhale, suck. A *kokyu-nage* is a breath throw, or, by extension, a timing throw, because it is done using only *uke's* momentum and *nage's* timing. *Kokyu-nage* techniques are a family of techniques which depend on timing, sensitivity, and *ki* extension rather than a joint lock. *Kokyu* is thought of as *ki* in motion, empowered by breath and its control. *Kokyu-nage* is known as *irimi nage* or as *ishi otoshi* in different styles.

kosa n.— cross, across from *ko*, cross, intersect + *sa*, finger crossing. *Tekubi- kosa-undo* is the "wrist-crossing-exercise." *Katate*, one hand + *kosa-tori* describes a "one-hand-grab." Compare with *katate-tori*.

koshi n.— hips. *Koshi-nage* is a "hip-throw."

koshin n.— moving backwards, from *ko*, backwards + *shin*, proceed. *Koshin-undo* is a series of exercises in which the student practices moving backwards while continuing to extend *ki* forward.

kote n.— hand, tips of hand, from *ko*, small + *te*, hand. *Kote-gaeshi* is a "wrist-bend" (wrist lock) which serves as a throw.

Kote sometimes refers to the entire forearm. In *Kendo*, a *kote* strike is a blow, not to the wrist but to any point on the gauntlets covering the entire forearms.

kubi n. —neck. *Tekubi* is the wrist, that is, the "neck" of the hand (*te*).

Kubi-uchi is a strike to the neck. *Ushiro kubi-shime* is a one-armed neck choke from the rear. In medieval Japan, *uchi-kubi* was decapitation, a shameful and humiliating death.

kumi-waza n. — *kumi*, a pair, partners + *waza*, techniques. See **hitori-waza**.

kyu n.— level, quality. In martial arts, *kyu* designates any rank below *shodan* (first black belt. In other areas, *kyu* can refer to level or quality. For example, an "*ikkyu* restaurant" would be a restaurant of the first quality.

kyo n.— teaching. The standard wrist locks, *ikkyo*, *nikyo*, *sankyo*, and *yonkyo*, are the "first-," "second-," "third-," and "fourth-teachings."

ma-ai n.— the proper ("harmonious") distance between *nage* and *uke*, from *ma*, space + *ai*, fit, harmonize. *Ma-ai* depends on the reach of the partners and the types of weapons being used; it is closer for a pair of short opponents than for tall ones; it is closer for unarmed combat than for swordplay.

Throughout Japanese culture, *ma-ai* is extremely important. In calligraphy, the space between the characters is just as important as the ink. In Japanese rock gardens (such as that at Ryoanji Temple in Kyoto) the spaces between the rocks are just as important as the rocks themselves.

mae n.— front [Japanese reading]. See **zen** [Chinese reading]. Opposite is *ushiro*.

men n.— face, front of head; *men-uchi* is a head-strike. *Shomen-uchi* is a strike directly down to the head. *Yokomen-uchi* is a strike to the head or face with a diagonal component.

mi n.— body. *Mi* is Japanese reading. See **shin** [Chinese reading].

michibiki n.—, from *michibiku*, to lead or guide, guidance.

misogi n.— purification ritual.

mochi n.— from *motsu*, to hold, have, possess. *Ryote-mochi* is a hold with both hands [*te*, hand].

mune n.— chest, midsection, thorax. *Mune-tsuki* is a punch to the chest or midsection. Western fighting, particularly bar-room brawl variety, emphasizes a sock to the jaw; Eastern styles emphasize a blow to the *hara* or *ki* center.

nage n.— (1) A thrower, the person who performs techniques. (2) A throw. *Nage* is a common designation for the partner who performs the *nage-waza*, throwing techniques.

nido n. — twice from *ni*, two + *do*, a measure, a time, a degree

naname n.— oblique. *Kokyu-dosa* or *kokyu-ho* is sometimes called *naname kokyu nage* or the "oblique breath throw."

nikyo n. — "second" immobilization technique, from *ni*, two, second + *kyo*, teaching. See **katame**. Also known as *nikajyo* or *kote-mawashi* in different styles.

ojigi n. — bow, from *o*, no meaning but honorific + *ji* (originally came from time) + *gi*, greeting. Formerly, *ojigi* meant seasonal greeting. Now it means a bow. *Ojigi-nage* are throws down simply by bowing politely in response to an attack. Featured in *Taigi* 4 (known as "The Women's Taigi").

omote n. — front, forward. Usually equivalent to *irimi* techniques. See **ura**.

one-point n. — the English interpretation of *hara* or center point of the body, considered to be about two inches below the naval, roughly the point of the hip joints. Japanese sometimes use *itten* which literally means "one-point." See **seika-tanden**.

onshi-no-gyoi n.— *onshi*, receiving from the emperor + *no*, of, possessive particle + *gyoi*, honorific gift of clothes.

oroshi n.—, from *orosu*, to drop downward; to put down. The technique *ude-oroshi* involves dropping the arm-downward.

po n.— variant of *ho*, direction. See **ho**.

randori n.— a multiple-person attack; free-style sparring, from *randoru*, to spar, from *ran*, chaos, chaotic, random, or disorderly + *dori*, from *tori*, grab.

renzoku n.— continuance, succession, a series, from *ren*, link, join + *zoku*, continuance.

ritsugi n.— *ritsu*, standing + *gi*, techniques [Chinese reading]. Japanese reading is *tachi-waza*. See **zagi** [Chinese reading for sitting techniques] and **suwari-waza** [Japanese reading].

ritsurei n.— *ritsu*, standing + *rei*, bow. See **zarei** (sitting bow).

ryo- pre.— both; *ryote*, "both hands" from *te*, hand. *Ryo-kata-tori* is a "grab to both shoulders." *Katate ryote-mochi* is a "grab with both hands" (two hands grabbing one hand) and *ryote-tori* is an attack *to* both hands (two hands grabbing two hands). See **kata** (pre. indicating one side, single).

samurai n.— a warrior. Originally it meant those who served the emperors with their lives. See **bushi**.

sankyo n.— the "third" immobilization technique, from *san*, three, third + *kyo*, teaching. Also known as *sanjakyo* or *kote-hineri* in different styles. See **katame**.

sayu n.— left and right, from *sa*, left + *yu*, right. *Sayu-undo* involves alternately shifting the arms to the right and left and dropping their weight underside to perform a throw.

seiza n.— the formal Japanese kneeling position, from *sei*, correct + *za*, sitting.

seika-tanden n. — *seika*, under the navel + *tanden*, the body part about 2 inches below the navel. *Seika-tanden* is the bodily source of *ki* energy.

sensei n.— instructor, teacher, from *sen*, before + *sei*, living or born, hence "one who was born before you."

senpai n.— from *sen* + *hai*, comrade, companion. The combination indicates anyone senior in a particular area. Hence, on the mat, you may be *senpai* to someone who joined the club before you did (regardless of *kyu* grade) but *kohai* to the same person who may be a "senior" at school, at work, or simply in age. See **dohai** and **kohai**.

shiho n.—four directions, all directions, from *shi*, four + *ho*, direction .

shikko n.— from *shitsu*, knee [Chinese reading] + *ko*, progressing. The Japanese reading of "knee" is *hiza*.

shinai n.—bamboo sword. A length of split and bound bamboo for sword practice. It makes a loud whack when it connects, but does not cause serious injury.

sinanju — an entirely fictional martial art. The original *The Destroyer* novels were introduced to the screen via "Remo Williams: The Adventure Begins." If you see someone actually advertising *sinanju*, smile and walk away.

shin-shin n.— mind and body from *shin*, mind + *shin*, body. Both elements have the same pronunciation but different characters with different meanings.

Zan-shin is the immovable mind, unbroken flow of *ki* and concentration on *uke* after the throw is completed; *fudo-shin* is the unperturbable mind.

Shin-Shin Toitsu Aikido is literally "Aikido with mind and body coordinated" from *shin*, mind + *shin*, body + *toitsu*, coordination + *ai*, harmony + *ki*, spirit, energy + *do*, way.

shindo n. — shaking, swinging, oscillation, vibration from *shin*, shaking, waving + *do*, movement. *Tekubi-shindo-undo* is the "wrist-shaking-exercise."

shite n.— Yoshinkan style uses this term to designate what other styles call *nage*. Pronounced *shtey*, it is the word used for the principle actor in a *kabuki* play.

shomen n.— front from *sho*, correct, proper + *men*, face, mask, side. *Shomen-uchi* is an overhand strike (*uchi*) attacking the "front" of the head. See **yokomen**.

sode n.— sleeve. *Sode-tori* is a "sleeve grab."

suburi n.— *su*, origin, essence, true nature + *buri*, from *furi*, swinging. *Suburi* means sword swinging (exercise) without a partner or an opponent; it is also applied to practice with baseball bats and golf clubs.

sudori n.— a passing through, from *su*, origin, essence, true nature + *dori*, from *tori*, passing. *-dori* (with long vowel) is not the same as *dori* (from *tori*, grab). *Sudori* is a type of forward throw in which *uke* passes straight through with no change in direction and no rotation — then falls.

suwari n.— seated. *Suwari waza* pertains to exercises done from *seiza*.

tachi n.— long and big sword. Originally written "big sword," now written "thick sword." *Tachi-tori* techniques are those designed to take away an opponent's sword. See **tanto**.

tachi n.— standing, from *tachi*, to stand *Tachi-waza* are "standing techniques." Also appears as *dachi*, hence *zagi han-dachi*.

taigi n.— *tai*, body + *gi*, techniques. *Taigi* generally refers to techniques without weapons in contrast to k*en-gi*, sword techniques or *jo-gi*, stick techniques. However, in the Ki Society, *taigi* refers to partnered exercises involving a series of attacks and defenses but designed to demonstrate flow and rhythm.

tanto n.— dagger, knife, from *tan*, short + *to*, sword. *Tanto-tori* are techniques for dealing with knife attacks.

te n.— hand; *kara-te* is the way of the empty, hence weaponless hand; *kata-te* is the neck of the hand, that is, the wrist. *Katate-tori* are attacks to the wrist. *Tegatana* or *tekatana* is the "hand-blade" or "sword" edge (or knife-edge) of the hand.

tekubi n.— wrist, from *te*, hand + *kubi*, neck. *Tekubi-kosa*, wrists-crossing; *tekubi-kiri*, a cut to the wrist.

tenchi n.— *ten*, heaven + *chi*, earth. *Tenchi-nage* is "heaven and earth throw," based on being powerfully rooted to the earth while extending towards the heavens.

tenkan n.— *ten*, turn + *kan*, to interchange, reverse. *Tenkan* is a "turning" outside *uke's* line of attack. Compare with **irimi**.

tessen n.— *tetsu*, iron + *sen*, fan. It looked like any folding fan, but its skeleton was of steel. It had two main outside ribs of sword steel to fend off sword blows, inner skeletal ribs of fine sword steel, thin and pointed so that when opened and used to strike at throat of foe, at least one rib would pierce the silk cover and slit the attacker's throat. The steel fan was used where more overt weapons were forbidden, and even played a critical part (as a *fin*) in the art of swimming in armor (*tachi oyogi*).

tobikomi n.— *tobi*, to jump + *komi*, entering, into [something]. *Tobikomi* usually describes a jumping in behind *uke*, as in *Kokyu-nage* Basic (*katate-kosa-tori irimi tobikomi*).

toitsu n.— unity, unification, from *to*, reign, govern + *itsu*, one. *Shin Shin Toitsu Aikido* is Aikido with mind-body coordination or unification.

tori n.— from *toru*, to grab, take, pick. *Katate-kosa-tori* is a grab of the opposite [cross] wrist; *kata-tori* is a grab of the shoulder or, as we think of it, the lapel.

tsuki n.— from *tsuku*, to stick. A thrust, poke, stab, punch as with a fist, *jo*, or knife; *mune-tsuki* is a chest-punch; *ushiro-tsuki* can mean a stab from behind or a thrust to the rear.

uchi n.— from *utsu*, to strike. *Shomen-uchi* is a frontal attack [to the] head while *yokomen-uchi* is a diagonal attack [to the] head.

uchi n.— inside. Opposite is *soto*, outside. An *uchideshi*, from *deshi*, pupil, disciple, is an apprentice living in the home of his master.

ude n.— arm; *ude-furi undo* is the arm-swinging exercise.

uke n. — receiving, from *ukeru*, to receive. In Aikido the partner who *receives* (techniques). The opposite is *nage*. See **nage.**

ukemi n.— (1) defensive, passive (2) the act of taking techiniques, from *ukeru*, to receive *ukemi*. *Uke* is the attacking partner who receives *nage*'s technique. *Ukemi* is the art of falling under control and refers to protecting oneself by falling safely. *Koho-ukemi* is a backwards roll or fall; *zenpo-ukemi* is a forwards roll or fall.

undo n.— exercise, motion, movement from *un*, carry, transport + *do*, motion.

ura n. — behind, in back of [something]. In styles other than Ki Society Aikido, *ura* techniques are often the named equivalent to Ki Society *tenkan* techniques. See **omote.**

ushiro n.— back, backwards, behind. *Ushiro* techniques all involve an attack from the rear such as a bear-hug from behind (*ushiro-tori*). The opposite of *ushiro* is *mae*.
Ushiro tekubitori describes a "wrist grab from behind."
Ushiro ryote-tori describes "both hands attacked from behind."
Ushiro ryo-kata-tori describes "both shoulders grabbed from behind."

waza n. — technique [Japanese reading]. *Hitori waza* refers to "single" person exercises such as *ikkyo-undo*, *funakogi-undo*. *Kumi waza* refers to "more than one person" technique, that is, throws involving an attacker and a defender. See **gi** [Chinese reading].

yoko n.— side, sideways, diagonally. *Yokomen-uchi* is a diagonal strike, *uchi* to the head, *men*. It actually begins as a straight forward strike, as does *shomen-uchi*, with an added diagonal component and a turning of the hips.

yonkyo n.— the fourth immobilization technique from *yon*, four, fourth + *kyo*, teaching.

yudansha n. — *yu*, from *yu-suru* to possess + *dan*, level + *sha*, person. Hence black-belt level students or "persons with *dan*."

zagi n.— *za*, seated, sitting + *gi*, techniques. Both *nage* and *uke* are seated in *seiza*. *Zagi-handachi* are techniques in which standing *uke* attacks kneeling *nage*.

zan-shin n.— the remaining or immovable mind. See **shin-shin.**

zazen n.— sitting meditation, from *za*, seated, sitting + *zen*, quietness, serenity. See **zen.**

zarei n.— a seated bow, from *za*, seated, sitting + *rei*, bow, etiquette, gratitude. See **ritsurei,** a standing bow.

zen n. — Originally this Chinese character meant that "emperors cleansed the earth and worshiped the heaven or heavenly God." It also meant "quietness" or "serenity". Nowadays, *zen* means to seek true senses or features by attaining a state of perfect self-effacement, and unifying spirit and soul.

zen n.— front [Chinese reading]. See **mae** [Japanese reading]. Opposite is *ushiro*. See **ushiro.**

zengo n.— *zen*, forward + *go*, backward, hence *zengo-undo*, "forward and backward exercise."

zenpo n.— forward, from *zen*, forward + *po*, from *ho*, direction. *Zempo kaiten* is a forward roll; *zenpo kaiten-nage* is a throw in which *uke* is projected into a forward roll. See **koho.**

Index

Aikido-Lite

Some favorite works by members of the worldwide Aikido-L cyberdojo.

Karate vs. Aikido in Haiku

— by Cady Goldfield vs. Michael Bartman

> *Foot pierces the void*
> *A bright flash! A blur of light!*
> *Taekwondoka rulz!*
>
> > — *Cady Goldfield*

> *Foot pierces the void*
> *Where's Aikidoka? What the . . .*
> *Taekwondoka falz!*
>
> — *Mike ("Hey, it's an Aikido list, what did you expect?)" Bartman*

> *Aikidoka gasps!*
> *His foe takes good ukemi.*
> *Taekwondoka rolz!*
>
> > — *Cady Goldfield*

> *Aikidoka grinz.*
> *Yes! Great ukemi indeed*
> *Let's go get a beer.*
>
> > — *Mike "a few one pint curlz?" Bartman*

> *Former foes embrace*
> *Match is over, time for brew*
> *Let's invite Kjartan*
>
> > — *Cady Goldfield*

> *Peace spreads like the rain*
> *Cools hothead competition*
> *Hey! Let's invite EVERYONE!*
>
> —*Mike "Does Jeff have a CyberBrew to recommend?" Bartman*

It's In Your Hips

— By Monica Norman

A new student questions her sempai to the tune of "It's in His Kiss."

Is it Aiki, I want to know!
How can I tell if it's Aiki-do?
Do I use my eyes?
Oh no! You'll telegraph.
Try to throw them high?
Oh no! You'll make them laugh.
If you wanna know,
To make it Aiki-do,
It's in your hips.
That's where it is.

Should I make a face?
Oh no! He'll use a fist.
Use a strong embrace?
Oh no! She'll just resist.
If you wanna throw, if it's really "do,"
It's in your hips.
That's where it is.
It's in your hips.
That's where it is.

Ah-ah-atemi,
Let him squeeze you tight,
Extend where you want him to go-o-o-o.
If it's do, if it really is,
The mat he will kiss.
How 'bout my kote gaeshi?
Oh no! You broke my wrist.
And you're not turning your hips when you twist.
If you wanna flow, if it's really "do",
It's in your hips.
That's where it is.
It's in your hips.
That's where it is.

Oh, oh, oh, lead her, sen sen no sen,
Blend and then you take her hara.
When it's "do", when you really flow,
It's there in your hips.

How 'bout this nikyo?
Ow! No, that's not the way.
And you're not list'nin to all Sensei say.
When it's Aikido, when you really flow,
It's in your hips.
That's where it is.
(Oh yeah)
It's in your hips.
That's where it is.

Climate & Geographic Superiority in Budo

— by Dennis Hooker, Aikido Schools of Ueshiba

After reading so much of the well thought out dialog by first and second year Aikido students (and some teachers who act like they are) regarding the proper way to study Aikido and the proper school to belong to, the social research lab at Middlelander University dedicated itself to identifying the best possible school of Aikido and what factors make it so. Given the dialog, the weight, and consideration it deserves, we offer the following.

Our science project has taken us all over this country. As we stand here at the southernmost tip of Florida and look to the north across this great nation we view the wondrous variety of its people. We look to the left and see the Left coast with all those strangely liberal people and their liberal ways. This is reflected in their Aikido, as it should be.

As we look to the right, we see the Right coast with all those bizarre conservative people and their conservative ways. In their Aikido you can see their conservativeness. They are reluctant to shift from convention and do strange things in new ways and call it Aikido, as do those liberal nuts on the Left coast. Those on the Left coast can not contain themselves with such absurd rigidity as those conservative quacks on the Right coast. They must reach out with their feelings and become Luke Skywalkerish in their thinking, as they strive to be Obi-Wan.

If we tilt our head just right, we can view the heartland with those wonderful moderate folks. They occupy the Middle Land, and though we consider ourselves part of them we are being totally objective in this study. They are the most wonderful people in the world (a good looking and intelligent people too). Their middle ways and logical thinking are carried over into their Aikido.

Being moderate, they can take from the strange Left and Bizarre Right those attributes deemed good and leave the rest. They can do this because they are from the Middle Land, a superior breed of people. It has nothing to do with religion, race, sex, or sexual orientation. It has to do with geography.

If a Left coast nut would establish residence in the Middle Land that person would soon lose their distorted method of thinking and acting and become a Middlelander.

The same applies to a Right coast conservative bizarro. Their tendency to kill and maim like the badass Niko and mighty Rambo would soon be lost among so many righteous people like the Middlelanders. The Middlelanders organize under different names as do the strange and bizarre peoples. However, there is a collective Middlelander thought shared by all groups. That is a knowledge of superiority over the Left and Right peoples.

The method of thinking is different between the Middlelanders and the strange Left and bizarre Right. The Middlelanders go with the old axiom that: "I disagree with what you say but I will defend to the death your right to say it."

The bizarre Right says:

"I disagree with what you say and I will kill you if you say it again."

The strange Left says:

"I disagree with what you say and if you say it again I will kill myself."

We think we are being extremely open minded in our evaluation of the Aikido population in this country. The logic of this rationale has to do with geography and climate-induced thought patterns. The strange Left coasters live much of their life outside. This is because the weather is so hospitable. With that much open sky and semi-clean air there is nothing to hold the mind inside. The thoughts drift out and open space drifts in (thus the term "air-head"). With so much free-radical Aikido thought floating in the air, held under layers of pollution, it is no wonder there appears to be spontaneous birth of Aikido Masters on the Left coast. We can find no other explanation for Sensei who have no history of Aikido study or identifiable teachers. Their Aikido Knowledge could only have been gained through osmosis brought on by geography and climate.

On the other hand the bizarre Right coasters spend much of their time indoors. Without the freedom of the open spaces, their thoughts are repressed inside during long cold winters and short hot summers. At the first sign of provocation, their pent-up repression comes pouring out in the form of a devastating right cross to the jaw (thus the term "radical right"). The Right coast also has its share of spontaneous *sensei*-ing of unsuspecting people. The geography and climate causes many days of isolation in dark cold dwellings where the osmosis takes place from the pages of books, magazines, and the glitter of the VCR.

The Middlelanders, however (by the way, did we mention we are part of them, but are being totally open minded in this study?), have a perfect balance between repression and liberation. Mild winters and warm summers provide a perfect balance for nurturing a complete and nearly perfect human being (thus the term "god-like"). The phenomenon of spontaneous sensei-ing does not take place in the Middle Land as there is always an opportunity to take at least one class and see at least one real *sensei* before becoming an Aikido Master.

The strange and bizarre peoples hold us (them) in awe, which is understandable now that we have shown beyond a doubt the scientific proof of geographic and climate induced superiority in budo.

—D. H.

Aikido Food for the Soul

Donuts

— By Michael Bartman, Ki Society

"Mike [insert quote here] Bartman" notes that: donuts would be a perfect Aikido Food. They are circular in overall shape as well as in cross section. No matter how you cut it, you get a circle! (or at least, an ellipse).

— Mike "of course, topologists think they are coffee cups..." Bartman

You may think they have no center, but of course they have a center! There's just no *donut* at the center...just an "empty cup". Without the donut, the donut center, or "hole", wouldn't exist. It is nothing, void, yet, when surrounded by donut, it becomes something more than just empty formless space. No donut, no donut hole, no donut hole, no donut. With donut and hole, a donut whole.

Both parts are required to have a donut. You must have the circular donut to define the hole, and the hole to constitute the calm empty center which defines the donut itself as a donut. The hole becomes whatever shape the donut requires it to take on...blending and conforming *exactly* to the shape required by that particular donut. The hole is not trying to be anything in particular, it just is, and in so being, lets the donut be a donut.

The donut, through it's circularity, defines the requirements for the hole to take on. A hole with preconceived notions about how big it wants to be, or where it wants to be located, will not make a good donut. Too big a hole and there's not enough donut to be worthwhile, or perhaps no donut at all. Too small a hole and you get a defective bun. A hole located too far from the center of the donut can form a croissant, but this off-balance pastry is not very Aiki at all...too wrapped up in itself.

In addition to all this philosophical stuff, donuts are also really good at rolling, both forwards and backwards, but, like Aikidoka, seldom very good at rolling sideways. They are also very stable when they've lowered their centers to the maximum extent possible, and can handle a push from any direction with equal ease and no discernible preference.

The ones who's centers are full of non-donut stuff aren't really donuts, though they are frequently found around real donuts. The fillings take up so much room that there's no room for the hole, and, as I said above, without a donut hole, there's no donut whole.

— Mike "See why I think donuts are the perfect Aikido Food?" Bartman

Breakfast Waza: Correct Buttering of Toast

George Simcox wrote: As one matures one begins to respect the views of others and sees the wisdom in choices other than their own. When I butter toast, for example, I hold the knife in my right hand, get a dab of butter by scooping from right to left across the surface of the tub and then butter the toast moving the knife blade from right to left. Now some folks do it other ways and that is OK, but I like my way and probably won't change. My point is; cool and really neato is something for each individual to decide. We must all be flexible and practice what we preach.

Chuck Gordon wrote: Dammit George! You know it's *left* hand, scraping the toast *bottom* to *top*. [Sigh.] How many times do I have to *tell* you!?

Beate Kawelke wrote: I really don't know why you 'mericans think that to be so important. The True Way (tm) is not about the direction. It's about choosing the right type of butter'n'toast and then truly feeling it, *becoming* it.... and don't forget to move the knife from your center [deep sigh]. How many times do I have to *tell* you!?

Wiley Nelson wrote: Amen! I've heard that some heretics have actually stopped using butter and use margarine or even [Gasp!] No-Fat vegetable spread! Without saturated fat and cholesterol, where's the reality? How can you call it an "effective" breakfast? Any *real* breakfast eater knows that if you eliminate all the risk from breakfast, then it is no longer really breakfast. You might as well be having "Brunch" with all the other *poseurs*.

Ben Calvert wrote: This is why it's important to restore the competitive aspect to toast-*do*. Cooperative practice is fine, but how can you tell if your breakfast is really good until you put it up head to head against your mother-in-law's?

Chris Brogden wrote: [meditative sigh] As you truly progress in your study of Bread-do, the butter and knife become unimportant, and the movements needed become smaller and smaller, and you begin to realize that pure technique lies *beyond* movement, beyond utensils. At this point, no one will be able to see you butter the bread until it is already in your mouth.

The Teacher and the Cowherd

— by Serban Derlogea

In a village of old, the peasants' cows were gathered every morning on the streets to walk to the grazing field under the supervision of the village's cowherd. Now, the cowherd, a simple man, directed the cows by noisily cracking his whip. The majority of the peasants were not disturbed by the noise, as they were themselves already under way toward the crop fields. But the village schoolteacher had another working schedule and liked to sleep a bit longer. He was very annoyed by the cowherd's early morning cracks so wanted to get the man to stop being a nuisance.

However it was not possible to tell him directly to be silent. The cowherd was proud of his job and would not accept remonstrations. He might even become violent if asked straightforwardly to proceed differently from what he thought best. The teacher thought a little over the matter and guess, what did he imagine?

He met the cowherd and said to him: "Hello, dear John! I have to tell you how much I like the noise you do with your whip. For me it is the best of music. I cannot stop enjoying it every time you walk the herd near my house toward the pasture field. I dare ask you to do me a favour: please crack your whip several more times, but louder, any morning you pass by my house. For your kindness I shall reward you with a glass full of brandy, which you will find on my doorstep when you walk by. OK?"

John the cowherd was a little bewildered by such unusual request. He said to himself that God's world is full of lunatics! However, as he was not disturbed in any way by the request and moreover, was going to have a profit, he accepted eagerly. So, from next morning on, the deal was performed for the best satisfaction of both sides: John whipped and cracked as best he could any time he went past the teacher's house, and drank in return the glass of good brandy he found regularly on the doorstep. This arrangement worked perfectly for some days.

However, one bright morning the brandy glass was missing! The cowherd was upset but for once he performed his best without the liquid reward, assuming it was only a mistake of the teacher. The following morning John first searched for the glass and finding none, was furious.

"Villainous and greedy teacher," he said himself, "you want to hear my beautiful cracks for free. Well, I shall not be your dupe! You shall not hear again my tune!" And he was very careful not to crack his whip ever again near the teacher's house.

So the village teacher escaped the danger to his morning sleep. Without quarrels, without insults, without court. Only through a sly handling of the problem. Through "soft violence," as defined by the old man of the village who told me the story. Without a confrontation, but with a Taisabaki. As we learn to do it in Aikido!

— *S. D.*

Is Your Radar On?

— By John Garner, Instructor, Motorcycle Safety Foundation

Out in the Real World, hazards can approach from any direction. In the MSF beginner course, the acronym SIPDE describes a strategy for dealing with hazards:

Scan, Identify, Predict, Decide, Execute

Experienced Rider classes combine the steps to get SPA:

Search, Predict, Act

Both strategies deal with risk management of hazards in time and space. However, they have one very important feature in common: Where to search. The answer is: Everywhere! We don't know if the hazard is in front, in back, or to the sides, so we must have two heads and four eyes, or so it seems, to be vigilant.

Imagine yourself going along in a straight line. Now draw a circle around yourself. Using clock positions, place 12:00 straight ahead, 3:00 to the right, 6:00 behind and 9:00 to the left.

Consider the aircraft controller screen. The circular screen has a line (the radius), sweeping in a counterclockwise direction. It doesn't miss a thing. We can mimic this by looking ahead, to the right and left, and in both the right and left mirrors. I'm going to pay special attention to the 11 o'clock position where most accidents happen, but I'm not going to forget about the others. So, my radar is on. Take that circle you've drawn around yourself and let's go for a ride.

1. ***Scan***. At cruising speed we're still searching using the radar analogy. Is that circle around you still appropriate?

    Not really. Threats from behind are much less likely, so think of a teardrop shape around you with the 'tail' behind. Place yourself about one-third from the tail, with the large rounded part in front. You will search this new shape or 'bubble" with your radar.

    Stop sign ahead! Slow using both brakes and downshift to first gear before stopping. What happened to your teardrop? Did it slowly become a circle, then reverse with the tail in front and the large rounded drop to the rear? I hope so, because now your biggest problem is, "Did the guy behind me stop?" The radar is focused more to the rear.

2. ***Predict***. If that truck doesn't stop, you're in first gear right?

    Did you include an escape route in your radar search? I hope so because now you must....

3. ***Act***. Ease out the clutch and go there!

    After the hazard is off your radar screen, what do you do? (Hint: Do they ever turn off the aircraft controller screen?)

- Hazards are everywhere. Scan continuously to find them!
- Use the radar screen analogy to help you do the search. Change your "circle" to the teardrop as your riding situation changes.
- Most important: Never turn off your radar!

On Learning

Motor Planning and Learning

— By Julie Herbert, OTR/L, BCP

How you learn a technique consists of three phases of motor planning:

- **Ideation**: You have to have an idea what you're going to do.

  In Aikido, that's fairly easy because the technique has a certain pattern. In theory, once it's named, you have an idea what you're doing. In reality, it is not quite that simple, but you'll at least get an idea based on a *shomen-uchi* or a *mune-tsuki*. You have an idea of what is possible to do with that attack.

- **Planning**: Being able to figure out what is involved with a particular technique in the mind's eye.

  Requires awareness that you are going through the technique in the correct pattern.

- **Doing**: Actually doing the technique.

  Requires the physical coordination to execute the technique as it is given.

Students can have difficulty with any or all of these and they can be helped in various ways.

For problems with the ideation phase of motor planning, written instructions with illustrations give the student an idea of what they're looking for if they cannot come up with their own idea of what those words mean.

A good proprioceptive system is extremely important when it comes to learning Aikido, especially in the planning phase. That is what gives you a good perception of your body position in space so that you can move in a coordinated manner within a technique and effective manner, as in leading a dance.

The proprioceptive system is primarily located in the muscles and joints. It helps maintain good posture. It is also behind positions such as Unbendable Arm where your arm is not extended completely through its full range of motion but is partially bent in a position of "co-contraction." That means that the muscles on the top and back of your arm are working as a team to maintain that position. Bending the arm all the way up or straightening the arm all the way out works only one set of muscles. Your brain gives feedback to these muscles and joints, telling you where your body is, helping you be aware of where you are within a technique.

Once you know where and how you are moving through space and time you are able to pay attention to what *uke* is doing and when he is doing it. Students who have problems with proprioception tend to move heavily on the mat, tend to move on their heels (rather than the balls of their feet), and tend to crash into *uke* (rather than getting off the line of attack). Timing is also very important. Proprioception allows you to determine how fast *uke* is coming at you and how much pressure he's applying to determine how to redirect his *ki*.

Visual learners[1] gain information from what they read, *auditory* learners pick up the spoken directional components of a given technique (down-up-down), but *tactile-*

---

kinesthetic learners use strong proprioception to imitate techniques just by watching them being demonstrated.

People with proprioception difficulties tend to rely heavily on the visual system to compensate for not having a true sense of where their body is in space; they need to *see* their body move through space. They may be so busy watching where they are putting their arms and hands and legs that they are unable to pay attention to what *uke* is doing or where *uke* is. In learning a throw which requires them to be in close, they don't understand how they're creating a gap because they're still trying to figure out where they are.

To reinforce motor memory of techniques, students need to learn what patterns are involved. Breaking the technique down so far that each placement of finger or toe is a separate action is too mechanical; the student loses sight of the pattern the body is to move through. Break it down, yes, but also practice the *complete* pattern to give the student a better sense of the whole pattern and its appropriate rhythm. This can be done through dance steps, giving a count to identify the beats and pauses within a technique and establishing its general rhythm.

In Aikido there are many waltz steps (3/4 time) and tango steps (5-part techniques). The Standard Response of Brush, Step Back, Draw Up is a three-part waltz-time rhythm. Another is *yokomen en-undo*, which consists of two sets of 1-2-3. The 5-part tango rhythm appears in *katate-tori ikkyo tenkan*. Not taking the time to pause briefly after drawing up and before stepping in throws off the entire rhythm of the technique making it more difficult to learn or perform. Music in the background during techniques could help to decrease some of the frustration for beginners trying to learn a new technique and feeling overwhelmed with the whole concept. Chanting the beats aloud as in *jo* exercises also helps to organize movement.

Learning techniques as *patterns* is similar to writing with cursive rather than printed letters. Although writing skills tend to be taught using printing before cursive, some students find the multiple steps involved in forming printed letters too confusing because each time you lift the pencil, a new step begins. Without good feedback from the muscle components of proprioception to accurately return the pencil to the beginning of another stroke, printing can become very slow and tedious.

Although cursive strokes change direction frequently, these strokes build on the natural development of writing through scribbling and generally include one step per word (unless crossing t's or dotting i's). Similarly, in Aikido, you can lead through the general pattern of a technique and add the details later. You can also break down the techniques and components into steps:

1. Standard Response,

2. Initial setup,

3. Moving *uke* to the mat.

---

1. Notice that Ms. Herbert differentiates between "being visual" as it's commonly understood, and being a "visual learner." The ability to "visualize" can be an issue of *imagination*, (the ability to create an *image* of something that isn't really there) rather than a learning mode. For example, making Unbendable Arm by "touching" a distant wall is easier for some students than requiring them to make up something "unreal" as they must do if asked to "extend through the wall." On the other hand . . .

"Visual learners" may *see* a demonstration but not make the connection between what they see and what their bodies should do and feel. These tend to be the bookworms and readers of the world. Do you remember the location of a sentence or picture on a page? If so, chances are that you will be greatly helped by working with handouts and other printed teaching materials. "Tactile-Kinesthetic learners" can translate what is seen directly into body feel and movement. Dancers, gymnasts and other athletes often excel at this skill. — *C. M. S.*

Students unable to learn a technique just "by doing" may need to be physically guided. For example, *uke* can "drive" while a third partner stands behind, directing arms and body to where they need to go, as slowly and as often as necessary.

Even clothing choice can make a difference; a heavier *gi* can reinforce proprioception because the added weight on joints helps increase awareness. On the other hand, a tank top and shorts can also help because air moving over the bare skin of arms and legs is felt more easily than while wearing even the lightest *gi*.

The concept of extending *ki* helps to "energize" your joints and muscles so that you get a sense of the best flow. You can also rev up your system via "heavy work exercises" that involve the components of pushing, pulling, lifting, or carrying. Any of these activities can increase awareness and get your body ready to do an action.

Improving on the *doing* aspect of motor planning, going through the motions with assistance rather than just trying to watch and do, may be easier. That's where putting in time as *uke* is very important because you get an idea of what you're actually trying to do with a partner. Going through the motions of *uke* makes a better *nage* because the student learns where to move *nage* and the most effective way to do that.

Props are also very helpful to learning techniques simply because they provide more physical reference to the technique, making the technique more concrete and easier to learn.

From an instructor's standpoint another aspect of sensory systems that may come into play during the doing phase is "tactile defensiveness." Some people are sensitive to touch to a degree that makes it difficult for them to interact with a partner, especially when contact is unpredictable, as in a *randori*.

Fortunately touch can be predicted most of the time because techniques have set patterns. Unfortunately, the defensive response can't always be shut down even when the person knows the touch is coming.

For students with tactile defensiveness, it is extremely important to practice a standard response before working through a technique. If they can make it through the standard response, the chances of their being able to do the technique while maintaining a relaxed state of mind is definitely enhanced. When defensiveness rules, you tend to react to the attacker rather than the attack. You recoil, or throw up *ki* as a *wall*, which derails the entire sense of *extending ki*, producing very different results.

"Tactile defensives" tend to rely on their eyes to help maintain an alert state similar to a scared animal. They find it difficult to relax and just go through the motions because they are always, in a sense, looking out for danger. This may not be at a conscious level, but you can easily see someone who tends to flinch as *uke* attacks or tries to move faster just to get the technique over with.

Sometimes it's helpful to exaggerate slowness. It's very easy to go through a technique too fast, making it one-step. Learning the techniques as a pattern includes the necessary pauses instead of trying to continue at a fast pace or accelerate from the moment of contact until the end.

Wearing a heavier *gi* can help a person who feels defensive because it provides a sturdier barrier to *uke*; in the role of *uke* it can be easier to accept touch and more physical contact through the thicker material. *Ki* development exercises with emphasis on "relax completely" can help to decrease defensiveness over time.

Slow Learning

—By Yael Shahar and Chris Pearce

All techniques are tougher when done slowly, but it's good practice. You just need to make sure that you've taken their balance all throughout the movement (which is more easily said than done, of course). It's perfectly possible with shihonage, although I can't perform it slowly too well.

— Jun Akiyama

Yael notes:

Learning Kung Fu when I was young I kept very few of the techniques that I learned in that class. But there was one *kata* that our instructor had us do a number of times as *slooooowly* as we could. When she did it she could stretch this 3 minute kata out for half an hour (sort of looked like she was operating in proximity to a black hole, only without the red shift).

So we all imitated her: *Slooooow kaaataaaa* . . . .

To this day my body remembers that single *kata* from beginning to end while I've forgotten almost all else from that class.

A fast technique should be the same as a slow technique —just done faster. This seems to happen naturally if the technique is repeated slowly enough and often enough. Perhaps "slow motion" goes straight into "long term" body memory, whereas "fast action" passes and is gone before the body has a chance to remember. After all most of our unintentional movements, such as getting knocked over, happen very quickly. These sorts of incidental moves aren't something we want to ingrain. But learned responses — intentional movements — are initiated by us slowly at first. And don't babies learn how to move by doing everything very slowly?

Gives a more positive aspect to being a "slow learner," eh?

And Chris Pierce comments:

Piano parallel. I am given to understand that to really memorize a piece, you have to understand the structure of it. The only way to know if you've got it memorized is to play it SLOOOOOWLY.

Playing at speed engages your "muscle memory," which is very unreliable. It's context sensitive, for one thing. Change pianos or change environments and you change the kinesthetic feedback that drives your fingers to the next place. And with muscle memory, if you lose it in the middle of the piece, you are totally lost. It is impossible to get back on track without starting over.

If you practice slowly, you can't engage your muscle memory. That's probably why you still remember that one kata to this day.

Personally, I am completely inept at music memorization. As far as I can tell, I have never successfully memorized a piece through anything except muscle memory. Given a piano keyboard but no music, I *cannot* play anything. This after about 15 years of study. Lots of classically trained pianists are in the same boat, actually. I *know* that for piano performance at least, muscle memory alone does not work.

A good page about memorization at the piano, perhaps applicable to aikido.

http://www.serve.com/marbeth/memory_methods.html

Afterword

I hope that you have found this sampler of Aikido Exercises useful and helpful.

If you have corrections or comments, or if you have an exercise, illustration, or anecdote that you would like to share for possible inclusion in future editions, please write me at:

> Round Earth Publishing
> P.O. Box 3855
> Dept. 150
> Merrifield, VA 22116
> e-mail: Aikido@Round-Earth.com

The Virginia Ki Society is a non-profit educational society located at:

> 2929-E Eskridge Road
> Merrifield, Virginia 22116

Adult Aikido and *Ki* Development classes are held daily. We also offer children's classes, and classes in *t'ai ch'i* and *kendo*. See schedule of classes and seminars and a complete map with pictures at: http://vakisociety.org or call (703) 573-8843 for more information.

The *dojo* is between Routes 50 and 29 a short distance from the intersection of 29 (Lee Highway) and 650 (Gallows Road). It is about a 15-minute walk south of the Dunn Loring Metro station, behind the Multiplex Theatre. Watch for the big orange and white relay tower which is next to our building.

From the Dunn Loring Metro,

1. Walk south (a right onto Gallows road outside the station).
2. Cross 29, turn right (west) down 29.
3. At the Multiplex theatre marquise, turn right down the service road (Old Lee Highway) 1 block.
4. Turn left on Eskridge Road and pass the orange tower.
5. Turn left into Eskridge Business Park. There are two rows of buildings; Virginia Ki Society is at the rear, in Unit E.

Drop by any time. Visitors are always welcome!

You may also write us at:

> Virginia Ki Society
> P. O. Box 2351
> Merrifield, VA 22116

For information on the Aikido-L mailing list, dojo listings, other styles and instructors, please see the Internet addresses listed on page 253.

Selected Books

Ki in Aikido—A Sampler of Ki Exercises
—C. M. Shifflett

Ki is the seemingly mysterious "force" behind the Japanese martial art of Aikido — and a powerful tool for daily living. *Ki* exercises are a simple but highly effective means of teaching mind-body coordination. The results of this discipline are calmness and relaxation, increased inner strength and personal effectiveness.

Ki testing provides a rare opportunity to actually test, measure and evaluate the otherwise elusive qualities of mind and spirit. However, many standard tests have never been documented while those that have are rarely presented in a manner designed for actual class application.

Ki in Aikido is the "lab manual" of *ki* exercises, designed for systematic and effective practice of *ki* development.

It is written in a simple user-manual format.

Text is clear, concise, and profusely illustrated with detailed line drawings.

Step-by-step explanations of testing techniques and the exercises are appropriate for beginning to advanced students and for individual, partnered, or classroom practice. A unique resource. **$16.95**

I congratulate you on an excellent work. I tried some of the exercises, with remarkable results in some instances. Thanks for the book and for undertaking an important work in producing it.

— David Lynch, *Aikido Journal*

A test's great value is that it lets you know what you do not know, and saves the embarrassment and danger of learning it later in real life. Tests in this handy little book go even farther. It is a great advance in testing since the first Unbendable Arm.

— Jay Gluck, *Zen Combat*

I am thrilled with it. I will make extensive use of it, especially teaching in the dojo. This is certainly the best book I have read on the subject — so much good sense, so many helpful exercises. Great drawings!

— Rev. Bill Bickford, Kingston Ki Aikido

Not just "do this" exercises, but class "experiments" — try this and see what happens. Then try this and compare results. The reader is invited to explore just what Ki can do in casual, simple situations. I think this text will prove to be invaluable to beginners, advanced students, teachers, and everyone in between.

— E. Izawa
"The Unofficial Ki Society Web Page"

This is definitely a book worth getting. Very good line drawings, clear instructions. Specifically designed for *doing Ki exercises* — a very fine book.

— M. Brandenburg
Kokon Ryu Renmei Aikido

Zen Combat
—Jay Gluck

A new edition of a classic. As the first American exchange student in Japan after WWII, Gluck began an enthusiastic exploration of Japan and its martial arts. Gluck is the author of the 1957 *True* magazine article, "Masters of the Bare Hand Kill" that introduced karate to America. *(True* editors asked Gluck to write a similar article on Aikido, but when they saw film and photographs of tiny Morihei Ueshiba effortlessly throwing burly American MP's, they dismissed the footage as "rigged" and "phoney.")

Zen Combat ranges from the 1957 *True* article that introduced karate to America, to Aikido, Tohei's discovery of Unbendable Arm, Firewalking Made Easy, cocktail-party *sumo wrestling,* and the truth about *ninja.*

A treasury of wry wit and eye-witness history – first-hand accounts of training with O'Sensei, Tohei and others, the historic meeting between Morihei Ueshiba and cartoonist Rube Golberg, and a newly expanded section on ki.

288 pgs. 4-1/4 x 7-1/4 ins. Softbound **$8.95**

Myofascial Pain Syndrome . . .
—David G. Simons, M.D.

Aikido is remarkably injury-free compared to other martial arts. Unfortunately, when injuries do occur, they may be soft tissue injuries with mystifying pain referral patterns. A pattern of pain in shoulder, triceps, scapula, and the fingers may have nothing to do with shoulder, triceps, scapula, or fingers but with nerve entrapment by the scalene muscles of the neck. Cause?

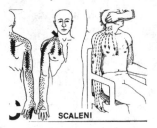

SCALENI

Perhaps too many neck-a-nages or balancing a phone on your shoulder. If you are hurting, consider this brief but excellent excerpt of a renowned two-volume medical textbook.
Written for medical professionals but illustrations and comments speak to professional and laymen alike.

39 pgs. 8-1/2 x 11 ins. **$5.00** post paid

Selected Videos

Hidden Fortress
—Director: Akira Kurosawa

A defeated and hunted princess who fights for her freedom and her clan inspired George Lucas' *Star Wars*.Toshiro Mifune is general Rokurota Makabe, who in *Star Wars* becomes Obi-wan Kenobi and Han Solo. Princess Yukihime becomes Princess Leia Organa, General Fujita, vassal to an evil lord, becomes Darth Vader, and the two hapless foot soldiers who aid the princess become C3PO and R2D2. The Source of the Force.

1958, B&W, 139 min., Japanese w/ English subtitles **$39.95**

The Seven Samurai
—Director: Akira Kurosawa

A village hires a band of *samurai* to protect them against the annual harvest-time raiders. A masterpeice of strategy, cinematography, psychology and the human soul, and considered to be one of the world's 10 best films.

1954, B&W, 208 min., Japanese w/ English subtitles **$34.95**

Sanjuro
—Director: Akira Kurosawa

In this rollicking sequel to *Yojimbo,* a gruff, rough *samurai* (Toshiro Mifune) aids a band of naive young noblemen. Mifune highlights the contrast between explosive action and relaxation, appropriate action and appropriate inaction, the error and danger of judging by surface appearances, and how mere Action Hero Solutions lead to tragic ends.

1962, B&W, 95 min., Japanese w/ English subtitles **$29.95**

Yojimbo
— Director: Akira Kurosawa

Gang warfare in Japan of 1860 with an American Western frontier motif. Mifune plays off one gang of genuinely bad people against another equally bad. The original Man With No Name in Japan's most popular film of all time was recast as *Fistful of Dollars.* **$29.95**

1961, B&W, 111 min. Japanese w/ English subtitles **VHS $29.95**

Selected Patterns

Japanese Hakama

The *hakama,* voluminous pleated pants with a rigid backboard, is worn by students of Aikido and other Japanese martial arts.

Our exclusive pattern includes illustrated directions for asembly, an information sheet for fitting women's *hakama,* and instructions for putting on and folding your finished hakama.

To order please include your waist and *hip* measurements taken over *dogi.* **$16.95**

Japanese Kimono

From Folkwear, a *yukata* of cool, lightweight cotton for men and women. Includes a list of fabric sources, and directions for traditional Japanese embroidery and decoration. Adaptable for *dogi* top by narrowing the sleeves. **$16.95**

Child's Kimono

From Folkwear, a child's kimono including instructions for tying and wearing the *obi* sash.

Pattern includes two cozy vests, one quilted and one knitted, with complete quilting and knitting instructions. **$16.95**

Japanese Hapi/Haori/Tabi

Simply elegant. The *hapi* is a man's short coat, *haori* a woman's thigh-length jacket worn over kimono. Tabi are the traditional split-toe slipper socks worn inside or with *zori* sandals.

Pattern includes designs and instructions for silk screen fabric printing and an extensive list of sources for dyes and fabrics. **$16.95**

Japanese Futon & Furnishings

Wonderfully practical bedding that can be folded away when not in use.

Pattern for folding foam mat, floor cushions, sleeping pillows, top quilt, *noren* (curtains), and *yogi* (quilted sleeping kimono) with instructions for *sashiko* quilting and *shibori* tie-dyeing. **$16.95**

Order Form

Books

Aikido Exercises for Teaching and Training	$19.95
Ki in Aikido — A Sampler of Ki Exercises, by C. M. Shifflett	$16.95
Myofascial Pain Syndrome, by D. G. Simons (post paid)	$5.00
Zen Combat, by Jay Gluck	$8.95

Videos

Hidden Fortress (A. Kurosawa) The inspiration for *Star Wars*.	$39.95
Sanjuro (A. Kurosawa) A rollicking samurai spoof.	$29.95
Seven Samurai (A. Kurosawa) The award-winning classic.	$34.95
Yojimbo (A. Kurosawa) The inspiration for *Fistful of Dollars*.	$29.95

Patterns

Hakama — Please include hip measurement taken over dogi.	$16.95
Hapi, Haori, Tabi — Men's/women's jackets and slipper socks.	$16.95
Kimono — *Yukata* style for men or women.	$16.95
Futon — includes pillows, quilt, curtains, and sleeping kimono.	$16.95

Name (Please Print):

Address:

City:	State/ZIP:
Phone: ( )	Dojo:

Total Merchandise:	$
Virginia residents please add 4.5% State tax:	$
Shipping: $4.00 for up to 2 items. $1.00 each additional item.	$
Total:	$

Credit Cards: Expiration Date:____/____

☐ VISA ☐ MasterCard   ☐ Discover ☐ AmExpress

Name on Card (PRINT):

Card Number:

☐☐☐☐–☐☐☐☐–☐☐☐☐–☐☐☐☐

Signature:

In U.S. FAX your order **TOLL FREE** to 1-(888)-542-4543
Aikido@Round-Earth.com   Voice: (703) 641-9169
Round Earth Publishing, P. O. Box 3855, Merrifield, VA 22116

Order Form

Books

Aikido Exercises for Teaching and Training	$19.95
Ki in Aikido — A Sampler of Ki Exercises, by C. M. Shifflett	$16.95
Myofascial Pain Syndrome, by D. G. Simons (post paid)	$5.00
Zen Combat, by Jay Gluck	$8.95

Videos

Hidden Fortress (A. Kurosawa) The inspiration for *Star Wars.*	$39.95
Sanjuro (A. Kurosawa) A rollicking samurai spoof.	$29.95
Seven Samurai (A. Kurosawa) The award-winning classic.	$34.95
Yojimbo (A. Kurosawa) The inspiration for *Fistful of Dollars.*	$29.95

Patterns

Hakama — Please include hip measurement taken over dogi.	$16.95
Hapi, Haori, Tabi — Men's/women's jackets and slipper socks.	$16.95
Kimono — *Yukata* style for men or women.	$16.95
Futon — includes pillows, quilt, curtains, and sleeping kimono.	$16.95

Name (Please Print):		
Address:		
City:	State/ZIP:	
Phone: ( )	Dojo:	
	Total Merchandise:	$
	Virginia residents please add 4.5% State tax:	$
	Shipping: $4.00 for up to 2 items. $1.00 each additional item.	$
	Total:	$

Credit Cards: Expiration Date:_____/_____
☐ VISA ☐ MasterCard   ☐ Discover ☐ AmExpress

Name on Card (PRINT):

Card Number:
☐☐☐☐ — ☐☐☐☐ — ☐☐☐☐ — ☐☐☐☐

Signature:

In U.S. FAX your order **TOLL FREE** to 1-(888)-542-4543
Aikido@Round-Earth.com   Voice: (703) 641-9169
Round Earth Publishing, P. O. Box 3855, Merrifield, VA 22116

Order Form

Books

Aikido Exercises for Teaching and Training	$19.95
Ki in Aikido — A Sampler of Ki Exercises, by C. M. Shifflett	$16.95
Myofascial Pain Syndrome, by D. G. Simons (post paid)	$5.00
Zen Combat, by Jay Gluck	$8.95

Videos

Hidden Fortress (A. Kurosawa) The inspiration for *Star Wars*.	$39.95
Sanjuro (A. Kurosawa) A rollicking samurai spoof.	$29.95
Seven Samurai (A. Kurosawa) The award-winning classic.	$34.95
Yojimbo (A. Kurosawa) The inspiration for *Fistful of Dollars*.	$29.95

Patterns

Hakama — Please include hip measurement taken over dogi.	$16.95
Hapi, Haori, Tabi — Men's/women's jackets and slipper socks.	$16.95
Kimono — *Yukata* style for men or women.	$16.95
Futon — includes pillows, quilt, curtains, and sleeping kimono.	$16.95

Name (Please Print):

Address:

City: State/ZIP:

Phone: (   ) Dojo:

Total Merchandise:	$
Virginia residents please add 4.5% State tax:	$
Shipping: $4.00 for up to 2 items. $1.00 each additional item.	$
Total:	$

Credit Cards: Expiration Date:____/____

☐ VISA ☐ MasterCard ☐ Discover ☐ AmExpress

Name on Card (PRINT):

Card Number:

☐☐☐☐ – ☐☐☐☐ – ☐☐☐☐ – ☐☐☐☐

Signature:

In U.S. FAX your order **TOLL FREE** to 1-(888)-542-4543
Aikido@Round-Earth.com   Voice: (703) 641-9169
Round Earth Publishing, P. O. Box 3855, Merrifield, VA 22116

Order Form

Books

Aikido Exercises for Teaching and Training	$19.95
Ki in Aikido — A Sampler of Ki Exercises, by C. M. Shifflett	$16.95
Myofascial Pain Syndrome, by D. G. Simons (post paid)	$5.00
Zen Combat, by Jay Gluck	$8.95

Videos

Hidden Fortress (A. Kurosawa) The inspiration for *Star Wars*.	$39.95
Sanjuro (A. Kurosawa) A rollicking samurai spoof.	$29.95
Seven Samurai (A. Kurosawa) The award-winning classic.	$34.95
Yojimbo (A. Kurosawa) The inspiration for *Fistful of Dollars*.	$29.95

Patterns

Hakama — Please include hip measurement taken over dogi.	$16.95
Hapi, Haori, Tabi — Men's/women's jackets and slipper socks.	$16.95
Kimono — *Yukata* style for men or women.	$16.95
Futon — includes pillows, quilt, curtains, and sleeping kimono.	$16.95

Name (Please Print):		
Address:		
City:	State/ZIP:	
Phone: ( )	Dojo:	
Total Merchandise:	$	
Virginia residents please add 4.5% State tax:	$	
Shipping: $4.00 for up to 2 items. $1.00 each additional item.	$	
Total:	$	

Credit Cards: Expiration Date:____/____

☐ VISA ☐ MasterCard   ☐ Discover ☐ AmExpress

Name on Card (PRINT):

Card Number:

☐☐☐☐–☐☐☐☐–☐☐☐☐–☐☐☐☐

Signature:

In U.S. FAX your order **TOLL FREE** to 1-(888)-542-4543
Aikido@Round-Earth.com   Voice: (703) 641-9169
Round Earth Publishing, P. O. Box 3855, Merrifield, VA 22116